Being Smart about Gifted Education:

A Guidebook for Educators and Parents

Being Smart about Gifted Education:

A Guidebook for Educators and Parents

Dona J. Matthews, Ph.D.
and
Joanne F. Foster, Ed.D.

Great Potential Press®

Being Smart about Gifted Education:
A Guidebook for Educators and Parents

Cover design: Mary Velgos Design
Interior design: The Printed Page
Copy editor: Jennifer Ault

Published by Great Potential Press, Inc.
P.O. Box 5057
Scottsdale, AZ 85261

Printed and bound in the United States of America using partially recycled paper.

Great Potential Press and associated logos are trademarks and/or registered trademarks of Great Potential Press, Inc.

13 12 11 10 09   5 4 3 2 1

At the time of this book's publication, all facts and figures cited are the most current available. All telephone numbers, addresses, and website URLs are accurate and active; all publications, organizations, websites, and other resources exist as described in this book; and all have been verified as of the time this book went to press. The author(s) and Great Potential Press make no warranty or guarantee concerning the information and materials given out by organizations or content found at websites, and we are not responsible for any changes that occur after this book's publication. If you find an error or believe that a resource listed here is not as described, please contact Great Potential Press.

Library of Congress Cataloging-in-Publication Data

Matthews, Dona J., 1951-
  Being smart about gifted education: a guidebook for educators and parents /
Dona J. Matthews, Ph.D. and Joanne F. Foster, Ed.D.
      p. cm.
  ISBN-13: 978-0-910707-95-4
  ISBN-10: 0-910707-95-2
1. Gifted children—Education. 2. Gifted teenagers—Education. 3. Parents of gifted children. 4. Teachers of gifted children. I. Foster, Joanne F., 1953-
II. Title.
  LC3993.M362 2009
  371.95—dc22
                              2009015609

Acknowledgments

As we revise our original manuscript, and prepare the second edition titled *Being Smart about Gifted Education*, we want to thank everyone at Great Potential Press for their ongoing confidence in our ability. We appreciate their vision and willingness to work earnestly with their authors, and we enjoyed bringing this project to fruition. Jim Webb, Janet Gore, Jen Ault, and Lisa Liddy have been dedicated in their efforts to help make this the best book it could possibly be.

There have been many important mentors along the way for us both. Dona would particularly like to acknowledge Dan Keating, whose extraordinary intellectual mastery and commitment to the largest best truth will always be a model; Rena Subotnik, whose thoughtfully perceptive wisdom and generous support create bountiful possibilities; Don and Joyce Matthews, whose commitment to learning and engagement in life are the foundation of everything else; and her colleagues at the Ontario Institute for Studies in Education of the University of Toronto (OISE/UT) and at Hunter College, City University of New York, whose friendship and support are invaluable. Joanne would like to acknowledge all those who offered ongoing encouragement and latitude in her broad-based consultancy practice; her colleagues at more schools than can possibly be mentioned here; the many individuals who have provided guidance and collaborative support at OISE/UT; and Clara and Nathan Stein, who instilled in her a lifelong love of learning that serves to underlie all personal and professional growth.

We would like to thank our readers, both in the preliminary stages and more recently. Many people come to mind in that category, but some who have been particularly important in this book as it has evolved are Linda Edwards, Carole Matthews, Winnie Mayers-Jones, and Luc Kumps and his EduRatio team in Belgium. We would also like to express our appreciation to all the wonderful educators, parents, and children with whom we have worked over the past 30 years. We are delighted to have this opportunity to share their voices and viewpoints with you. And a special thanks goes to all of our friends and extended family members who were always there to cheer us on, and sometimes just to listen.

Our husbands have been an integral part of the process of writing and revising this book. We cannot say enough to thank Stephen Gross and Garry Foster for their boundless support and patience, and for being there with humor, perspective, inspiration, comfort, and love every step along the way.

Finally, we would like to dedicate this book to our children. We have learned more from Robin, Erin, Eric, and Michele than they will ever realize—until perhaps one day when they have children of their own.

Contents

List of Tables

Foreword

Psychology has lots to offer gifted child studies and gifted education, and it always has. Most of the patriarchs and matriarchs of the field were trained in the discipline, as were many of their rebellious "sons" and "daughters." This wonderful volume continues that tradition by promoting evidence-based practices that have been carefully culled and vetted through psychological science, education, and evaluation research, as well as by the deep expertise of the authors.

Dona Matthews and Joanne Foster's conceptualization of "mastery" versus "mystery" approaches for gifted education and gifted child studies unveils the source of conflicting outcomes we see in the gifted education literature. They make it clear that unless the preparation provided to teachers and the consultation we provide to parents are grounded in some form of definitional consensus, our field will undermine its ability to play a greater role at the table of school reform and policy development.

The authors explicate the arena of gifted education in a number of constructive ways. They do not accept hearsay or ideology as an excuse for promoting practices in identification, curriculum, evaluation, or counseling services. They provide solid advice to parents, educators, and decision-makers in language that is accessible to all interested readers. Every reader, from those with little exposure to the field, other than experiences with their own children and their children's teachers, to those who have been immersed for decades in serving the needs of gifted children will find this book a welcome reference.

Rena F. Subotnik, Ph.D.
Director
Center for Gifted Education Policy
American Psychological Association

Preface

Based on 25 years of experience with students who have exceptionally advanced learning needs, as well as their parents and educators, we wrote *Being Smart about Gifted Children* (2004) for parents and teachers, and also for teacher educators, educational administrators, school psychologists, and educational policy-makers who are interested in gifted-related issues. We wrote it out of a concern for children's development, in response to widespread misconceptions about the nature and needs of gifted development, as well as the well-intentioned but sometimes misleading practices that we were encountering. We included the voices and viewpoints of many different stakeholders in children's education as we carefully considered how to support optimal development in those who have been labeled gifted and those who have not.

In revising the book for a second edition, we have reflected on what we wrote previously, all the while thinking about what our readers and reviewers have said about the book, as well as about how the field has changed. The response to the first edition has been enormously gratifying. Parents and teachers have let us know that our ideas help them make sense of the problems they encounter and the questions they pose. Just as encouragingly, in the intervening years, a burgeoning of research about brain development, expertise, and giftedness confirms the importance of the mastery model of giftedness that we introduced five years ago. Because of this, we have changed our title to *Being Smart about Gifted Education*. In this new book, we provide an added number of current references to support the mastery model, as well as new ideas that we have developed from our ongoing work in the field. Our fundamental principles and positions are the same, but here we've provided an updated set of ideas, references, and resources.

One of the themes you'll see running through this edition, as with the first, is that there is no single formula for living or working with gifted learners. People who want to support gifted-level development for the children in their lives—that is, to provide them with the best possible guidance, challenges, encouragement, and education—must begin by reflecting upon individual differences, including emotional, social, academic, and developmental. They can then consider the perspectives and understandings that will help them make the best informed decisions, and they will find new ways to enable children to experience their world fully as an engaging place in which to live, laugh, and learn.

Although we have significantly updated all of the chapters and sections of this book, it is Section II that has changed the most from the first edition to the second, as we incorporate some newly evolved understandings of the mastery model. The title of that section has changed from "Being Smart about Testing, Identification, and Labeling" to "Being Smart about Diagnosing Mismatches." We know that people sometimes grapple with the mystery model and its attempt to categorize some children as gifted and others as not gifted, but (illustrating the way that paradigms shift and evolve over time), we now see that our use of some of the categorical terms did not sufficiently reflect mastery model thinking. For example, in the first edition, we sometimes focused on identifying giftedness, rather than on assessing developmental levels and abilities. In this edition, you'll see fewer categorical mentions and more emphasis on what we've come to see as a fundamental difference—diagnosing mismatches between a child's educational experiences and that child's level of functioning, rather than labeling giftedness.

We have also incorporated Carol Dweck's exciting new work on mindsets, as well as recent research findings on expertise and cognitive neuroscience that show the importance of habits of mind in cognitive development. We have added sections on nonverbal tests and radically changed our section on aptitude tests. We have also incorporated perspectives from several other recent publications that illustrate the continued movement in the field from mystery to mastery, including the ways that the mastery model is more inclusive. We illustrate how this approach opens doors to gifted learning possibilities for diverse learners, many of whom were too often excluded from gifted programming in the past due to test criteria they could not meet.

In this book, we discuss many topics that parents, educators, and policy-makers have asked about, including some that are seldom covered in other books on gifted development. For example, testing, assessment, and identification issues are the objects of much interest as well as confusion, so we devote an entire section of the book to these topics. We offer alternative approaches to gifted programming, ideas about teacher training initiatives, advice about advocacy, thoughts on the relationship between creativity and giftedness, and a description of a dynamic scaffolding approach to gifted consultancy. We also discuss matters that affect children's well-being, including social, emotional, extracurricular, and motivational factors. Throughout the book, you will hear real voices that belong to the adults and children with whom we have worked, and you will read vignettes of experiences of giftedness and its development.

Throughout these pages, we challenge much of the conventional thinking about gifted education and include only those policies and practices which are solidly grounded theoretically and empirically. As you read this book, you may recognize that some of our perspectives differ from those popularized by others in the field of gifted education. Over the past 30 years, we have been observing a paradigm shift in the field of gifted education that has accelerated in the five years between our first edition and this one. In the first chapter, we introduce the mystery and mastery models of gifted education and discuss the growing movement toward the latter, which we then revisit throughout the book. In this, the second edition, we incorporate feedback we've received about the mystery/mastery distinction, and we continue the discussion. As we wrote in the first edition, we welcome controversy and other opinions and think that continued discussion of these ideas is healthy and positive.

In the first edition of *Being Smart*, we wrote about a double mission in gifted education. One, there is an important and primary focus on nurturing exceptionally advanced ability that is already evident by understanding and supporting exceptionally capable learners' development and education. This is the conventional role of gifted education. However, equally important is the second mission—that is, using what we know about gifted development to encourage it in other children. It is vital that we provide opportunities for every individual to develop his or her abilities and that we empower all children to engage in their own learning. We must teach them to seek knowledge, embrace determination, and reach beyond the status quo. U.S. President Barack Obama, in his inaugural address in January 2009, emphasized the role of "risk-takers, doers, and makers of things," and stated that "Greatness is not given. It must be earned." In the spirit of these statements, we believe that all of us have a responsibility to give children the tools with which to become proactive, and to then affirm and reaffirm their abilities.

By knowing how children and giftedness develop, parents, educators, and others can make informed decisions and foster advancement much more broadly, including in those whose exceptional abilities might not otherwise be optimally developed. Grounded in our backgrounds in teaching, special education, developmental psychology, and educational psychology, we build a foundation in this book for readers to learn more about many of the complexities of gifted development.

Being Smart about Gifted Education emerges out of many years of work with high-ability children, their parents, and educators, and also from a shared sense of the joys, challenges, diversity, and uniqueness inherent in this field. We believe that the gifted educational enterprise should be encouraging and inclusive, working to support the optimal development of all children, while at the same time paying particular attention to those already recognized as exceptionally capable learners. This book is about helping those learners find a healthy balance in their lives—one that respects and nurtures their exceptional ability and that also fosters their well-rounded development.

Canadian poet Irving Layton wrote, "They who are driven dance best." Those six words beautifully convey our passion and enthusiasm, and that which we observe in the parents, educators, and children with whom we work—the people we write about in our book—those movers and shakers who are driven to find the best ways to keep on learning and teaching. We are delighted to share with you here our own views, as informed by this rich collective experience.

Dona J. Matthews and Joanne F. Foster
Toronto, Canada
March, 2009

Section I

Being Smart about Giftedness

Chapter 1

Perspectives and Paradigm Shifts

---

*Does genius make history or
does history make the genius?*[1]

What Is Giftedness?

There is no such thing as a "typical gifted child." We have seen over and over in our work in gifted education that giftedness is an individual differences phenomenon. Developmental histories and pathways, including how a child feels and responds to things and what he needs in order to thrive in a particular situation, are highly individual and even unpredictable. Certainly, there are general guidelines and principles, but parents and teachers who understand that there is no single approach that applies to all children are much more likely to make good decisions for the children in their lives than those who think that there might be any one "right" answer to the questions they have.

Parents often have mixed feelings, difficult questions, confusions, and concerns about the term "gifted" that is in use in their children's schools. Here are some of the inquiries and concerns that we frequently hear from parents:

> *"How are gifted kids different from other kids, if at all?"*
> *"I need to know what to expect, what I should worry about with my child."*

> *"My other son isn't 'gifted,' even though he seems to be just as bright as his brother in many ways. Is there anything I should do?"*
>
> *"Gifted children do not wish to <u>work</u> more; they wish to <u>learn</u> more."*

Teachers' questions and concerns are similar:

> *"How are gifted kids any different from other kids?"*
>
> *"If a so-called 'gifted' student doesn't finish all her work, she really isn't gifted, is she?"*
>
> *"What am I supposed to do with the gifted kids in my classroom? I have 28 whose work is average or below and just two who are identified as gifted. I can't design a special program for each student!"*
>
> *"I'd like to know how to help some of these gifted kids improve their social skills."*
>
> *"I feel the really bright ones can manage with an extra challenge here or there, so I usually pay more attention to the students who are struggling with their work. The slower kids need more help."*

And, of course, some of the most poignant questions and concerns are the ones that we hear from the children themselves:

> *"How are gifted kids special?"*
>
> *"If I don't understand the math work, does that mean I'm not really gifted?"*
>
> *"Why does everyone expect so much of me all the time?"*
>
> *"Other kids call me 'brainer' or 'nerd.' I'd rather be cool than gifted."*
>
> *"I'm embarrassed when people ask me about being gifted."*
>
> *"I'd rather not be different."*

If we are to understand exceptionally capable children and support them in their development—that is, provide them with the best possible guidance, challenge, and encouragement—we must start by reflecting on their individual differences. From that baseline information and starting point, we can then consider various factors and options at school, at home, and in the world. But first we should talk about what it means to be "gifted."

Two Perspectives: Mystery and Mastery

One might think that the question "What is giftedness?" is one that any expert in this field could answer quickly and easily. Offer a simple definition, and then move on to more interesting things. But wait. It is not so easy. Not only do kids, parents, and teachers all give different explanations of what giftedness is, but the experts disagree as well.

Here are some perceptions of giftedness from a few teachers:

"Smarter than others."
"Born with the ability to learn incredibly fast."
"Has a higher IQ than others, that's all."

These voices reflect what we have decided to call the "mystery model" of giftedness. From the mystery model perspective, gifted children are born with high potential and will usually score in the superior or very superior range of intelligence tests. Their ability stays relatively constant over time.

The mystery model is implicit in those approaches to gifted education in which children are categorized as simply "gifted" or "not gifted," without any clear links to specific educational programming based on their particular strengths or abilities. Often, teachers assume that these children are gifted or have the potential to operate at a high level in all areas. With this assumption, a high-scoring child may be placed in a gifted program with others who achieve high scores on the same intelligence tests, even though that child's areas of ability may differ greatly from the other children's. We think of this approach as "mysterious" because it is very difficult to figure out exactly what giftedness means using this model, as well as what to do about it when it is identified.

Now we consider some other responses to our question about what being gifted means from children and adolescents who have been identified as gifted, as well as their parents:

"Smarter in some areas and closer to average in others."
"It's not what you have, but what you do with what you have."
"School is almost always boring, 'specially math."

These answers are closer to what we call the "mastery model" of giftedness. It was while developing our first draft of *Being Smart about*

Gifted Children that we coined the mystery/mastery terminology. Under the mastery model, the term "gifted" simply denotes a mismatch between a child's current level in a given subject area and the educational programming that is usually offered at that student's age and grade level.

The mastery model aligns well with best practices in special education, where the focus is on learning differences at a given point in time that require special educational adaptations. From this perspective, a child is considered gifted when her learning needs in a given subject area are so advanced relative to those of her classmates that her academic development will be stalled or impeded unless the educational programming is somehow modified and adapted to meet those learning needs.

There is no mystery about what giftedness means from the mastery model's perspective; it is developmental advancement at a certain point in time in a particular context that requires academic adjustment. We should add that although the mastery model's defining focus is intellectual advancement, it does not preclude attention to other ways of excelling, such as musical virtuosity, athletic prowess, leadership skills, or any other socially valued ability.

There are social and emotional consequences and concomitants of giftedness, as there are with other exceptionalities. Just as we pay attention to social and emotional dimensions of learning disabilities and sensory impairments, so we must attend to these issues with exceptionally advanced learners, which we address in Section IV, Being Smart about Gifted Development. From a mastery model perspective, however, with a focus on children and their schooling, the essence of giftedness is cognitive.

The best way to describe the important elements of the mastery model, and to explain why we are making the distinction here, is to compare it with the mystery model.

1. *Origin.* Most educational practitioners today accept that both genetic predispositions ("nature") and environmental supports ("nurture") are important influences on intelligence. The mystery model emphasizes the "nature" component, assuming that giftedness is innate—that some children are born with brains that work unusually well, just as some children are born with advantages that help them become better athletes. In the mastery model, explanations like this are not relevant because the mastery perspective focuses on finding the best learning match for each child. When mastery model practitioners discuss an

explanation for superior intellectual ability, they tend to put more emphasis on children's opportunities to learn—the "nurture" factor.

2. *Duration: Dynamic or Temporal Factors.* The mystery model implies an intellectual superiority from birth to death and across all contexts, as expressed in the saying "once gifted, always gifted." The mastery model, which emphasizes giftedness when it requires educational attention, makes no assumptions about the duration of giftedness because it is defined as a current need for special educational programming—something which can change over time.

3. *Extent: Domain Strength.* The mystery model encourages those who work with the child to focus on global intelligence and assumes that giftedness means superior thinking in most or all domains. "He is gifted," would imply excellence across all tasks that require analysis or synthesis, from reading a map to deciphering a Shakespearean sonnet to learning advanced algebra. A main tenet of the mastery model, on the other hand, is that, for most people, intellectual competence varies considerably across areas. Thus, a person gifted in algebra is not necessarily gifted in reading maps or understanding Shakespeare. Under the mastery model, the term is usually accompanied by a subject area designation—for example, a child might be described as gifted in mathematics or science.

4. *Identification Timing.* From the mystery model perspective, it is possible to specify which children are gifted and which are not, and the sooner in a child's life that giftedness is identified, the better. A mystery perspective emphasizes early identification in order to make sure that innate giftedness is not lost or wasted. The mastery model perspective focuses on remedying educational mismatches, so the emphasis is placed on identifying exceptional educational needs as they develop. Identification of giftedness is seen as an ongoing process—an important part of a child's education from the early years right through to graduation. Increasingly, practitioners are moving to the latter perspective and advocating ongoing identification and assessment practices rather than once-and-forever identification in the early years.[2]

5. *Identification Measures.* Historically, the best measure of gifted-ness for advocates of the mystery model was IQ. For mastery model practitioners, the best way to identify giftedness is by using multiple measures, including a combination of dynamic classroom assessment, high-ceiling tests of academic reasoning, and parent-generated information that can provide targeted teacher-friendly input about appropriate curriculum to match gifted learning needs. We discuss testing at great length in Chapters 3 and 4 and in Appendix I.

6. *Identification Implications.* In the mystery model, gifted identi-fication practices and educational programming operate separately, and the only educational implication of making the gifted cut-off score in some jurisdictions is the categorical des-ignation of "gifted." This designation is then used as eligibility for whatever gifted programming is available. Fortunately, an increasing number of jurisdictions are now moving closer to the mastery model, in which identification methods lead directly to educational planning and targeted decision making.[3] The mastery approach identifies children's areas of exceptional strength (and proficiency, and sometimes areas of weakness) such that the necessary curriculum adaptations can then be designed, and appropriate learning opportunities can be provided.

7. *Placement and Curriculum Implications.* The usual best place-ment under the mystery model is a segregated gifted class or some form of gifted enrichment such as a pull-out (or send-out) model, in which gifted learners go to a specialist teacher for a period of time, or the regular classroom teacher is to provide enrichment or more challenging work. However, all too often, teachers who are expected to implement the gifted program or devise the adaptations receive little training or sup-port. In many jurisdictions now, a segregated gifted class is seen as only one of many possibilities within a broad range of options, with the placement depending on a child's individual special learning needs. The practice of matching the program to the child's needs is consistent with the mastery model.

8. *Coherence.* Under the mystery model, there is little or no connection between the definition of giftedness and the way it is identified, or between identification and actual programming; these three foundation points—definition, identification, and programming—operate quite separately from each other. One advantage of the mastery model is that it is defined as educational exceptionality, and educational programming recommendations are based on understanding individual children's learning needs, which are assessed through a multifaceted identification process designed to inform instruction. The three foundation points are integrated and interdependent, forming a coherent approach.

9. *Elitism and Political Implications.* Under the mystery model, educators of gifted learners often face considerable pressures relating to charges of elitism, including the scapegoating of gifted programming and unstable funding. Because the mastery model is clearly and coherently tied to special learning needs, educators who work from a mastery perspective are less likely to incur these kinds of social, political, and funding problems. When gifted learning options are (and also are seen to be) flexibly targeted to special learning needs and include all of those students for whom they are appropriate, people have fewer problems with gifted education.[4]

10. *Evaluation.* Evaluation has been a chronic problem in gifted education.[5] When definition, identification, and programming are amorphous and disconnected, as they are in the mystery model, it is hard to figure out if something is working or not, much less what needs improvement. As a consequence, for far too long, the only gifted program evaluations were user-satisfaction measures, in which students, parents, and teachers in gifted programs were asked if they were satisfied. People who are selected for an enriched and challenging program generally like their new program, which of course is good but does not provide objective information about the nature or degree of effectiveness of the program. From a mastery perspective, on the other hand, program evaluation is more objective and defensible: does the programming match individual children's learning needs on a subject-by-subject basis?

In Table 1.1, we summarize our comparison of the mystery and mastery approaches.

Table 1.1. A Comparison of the Mystery and Mastery Models of Giftedness

Factor	Mystery Model	Mastery Model
Origin	Nature focus (i.e., genetic, innate), with some nurture/environmental influences	Nurture focus (i.e., appropriate opportunities to learn) in context of genetic predispositions
Duration	Static; "once gifted, always gifted"	Dynamic; changing over time
Competence Domains	Most or all intellectual areas	Domain-specific (e.g., mathematical giftedness)
Identification Timing	Once, as early as possible	Ongoing, as needed
Identification Measures	Intelligence tests; checklists; creativity tests	High-ceiling academic reasoning tests and ongoing dynamic classroom assessment, supplemented by IQ tests as necessary
Identification Implications	Categorical ("gifted" or "not gifted")	Special education needs at a specific time in a specific area of functioning
Curriculum/ Placement	Enrichment; segregated gifted class if possible	Range of options; regular class if possible
Coherence	Definition, identification, and programming disconnected	Definition leads naturally to identification and programming, forming a coherent whole
Political Implications	Some charges of elitism, as well as scapegoating and funding concerns	Easily defensible
Evaluation	User satisfaction measures	Academic and cognitive measures of learning

The following vignettes illustrate the differences between the mystery and the mastery models. We show how each model might play out in the life of one child.

Raqi's Story, Version 1 (Mystery Model)

Raqi was an early talker and a very early reader. When she entered kindergarten, she was already reading chapter books and more than ready for "real work." She was lucky to have a kindergarten teacher who enjoyed her precocity and encouraged her to read while the rest of the class participated in learning their letters and other reading readiness activities. Grade 1 was a good year for her, too, again thanks to a teacher who knew how to keep her challenged and learning and who was able to be flexible in her demands.

Grade 2 wasn't so successful; there were no special accommodations for gifted learners, and Raqi just had to wait it out. She had arguments with her teacher, who was irritated by her extraordinary mathematical ability and who tried to trap Raqi by giving her problems she couldn't solve. Raqi survived through the second and third grades until the system-wide gifted identification process was available. She sailed through the gifted assessment process with flying colors, achieving an IQ score of 143. There was no question about her identification as gifted, and she was happy when her mother decided to allow her to attend the full-time gifted magnet program that was offered at another school.

Raqi loved the idea of going to school with other kids who were as intellectually curious as she was, who were keen to learn about *everything*, and who insatiably gobbled up books and wanted to talk about them. She waited impatiently all summer and strode off to school on the first day of fourth grade with very high hopes of having a teacher who understood her and friends she could really talk to.

But after that first day of school in the gifted class, Raqi came home dejected.

"Mom," she said, "I *hate* my teacher. She's nice, but she's really dumb, and she won't let us do *anything*."

Over the course of the next few weeks, Raqi's opinion of this teacher did not improve. She was even more dismayed to find that the kids in the class did not share her interests or enthusiasms and that their vocabularies were not much different than those of the kids she knew at her old school. Most of them didn't know what she was talking about unless she talked silly, and of course (being Raqi), she would not stoop to that level. As if all that weren't bad enough, she had some unhappy experiences in which she discovered that the other kids and teachers in the school openly resented the kids in the gifted program, especially the ones like her who refused to pose as less intelligent than they were.

Raqi's mother went into the parent-teacher conference in October hoping to help Raqi's teacher deal with her daughter, whom she knew to be difficult when she felt that her time was being wasted, but also to be wonderful when she was learning and engaged. Raqi's mom found that Miss Pinkerton was very young, and this was her first year working with gifted learners. She was an enthusiastic teacher who was following a set of curriculum materials obtained through the district office. The teacher explained very nicely but quite firmly that she wasn't able to create a special curriculum for each of the children in the class, and that even if Raqi already knew the material they were covering, she would be expected to go through it with the class, doing all of the homework and assignments. Raqi would be allowed to do extra work if she wanted to, of course, although Miss Pinkerton would have little time to mark it or to talk with her about it.

Raqi stayed in a gifted class for the next few years, feeling a bit lost and desperate and even weirder than she had felt in the regular classroom. She had hoped that once she was in a gifted classroom, she would meet kids like her and have teachers who understood her insatiable hunger for learning deeply and broadly. Those hopes were not realized. Sadly, it wasn't until high school that Raqi began to enjoy school again and find opportunities for real learning at school.

As with all of the vignettes that we share in this book, Raqi's story can be read in various ways. Like life itself, each story is complex, with different threads that can be pulled out for further consideration. We include Raqi's true story (version 1), not to show how terrible full-time gifted classes are—because many parents and children have told us that such classes have saved their lives—but rather to illustrate that gifted programs are not always the salvation that parents hope they will be, and that it is not enough simply to get a child labeled as gifted and put into a gifted class for all of her gifted learning needs to be met.

Here is a far happier version of Raqi's story, one that will illustrate what the mastery model looks like in practice. The significant difference is not so much the programming model, but rather the attitudes and approaches that are taken by the educators involved.

Raqi's Story, Version 2 (Mastery Model)

Let's replay Raqi's story as if her school district were providing gifted education designed to match her exceptional learning needs, consistent with a mastery perspective. We have the same little girl, a precocious talker and reader, hungry to learn everything she can from her earliest days on, devouring mathematics and literature, foreign languages and geography.

We don't have to retouch the first two primary school years at all. Raqi's kindergarten and first-grade teachers did all the right things by responding flexibly to what they observed and providing opportunities for Raqi to keep on learning, even though she was advanced in so many ways compared with her age peers.

In this second version of the story, let's suppose that Raqi's Grade 2 teacher realized that she was out of her depth and called in the special gifted education consultant, who worked with her to identify Raqi's areas of exceptional strength. Together with Raqi and her mother, they worked out a plan that compressed some of the aspects of the curriculum that Raqi had already mastered. This included designing a program that allowed her to work with the fourth-grade teacher, who was a math specialist, in a special weekly math challenge group that was working toward participation in a district-wide math contest. They gave Raqi some flexibility around classroom assignments and allowed her to choose her own reading material with the help of the school librarian, who worked with her to develop a meaningful reading plan for the year.

The special gifted education consultant worked with Raqi and each of her teachers for the next several years until Raqi was ready for high school. She accelerated through one complete

> grade and was ready to begin doing Advanced Placement courses in mathematics by the time she reached high school. She'd had a very happy and successful elementary and middle school experience. She was looking forward to continuing with the exploration of her interests at a local high school that had a wide range of subject area possibilities and a flexible administration that was willing to support the development of her many and varied interests and would allow her to take courses at the local community college when it seemed appropriate.

Through the years since *Being Smart* was first published, we've asked teachers and parents for their responses to various aspects of the book. The Raqi story is mentioned more frequently than just about anything else, sometimes with annoyance, because it seems to suggest that full-time classes don't work (and we are NOT trying to make that point!), but more frequently with an "Aha! *That* is the difference between the mystery and mastery models." Here are two of the comments that people have written about this:

> *"I can embrace the mastery model concept. In particular, I like the idea that giftedness is fluid and relative, and the aspect of domain strength is important. This is a realistic notion of what giftedness is because it is nonjudgmental, allowing for growth and change, in addition to average achievement at certain times or in certain subject areas."*
>
> *"The mastery approach makes a lot more sense because it accommodates kids' subject-specific abilities. Because it is also so inclusive, I think it is a viable and useful way to think about and identify giftedness."*

Shifting Paradigms

By definition, paradigm shifts are disturbances of the status quo. It is always difficult to identify when a paradigm shift begins to happen; it is easier to see it in retrospect. With its focus on domain-specific abilities rather than general intelligence, the Marland Report[6] from the U.S. Department of Education laid early groundwork for the beginning of the mastery model. Another early and important influence in this paradigm shift was the work that Julian Stanley and colleagues at Johns Hopkins University did with the Study of Mathematically Precocious Youth.[7]

Similarly, in 1982, Nancy and Hal Robinson outlined their optimal match concept.[8] These authors argued for providing a range of options for gifted learners and matching programming to individual learning needs. The following year, Howard Gardner proposed his theory of multiple intelligences, which changed the way educators think about intelligence.[9]

Then, in 1989, Jim Borland published *Planning and Implementing Programs for the Gifted*,[10] in which he talked about gifted education in very similar terms to those that we use here. He described himself as "a special educator whose population of interest is gifted children" (p. 2). He enumerated seven underlying principles, all of which are consistent with the mastery model, and we find that it continues to form a strong foundational base. We applaud Borland's foresight and perspectives, and yet we respectfully make a few small additions or refinements, noted here in italics:

1. The education of…gifted *learners* is a form of special education.

2. Children's current educational needs, not their prospects for future eminence, should guide our practice.

3. The nature of the children served will and should vary from school district to school district.

4. No single program model can be appropriate for all *children or all* school districts.

5. Programs for the gifted should be based on information gleaned from formal needs assessments, *which can include informal measures*.

6. The needs of gifted children are best addressed in the company of their age and/*or* ability peers.

7. Curricula for gifted students should stress the acquisition of important *and relevant* knowledge.

Borland stressed the centrality of these principles, saying, "No other way of conceiving of the education of the gifted, I believe, offers as defensible a rationale or as workable a framework for special programming."[11]

Michael Howe's *The Origins of Exceptional Abilities* (1990) provided further highly persuasive evidence for a domain-specific developmental perspective on gifted-level ability.[12] About the same time, the inaugural issue of *Exceptionality Education Canada* (1991) contained several frequently-cited and thought-provoking articles, including those by Dan Keating and David Henry Feldman.[13] Each of these articles made effective and controversial arguments for the need to move to a mastery perspective.

Other perspectives in gifted education are consistent with important elements of the mastery model. These include the talent development approach[14] and the integrated curriculum model.[15] Renzulli's enrichment triad model is a widely-used approach to giftedness that, in our opinion, provides something of a bridge between the mystery and mastery models.[16] Recent findings on the importance and validity of acceleration further illustrate the paradigm's shift to the mastery model, with its emphasis on ensuring a good match between a child's subject-specific developmental level, on one hand, and the academic challenges provided, on the other.[17] An increasing focus on expertise as a way to understand high-level development provides yet another example of the shift toward the mastery model of giftedness.[18]

In *Mindset*,[19] developmental psychologist Carol Dweck pulled together findings in neuropsychology, developmental psychology, and education that distinguish between a fixed mindset, in which some children are categorized as inherently smart (analogous to the mystery model), and a growth mindset, in which intelligence is seen as developing over time with appropriately scaffolded opportunities to learn (mastery model). Dweck's research, along with that of her colleagues, provides a remarkable confirmation of the validity of the mastery model; the fixed mindset (or mystery model) is associated with lower achievement and self-esteem, and the growth mindset (mastery model) is associated with greater confidence, risk-taking, and higher academic and career success over time. Dweck has written elsewhere about the application of her groundbreaking mindset findings to gifted education.[20]

Over the past several years, many experts in gifted education have written about the need for major changes in perspective,[21] with some describing the changes underway as a paradigm shift.[22] For example, in discussing his observations of a paradigm shift in progress, David Henry Feldman wrote, "Recognition that the field of gifted education is holding an increasingly untenable position appears to be growing, perhaps to the critical point at which real change becomes possible, even necessary."[23] He posited (as do we in this book) that it is important for the ongoing viability of the field that educators interested in high-level development pay attention to the developmental aspects of giftedness and the evolutionary movement of gifted education. We suggest that the mastery model provides a good way to do just that, as well as to simultaneously clarify some confusion that exists for many parents and educators.

Origins: Nature or Nurture?

Children's joy in the learning process is the ultimate goal, without which, we believe, giftedness will not easily be evidenced.[24]

For many years, there has been an ongoing debate about the relative weight of genetic and environmental influences on intelligence. Current research describes the inextricable and highly complex dynamic interconnection of nature and nurture over time.[25] The findings on high-level development come together in interesting ways. They suggest that high IQ most frequently results from children with the necessary neurological predispositions being listened to, cared about, respected, and provided with opportunities to learn and explore in age-appropriate ways.[26] There is good reason to think that giftedness rarely evolves unless some combination of "cognitive ability, motivation, and enriched environment co-exist and meld together to foster its growth."[27] Extensive longitudinal research findings indicate that if parents want to encourage giftedness, they should be careful observers of their children's development, responding to it and enhancing it without inappropriately demanding achievement.[28]

Giftedness can develop for other complicated reasons, too. For example, high achievement can be motivated by a drive to overcome some kind of obstacle (perhaps poverty, disability, or social or emotional deprivation). In a book exploring the reasons for, influences on, and various aspects of high-level development, Simonton considers the prevailing "common sense" notions and myths about such development, as well as the research findings for myriad possible effects on it, including (among many others) genetic inheritance, gender, birth order, creativity, age, intelligence, personality, psychopathology, relationships, and opportunities.[29] From Simonton's work, we learn to appreciate that the pathways to gifted-level achievement are as diverse and unpredictable as the achievements themselves.

The research on exceptional ability as it manifests itself in adult achievement outcomes is similarly interesting. Giftedness may not show up until middle or even late adulthood.[30] In fact, many of those who end up succeeding at very high levels in most real-world domains (with the exception of math, music, and sports) are persons whom teachers or parents did not recognize as exceptionally advanced when they were children.[31] Therefore, when children are not identified by schools as gifted, parents should *not* conclude that they are ineffective parents or that their child has less genetic potential than others. Giftedness as seen from the mastery perspective is about exceptional learning needs at a given point in time that require special educational adaptations; it is *not* about predicting future success or possible eminence.

Domains of Competence

Over the last few decades the definition of giftedness has changed from being a one-dimensional conception linking giftedness to high intelligence to multi-dimensional conceptions acknowledging the existence of outstanding ability in various domains.[32]

The concept of intelligence as multifaceted is not new and has been proposed by many people in many forms.[33] Howard Gardner captured popular imagination with his theory of multiple intelligences.[34] He argued that a single measure like IQ is inadequate and misleading in describing a person's many different abilities. When trying to understand or assess a person's intelligence, there are many intelligences or ability domains that should be considered somewhat separately.

Gardner acknowledged that the boundaries among the various intelligences are contentious and arguable and that there are many possible candidate intelligences. He developed criteria to designate an area or domain as an intelligence, including evidence that the domain is: (1) useful and important, at least in some cultural settings, (2) somewhat neurologically separate from other areas, and (3) considered to be a functional domain by test-designers, psychologists, or social historians. He initially proposed seven intelligences that met these criteria: linguistic, logical-mathematical, spatial, bodily-kinesthetic, musical, interpersonal, and intrapersonal. He has since nominated three other intelligences as candidates for this list, including naturalistic, existential, and spiritual intelligences.[35] It is possible that a given individual can be gifted in one, two, or even several of these domains but not in others, but very few people (if any) are gifted in all areas. Children's profiles of abilities *are* different, and Gardner provides a model for thinking about that.

Even among those who are identified as gifted because of overall high IQ scores, most are not gifted across all school subject areas. In fact, many children identified as gifted are quite average in some areas—a phenomenon called *asynchronous development,* and this increases with degree of giftedness in one domain or another.[36] By the time they reach adolescence, gifted young people who are good at everything are more the exception than the rule, and as they get older, there are only a very few who can be considered gifted across most or all subject areas.[37] Increasingly, gifted education experts are advocating that educators consider multiple intelligences perspectives rather than the global giftedness focus assumed under the mystery model.[38]

Is Learning Easy?

> *"I can't get math now. I guess that means I'm not gifted anymore."*
> *"My homework takes me soooo long, and my friend does it in five minutes. Could the tests be wrong? Maybe I'm not gifted after all."*
> *"I failed the geography test yesterday. Am I still gifted?"*

Contrary to popular belief, being gifted does *not* mean finding all learning easy. Gifted learners may find it simple to achieve or even exceed some or most age-normal expectations, but they experience the same challenges as anyone else in moving from their current level of mastery in a subject area to the next higher one. However, they may have some advantages in doing so. For example, they often have a larger and more conceptually complex foundation of knowledge than their age peers, as well as the confidence that comes from previous learning successes and from overcoming challenges. Nevertheless, it seems that real mastery involves effort and persistence.[39] Investigations of the lives of even the most highly gifted individuals inevitably conclude with observations of the tremendous investment of time, energy, and attention to the learning process that has been made. The lives of Beethoven, Einstein, and Picasso, for example, all illustrate the fact that high-level achievement reflects a huge commitment and countless hours spent mastering their respective domains of competence.[40]

In their book *Cradles of Eminence*, Goertzel, Goertzel, Goertzel, and Hansen discuss various kinds of shaping experiences in the childhoods of hundreds of prominent figures, and they consider what elements might lead to eminence.[41] They find that personal strengths, abilities, and ambition were valued in the homes of many of the individuals described, and their homes were places where ideas and opinions mattered. Love of learning was nurtured, and parents respected and largely encouraged perseverance and achievement.

No matter how easy learning might be for any given child, the moment always comes when a person who has previously found learning to be effortless comes across something that is difficult to master. Some children experience this when they first encounter algebra or a second language; others may become discouraged when they tackle philosophy or creative writing. If they are lucky, they have an experience of failure sooner rather than later. Sometimes when that first real difficulty is encountered, children previously identified as gifted think that they are no longer gifted. We do these children a disservice if we allow them to go through years of schooling without experiencing the challenges that can help them learn how to work hard, persevere through challenges, and surmount obstacles. Resilience and persistence are not learned by facing only easy tasks. One teacher got it right when he made the analogy that if failure is not encountered early on, then, like a nail lodged in a tire, it can become more difficult to deal with later on and may even cause irreparable damage.

The most important component of gifted-level achievement is hard work done consistently over many years with an attitude of problem finding and problem solving. "Even highly gifted children have to learn the hard way. Mozart still had to learn and work very hard for an extended time (more than 10 years) before he was able to produce his first masterpiece."[42] Exceptionally high-achieving adults have more failures than other people (as well as more successes) and also have a different reaction to them. Specifically, they work to master the skills that they have trouble with—a mastery orientation—rather than deciding that they aren't capable in that area.[43]

We'd like to share two perspectives that were sent to us in response to our earlier book. A new teacher wrote:

> *Without realizing it, I think I had adopted a mystery model perspective. I was struck by this as I read about how giftedness is domain-specific and can change over time. I now recognize how important it is to engage in ongoing assessment and identification practices. The sentence "The most important component of gifted-level achievement may well be hard work done consistently over many years with an attitude of problem-finding and problem-solving" jumped out at me. The emphasis here is on the interaction between the student's innate abilities and the nurturing and support required in order for them to develop. I'd always thought of giftedness as being more passive, as if it were bestowed upon someone. Engagement and effort really do matter.*

A former identified-gifted student wrote:

> *Ever since I was young, I've had a tendency to back off from work, especially when it's difficult. Now, after reading this section, I understand why. I wish my teachers had challenged me to achieve mastery and helped me to recognize that failure is an important part of learning.*

Another component of whether gifted-level achievement is easy or hard seems to be the age of earliest exposure to a domain, such that sensitive periods in brain development are maximized. An important variable is temperament, particularly as it interacts with and is shaped by the environment.[44] You can reassure young people who are worried about losing their giftedness by telling them that the best way to stay smart is to work hard at things they're curious about, and that no worthwhile learning comes easily. There is no real learning without failure; in fact, it is how we respond to failure that makes the difference between achieving at a high level and being mediocre in our achievements.[45] As a colleague who is also a parent says, "This is so important! It speaks to our impatient culture of instant success with minimal effort. So often, bright kids figure they should comprehend instantly, and they feel stupid if they have to reread something."[46]

Other Terms

"I don't believe in the term 'gifted.'"

We hear this comment frequently from parents, teachers, and children. It is one that we welcome, because when people say this, it often means that they are beginning to seriously think about what giftedness means. The term is controversial, and for good reasons.[47] Many who work in this field have trouble with it because it implies that "the gifted" share certain universal characteristics, and it simultaneously establishes an implicit category—"not gifted"—for everyone else. There is also a problem with the relationship between "gifted" and "gift": the term implies that the gifted person has received a gift. He or she therefore cannot take ownership of it or even feel proud of success. The gifted label carries a risk of intellectual identity detachment—a feeling that the gift must be used but cannot be owned and that accomplishments are handed out rather than earned. It can also bestow a burden of responsibility that the person has to use this gift wisely.

There are many other terms used to refer to high-level development. Here are some:

1. *Precocity* means *knowing ahead of time.* Precocious readers, for example, read sooner than expected, and doing something ahead of the age at which it is expected is commonly thought to be a sign of giftedness. Although reading early does give a child a big advantage in independent mastery of the world of learning, not all precocious readers go on to become gifted learners. Conversely, not all of those who go on to gifted-level achievement are early readers.

2. *Prodigy* is a word used to describe a child whose *achievement in one area is truly extraordinary for his or her age*, at a level expected of a much older expert. Thus, a musical prodigy might

play a violin solo with the kind of technical virtuosity that an older, already-accomplished violinist would use. A math prodigy might have skills usually exhibited by someone who has been studying mathematics for years. For various reasons, prodigies do not always live up to the promise of their youth,[48] and not all of those who achieve prodigiously as adults were considered remarkable as children.[49] Early expertise in structured or formal domains has little to do with high IQ and does not guarantee future success. Ability, passion, temperament, and learning opportunities all fuel the fire for prodigious accomplishment.[50]

3. *Genius* is a term reserved for someone who has *demonstrated enormous achievement in an important field of endeavor*, such as Mozart, Einstein, Gandhi, Mandela, or Freud. A child is not usually described as a genius.

4. *Superiority* is a psychometric term meaning *at least one and one-half standard deviations above the mean*. "Very superior" is the psychometric category used to refer to scores that are at least two standard deviations above the mean. We discuss these terms more fully in Section II.

5. *Talent* is typically associated with giftedness in the arts or sports, such as musical strength or athletic prowess. Gardner argued that these other dimensions of one's development are *integral and not peripheral to human intelligence*, and that in fact there are many ways to be intelligent.[51] "Talent development" is the term being used increasingly by experts in gifted education as they investigate the dynamic and developmental dimensions of all areas of ability.[52] Most of the work in talent development is consistent with the mastery model approach because of its focus on understanding and supporting domain-specific high-level development and on individual developmental differences.

6. *Advancement* refers to *competence or achievement that is ahead of what is expected* for a child's age. It is similar to precocity, without the mystery undertones.

Of these terms, advancement is probably the best for our purposes. From a mastery model perspective, "gifted" means that a child is advanced academically in what he understands and can do. He is ahead of what is expected for children his age in one way or another. However, because "gifted" is the term that is used in most educational jurisdictions, we use it somewhat interchangeably with other terms like "high-ability learner" and "advanced learner."

Very few people would argue with the observation that there are enormous individual differences in children's personalities, abilities, developmental pathways, interests, attitudes, and ambitions. However, not everyone recognizes that this is just as true for those with the gifted designation as for all others. Addressing the needs of gifted learners means paying careful attention to those individual differences and thinking beyond the widespread misconceptions that are, and have been, embodied in the word "gifted." For these reasons, we do not include any charts or lists of common "characteristics of the gifted," and we tend to stay away from talking about *the* gifted.

Historical Perspective

"People call you 'brainer' or 'smart kid.'"
"I don't like being treated like I'm different."

The concept of giftedness was not formally studied until the early twentieth century. In a longitudinal study called *Genetic Studies of Genius* (1925-1959), psychologist Lewis Terman examined the developmental characteristics of gifted children.[53] He believed that intelligence was genetically determined, a blueprint of a person's mental capacity, and measurable with IQ testing. This view prevails today in much of what is written about gifted education, and many educational jurisdictions continue to rely on IQ as a primary instrument for identifying gifted-level intelligence. Around the same time period, stretching back to 1926, Leta Hollingworth made significant contributions to the fields of psychology and gifted education. She focused on the guidance and counseling needs of gifted children. Rather than asking, "Who are the gifted?" (which was Terman's focus), she concentrated on finding out: "How can we meet the needs of gifted children?"[54] Her work is still highly regarded, and its impact is widespread.[55]

In the intervening years since Terman and Hollingworth conducted their studies, interest in giftedness has waxed and waned, and social and educational perspectives on it have varied greatly. One notable influence is the 1972 Marland Report.[56] This document focused on problems resulting from discrepancies between children's abilities and educational program offerings, stating that children who are exceptional in one or more designated categories should be provided with special educational services. The Marland Report included these categories: (1) general intellectual ability, (2) specific academic aptitude, (3) creative or productive thinking, (4) leadership ability, and (5) visual and performing arts. These categories have been used by educators for more than 30 years as a broad guideline for determining who might have gifted learning needs.

Today, many parents want to give their children every intellectual advantage, and a huge industry is thriving on marketing educational and technological toys, games, and programs that claim to make children smarter. Large regional talent searches are popular throughout North America and around the world. These programs typically identify academically gifted learners at early adolescence and support them into early adulthood. However, even though there is great interest in supporting high-level development, it is also politically incorrect in many places to even mention giftedness, much less to devote educational resources to addressing the needs of gifted learners.

Many people working in the field of gifted education are seriously concerned about the emerging consequences for gifted learners of the American federal *No Child Left Behind* (NCLB) legislation, which puts strict rules in place for schools regarding minimum learning outcomes for all students.[57] Unfortunately, this legislation has had, and continues to have, unintended consequences: gifted learners and those with learning disabilities (sometimes one and the same) are at the margins of schools' planning, of society's attention, and of policy-makers' consciousness in crafting policy. Without appropriately targeted learning opportunities, neither group achieves the depth or breadth of which they are capable.[58]

One troubling sign of the times is that many parents are actually embarrassed to discuss their child's intellectual giftedness with friends and family or with their child's teacher at school. Interestingly, they would not be reluctant to discuss a similar level of athletic or artistic exceptionality. Kids are often embarrassed to talk about being smart, too:

> *"I try not to let anyone know I'm in a gifted program."*
> *"It's not fun to be called a geek."*

> *"Some kids 'dis' the congregated gifted, calling us nicknames like 'nerds' and 'smart people.' And sometimes they say we're really stupid."*

Many educators who work with gifted learners tell us that their colleagues consider their work with these learners to be peripheral and elitist, and we have certainly seen this attitude ourselves. It is unfortunately true that much that has been done in the name of gifted education is not evidence-based and is in fact peripheral to what goes on in the rest of education. A "gifted enrichment activity" that focuses on building kites might be fun and interesting for some participants, but too often, little or no serious thought or effort goes into connecting the activity with seminal aspects of the curriculum. Students who describe this kind of activity as not only unproductive but also trivial or insulting are not entirely wrong. However, there are many teacher-friendly and evidence-based suggestions for adapting curriculum for gifted learners in ways that are not peripheral and that are well-grounded in theory. We describe these in detail in Section III.

Using the mastery model approach, identification and programming practices work toward matching a child's ability level to specific curriculum. For instance, some third graders appreciate the opportunity to read and discuss literature that is typically assigned to much older children. When such an approach is used, the majority of parents and teachers are not likely to see this as elitist.

If there is a bright future for gifted education (and we hope there is!), the current problems in the field, such as programming that embarrasses children or invites political sniping or elicits charges of elitism, must be overcome. One way of doing so is to make it an explicit goal to ensure that the learning needs of *all* children are known and well-met and that what is understood about gifted development is shared widely.

Guidelines and a Definition

> *"All children are gifted."*

Most people would agree that every child—even one with limited intellectual ability—has substantial learning potential and that we ought to encourage the best possible educational outcomes in all children.[59] This does not mean, however, that "all children are gifted." Using the mastery approach, those with gifted learning needs are those whose exceptional abilities are so advanced that they require specific educational adaptations to ensure a level of instruction that matches their observed performance. As an analogy, very few people would consider placing normally developing children in special programs for developmentally delayed learners.

So what exactly do people mean when they talk about giftedness? One definition—but one that we have problems with because of its generalities and focus on the concept of wide-ranging potential—is: "A gifted pupil is one who has been identified as possessing an unusually advanced degree of general intellectual ability that requires differentiated learning experiences of a depth and breadth beyond those normally provided in the regular school program to satisfy the level of educational potential indicated."[60]

Here is another definition that gives us pause: "The term 'gifted pupils' shall mean those pupils who show evidence of high performance capability and exceptional potential in areas such as general intellectual ability, special academic aptitude and outstanding ability in visual and performing arts. Such definition shall include those pupils who require educational programs or services beyond those normally provided by the regular school program in order to realize their full potential."[61]

While both of these definitions have the advantage of being flexible and tied to appropriate programming modifications, each one is also ambiguous. What does "unusually advanced degree" mean? Or "general intellectual ability"? Or "potential"? Indeed, how can we possibly know with any degree of certainty who is going to accomplish what, or to what extent they will excel?[62]

The primary mandate of educators is the academic development of all students. Their job is to think about and provide what children need for their academic and intellectual development. This means offering those children learning opportunities rather than creating a hierarchy or ranking of children's potential life achievement. (In Chapter 10, we address the important social and emotional issues associated with gifted development and education, but for now we are trying to define the term.)

With due regard to how the mystery model has shaped thinking about gifted education over the years, and with a sense that a paradigm shift is well underway, we have formulated a mastery model definition for giftedness. We have developed some basic guidelines, grounded in our work in educational psychology and developmental psychology. The definition must:

- reflect what we know about high-level cognitive development and individual differences
- incorporate the domain-specific nature of intelligence
- respect the dynamic and context-specific nature of intelligence
- not place limits on a child's potential
- focus on academic proficiency relative to others
- lead logically and directly to identification practices
- lead logically and directly to educational programming implications
- minimize the categorical dichotomy between "gifted" and "not gifted"

We suggest the following working definition of giftedness—one that incorporates all of the suggested guidelines.

The Mastery Model Definition of Giftedness:

Giftedness is exceptionally advanced subject-specific ability at a particular point in time, such that a student's educational needs cannot be well met without significant adaptations to the curriculum or other learning experiences.

> *Note: Those familiar with special education for students with learning problems will recognize that this approach is consistent with what is often called "Adaptive Instruction" and the prevailing approach to best practices in special education.*[63]

We have observed that schools that use the mastery model (or adaptive instructional) approach to giftedness experience fewer problems (such as elitism, political and funding tension, and parental pressure to get children into gifted programs). At the same time, academic curriculum for all students, including those who are gifted, is enhanced. Because the program is focused on matching precious resources to clearly defined and designated learning needs, there is less mystery to the gifted enterprise and consequently less resentment and sense of exclusion from resources from which all children might benefit.

What gifted learners—and in fact *all* learners—need are learning opportunities that challenge them sufficiently and appropriately, along with the right kinds of guidance and support so that they can meet and enjoy those challenges and feel good about themselves at home and at school.

Since the first edition of *Being Smart* was published in 2005, we have been gratified to have colleagues discuss the advantages of the mastery model approach,[64] and also to hear from parents and teachers about the difference it makes in their practice:

> *The mastery viewpoint stresses that the student has shown exceptional mastery of a subject and requires special programming to meet his learning needs. It eliminates implied value judgments concerning a child's overall "superiority" and is more equitable for every student.*[65]

> *With the mastery model, learning disabilities do not disqualify students from participating in a suitably advanced program. A label is no longer an issue. The focus is on keeping students appropriately challenged in all subject areas, and they're rewarded by experiencing the joy of learning.*[66]

A mastery perspective on giftedness in no way devalues the essential mystery of humankind, and we marvel as much as anyone else at the magic of everyday life and at the achievements of which people are capable in every domain. There is so much about human development that remains mysterious, so much we still don't know about what fosters expertise, exceptional accomplishment, and creativity—all components of gifted-level development. There are encouraging findings, however, that can help parents and educators in supporting gifted development, and that is what we emphasize in this book as distinguishing a mastery model from a mystery model. In the next chapter, we consider the nature of creativity from a mastery perspective in the context of its connection to giftedness.

Chapter 2
Creativity and Giftedness

> *The present belongs to the sober, the cautious,*
> *the routine-prone, but the future belongs to*
> *those who do not rein in their imaginations.*[1]

People often see creativity and giftedness as disconnected concepts, thinking of "creativity" as referring to artistic ability and "giftedness" as applying to exceptional academic intelligence. Our work in this area suggests that, in fact, these concepts are symbiotically intertwined. Creativity is an important component of actualizing giftedness in every domain, and domain-specific mastery is a prerequisite for high-level creative work. Rather than thinking of giftedness and creativity separately, our perspective is much closer to that expressed by David Henry Feldman:

> *To be creative means to use your full set of capabilities for some valued and valuable purpose, the consequences of which make a significant difference to an established field of endeavor.... Creativity is quintessentially a matter of devotion, mastery, patience, persistence, and talent...applied in full measure over a sustained period of time.*[2]

Over the course of history, there has always been a fascination with creativity. Toynbee hailed outstanding creative ability as "mankind's ultimate capital asset."[3] He argued that progress in confronting the problems of our world will be "spearheaded by some of the most advanced thinkers of our times," and that therefore, "to give a fair chance to potential, creativity is a matter of life and death." When we consider the riches that humanity has created over the ages in every area—in art, science, philosophy, music, literature, and other domains—we see the achievements of those whose creative work has stood the test of time.

People are experiencing more rapid and profound change in their lives than ever before. The nature of the current changes, particularly in communications technology, suggests that this change rate will continue to increase dramatically. One of the educational implications of living in these rapidly changing times is that it is essential that parents and educators who are interested in supporting gifted-level development encourage children to develop their capacity to adapt to changing circumstances. Creativity and creative habits of mind are vitally important means to that end.

What Is Creativity? And How Does It Connect with the Mastery Model of Giftedness?

Over the years, many people have directed our attention to children's creative efforts. Comments we hear from students, parents, and teachers include ones like these:

> "*I want to enter the creative writing contest, but I know I won't win.*"
>
> "*Look at my picture! I'm not creative at ALL! You should see the pictures my friend draws—people with three heads, blue monsters, and cars with wings. She's really creative.*"
>
> "*Other kids call him weird. I've even had adults tell me they think he's weird. But I think it's because he looks at the world differently, more creatively.*"
>
> "*I don't want to stifle her creative spirit.*"

In addition to David Henry Feldman, some authors who have explored the creativity field in ways that are consistent with the mastery model of giftedness are Teresa Amabile, Tom Balchin, Mihalyi Csikszentmihalyi, John Feldhusen, Howard Gardner, Dan Keating, David Perkins, Jane Piirto, Dean Keith Simonton, Robert Sternberg, and Robert Weisberg.[4]

One way of thinking about it is to distinguish between big-C Creativity and little-c creativity.[5] Big-C Creativity occurs only when a field has been fundamentally changed in a substantive way. Leonardo da Vinci, Martha Graham, Martin Luther King, Jr., and William Shakespeare would all be considered Creative by this definition. Such high-level creativity does not occur, however, until someone has acquired a rigorous or high level of mastery of a domain, which rarely (if ever) happens until the person has been working hard in that domain for at least 10 years. Only then is there a large enough foundation of knowledge and skills that the potentially creative individual has mastered the tools and has the complex conceptual understanding required for important and interesting innovation in the field.

On the other end of the rigor spectrum, little-c creativity is the ability to generate novel ideas or unusual products. For example, suppose that a teacher or parent asks a child to devise new ways to depict a character in a story that the child is reading. If the child generates something that appears to onlookers as unusual and unique, like a poorly-written poem about a person with three heads, then the child and her ideas might be considered creative. Although it would be accurate to describe the poem as representing divergent thinking and to say that this kind of divergent thinking has a place in defining creativity, it would be a mistake to equate the two. Divergent thinking is necessary but not sufficient for productive creativity.

Keating defined creativity as an interplay of four factors which he called the "four faces" of creativity.[6] His position synthesizes many of the competing definitions that are still in vogue, and in its practical implications, it connects directly to a mastery model of giftedness. He proposed that creativity involves: (1) content mastery, (2) divergent thinking, (3) critical thinking, and (4) effective communication.

This perspective incorporates the argument that creativity is built upon mastery of the knowledge and skills needed to be creative—the same knowledge and skills that are components of gifted development. It recognizes divergent thinking as an essential component of creativity, and certainly by most definitions, one must be thinking laterally or "outside the box" and generating innovative ideas in order to be doing creative work. People who are considered creative must be good at divergent thinking, but they must also be good at selecting their most promising ideas from the merely unusual or novel ones. As Keating argues, creativity requires people to analyze, synthesize, and evaluate their divergent ideas. They have to be able to think critically about which ideas are worth further time and energy. And once an important idea has been generated and identified as promising, they must then be able to communicate it effectively enough for others to understand it or recognize its value.

When defined in this way, creativity applies to science, business, and other domains as much as it does to the arts. If one cannot communicate one's good ideas so that others can understand them, they are not very useful. Poorly written poetry, therefore, is *not* creative. It may show promise, perhaps, that with further work, the writer might be able to do something better, but, by Keating's criteria, a poorly executed poem is not in and of itself creative.

Yet another approach to understanding creativity is to examine the lives of highly creative people and consider how they experience creativity. Creatively successful people in a number of domains often describe an experience of being so fully engaged in their work that consciousness of time disappears and they experience a profound sense of well-being. This sense of well-being and fulfillment is called "flow" by Mihaly Csikszentmihalyi, a psychologist who has written extensively about creativity. Flow is the feeling that motivates a person to do the work in which personal creativity is embedded, and it occurs when one experiences a balance between the challenges in a situation and the capacity to take action on them.[7] Csikszentmihalyi identifies the following essential components of a creative flow experience:

- clear goals along the way
- immediate feedback
- a balance between one's challenges and one's skills
- a merging of actions and awareness
- the exclusion of distractions from one's consciousness
- no concern about failure
- no self-consciousness
- a distorted sense of time
- a sense of an activity as its own reward

According to Csikszentmihalyi, these components combine in ways that are so fully absorbing that a person in a flow state can temporarily lose track of time and place, and even a sense of the world itself. In a spirit of authentic inquiry, voluntary engagement, and emerging awareness, flow can evolve into surprising realizations. There may be no other purpose to flow than to inspire a person to keep on flowing,[8] thereby fueling intrinsic motivation and furthering creativity.

Can We Measure Creativity?

"How on earth can I grade my students' assignments for their creative worth?"

"I think there is danger in seeing creative activities as somehow distinct from activities that involve careful thought and problem solving."

"I don't think creativity is something that can be packaged, then put on a scale or placed alongside some kind of measuring grid to be given a mark."

We know one educator who assesses creativity by observing her own reactions to her students' work. If she has what she describes as "spine-tingles," the student gets bonus marks for creativity. No tingles, no bonus. We suspect that we're not alone in worrying about the reliability and validity of this kind of measure, but we are often surprised by competent practitioners who think they can somehow rank their students' creativity and decide which ones are more and less creative than others.

Although there are many tests of creativity, none of them comes close to assessing the actual qualities of creativity in any kind of valid or meaningful way. In order to fit into a standardized, paper-and-pencil, group-administered testing mode, most standardized tests of creativity focus on decontextualized divergent thinking tasks. For example, a child may be asked to do as many things as possible with a circle or a paper clip in a limited time period. There is no sense of authentic challenge involved in such tasks, and those who accomplish truly creative work typically do not find such tasks worthy of much effort. Piirto[9] and many others who are engaged in creative work and/or the study of creativity observe that truly creative people are not likely to score very well on creativity tests.

The following story about Joel, a child we worked with who has many creative hobbies and interests, illustrates the problem with creativity tests.

A Parent's Thoughts about Creativity Testing

My son, Joel, is in Grade 4. He excels in math, sculpting, and other tactile activities, but he was recently excluded from his school's gifted program because he "failed" a creativity test. He did great on the academic ability and task commitment assessments, but his teacher told us that his score on the test of creativity was unusually low. My younger daughter, Kate, has not really been exposed to many of these things yet, so I'm not sure what her strengths are in those or, for that matter, other areas. For all I know, she may be outstanding, too.

My point is that age and context are big factors here, and in any case, not all creativity is consistent. I'm upset that Joel did badly on a creativity test and that that's why he didn't qualify for the gifted program. I'm not sure his performance means a darn thing other than the fact that now he's being penalized for it in much the same way that a great author may write a poor book and be faulted for that. Some people have the potential to think in new and exciting ways but may not be able to show it on cue or in a test situation for a variety of reasons.

Joel's Thoughts about Creativity Testing

I love Legos! It's my favorite thing. I also like to make stuff out of popsicle sticks, bubble wrap, and duct tape. Sometimes when I'm bored I build forts with the furniture. It drives my mom crazy.

The other day, the teacher gave our class this dumb assignment. She handed me and each of the other kids a piece of paper with a bunch of circles drawn on it. She said, "Make as many things as you can, all different." How stupid! I looked at Sam. We shook our heads and groaned. So I quickly drew some faces and a couple of bikes and a sun to make my teacher happy.

You're not going to believe this but my mom says I'm not allowed in the gifted program because I'm not creative. She says that circle thing was a test, and it proved I'm not creative. Well, I think the test is not creative, so there! Why didn't they just ask me to build something?

We agree with Joel and his mother that creativity is hard to measure. Creativity is too idiosyncratic, too rooted in particular tasks and situations to be easily quantified. Tom Balchin, who has investigated creativity extensively in Great Britain, wrote, "There is as yet no conclusive 'set of criteria' for evaluating creative products."[10]

Nevertheless, there are various measures that can help educators assess specific aspects of creative endeavors in ways that help them foster their students' creative productivity. One such tool (Balchin's Creative Product Grid)[11] assesses students' products' uniqueness, insights, and risk-taking, as well as potential functionality, well-craftedness, and attractiveness.

Another promising approach to assessing creative work is to focus on the actual process in an authentic context of application. Although creativity is too contextual, too individualistic in essence and form to ever be quantified by standardized pencil-and-paper tests, there are indications that creative and artistic potential in performing arts talent can be assessed validly and equitably with the Talent Assessment Process[12] in dance, music, and theater.

Creativity is too complex to be pigeonholed and quantified, too interconnected with psychological factors such as motivation, attitude, and the potency of perceived challenges. Far better to appreciate, understand, and foster creativity than to busy oneself trying to assign a numerical value to it. If we want to measure creativity, the best we can do may be to assess Keating's four factors—content mastery, divergent thinking, critical analysis, and communication skills—in an authentic problem-solving context that has relevance to the individual test-taker.

Nurturing Creativity

"Creative work can be incredibly difficult for students. I've found that I first have to establish a really supportive and encouraging environment before their creativity emerges."

"Students who are simply told 'be creative' often give safe answers first. Only after seeing how far they can go without being 'wrong' do they begin to stretch their ideas."

"Creativity is not only important in elementary and secondary schools, but also in many workplace situations. Teachers need to value and respect the idea of adopting and modeling creative approaches to learning."

Over the years, teachers have expressed their concerns to us about how challenging and yet how very important it is to give children's creative imagination room to grow. Science teacher Namrta Bhardwaj wrote the following:

> *I fear that there is not enough creativity in science classrooms. Students are rewarded for memorizing or learning facts, not for unique insights or creative ideas. This is very unfortunate, because for someone to develop into a good scientist, unique and creative ideas are truly essential. For example, researchers have to be able to see solutions that are not obvious. If we want students to become effective scientists, we need to help them develop their creativity right from the start.* [13]

Most educational researchers writing today would agree with Ms. Bhardwaj. In a review of evidence-based best practices in gifted education, Ann Robinson, Bruce Shore, and Donna Enersen wrote, "Even as we admit that the complexity of creativity makes defining it difficult, there is agreement that creativity can be nurtured and developed in a person, or it can be repressed and even lost. For all children, creativity training and recognition of production is important."[14]

In the 1980s, North American educators invested a lot of time, energy, and money into teaching creative thinking skills. However, the research done at that time demonstrated that creative thinking strategies do not usually transfer to other tasks. In spite of our best efforts, it seems that we cannot teach people to be creative, or for that matter analytical, in a vacuum. Creativity must be applied in domain-specific areas, building on rich content knowledge.

Creativity can be elusive, and it requires hard work. It involves preparation, incubation, illumination, and verification.[15] Too often, the impetus is on the final product instead of on the creative process itself. As with any expertise, fostering creativity involves nurturing the following habits of mind:[16]

- active engagement in learning and experimentation
- the progressive tackling of higher-level problems
- a matching of talents and task demands
- *practice, practice, practice* ("the way to Carnegie Hall")

The importance of these domain-specific habits of mind in generating high-level creativity has been demonstrated over the past few years in a number of fields from a number of different angles, including talent development,[17] expertise,[18] equity and diversity,[19] and wisdom.[20] Parents and educators who want to encourage children's creativity will do well to pay attention to these four basic principles: actively engaging children in many kinds of learning and experimentation, progressively raising their levels of challenge, matching schooling demands to ability level on a subject-by-subject basis, and emphasizing the importance of hard work and effort sustained over long periods of time.

Robert Sternberg has written about creativity as a choice.[21] He argues that we can decide to be creative (or not). He points out that as the world changes, people must acquire a flexible and creative attitude to their work, and also to life's other demands. Creativity can be developed, and creative decision-making processes can be taught.

Sternberg lists 10 ways that people can decide for creativity. We present them here, accompanied by our own short explanations:

1. *Redefine problems* so that you do not remain "stuck" in one place.

2. *Analyze your own ideas*, extending and improving upon them through reflection and critical analysis.

3. Be willing to *sell your ideas* by demonstrating their value to others.

4. Recognize that *knowledge is a double-edged sword*—that expertise can interfere with creative thought if it impedes flexibility and open-mindedness.

5. *Surmount obstacles* knowing that opposition can help you refine your ideas and forge new ones.

6. *Take sensible risks*, playing it safe when necessary but daring to stretch beyond your comfort zone.

7. Embrace a *willingness to grow*; instead of concentrating on being right or clinging to a certain viewpoint, be on the lookout for new problems and solutions.

8. *Believe in yourself* and your ability to produce creative ideas.

9. *Tolerate ambiguity*, recognizing that here are always rocky stages of uncertainty and muddle in the creativity process.

10. *Find what you love to do and do it*; creativity is built on passion, aspiration, and perseverance.

Sternberg acknowledges that the impetus for being creative varies from one person to the next, and thus the enabling factors for it also vary. This list is a starting point for thinking about how we can choose for creativity.

There are also a number of questions that parents and teachers can ask, both of themselves and of the children in their lives. We suggest five questions here, but you can generate more by thinking creatively about the ideas we discuss in this chapter and how they apply in your life. The answers may help you to understand what creativity is all about, what makes it happen, and how to encourage it in yourself and others.

Questions to reflect upon:

1. How do you know if you're involved in a creative process?

2. What would teaching and learning be like without creativity?

3. In what ways can creativity be frustrating for children or hamper their learning?

4. Under what circumstances can creativity enhance learning?

5. What is the connection between creativity and effort?

Paradoxically, the optimal environment for fostering children's creativity is one that feels both safe and challenging. Whether at home or at school, such environments have some common features:[22]

- acceptance and celebration of diversity

- errors seen as opportunities for learning

- opportunities for independent learning as well as collaboration

- flexible tasks

- time to listen, reflect, focus, and refocus

- encouragement of children's input

- requirement to defend positions with facts and logic

- serious attitude toward children's questions

- opportunities to work with varied materials under different conditions

- rewards for courage and reasonable risk-taking, as much as for correct responses and compliance with task demands

So how are creativity and giftedness related? Competence in a domain is the first step toward creativity. The next step involves stretching beyond the domain's frontiers to break new ground and generate fresh ways of looking at the world. Being gifted is not the same thing as being creative, but it is a very good beginning.

We have reviewed only a sampling of the current work on creativity, but many other resources have been designed to help teachers encourage creativity in their students. We provide further references for some of these on our website (www.beingsmart.ca). They will also be useful for parents who want to stimulate their children's creativity at home and elsewhere.

Creative Parenting and Teaching

Fostering creativity should not be reduced to a collection of set exercises carried out at fixed times as part of a 'creativity program.'[23]

"I think that children who are given opportunities to play with lots of toys tend to develop more creative problem-solving skills."

"I always enjoyed creative drama when I was younger. I try to involve my daughter in role-playing activities because it's a good way to increase her creativity and her understanding and tolerance of others."

Being a creative parent or teacher who supports the development of giftedness means learning a lot about the content of the parenting or teaching domain and then continuing to learn more. It also means looking at problems and failures as opportunities to broaden horizons—in fact, welcoming problems as possibilities or as ways of identifying what you can do better. It is by pushing one's competence and by being open to new ideas that people grow, expand, and invent new approaches and ways of doing things. Remember Keating's analysis of creativity as a combination of: (1) achieving a high level of mastery in a domain, (2) engaging in critical analyses of our behavior and its outcomes, (3) opening our minds to divergent possibilities, and (4) communicating effectively.[24] These factors are as valuable in our own work and daily lives as they are when applied to children's efforts. Being creative in these ways (and modeling all of this for children) can keep us fresh, eager to keep on learning, and enthusiastic about living and working with the children in our lives.

Section II

Being Smart about Diagnosing Mismatches

Chapter 3

Questions and Answers about Testing

Identifying gifted students is,
predictably, a can of worms.[1]

In gifted education (as in education generally today), testing and assessment are highly controversial and can be intensely anxiety-provoking. We think that this problem has a lot to do with the traditional mystery model perspective that "gifted" is a special category that some people belong to and others don't, such that it is possible to ascertain through testing who meets the criteria and therefore is gifted versus who fails. Categorizing people as either gifted or not gifted is responsible for much of the confusion, controversy, discomfort, ambivalence, and anxiety concerning gifted education.[2]

Slowly, as the paradigm shifts from a mystery to a mastery point of view, educators and parents are realizing that the important questions do not concern whether or not a child belongs in the gifted category, but rather how his or her individual learning needs might best be met.[3] In connection with testing, the field is moving from a focus on categorization to a focus on discovering and diagnosing educational mismatches.

In this chapter, we address the *who, what, when, where,* and *why* questions that parents and educators ask, thinking about our answers in the context of mismatch diagnostics rather than the traditional focus on categorical identification. Next, in Chapter 4, we address questions concerning *how* to assess learning needs intelligently, and in Chapter 5, we discuss how mismatch diagnostics is preferable to gifted labeling.

Who Needs Testing?

> *"I'm just not sure whether or not to put my son through the testing process."*
>
> *"Rob tested at 129, so he's not considered gifted. His friend's score was 130, and he is supposedly gifted. That doesn't seem right."*
>
> *"I dislike the gifted label, but I can see that Adrianna is way ahead of her classmates and bored with her grade-level work. But does she need the label to get the type of education she needs?"*

Parents and teachers often have questions about the educational testing enterprise, and nowhere is this more true than in gifted education.[4] People are uncertain about the tests themselves, the whole assessment process, and the cut-off scores that are used to designate giftedness—or lack thereof.

The questions and uncertainties reflect valid concerns. Adults should think carefully before putting children through the time and trouble involved in the testing process, to say nothing of the expense incurred by parents or the school. Nonetheless, for exceptionally capable learners, test results are important.[5] They can show where areas of strength and weakness lie, and if used properly, they can provide guidelines for intelligent decision making and programming applications.

In thinking about testing processes, it makes sense to begin by asking these two guiding questions:

1. "If this child is *not* tested, what is likely to happen?"

2. "If we *do* test, how will the information be used?"

Although these questions should be answered on a situation-by-situation basis, there are a few basics that can help guide decision making. Sample scenarios follow.

The Child Who Is Unhappy

> *"I used to like school. Now I hate it. Nothing but blah blah."*
>
> *"I like spelling. But the Grade 2 spelling words are too easy, so I write them backwards."*

> *"I was doing a math experiment I invented in the school wash-*
> *room. I was counting the number of flushes, but the toilets*
> *overflowed and I got a week of detentions. It's not fair."*

If a parent or teacher observes that a child is chronically frustrated, bored, or unhappy at school, then it is time to consider an assessment.[6] Guiding question #1 (If this child is *not* tested, what is likely to happen?) is at the fore here because the unhappiness indicates that he might have learning issues (possibly giftedness, perhaps as well as learning disabilities or other concerns) that need to be addressed sooner rather than later in order to prevent more serious problems down the road. An assessment by a good educational psychologist can help to uncover the child's strengths and challenges, leading to specific recommendations for productive learning.

The Child Who Is Doing Well

If a child appears to be learning and thriving at school, and if her developmental needs seem to be well met without making any changes, testing may not be necessary at all, at least for the time being. This is where guiding question #2 can be helpful (If we *do* test, how will the information be used?). Are things moving along happily and well? Do the teachers and school appear to understand the child's learning needs? Are they providing what is needed for her to continue to learn and progress commensurate with her ability level? If so, then why bother going to the time, trouble, and expense of an assessment? If a child does not need the exceptionality label in order to get the education that she needs, it makes more sense to wait until assessment information will be more useful—for example, if problems occur with some aspect of her learning or school experience, or if there are other indicators that more (or less) challenging curriculum is warranted.

In some circumstances, however, a proactive assessment can be helpful.[7] Sometimes a child appears to be doing just fine but *does* need something more if he is to be appropriately engaged in learning, a possibility to which parents and teachers should be attentive. High-ceiling subject-specific reasoning tests (as discussed later in this section) can be helpful in discovering gifted learning needs that may not otherwise be apparent. Where such tests are not in place, a psychoeducational assessment can be useful.

Individual Differences

> "*He feels that he is different from everyone else and worries that others do not accept him for the way he is.*"
> "*Sometimes she seems 'off the wall.' She just sees things differently.*"

Schools vary tremendously in their readiness, willingness, and ability to consider and address individual differences, even if testing has shown that a child is exceptional in one or more areas. An important factor in making a decision about whether to assess an individual child is whether or not anything productive will be done with the results (guiding question #2). This is not always easy to know ahead of time. Some schools pay lip service to diversity and to "educating the whole child" but in reality provide a "one size fits all" kind of education, with little or no adaptations made for individual differences. Some schools convey the attitude, "If you don't like what we provide, you can go elsewhere." Other schools welcome assessment information and work actively with teachers and parents to adapt programming and develop options that facilitate learning for each student.

Parents can find answers to our two guiding questions by becoming actively involved in discussions with the child's teacher, the principal, special education personnel, and possibly other parents, combining what they learn as a result with their own observations and interactions with their child.[8] In general, the more open, flexible, and accommodating the school climate, the more likely it is that assessment recommendations will be implemented.

Who should be tested, then? The strongest candidates for testing are those who: (1) are having difficulties that cannot readily be investigated or solved by parents and educators using their own knowledge of the child, and (2) exhibit problems over a sustained period of time, such as:

- difficulty at school

- boredom or unhappiness at school

- anxiety or signs of other psychological stress

- learning needs that may not be matched by the learning experiences at school

Testing makes more sense for students whose schools are prepared to make the necessary changes if they are provided with information about exceptional ability than for those who attend schools with little or no programming flexibility.

What Are the Key Concepts?

> *"There are so many different kinds of tests. I don't know what any of them are."*
> *"How do we get the test results? Will someone explain them to us?"*
> *"The school wants to test Maya, but I'm not sure if that's a good idea."*

A *test* is a specific instrument, such as the Stanford-Binet Intelligence Scale,[9] the Wechsler Intelligence Scale for Children,[10] the Woodcock-Johnson Psycho-Educational Battery,[11] or any of the academic achievement tests that are routinely given.

An *assessment* of a child's abilities is much more comprehensive than any one test and includes several different measures, some of which may be tests. A full psychoeducational assessment usually includes an intelligence test; one or more academic achievement tests; various measures of learning styles, self-concept, and attitude toward school; and a consideration of the child's functioning at home, with friends, and at school. It may include observations of the student and interviews with the parents and teachers as well. Parents are usually asked to provide medical and anecdotal history and to comment on the child's interactions with siblings.

Standardized Tests

Standardized tests are designed to allow reliable comparisons of individuals with others of the same age or grade level. They are standardized in both the administration and the scoring procedures. There are very detailed rules about how to administer and score each item so that the test conditions are as close as possible to identical or "standard" for all those who take the test. The advantage of standardized tests is that they provide a standard against which to measure an individual's ability. The disadvantage is that they allow no flexibility in administration or scoring.

Percentiles

A percentile designates where one person's score falls relative to other people's scores. If a child scores at the 60th percentile, it means that she has scored as high as or higher than 60% of others who have taken the same test and who are included in the comparison group. If someone scores at the 98th percentile, she has scored as high as or higher than 98% of others. These percentiles do not mean that the child knows 60% or 98% of the information being tested, but rather that she has done better than that percentage of the comparison population.[12]

Standard Scores

Intelligence and academic test results are usually reported as standard scores, which are based on a normal, bell-shaped distribution. As with percentiles, a standard score shows a person's functioning on a given test as compared with other test-takers, usually of the same age or grade. For many tests, including IQ, the standard score is based on a test mean of 100. Thus, a score higher than 100 is above the average. However, since tests always have some possibility of error ("error variance"), IQ scores are usually expressed as belonging to a range. Thus, the Average range includes IQ scores from 90 to 109, Above Average includes scores from 110 to 119, Moderately Above Average includes scores from 120 to 129, and Significantly Above Average includes scores above 130.

Standard Deviation

Standard deviation is a statistical term describing the distribution of scores around the test mean. With tests like intelligence tests, in which the test mean is set at 100, the standard deviation is usually 15. Most people (68% of the population) score within one standard deviation (15 points) above or below the mean (that is, between 85 and 115). The farther from 100, the more exceptional a standard score is. Mental retardation is usually considered when scores are two or more standard deviations below the mean (70 or below). Giftedness is usually considered when scores are two or more standard deviations above the mean (130 and above).

Intelligence Quotient (IQ)

Historically, the "quotient" in IQ referred to the relationship between a person's so-called "mental age" (as determined by his score on the test) and his actual chronological age. While that computation is no longer used, the term intelligence quotient (IQ) remains and is widely used to designate a standardized measure of intelligence. The two most valid and reliable tests of intelligence for school-aged children are the Stanford-Binet Intelligence Scale[13] (currently in the fifth edition) for ages 2 to 90, and the Wechsler Intelligence Scale for Children (WISC)[14] (currently in the fourth edition) for ages 6 to 16.

Group vs. Individual Tests

Group-administered tests can be given to many people at once—in a classroom setting, for example. They are time- and cost-efficient to administer, although they provide little or no opportunity to consider individual differences in response styles or reasons for making errors. Their administration does not require specialized training.

Individual tests are administered privately, one-on-one, by a highly trained and experienced test administrator (a psychologist or psychometrist). Individual tests are significantly more expensive than group tests but provide much better opportunities for observation of a child's individual learning style, attitudes, strengths, and problems, and they therefore provide much richer information for assessment purposes.

What Purpose Does Testing Serve?

> *With a current national and international focus on testing and assessment and standardization of curriculum, we can kill the joy that our most able students have both in school and in creative endeavors.*[15]

Tests can provide valuable information about exceptional learning needs. Or not. The value of test scores lies in the way they are interpreted and used to inform educational programming and decision making. As with so many areas, the numbers are meaningful, but they can easily be misinterpreted or misunderstood. One of the most confusing aspects of an assessment report is the number of scores provided; figuring out which ones matter most and how they all come together is one of the most sophisticated demands of assessment interpretation. The importance of having a wise and thoughtful interpreter cannot be overstated.

Typically, a psychoeducational assessment report is several pages long and includes: (1) scores of several subtests and tests (reported both in percentiles and in standard scores), (2) written descriptions of the child's areas of strength and weakness, and (3) recommendations for home and school.[16] Although jurisdictions vary in what specific cut-off score is used for gifted identification, there is usually a requirement that certain scores be above the 98th percentile.

Whether or not the official label of "gifted" is used, when major scores[17] are above the 98th percentile (or standard scores are above 130), parents and educators should consider the child's needs—educational and otherwise—as it is quite possible that the school program is not sufficiently stimulating or challenging. An unusually high intelligence test score, for example, is an indicator—a warning flag—that caring adults need to investigate the match between the child's ability and the learning opportunities that she is being given. Children who score above 150 are highly likely to have special educational needs, as well as being at risk for social/emotional difficulties, particularly at early adolescence.[18]

It is also important to realize that when a child's IQ is below 130 (or any given cut-off), it does not necessarily signify the absence of an educational mismatch for that child at that time. IQ tests can have low scores for many reasons, such as fatigue, distractions, poor motivation, or for medical reasons, and careful test interpretation is essential. Test scores can be useful provided that they—as with other information generated—are wisely considered and carefully communicated to those who are making decisions.

When to Test?

There are many ways to answer the *When?* question. We consider the child's age, comfort with testing situations, retesting, the time of year, and whether advance preparation is required.

Age

> "We've been told that our four-year-old is showing signs of giftedness. Should we have her tested?"

"Do schools typically test smart kids in the primary grades?"
"My son is 13 and has never had an IQ test. Is it too late?"

Although intelligence testing can be done when a child is as young as two and a half, it makes sense to only test that early when there are reasons for concern. If a child's development is generally proceeding well and he seems happy and interested in learning, it is not the time to think about testing.

There are huge individual differences in many dimensions of maturation—differences which make it hard to score test behaviors in standardized testing situations, particularly at younger ages. For example, some independent and curious youngsters are not much interested in complying with a stranger's requests that they follow the directions to manipulate blocks in a certain way. They would rather invent their own block designs than copy the ones the examiner shows them. Alternatively, they may not be interested in solving puzzles as quickly as possible, which is necessary to score well on many standardized tests. Although gifted assessments are sometimes conducted in the preschool years, there is less than desirable test reliability until about age seven.[19]

We discuss these issues more fully in Chapter 5, in connection with early identification, and we illustrate some of them with this vignette.

When to Test?

Parent

Jake is six years old and in Grade 1, and I'm wondering if he should be tested. He is currently reading chapter books at the Grade 4 level. He wants to write his own chapter book and has a title and story idea in mind. His teacher is supportive and is encouraging him to do so. She also goes out of her way to find interesting materials and activities for him.

Jake has always been very verbal. He is extremely focused and intense. He gets frustrated, but at the same time, he has a lovely sense of humor. Socially, he is well adjusted, but we are beginning to notice that a lot of his friends don't have the same desire to remain at various activities for the length of time that he does. He appears to be strategy-oriented (he likes chess) and looks for patterns everywhere. He loves statistics and has taught himself many things, particularly in the sports world—the ins and outs of baseball and hockey, as well as names of all the players and their info. He is very self-challenging (for example, with computer games, he won't rest until he has completed each level of difficulty), and he loves it when he's successful.

As Jake is our first child, we don't know if his attributes are that different from others his own age. So far, he is happy and loves school. However, he is quite mature for his age in some areas (he can reason like someone much older, and he's always thinking ahead). He is also the multi-tasking king. He can follow a hockey game (or two) on television while playing on the computer, and he can still carry on a conversation.

If you could shed light on any of this, it would really help.

Our Response

Jake sounds wonderful. Although he might well test at the gifted level, we do not recommend testing at this point. As long as his learning needs are being met and he is doing fine in other ways (and he sounds like the kind of child who goes more than halfway to ensure that!), our position is: "If it ain't broke, don't fix it."

As he gets older, if you notice signs of unhappiness, boredom, frustration, aggression, or depression, then it would be a good time to consider testing. In the meantime, it sounds like your instincts are excellent and that he is in home and school environments that are meeting his needs very well. So keep doing what you are doing! You also might want to take a look at some of the resources we provide on our website and consider joining your local chapter of the Association for Bright Children (ABC).

Although we have focused predominantly on young children in this discussion, there is no upper limit to the appropriate age for testing. Adolescents are not too old. Even adults who perceive a mismatch between their abilities and learning or career opportunities can sometimes benefit from assessment information.

Comfort with the Testing Situation

> *"I had a fever the day of the test, but I never told anyone I felt sick 'til later."*
> *"When I got tested last time, the lady had an accent, and I couldn't really understand her."*
> *"I wanted to make sure the stupid test was done in time so I wouldn't miss any of lunch period."*

A child who is sick or distracted or who decides to rush through the testing in order to do something she really wants to do (lunch, gym, recess, photography club, a music jam session, or maybe math) is not going to perform as well as she is able, and her test scores will be lower than they would otherwise have been. A child who is uncomfortable with the test administrator, feels pressured, or has trouble understanding the instructions might also have difficulty doing well in such a testing situation. Standards of professional assessment practice include that a child should be physically and emotionally comfortable and that she understand the instructions.

Retesting

> *"Can we have Christopher retested on the WISC?"*
> *"Emily took the Stanford-Binet six months ago. She has matured a lot since then, so we want her to redo it."*
> *"Sanjay took an IQ test back when he was six. He's going to high school next year. Does it make any sense for him to do it again now, or will the results be the same?"*

Intelligence tests are not tests of academic content mastery, such as mathematics or English language or science. Instead, they are designed to provide information about a child's cognitive processing, including his reasoning ability, when faced with novel puzzles and problems. In order to provide valid scores, the tasks must be new to the child, and because of this, the same test cannot be given too frequently. In many cases, the rules governing test practices actually prohibit re-administering a given test before a minimum of one year. Some jurisdictions are more conservative than this and will accept the results of a retest only if it has been at least two years since the previous testing using the same instrument. This prevents giving a scoring advantage to children who have been recently tested.[20]

If children are assessed when they are young, it is sometimes necessary to repeat the testing later. Generally, assessments that are two or more years out of date are not considered adequate for making current programming decisions. Children grow and develop in ways that cannot always be predicted, and children's test scores (including IQ) can change over time, occasionally dramatically, sometimes rising, sometimes falling. However, there is rarely a good reason to do "regular" intelligence testing or to retest a child at all unless there is a decision to be made that requires new information.

Time of Year

> *"Should children be tested at the beginning, middle, or end of the school year?"*

The best time to test a child is when the need for it is recognized. Experience has shown us that in schools that use a September-June calendar, the two peak months for testing are October and May. If classes begin in September, problems tend to surface by October, so parents and teachers identify reasons for assessment at that time. In the spring, people begin thinking about and planning for the next school year. There is enough lead time then to incorporate any necessary changes into educational planning for the fall.

If testing is being done by the school rather than by a private practitioner, there is usually little individual scheduling choice. As might be expected, there tend to be waiting lists for individual assessments, particularly if the referring issue is giftedness, which is very often seen by schools as less urgent than other kinds of schooling issues.

Advance Preparation

> *"What can we do to make sure our child doesn't 'fail' the gifted test?"*
> *"Are there practice tests our son can work on?"*
> *"How can we reduce text anxiety?"*

Sometimes parents ask how to prepare a child for testing. Our answer: "Make sure she gets a good sleep the night before and eats a nutritious breakfast." There is little that one can study that helps prepare for an intelligence test.

Intelligence tests are designed to assess a child's reasoning ability and knowledge in several areas. Preparation is what has occurred all through the child's life up to the time and date of testing. A child who feels loved and listened to, whose curiosity has been encouraged, and whose questions have been addressed is as ready as he can be. If his learning has been supported and he has been exposed to a variety of situations and learning opportunities, then he has done the best homework or preparation possible.

In fact, studying for an intelligence test is more likely to make a child anxious and so reduce the score rather than improve it—unless, however, an unscrupulous person who has access to the test coaches the child in the actual test items or similar tasks. Even when parents are willing to collude in this unethical practice and find someone willing to prepare their child in this way, they do the child no favor. If they succeed in artificially boosting the child's score into the gifted range, she is likely to find herself struggling to keep up with the others in a gifted program. She runs the risk of going from being one of the most competent members of a regular class to being the least capable learner among those who are more advanced. Even though tests and scores are problematic in many ways, if they are the standard that all children are being held to, it is not usually an advantage to be the least competent in the group at meeting that standard. For obvious reasons, this kind of situation can seriously damage a child's self-esteem, learning, and eventual achievement.

Another concern about test preparation relates to test anxiety. Some children become anxious just because they are being tested or as soon as they see a stopwatch being used to time them. Parents can help prevent or reduce anxiety (and its possible score-lowering effects) by making sure that their child is comfortable, well-rested, and well-fed on the day of testing. They can also help by modeling a calm, poised, and curious attitude toward the assessment session, as well as explaining the reasons for doing the testing. It can be helpful to chat with the child in a reassuring manner, ensuring that there is not too much emphasis placed on performance outcomes. One way to talk about the testing process is as an exploration of how the child learns in order to think together about the most reasonable educational plan.

When parents ask us what to tell their child about what he will be doing during an assessment, we suggest saying something like, "We're hiring a learning detective who needs your help to find some clues. The learning detective will ask you to do some puzzles, thinking activities, and quizzes. You'll be working together to figure out how you learn best. We want some ideas about that and some information that we can share with your teachers." Most children like the idea of working with the psychologist to help figure themselves out.

Most curious and intellectually engaged children actually love assessment tasks, and many of them ask their parents on their way out of the testing if they can come back another day or do this instead of going to school. Generally, the only children who dislike the process are those who have had bad testing experiences already, who are experiencing too much pressure to do well, or who feel that their weaknesses are being investigated and exposed.

Life itself is the best preparation for an intelligence test, and being fresh and relaxed helps, too.

Where to Test?

> *"Are the tests done by the school the same as the ones done by private consultants?"*
>
> *"Jill was tested two years ago, and the school psychologist concluded that she had emotional problems. Since then, none of her teachers has even thought about her giftedness. Instead, all they do is focus on her so-called emotional issues."*
>
> *"Does it matter where he takes the test? Will the scores be part of his school record?"*

In some school settings, parents who want an assessment for their child have no choice other than to hire a psychologist in private practice. In other settings, there are school psychological services available, and at no charge.

Some parents, however, may have legitimate concerns about testing that is conducted through the school. Once the testing has been done, test results can become part of the child's permanent school record unless parents request that they be excluded—and requesting their removal is not always an easy process. Whether the results automatically become part of the child's record or not, parents may worry that educators will misinterpret the findings or use them to support programming that they (the parents) don't believe to be appropriate. There is some variation in these practices across jurisdictions, so this is something that parents should check into with their child's school, especially if it is a concern.

If there are concerns about what the assessment results will be or how they will be used, it is good to discuss matters in advance with the school psychologist, as well as to consider the possibility of hiring a psychologist in private practice to conduct the assessment. When a private assessment is indicated, it is important that there be a good fit between the child and the person doing the assessment. Choosing a competent and caring professional can be a time-consuming and stressful process. It requires some patience and effort, as well as considerable knowledge about what to look for. We discuss how to go about the process of seeking professional help in Chapter 11.

Why Test?

> *"I know my son is smart, but his grades are terrible."*
> *"My daughter is really creative, but she's always getting in trouble at school. The teachers just don't seem to like her."*
> *"I have this one student who never hands in his homework. He's the class clown. I think he's really bright, but how can I know for sure?"*
> *"There's a kid in my class who's driving me nuts with her questioning. She's becoming a real behavior problem. I need to know how to program for her."*

Most teachers have little or no training in gifted development, and so their personal biases and assumptions influence their perceptions of what a gifted child is like. Such characterizations can prevent them from recognizing and identifying the advanced or gifted learners in their classrooms. Testing can provide helpful information in these situations, as long as the testing information is presented in teacher-friendly form and the teacher is given appropriate support in thinking about programming implications of the findings.

Where the mystery model is in place, there can be students who are exceptionally advanced in their learning ability but who don't qualify for gifted programming. Some of the most capable learners are so bored and frustrated by what they are asked to do at school that the last thing they appear to be is keen, curious, task-committed, or high-achieving— attributes that are often regarded as typical characteristics of "the gifted."[21] Some advanced learners' grades are appalling except when they happen to like the teacher, the assignment, the subject, or some other extrinsic motivator like grades or recognition.

The best way to answer the "Why?" question concerning testing for giftedness is that test scores can show what kind of gifted learning needs a student might have. As David Dai and Joseph Renzulli write, "In static models of gifted education, assessment (identification) and educational provisions are separate processes, but in dynamic models of gifted education, they inform each other and thus become an integrated system."[22] From a mastery model perspective, standardized test scores can be used diagnostically to show:

- exceptional subject mastery relative to age peers

- students' areas of strength and weakness

- level and type of educational accommodation that may be needed in specific domains

Testing can be useful to indicate a child's areas of mismatch. The important question to ask then is: "What learning opportunities does this child need in the mismatched areas?"

A Sampling of Student Testing Scenarios

Each of the following students was identified as gifted, and it is interesting to see that the reasons for testing, procedures used, children's experiences, and consequences were all quite different.

Dana

Dana was a lively and energetic 10-year-old who had always achieved at a high academic standard at the private school she had been attending since kindergarten. Her parents believed that a full-time gifted program in the public school system would be comparable to the program in the private school, and at considerable financial savings. Accordingly, Dana's parents arranged for a psychologist to administer the Stanford-Binet Intelligence Scale during the summer. Dana met the criteria for her public school's gifted program and was granted entry. Her family treated the test "simply as an entry exercise" required in order for her to move from a private school to a public school. She loved the new environment and found it challenging because her teacher used the testing information to help design suitable programming for her.

Mariana

Mariana, a fourth grader who described herself as "mostly bored" at her local elementary school, was involved in a weekly challenge program that provided enrichment to a group of children on a pull-out basis. The special program teacher believed that Mariana was a suitable candidate for full-time gifted programming and nominated her for testing. Mariana took part in assessment procedures, and on the basis of a WISC score above the 98th percentile, she was identified as gifted. Mariana's parents wondered if they should leave her in the part-time challenge program and the regular classroom or move her to a full-time gifted placement. As far as Mariana was concerned, she was ready to "start fresh." After careful deliberation, Mariana and her parents decided to accept the gifted placement. From fifth grade onward, Mariana went from being mostly bored to being happily challenged. She compared work demands, reporting that they had previously been "effortless," whereas they became "a lot harder and much better than before."

Corey

Corey was a feisty nine-year-old who described school as "yawwwn, zzzz, ahhh! It's boring, exhausting, and far too much work." His report card indicated a range of achievement levels from A to D, as well as inconsistent work habits. He loved mathematics and all things to do with computers, although his school grades did not reflect this. Corey had almost no friends, and he perceived school as a place that he was obliged to attend but which served little purpose socially or academically. "I like school because it ends," he told us. Corey's gifted identification procedure consisted of a group intelligence test at school which he described as "managing bits of information." After a long wait, the school informed Corey and his parents that he had been

> selected for placement in a gifted classroom. Corey was hopeful that being in a full-time gifted program would make school more interesting and enjoyable; however, a year into the gifted program, he told us that nothing much had changed. He still had not made any friends, and his advanced abilities in math and computers were not being addressed at school. He said, "The only place I learn anything worthwhile is at home in front of my computer."

Although intelligence test scores are not always used intelligently (as in Corey's case), when they are seen in the context of other information, they can help parents and educators understand a child's learning strengths and any problems that she might be experiencing. It is important to keep in mind that the only good reason to test gifted learning needs is to figure out how we can better meet those needs, putting our focus on diagnosing possible mismatches rather than categorizing children as gifted (and not gifted). Testing merely to discover an IQ score does not help a child, parent, or teacher understand precisely what kind of educational programming is needed.

Now that we've considered the "Who, What, When, Where, and Why" of testing, we look at the "How?" question—that is, how to understand assessments and tests.

Chapter 4
Assessments and Tests

In Chapter 3, we introduced many of the terms, concepts, and issues connected to the complex area of assessing gifted learning needs. Here we discuss the way in which assessments are actually done, the various tests and measures that are used, and how to make sense of the scores and results that are generated. Again, we emphasize the mastery model's shift in focus, as the field moves away from the mystery model's focus on identification of children as gifted or not gifted toward an emphasis on what we call mismatch diagnostics.

It Starts with the Teacher: Dynamic Classroom Assessment

> *"Madeline absorbs everything I give her. I know she's ready for more, but I don't know where to start."*
> *"I know that all the students in my class have been identified as 'gifted,' but I don't know what that means when it comes to what math I should teach them."*

Learning is a dynamic process that happens in a particular context or environment.[1] In a school setting, it is deeply influenced by the learner's relationships with the teacher and other students, as well as by personal history, interests, and abilities. Identifying academic and other needs begins with ongoing dynamic assessment in the classroom.

In dynamic assessment, the teacher engages with the student as an active partner in an ongoing, cyclical process:

- informally assessing students' learning needs
- teaching to students' optimal levels
- assessing learning outcomes
- teaching to students' optimal levels
- assessing learning outcomes
- and so on, in a continuous loop of learning and growth

In this way, instruction and assessment inform each other, and each is grounded in a clear understanding of what the individual already knows and can do. Once a student has mastered a section of curriculum or skill, he is given (or helps the teacher discover or design) new and ever more challenging material. By keeping close track of student learning in this way, teachers and students can work together to make informed decisions that match curriculum demands to learners' developmental levels.

This approach has obvious benefits for all students, but it is particularly important for gifted learners, whose exceptional learning needs might otherwise go unnoticed by the teacher. By enabling students to confront new and appropriate challenges, this strategy both encourages gifted students' ongoing growth and helps to prevent boredom, frustration, and tuning out.

Dynamic classroom assessment minimizes the need for formal testing, labeling, or withdrawal of students from the regular classroom. There are several advantages to using ongoing dynamic assessment with gifted learners:

- Learning assignments can be more readily tailored to a child's temperament, personality, motivation, and interests.

- It significantly reduces the cultural and socioeconomic status biases inherent in standardized testing (as we discuss later on).

- It provides a more targeted indicator of ability in specific areas (such as math reasoning or reading comprehension).

- Dynamic classroom-based assessment is directly related to each child's learning needs, providing specific implications for where and what kind of instruction or intervention is appropriate.[2]

The Student Portfolio

One dynamic classroom assessment approach involves the use of portfolios, or compilations of students' efforts that demonstrate their progress in one or more areas.[3] Students are responsible for putting samples of their various efforts in their portfolios in collaboration with the teacher; the degree of student responsibility and involvement depends on age and other individual factors.[4] A personal folder, box, or other kind of holder can contain whatever the student (in consultation with the teacher) deems relevant artifacts of the learning process.

A portfolio might contain work samples, journals, audio or video recordings, pictures, test results, teacher assessments, or descriptions of achievements and learning experiences (including self-ratings and reflections). It is a "purposeful collection of student work that exhibits processes, strategies, progress, achievement, and effort over time."[5] In planning for the portfolio, the student is managing her own work and setting personal goals—both important life skills. She learns to take ownership and pride in her accomplishments, moving away from a dependence on outside evaluation from teachers or parents.

Portfolios generally reflect instruction, responses, and tasks that are authentic—that is, they are personally meaningful to the individual and connected to some kind of real-world outcome. For example, a typical student portfolio might contain initial plans for a project; several written drafts; self-evaluations; feedback from peers, teachers, and other experts; finished products; and possibly plans for subsequent activities. These materials can be kept by the teacher or the student, depending on maturity level, and can always be revisited. By sixth grade or so, a child should be fully responsible for assembling, maintaining, and updating his own portfolio.

With the portfolio approach, parents and teachers are able to recognize an individual child's abilities and developmental pathways in particular areas over time.[6] Increasingly, portfolios are being recognized as useful for student learning and dynamic classroom assessment purposes, as well as in parent-teacher conferences to showcase a child's learning.[7]

Performance Assessment

Performance-based assessment...represents an indispensable approach for assessing gifted learning.[8]

> *Performance assessment offers the most*
> *meaningful evaluation of higher order thinking.*[9]

As its name suggests, performance assessment is embedded in what students are actually doing or creating in their learning activities. Such assessments "focus on challenging open-ended problems that require high-level thinking and problem solving, and put an emphasis on the process the student uses to come to an answer rather than on whether or not the student can quickly find the right answer."[10]

One of the best known approaches to performance assessment is "Understanding by Design"[11] or backward planning, a three-stage approach to designing authentic and dynamic assessment. A teacher starts by identifying the learning outcomes that she is working toward and then works backward from there, creating a scaffolded structure for the learning process. The teacher must: (1) identify desired results, (2) determine acceptable evidence, and (3) plan learning experiences and instruction. Architectural metaphors are often used when this model is applied to education, with the teacher seen as an architect who starts with a vision of the completed building and then carefully works backward, thinking about content, scope, process, and coherence, as well as how these might be authentically assessed.

In addition to being a good way to implement dynamic assessment for all children, performance assessment is a promising way to include more diversity in gifted programming. Some of the features of performance assessment (as with other forms of dynamic assessment) that contribute to its being more inclusive are that:[12]

- it rewards fluency and complexity rather than speed
- it acknowledges multiple right responses rather than "one right answer"
- it involves manipulating materials as a pathway to solution-finding
- it employs preteaching (dynamic assessment)
- it focuses on higher-level thinking and problem solving
- it incorporates self-reflection

Day-to-Day Diagnostics

Effective teachers know that they can understand a lot about where students are in their learning through meaningful daily interactions with them. There are four key aspects to what we call day-to-day diagnostics: (1) careful observation, (2) active listening, (3) open dialogue, and (4) reflective responsivity.

Teachers can pay attention to how children react in various learning situations (for example, working in small or large groups or independently) and how they respond to certain teaching methods (such as direct questioning or written assignments). By observing students in action and recognizing what works and what doesn't, a teacher can get a better sense of how a child learns and what she knows.

Listening carefully to what children say to each other, to the teacher alone, to the class as a whole in the context of classroom activities, and within small group settings can also be illuminating. Active listening is an art that a wise teacher masters, and it starts with a willingness to really hear what children are saying. There is no better way to learn about others than to learn how to listen to them.

Communication that involves open discussion and two-way dialogue is another informal but highly informative assessment method. By talking with children, engaging them in meaningful and respectful dialogue, and being emotionally available and open to their questions, teachers can encourage them to demonstrate what they're thinking about what they are learning and thereby discover what the students don't yet understand.

Finally, reflection is an integral component of a teacher's informal assessment repertoire. Students can be encouraged to be reflective, to think about what's being taught, and to ask questions as they engage with the material, thus providing another meaningful indicator of where they are conceptually. And teachers who reflect on their students' questions and learning needs are in a better position to respond with appropriately targeted curriculum and assessment.

These processes—observation, listening, dialogue, and reflective responsivity—are perhaps the best assessment tools available, giving teachers a heightened attunement to individual learning needs and allowing them to gather considerable information about the children with whom they work. Employed on a daily basis, these informal child-focused methods provide a solid and authentic foundation for understanding and identifying many gifted learning needs.

Standardized Tests

> *"Tony loves school and does really well, but I'm not sure whether*
> *he needs harder work."*
> *"I'd like to know the actual benefits of achievement tests."*

Unlike dynamic assessment methods that teachers can use in their classrooms, standardized tests are not flexibly responsive to a single individual or context. By their very design, they cannot reflect the authentic, interactive, and dynamic nature of learning. What they do accomplish, however, is important. There are many different kinds of standardized tests, and we discuss a few of the most relevant here.

Academic Achievement

Standardized academic achievement tests provide a standardized way to measure how well a student is mastering school curriculum compared with the norm for children at his age and grade level. Used wisely, they constitute an important supplement to classroom-based assessment, providing a reference point and source of accountability for parents and educators.[13]

Standardized academic achievements tests are typically pencil-and-paper tests administered by a teacher to an entire class at one sitting. They might be scored electronically or by a teacher. They measure how well a student is learning, and they indicate grade level of content mastery and reasoning ability by subject area.

Because of the time, effort, and expertise that go into their construction, standardized academic achievements tests are generally much more reliable in their design than teacher-made tests. They can therefore yield direct and useful information about where a teacher ought to be targeting instruction. They are also useful for comparing schools and programs within and among districts, as well as for providing standards of accountability. If, for example, a school discovers that 75% of its fourth graders are scoring below the fourth-grade mean in mathematics, the school has some important information for thinking about possible reasons for this and for encouraging improvements in the fourth-grade (and first-, second-, and third-grade) mathematics curriculum.

In theory, and provided that scores are interpreted carefully, academic achievement test scores can indicate what a child knows about a certain subject area. But because these tests are standardized, they may or may not be directly related to what a given student has been taught in a particular school; a student's low score on a standardized test is not always a good measure of how well she has learned what she has been taught, because she has not necessarily been taught what the test is measuring. As with other kinds of assessment, there are many reasons for a child to score poorly on these tests—reasons that have nothing to do with a child's actual ability. Nevertheless, standardized academic achievement tests are an essential information source for thinking about how best to match individual learning needs with educational programming.

High-Ceiling and Above-Level Testing

> *"I can see that Juan needs more challenging work in math, but I just don't know how far to advance him."*
> *"I think Zaria is capable of doing sophisticated reading comprehension activities. But she's only in Grade 3!"*

When academic achievement tests are used to assess giftedness, they must be able to differentiate between those students who are excellent grade-level students from those whose abilities are far beyond the current grade level. If a child scores the maximum possible score on a test, he is said to be scoring at the test ceiling (sometimes referred to as "topping out" on the test). When this happens, one can't tell how much more the child knows because the test does not have enough items that are sufficiently difficult to measure the upper extent of his ability

Academic achievement tests that are designed to assess students' mastery of one grade level of curriculum are meant to do just that. They cannot be used to identify whether students should be placed at higher grades, or at what level. For example, if a child is in third grade but is functioning at the tenth-grade level in reading comprehension, she will score very well on a third-grade reading achievement test, probably topping out at the ceiling. However, so will the child who is working at an early fourth-grade level. High scores on a third-grade achievement test do not allow a teacher to distinguish between the student who has gifted educational needs (the one who reads at a tenth-grade level) and the one who is doing very well at or slightly above grade level without any significant modifications.

However, there are achievement tests that assess a wide enough range of grade levels that they are useful for identifying the actual grade level at which a student is functioning in any given subject area. The Stanford Achievement Tests[14] are an example of a set of measures (sometimes called a test battery) that satisfy the three essential properties of such tests:

- *very high ceilings*, which means that they have enough very difficult reasoning items to allow for differentiation between excellent grade-level students and those whose ability would be better matched by considerably higher grade-level curriculum

- *norming flexibility*, so that students can be compared with their age peers and also grade peers

- *assessment of reasoning separately from content knowledge*, providing information about a child's level of conceptual mastery somewhat independently of his opportunities to learn the actual content

High-ceiling tests are an approach to using academic achievement tests that can provide useful information about which students have gifted educational needs and what curriculum level best matches their learning abilities. Tests that focus more on reasoning than on content knowledge can help identify a younger child who has not yet been exposed to curriculum at higher grade levels but who can master it conceptually.

Another approach that is sometimes used is above-level testing—i.e., using tests that are aimed at a higher grade level than the child's age would normally suggest. Consider, for example, the two children described above who score very well on a third-grade test of reading achievement but who are widely different in their actual learning needs. If they were to take a fifth-grade, or seventh-grade, or even a ninth-grade reading achievement test, the difference between their scores would become evident. This kind of information enables educators to plan ways to differentiate curriculum effectively.

For curriculum planning purposes, a teacher needs to understand the extent of a child's development in order to provide appropriate learning opportunities. This prevents children languishing in classrooms where they already know the material being taught.

Some of our colleagues and readers are working to bring this approach to the system-wide level. Here is an example.

Taking It to the Next Level

Luc Kumps is a parent in Belgium who was very concerned about his son, Felix, a young boy who was exceptionally advanced in his academic development but seriously unhappy at school. The school seemed blind to the child's advancement and was focusing on his behavior. In the process of addressing their own concerns, Luc, his wife Ingrid, and a teacher friend, Magda Vandoninck, formed EduRatio, a small support group for parents and teachers concerned about gifted education issues. However, they have since become much more than that; they design and deliver sold-out workshop series to parents and teachers, have an active website,[15] and are involved in effective political advocacy.

Luc and his colleagues have now moved into research. They want to see above-level testing implemented nationwide, and they are currently conducting testing in schools to investigate both how easy it is to do above-level testing and also how many children can benefit. They are focusing for now on Grade 4 students and, as part of their experimentation, have added 10 Grade 5 test items to the 60-item test that is routinely administered to all Grade 4 students. Preliminary results from pilot testing look very good, showing that the children who have been identified in other ways as having advanced-level ability are doing very well on the additional above-level items. If their wider implementation of this study confirms these pilot test results, Luc and his colleagues will argue that this simple modification is an inexpensive screening test that indicates the need for further assessment of gifted learning needs.

From a mastery model perspective, children's learning needs can be met if they are assessed using a combination of dynamic classroom-based assessment and standardized high-ceiling subject-specific achievement tests. With this approach, students capable of handling and benefiting from sixth-grade work in science or math, for example, are given the appropriate learning material, regardless of whether their age pegs them in second grade or tenth grade. They are encouraged to study, learn, and progress at their own pace, going through the curriculum as quickly or as slowly as necessary. Where teachers have the training, perspective, and support required to implement this approach, many of the problems associated with giftedness (and other exceptionalities) are alleviated.

Intelligence Testing: What It Is and Is Not

> *"Justin is good at everything he tries. I know he's really, really*
> *smart, but I have no idea how well he'd do on an IQ test."*
> *"Katelyn used to be smart. She had a high IQ when she was five*
> *years old, but I sure don't see signs of that now."*

Intelligence as measured by intelligence tests is a much more limited concept than the name of the test suggests. Many years ago, Stephen Jay Gould wrote compellingly about the limits of intelligence testing and the changeability of IQ scores.[16] Many scientists since then have confirmed his findings, including the fact that people's IQ scores can change quite dramatically over time.[17]

How much emphasis should be put on intelligence tests? Most important aspects of successful careers and lives are not measured by intelligence tests. These aspects include motivation; social/emotional development; creativity, leadership, musical, athletic, and artistic ability; interpersonal skills; decision-making ability; and independent thinking.[18] Rather than seeing IQ as a true measure of a person's intelligence and as some kind of "real" indicator of a person's innate and permanent general cognitive ability, it is more accurate to see it as describing a child's functioning at a certain time on a certain number of specific tasks. When asked to comment on the intelligent use of intelligence tests, Carol Dweck wrote:

> *The real danger of these [IQ] tests is that many educators come*
> *to believe (erroneously) that they are a good index of how*
> *intelligent children are and what their intellectual potential is.*
> *The public needs to be educated; the fact is that nothing can*
> *measure intellectual potential. It is something that unfolds as*
> *children work hard and learn. Moreover, scientific research is*
> *showing that many of the most basic parts of intelligence can*
> *be changed with training.[19]*

Intelligence tests can be a good interactive tool for assessing how well children and adolescents learn in many important areas. Although they certainly have limitations and miss much of what is important about gifted development,[20] when used in conjunction with other measures of academic achievement and observations of social and emotional functioning, these tests can provide useful information. By using a combination of assessment approaches that includes intelligence testing, it is possible to identify a child's learning styles, strengths, and weaknesses in a way that informs both short- and long-term educational planning.

Group-Administered Intelligence Tests

"I'm confused about all the different kinds of intelligence tests."
"Is a group test as good as an individual one?"

Examples of group-administered intelligence tests are Raven's Standard Progressive Matrices[21] and the Cognitive Abilities Test (CogAT).[22] Such tests often include the words "intelligence" or "cognitive ability" in their name. They attempt to measure an individual's abstract reasoning ability, differentiated as much as possible from academic opportunities to learn. Group intelligence tests have the usual benefits of group-administered tests—they are cost- and time-effective.

However, group tests are problematic for identifying gifted learning needs. To begin with, there is no direct connection to academic curriculum, and these tests provide little information about a curriculum mismatch for a given child. They offer no opportunities for the child to interact in any dynamic way with the material or the test administrator. Therefore, these tests miss the divergent or creative gifted thinker who looks at questions differently than others or who thinks in more complex ways than the "right answer" exemplifies. Because of the paper-and-pencil format, they miss the child whose reasoning ability is exceptionally advanced but whose reading and/or writing skills are not developing as well as might be expected. They almost always miss the child with double or multiple exceptionalities—for example, the child who is both gifted and learning disabled.

Group intelligence tests can perhaps be useful for preliminary screening, as long as educators realize that some children will fall between the mesh-lines and will need to be "searched for" below the cut-off score. There are ways to reduce the problems associated with rigid cut-off scores by being flexible in assessment interpretation and identification. We discuss these issues in the remaining pages of this chapter, and also in Chapter 5.

Individual Intelligence Tests

Individual intelligence tests have several of the same validity problems as group-administered intelligence tests—in that they measure primarily the ability to do well on intelligence tests. Additionally, they suffer from some of the same diversity-fairness issues as group intelligence tests, such as cultural differences in opportunities to learn. No matter how a test is redesigned or the scores adjusted for life experience, children will not do well if they do not know the material being tested or if they have not had a history of the kinds of learning opportunities that prepare them for effective test-taking. Although test developers have worked hard to meet such criticisms, many observers are concluding that trying to make conventional intelligence tests culture-fair may not be a productive endeavor and that gifted identification itself is fraught with serious problems.[23]

At the same time, however, individual intelligence tests *do* have strengths. To begin with, individual intelligence tests are interactive in their design. The test administrator has an opportunity to observe a child's learning in a novel cognitive performance situation. Extensive training is required in order to administer individual intelligence tests, and an experienced clinician observes the child's approach to receiving, manipulating, and communicating information. The testing process takes an hour or two (depending on the child and the subtests administered). It consists of oral questions, as well as tasks requiring manipulation of various objects and puzzles, with several subtests measuring various kinds of abilities. Throughout the process, the examiner's role is to observe the test-taker's response style, noting relevant dimensions of cognitive and emotional functioning. When considered along with the test scores, these factors can be used to inform placement and programming decisions.

Another important benefit of the major individual intelligence tests is that they are highly reliable measurement instruments. If the scores are interpreted carefully, taking individual and cultural factors into account (such as tiredness, illness, test anxiety, and language spoken at home), they can provide an effective indication of a student's exceptionality.

When an IQ is extremely high, some kind of exceptionality exists that implies special educational needs. However, exactly what cut-off designates exceptionality is contentious and frequently debated. Nevertheless, when a student's score is more than two standard deviations above the mean (an IQ of 130, at the 98th percentile), there is good reason for parents and educators to examine the nature of the learner-learning match. And an IQ score above 145 (three standard deviations above the mean) is even more compelling in its suggestion of a probable mismatch.

There are two major individual intelligence tests in use, both of which have excellent test design and normative properties: the Wechsler tests, and the Stanford-Binet Intelligence Scale. Wechsler tests currently in use include the Wechsler Preschool and Primary Scale of Intelligence (WPPSI),[24] designed for children ages 2 to 6; the Wechsler Intelligence Scale for Children (4th edition, WISC-IV),[25] designed for children ages 6 to 16; and the Wechsler Adult Intelligence Scale, Revised (WAIS-R),[26] for ages 16 and over. The Stanford-Binet Intelligence Scale (5th edition, SB:V)[27] is designed for ages 2 to 90. Tests in both systems are in a constant state of revision, which is why their names include designations like "4th edition."

Individual Testing: A Case Study

Zachary, a five-year-old, was taking the Stanford-Binet Intelligence Scale. The reason Zachary's parents sought an assessment was to find out if there was something wrong with their son's cognitive processing that might lead to his having problems at school. At home and elsewhere, they observed an insatiable curiosity and appetite for learning, in combination with an extraordinary intensity of focus when he was interested in something. However, his kindergarten teacher described him as unexceptional—other than being a behavior problem in her class.

On one of the early items of the intelligence test, Zachary was asked to put together a puzzle that depicted a person's face. He did very poorly on this item, getting very few of the puzzle pieces in the right place. The test-giver was dismayed. Was the child's visual/spatial perception distorted? Did he have some kind of emotional problem that led him to misperceive human faces?

The little boy, however, seemed quite pleased with himself as he pronounced, "I made a face like Picasso would do it!" He then went on to discuss in some detail Picasso's work, including listing his reasons for preferring the work of Camille Pisarro to that of Pablo Picasso.

Through Zachary's conversation with the test administrator on this and other test items, it was obvious that he was extraordinary in his knowledge and interest in a wide range of areas. If a group-administered test had been given instead of the individual test, he would probably have had the same kind of fun thinking up interesting answers. But items in such a group test would simply have been marked wrong, and Zachary wouldn't have had anyone with whom to discuss his answers. It is likely that his parents would have been informed that the teacher was right—his intelligence was average (or perhaps below!), and his problems were emotional, maturational, and/or behavioral. Although his score on the individual test was considerably lower than he was capable of achieving, it was possible—because the test was administered orally and one-on-one—to provide an intelligent assessment of Zachary's exceptional curiosity, knowledge base, and inventiveness. It was also possible to make a strong recommendation for gifted programming for Zachary. He was clearly the kind of child who needed more challenges and who would continue to create his own!

Zachary is now 14 years old. He has had variable learning experiences over the past few years and continues to be a delight—and also a challenge—to his parents and teachers. It seems that when he has patient and flexible teachers who enjoy working with a lively, curious, intelligent student, he does very, very well. Otherwise, his school performance drops precipitously. We predict that this pattern of ups and downs will continue for the next several years, until he is finally out of high school or in circumstances in which he gets to choose what he is learning and has more autonomy about how he learns it.

Nonverbal Tests

The most widely used nonverbal tests in gifted identification are Raven's Standard Progressive Matrices,[28] the Naglieri Nonverbal Ability Test (NNAT),[29] and the Universal Nonverbal Intelligence Test (UNIT).[30] These are tests of figural or visual/spatial reasoning and working memory that require test-takers to solve matrices, mazes, and other figural and spatial tasks.

The past several years have seen considerable controversy concerning nonverbal tests when they are being used to identify giftedness. Their proponents[31] have argued that nonverbal tests are more inclusive than other measures and should be used in gifted identification in order to address concerns about under-representation of students from minority, English as a second language, and low socioeconomic status families. This argument has been challenged from both an empirical and a theoretical point of view.[32]

From a mastery model standpoint—in which the emphasis is on diagnosing a mismatch between a student's learning needs and her educational provisions—there is an obvious disconnection between visual/spatial reasoning and the majority of academic demands. If a child does well on a nonverbal test but is not doing exceptionally well on other measures of academic skills and abilities, it is a questionable advantage to assign her to a program in which she receives an advanced level of curriculum that is likely to involve many verbal skills.[33]

Advocacy for nonverbal tests in gifted identification rests on two mystery model assumptions: (1) that intelligence is innate (and thus can be measured if only we find the right tool—the one that transcends prior learning and other cultural advantages), and (2) that the goal is to identify and categorize children as gifted (and not gifted). A shift to mismatch diagnostics and a noncategorical mastery model is particularly valuable for those children who come from the diverse backgrounds that nonverbal test advocates are concerned about.[34]

Creativity Testing

Pencil-and-paper tests purporting to measure students' creativity are simply not useful long-term predictors of children's creative talent, ability, or achievement.[35] The best judges of creativity are experts in a particular domain. If we want to know if a child is artistically creative, for example, the best way to find out is *not* to ask the child to do a creativity test, but rather to assemble a panel of experts and ask them to comment on the child's work, just as a teacher might evaluate a child's academic portfolio. The same goes for musical, scientific, and other forms of creativity. The extensive literature on this topic shows that domain-specific ratings by experts are the best predictors of subsequent achievement.[36]

Creativity assessment has very little place in an academic assessment of gifted learning needs, unless it is an apparent trait, as in Zachary's case described above. As we discussed in Chapter 2, although creativity is an important component of high-level real-world achievement, it does not make good theoretical or practical sense to attempt to quantify it as a component of gifted identification for placement in a program for gifted learners.

There is a place, however, for a systematic approach to assessing creative and artistic potential if the objective is to select students for high-level performing arts programs. The Talent Assessment Process approaches in dance (DTAP), music (MTAP), and theater (TTAP)[37] have been used in New York City for the past 13 years and are now mandated by the Ohio Department of Education[38] for gifted and talented identification for students in the visual and performing arts. These are multi-session and multi-observer assessment processes that have proven to be valid and reliable with diverse student populations and limited access to arts instruction. In its focus on current readiness for advanced instruction for a particular domain, D/M/TTAP is consistent with the mastery model of giftedness.

Career Interest Inventories

> *"Monique isn't sure what she wants to study after high school. There are so many options open to someone with her talents and abilities. How can I help her decide what to do?"*
> *"Cole wants to be a lawyer. But he also wants to be a musician. AND he wants to be a scientist. Now he has to make course choices that will eliminate one or more of these possibilities. Help!"*

A student with multiple and diverse interests and abilities can have difficulty figuring out which future direction to choose and which areas of interest to sideline. As highly capable children become adolescents and young adults, choosing a college major or a career path can be complicated and potentially troubling. Consider, for example, the dilemma faced by a student who loves chemistry and is being encouraged by her science teachers to become a pharmacist or scientist, but who also loves writing and has been told by her English teachers that she could be a great journalist. At the same time, her drama teacher has suggested that she think about becoming a professional actor because of her thespian talent and passion. This young woman is in a quandary, in part because she must choose high-level courses and focus her attention more narrowly in her areas of serious interest as she approaches the end of high school and considers her post-secondary education.

There are career interest inventories and other tests designed to help with this process, though they are not generally appropriate for children younger than age 15. Unfortunately for exceptionally advanced students, such measures are designed to identify more conventional career paths and typically do not include highly specialized occupations like biochemical engineer, neuropsychologist, or international investment banker, any of which might be appropriate and interesting vocations to consider.

Career decision-making instruments can provide a framework to stimulate a young adult to think more systematically about his options and interests if used in combination with other experiences that encourage career exploration, accompanied by guidance from someone who understands high-level development. Some of the ways in which adolescents who exhibit multipotentiality can get the support they need in order to make informed decisions include mentorships, career days, job shadowing, and part-time opportunities in their areas of interest.

Parents and educators can help by encouraging students to explore unconventional options and to think and talk about ways to combine two or more areas of ability. Career education is on nearly every list of best practices in gifted education,[39] but the focus is on helping students develop the self-awareness and self-regulation skills that go into good decision making rather than on career interest inventories.

Nonstandardized Measures and Other Information Sources

"Jordan has been failing math all semester. I'm afraid his attitude is creating a block for new learning."

How a student approaches learning tasks can be more useful than test scores when diagnosing a learning mismatch. Error analysis (noticing where a child is making errors and why) and reactions to different kinds of tasks can be informative. Some of the reactions to attend to include how a child handles easier and harder kinds of tasks, her responses to timed tests, and her preferences for different kinds of activities. Some children perform much better on the harder items on some subtests yet make careless errors on the easier items. Even though this pattern can lead to a low or mediocre test score, it clearly indicates a need to be intellectually challenged.

Surveys and Inventories

There are many kinds of surveys, questionnaires, and inventories available to help educators learn more about students' learning needs. These include measures of self-concept, orientation to learning, school attitudes, past experiences, and learning styles. There are questionnaires that include questions about hobbies and extracurricular activities, preferred school subjects, and various aspects of daily school life. These kinds of inventories are informal and do not provide reliable scores. Nevertheless, used in combination with other tools, they can be important and useful additions to understanding a child's learning needs in order to make good academic recommendations.

School Reports

"Corinne's poor marks are becoming a regular thing. How can we break the cycle of negative feedback?"

"I can't wait to see my daughter's report card. It lets me know how well she's doing in school and how I can help her to improve in some subjects."

> *"It's not fair. I think teachers play around with report card marks,*
> *and parents don't even know it. I got a B on my science project*
> *because my teacher had a problem with one little part of my*
> *presentation, but Dean got an A just for trying!"*

Report cards are another source of potentially useful information about whether or not a child is experiencing a learning mismatch at school. Sometimes they are helpful as written, but sometimes they require a parent to have advanced decoding skills. It is not unusual for parents of gifted learners to see report card comments like "fails to complete his homework," or "is often disruptive in class," or "spends her time daydreaming." Knowing that the child in question is competent, such comments can signify that the student may not be sufficiently challenged by school tasks and needs adaptations to the curriculum.

Teacher-assigned school grades can indicate gifted-level ability, as in the case of students who consistently achieve extremely high marks. However, one problem with using high academic grades in identifying gifted learning needs is that (like grade-level achievement tests) they do not, in and of themselves, differentiate high achievers working at grade level from children who are working way beyond it. It is important, too, to remember that children who already know most of the material being presented in class or who are exceptional in other ways as well as giftedness (such as gifted/ADHD) are very often disinterested, bored, or frustrated. As they get older, these students may put little effort into their schoolwork. They may not even pass their courses, much less demonstrate gifted-level achievement. We have known many highly gifted middle and high school students in particular who received below-average or even failing grades. Still others drop out of school entirely from the futility of seeking a place of new learning, even if it means underemployment in the workforce.

The use of high academic achievement and high task commitment as criteria for gifted programming can trap students who need to demonstrate motivation in order to have their learning needs met but are not motivated *because* their needs are not being met. Consider the comments of classroom teachers who have argued against gifted programming for some exceptionally able children:

> *"She doesn't even DO all of her schoolwork, much less do it*
> *creatively."*

> *"He never pays attention to what we're doing in class. He's cer-*
> *tainly not task-committed."*
> *"She never finishes anything. She'll start a project and then lose*
> *interest halfway through."*
> *"He needs to learn good work habits before he goes to a gifted*
> *program."*

Rather than showing that the child should *not* participate in a gifted program, these comments reflect a desperate need for gifted educational adaptations. In each of the above cases, for a variety of reasons, we had evidence that the child was in fact highly creative, could pay attention for long periods of time, and had all of the necessary skills to work very hard—when given appropriate intellectual challenges. However, their report card marks and comments did not reflect this.

Another concern about report cards is that although a grading system does provide a kind of yardstick enabling parents to know how a child is performing at school and in comparison to other children (which can be useful), grades can be highly subjective. The underlying message of teachers' comments can be difficult for parents to figure out. And marks are inevitably and directly tied to teacher expectations, which can be quite variable. For example, what exactly is an excellent mark? A? A+? Does a child have to *exceed* grade expectations to earn an A or A+? School reports, like every other measure, can provide useful information, but they have to be interpreted carefully.

The nature of the traditional report card is, to some degree, in flux. Technological advances have changed the face of reporting, and parent-friendly online or edline access to student progress throughout the school year provides a window of opportunity for parents to stay apprised of children's work and achievement levels. Some schools use process folios in place of report cards. Such portfolios represent the learning and efforts of a single individual over time and do not lend themselves to being ranked or compared, because in effect, each student is competing against his own past achievement record. A student will participate in determining the criteria by which work is evaluated and then can use it to reflect upon strong performance, weak performance, and ways to change and improve performance.[40] A student learning profile, in the form of teacher-documented descriptions of a child's progress through the stages of the learning process, may supplement the portfolio. A teacher can prepare this using baseline data, annotations from conferencing, and notes on processes, final products, and celebrations of successes.

Aptitude Approach

"I'd like to find out Madison's potential. Should she take some kind of aptitude test?"

Aptitude implies a readiness to learn or to perform well in a particular situation. This means that the person not only is capable of performing well in the situation, but actually is in tune with it. There is a beneficial match between what the situation demands or makes possible and what the person brings to it.[41]

Aptitude is a much broader concept than intelligence or ability. It includes extracognitive factors such as motivation, drive,[42] interest, and persistence in a particular domain, as well as the cognitive strengths such as reasoning ability and prior knowledge that are required to succeed in that domain.[43] It also takes into account the context in which learning takes place, including the kind of teaching that the student has been exposed to (didactic or problem-based, emphasis on rote memorization or critical thinking, etc.). "The term aptitude does not refer to a personal characteristic that is independent of context or circumstance. Indeed, *defining the situation or context is part of defining the aptitude.* Changing the context changes in small or large measure the personal characteristics that influence success in that context. Aptitude is thus inextricably linked to context" [italics in original].[44] The notion of aptitude encompasses both the cognitive and extracognitive skills that go into gifted-level accomplishment, and that attract different people to different disciplines and learning environments.

By including drive, motivation, and persistence, as well as cognitive ability and context, an aptitude perspective on thinking about giftedness is consistent with current findings in developmental psychology and cognitive neuroscience that demonstrate the importance of these extracognitive dimensions in the development of high ability.[45] It is also consistent with the mastery model, in putting the emphasis on the attitudes and habits of mind that foster giftedness, rather than on a mysterious inherent superiority that some children have (and others supposedly do not have).

An aptitude approach to assessment makes sense for many reasons, including that the variables that predict academic success for children from minority families are the same as those that predict success for others.[46] These variables are domain-specific and include prior learning and achievement, ability to reason, interest, motivation, and persistence. In order to assess students' aptitude for mathematical giftedness, for example, and their need for advanced mathematical programming, the best predictors are mathematics achievement measures (standardized test scores and grades), scores on tests of quantitative reasoning, interest in mathematics, and teachers' ratings of motivation and persistence. This is true whether or not the students fall into one of the under-represented categories (e.g., Black, Hispanic, low socioeconomic status, or English as a second language).[47]

Like the difference between assessments and tests, it is important to distinguish between an aptitude *approach* and an aptitude *test*. We advocate an aptitude approach to assessing giftedness (that is, taking into account the extracognitive and cognitive factors that lead to successful learning outcomes), but not the pencil-and-paper "aptitude tests" that include a mix of reasoning and content mastery test items. These tests are similar in their format and appearance to academic achievement tests and group-administered intelligence tests—they are standardized in administration and scoring, and teachers can both give and score them. Aptitude tests do not test aptitude in the broad sense of the term, however, or incorporate meaningfully the defining features of the aptitude approach—domain-specific motivation, drive, engagement, persistence, and context—all of which require different kinds of assessment tools that together go into the multiple measures approach that has become a standard of practice in the field.[48]

A Synopsis

The following chart provides a synopsis of the benefits and challenges of the various kinds of tests that we have discussed.

Table 4.1. A Synopsis of Assessment Tools

	Benefits	Challenges and Concerns
Informal Classroom-Based		
Dynamic Classroom Assessment	Cyclical; collaborative; responsive; elastic	Teacher training and support needed; time-intensive; non-systematic; subjective; unreliable
1. Student portfolios	Cumulative; authentic; purposeful; evolving; child-created	Time-intensive; non-systematic; subjective
2. Performance assessment	Involves backward planning; embedded in action; addresses diversity	Teacher as architect requires training and time commitment
3. Day-to-day diagnostics	Heightened attunement to individual learning needs; child-focused; highly individualized; organic and authentic	Teacher training needed; time-intensive; non-systematic; subjective
Formal Assessment Measures		
Standardized Tests	Norm-referenced (allows comparisons with others); reliable; objective	Usually no connection to students' learning context or content taught; anxiety-inducing
1. Academic achievement tests	Subject-specific and targeted information for curriculum decision making (if sufficiently high ceiling)	Test items may not reflect what has actually been taught
2. Intelligence tests – Group	Cost- and time-effective; useful for preliminary screening purposes	No direct connection to curriculum; no interaction with material or administrator
3. Intelligence tests – Individual	Interactive; reliable; regular revisions; individual interpretation possibilities; information on reasoning ability independent of content	Questionable validity for academic decision making; diversity and culture fairness issues; costly; tend to be over-weighted in decision-making processes
4. Intelligence tests – Nonverbal	Appear to be more inclusive and culture-fair than other intelligence tests	Measure figural reasoning rather than constructs of greatest educational concern (language and quantitative development)
5. Creativity tests	Questionable when paper-and-pencil methods used	Not predictive of creative talent or ability
6. Career interest inventories	Starting point for thinking about possible career paths	Need to be combined with counseling and guidance; tend to include mostly conventional careers

Non-Standardized Measures and Other Information Sources	Criterion-referenced; responsive to individual differences and contexts	Unreliable; compromised comparison across settings
1. Surveys and inventories for example, attitude, self-concept, and orientation to learning)	Provide information on learning preferences, experiences, outlook, interests, and motivators	Static measures of dynamic constructs; limited information; questionable reliability of self-report data
2. School reports	Information on actual school performance and work habits	Subjective; variable in format
3. Aptitude approach (not aptitude tests)	Reflects context and extracognitive as well as cognitive factors that lead to successful learning outcomes; multidimensional; includes multiple measures	Similar concerns as with dynamic assessment approaches because it is assessing many of the same attributes (motivation, persistence, etc.)

We conclude this chapter with some cautionary advice: Remember that the real value of test scores is in their interpretation.[49] Only when test interpretation is done with sensitivity to an individual child's unique situation can test scores be used intelligently to diagnose an educational mismatch and inform educational decisions.

Chapter 5

Mismatch Diagnostics:
Moving away from Categorical Identification and Labeling

By all means, use tests to diagnose what children need to learn, but not simply to label them or to place them into fixed categories.[1]

The mastery model moves away from categorizing some children as gifted (and some therefore as not gifted) and instead focuses on identifying current subject-specific gifted learning needs using the ongoing dynamic assessment approaches discussed in Chapter 4. Educators using this model pay attention to what their students already know and where they might require differentiation for gifted learning needs, as well as learning problems. We call these educators mismatch diagnosticians; they diagnose mismatches between the child's needs and the school curriculum.

The Way It Ought to Be: Diagnosing Mismatches

"It would have been interesting to have had someone to go through the test results with us so we could've figured out how to cater to her learning by zeroing in on how she learns."

"I'm sure I know more about Morgan than any tester. Yet it seems to me that schools value those 'official test results' more than what parents have to say about their child's abilities."

"Are intelligence tests the only way to evaluate whether or not my son is gifted?"

How *should* gifted learning needs be assessed and identified? (Note that we put the focus on gifted *needs* rather than gifted *persons*.) Because giftedness is an exceptional subject-area advancement that requires educational adaptations at particular points in time, we recommend looking for subject-specific capabilities indicating that the individual requires more challenge than she would otherwise be getting. We suggest putting the assessment focus on finding students' "zone of proximal development" (ZPD) in various subject areas. The ZPD is that learning space wherein an individual's experience is both *challenging enough to be interesting* and yet *familiar enough to be mastered with some help.*[2]

The major goal should be to find those students who are working well past the usual learning zone within which the teacher is teaching. These students are working so far above grade level in certain subjects that they are learning little or nothing from classroom activities, and they would benefit from studying different material than what is being given to those who are working well at the normally targeted zone. When a child's day-to-day learning experiences are not providing much educational value, then it's time to consider instructional adaptations. These can be hard to figure out unless you know what to look for and how to look for it.

For *all* learners, the optimal assessment approach occurs in a comfortable place and in a way that is sensitive to their individual differences and developmental levels. For exceptional learners, as well as for those who are closer to average in their abilities, the best assessment is an ongoing process, by subject area, and clearly integrated with curriculum.[3] There are clear and measurable educational benefits of assessing students' zones of proximal development in each subject area and then offering guidance and learning opportunities accordingly.[4] Looked at in this way, the identification process—ongoing diagnostic assessment integrated into the classroom—is formative, practical, and an integral part of the learning process.[5] With this kind of practice, there is a natural match between a student's developmental level and his education, and therefore, in many cases at least, no need for formal labeling as gifted.

In the past several years, considerable effort has been invested in establishing more inclusive assessment processes in the classroom. In its emphasis on meeting diverse kinds of gifted learning needs within the contexts of the child's community and school environments, the mastery model solves many of the historic problems associated with the under-representation of minority children in gifted education. Some specifics of the non-discriminatory assessment approach that align well with a mastery model approach include the use of authentic and alternative assessment procedures, the clear link between assessment and program design, provision of opportunities for learning, and ongoing assessment being used to inform instructional interventions.[6]

In order to diagnose learning mismatches, teachers need to: (1) be very familiar with the domain or subject being assessed, (2) have a good understanding of content and procedures across several years' worth of curriculum, and (3) have access to excellent diagnostic measures, or (4) receive support and resources that can provide this kind of knowledge and expertise. Sadly, however, it is too often the case that even when (1), (2), and (3) are in place, teachers are faced with administrative hurdles that make it impossible to implement these policies. In some districts, all teachers in a grade level are required to be on the same chapter in the required book at the same time of the same day for *x* number of minutes, and the administrators send people around with stopwatches to slip into the classroom to time the teachers. We acknowledge that it is extraordinarily difficult in such a setting for a teacher to differentiate for gifted learning needs. At the same time, our experience suggests that there is usually a back door or a window of opportunity that can be used—something we discuss in Chapter 12 in connection with teacher development.

The Way It Too Often Is: Mystery Model Identification

> *"I never perform well on tests. I get really nervous and tense, and I sometimes have mental blocks, even when I know the stuff being tested."*
> *"What if I throw up?"*
> *"We recently moved, only to find that our daughter is no longer eligible for gifted programming in this district. That makes no sense! What should we do?"*
> *"Demarco was tested in Grade 6 at his new school, and they want to place him in a gifted program. It seems strange to*

> *think that he suddenly became gifted. Now we wonder*
> *what educational opportunities he's been missing."*

In many jurisdictions, gifted identification procedures take place at one age or grade level for all students. Children who achieve the designated cut-off score become eligible for special programs, and those who don't do not. This one-time-only identification designates as "permanently gifted" those children who test better than their peers at that point in time. But snapshot assessments miss all those whose need for advanced programming is not evident at the time of identification for any number of possible reasons, not the least of which is the fact that children's maturational timing varies tremendously. Other possible reasons why a child might miss a certain gifted cut-off score (reasons that have nothing to do with a child's actual intellectual ability or with her need for gifted programming) include:

- domain-specific (rather than global) ability (such as mathematical or linguistic giftedness)

- maturational differences (there are early and late bloomers)

- poor test-taking skills

- test anxiety

- learning or attention problems

- motivational factors, including a desire not to be identified as gifted

- environmental test-taking factors (such as heat, comfort, or noise)

- personal factors (such as hunger, tiredness, or illness)

- differences between a child's first language and the language spoken at school

- problems with personality fit with the test administrator

- cultural differences

Another common problem with mystery model gifted identification practices occurs because cut-off scores or identification methods differ from one school district or jurisdiction to the next, so children can "become" gifted or lose the label as their families move. Losing the label can feel like a serious problem to a child or his parents when it is seen as designating something real and innate (as it is with a mystery model definition). Even within a single jurisdiction, gifted identification practices change over time, leading to situations in which children are moved in or out of gifted program eligibility for political reasons, such as changing financial priorities and educational philosophy, as well as other factors that have nothing to do with whether or not children require educational differentiation.

The Typical Identification Process

"Why doesn't someone tell us more about these tests before they give them to us? It would be nice to know what to expect."

For the most part, the typical gifted identification process happens once or perhaps twice in a child's schooling and goes something like this:

- A child takes a preliminary screening test—usually a group-administered cognitive or academic abilities test or a spatial reasoning test—along with classmates, most commonly in the third or fourth grade.

- If the child achieves above a designated score on the screening test (e.g., above the 95th percentile), the next step is usually further testing, often on a more complex and better designed intelligence or cognitive abilities test, yielding a norm-referenced summary measure of intellectual ability.

- If the child achieves the requisite score (usually a standard score of 130 or 135, or above the 98th or 99th percentile), he or she is designated as "gifted." Other measures may be included in the determination, such as parent inventories, teacher checklists, creativity tests, etc. In practice, however, these additional measures are rarely used for decision-making or programming purposes, but rather to demonstrate that multiple broad measures have been included in the process (consistent with Public Law 94-142 in the United States, and standards of professional practice).

- Following the school's formal identification process, the child has the required ticket for admission to enriched academic learning opportunities, whether those opportunities actually match the child's advanced learning needs or not.

Other Questionable Approaches

> *"Our neighborhood school has no gifted identification policy in place."*

Some schools have an official anti-giftedness policy rooted in a well-meaning but misguided belief that *all* children are gifted, and they do not want to show favor to some children over others. Other schools—often private schools or elite public schools—have the attitude that children's high-level learning needs can be well met by the excellent education that they provide for all of their students, without considering the enormous individual differences in their students' learning capacity. In these situations, schools take an explicit or implicit (and often uncompromising) position that they do not need to assess or provide accommodations for gifted learning needs.

In other situations, there is a gifted identification policy and process in place that works against meeting the learning needs of many of the most advanced students. We include here a story from our case files—a situation that worked out well in the end but cost a lot of time, dedication, and effort on the part of the parents and educators involved.

A Case for a Tribunal

Logan was exceptionally advanced in many respects, and his parents were concerned that his learning needs were not being met at his local public school. He had failed to make the 130 IQ gifted programming cut-off score and was deemed to be ineligible for any gifted programming. However, the legally-mandated definition of giftedness in the jurisdiction was (and still is): *"An unusually advanced degree of general intellectual ability that requires differentiated learning experiences of a depth and breadth beyond those normally provided in a regular school program to satisfy the level of educational potential indicated."*[7]

Logan's parents discovered that the official policy regarding gifted identification called for:

1. evidence indicating a student's functioning to be at an advanced academic achievement level (at least two years or two grades higher than chronological age)

2. the possibility of nomination by the child's parent, a peer, or a teacher

3. evidence of strengths in areas other than those measured by an IQ score (such as social perceptiveness or advanced social interaction skills or athleticism)

4. demonstrated creativity

5. task commitment, as related to persistence in activities or pursuits (academic or otherwise)

Rather than accepting evidence on the basis of any of these five points, however, Logan's district relied on only one criterion for gifted identification: a minimum of 130 on an IQ test. Because the official policy had not been followed, Logan's parents objected. They advocated for Logan's right to suitable programming, and against the use of IQ scores as an exclusionary criterion. They took their case all the way to a provincial tribunal, where a panel of judges listened to both sides of the case. The lawyer for Logan's parents argued that one test should never be used as the basis for a decision about a child's educational placement and that gifted identification should be a multifaceted process.

Logan's requirement for learning opportunities that matched his level of ability could not be denied, and in the end, it was not. The final decision was in Logan's favor. It was mandated that he be deemed gifted, and he was invited to participate in gifted programming. It is unfortunate that the initially narrow approach to gifted identification resulted in the case being taken all the way to a tribunal, with the attendant expenditures of time, effort, and money on both sides. However, the positive result encourages optimism that educational institutions may be in the process of becoming less tied to outdated practices, less tolerant of bureaucratic arrogance, and more attuned to the needs of individual learners in ways that are consistent with mastery model recommendations.

In the end, this case acts as a reminder to educators, advocates, policy-makers, and other stakeholders that parents like Logan's can do something to change inappropriate policies. Sometimes it requires lengthy legal wrangling and dogged persistence, whereas other times, negotiations are relatively smooth and uneventful by comparison. The good news is that as time goes by, more and more schools are taking judicious, carefully reasoned steps in the right direction.

Labeling

The greatest problem with any school label, official or unofficial, is that the term will begin to take on an existence of its own and overshadow the actual needs of the child.[8]

"Is the gifted label a good thing?"
"I was so happy when I found out I was gifted!"
"I do NOT want to be one of those nerds! If I pass the gifted test, I don't want anybody to know, and I will NOT go into the gifted class."

Labeling certain children as gifted is troubling for several reasons, including that it implies that other children are not gifted. At the same time, however, it can be difficult to make the case that children require special academic accommodations unless they are given labels that designate the nature of their special needs. When there is no official label, too often the necessary programming adaptations are just not provided.

All labels carry awkward connotations. Labels designating learning problems have their own issues, but the gifted label is particularly provocative for many parents and educators. It implies that the majority of children (all those who are not in the gifted category) lack special abilities or gifts, and so it can evoke negative reactions from peers, teachers, and others.[9] Just as troubling, it leads too many children to believe that they do not have to work hard at school, or to choose simple courses so that they can succeed easily.[10]

There is no single viewpoint on the gifted labeling experience. Children are often unsure of what to expect once they have been given the gifted label. Responses include pride, confusion, embarrassment, and fear. Many children have social concerns, wondering, "Will I be accepted?" "Will it be hard to adjust to a new learning environment?" or "Will I be able to keep pace with other gifted kids?" Other children worry about academic workloads. Many parents have similar concerns and uncertainties about what lies ahead.

We share here some different personal perspectives on gifted labeling. First we consider it from students' points of view:

> *"It's a cool thing."*
> *"I'm not the norm, but I'm not 'gifted.' I feel like I'm the only person like this."*
> *"I don't consider myself smart. I consider myself a quick learner."*
> *"If I had not been identified, I might have considered drugs."*
> *"The gifted label helps university acceptance."*
> *"I feel embarrassed when people ask if I'm gifted."*
> *"Because I'm gifted, I can only have one label: Gifted. Not cool."*
> *"People respect me more. It makes me feel good."*

Now let's consider parents' views:

> *"We felt vindicated but worried. He felt vindicated and relieved."*
> *"She was proud and embarrassed."*
> *"He feels that he is different from everyone else and worries that they won't accept him the way he is."*
> *"I was extremely happy and proud of her."*
> *"She felt special and excited. It's a great opportunity."*
> *"Not a big issue. Not at all surprised. She didn't display much emotion one way or the other."*
> *"The concept of labels should be taken lightly."*
> *"We had a number of questions and no one to put them to."*
> *"I only hope the gifted label opens doors for her in the future."*

The Label: A Mixed Blessing

Many people think of giftedness as a good thing and of the gifted label as an enviable achievement. However, like a beautiful rose with surprisingly sharp thorns, the gifted label can be accompanied by unexpected difficulties. It is important that adults deal sensitively and patiently with their children by listening to and communicating honestly with them. Knowing what the concerns might be and how to find appropriate resources can make a big difference in how positive the gifted experience is for a given child or her family.

Most children experience a mix of pluses and minuses to being labeled as gifted—a mix that can change over time with shifting circumstances, opportunities, and maturation. The following benefits came to light in a series of in-depth interviews with children and their families about their reactions to the gifted label and its consequences:[11]

- validation of abilities
- reduced boredom and frustration due to programming modifications
- enhanced learning opportunities
- bolstered self-confidence
- a confirmation and affirmation of feelings of differentness
- opportunities for interaction with intellectual peers

There were also many problems identified by the children and their parents. Here is a sampling:

- the need to change schools to get gifted programming
- programming uncertainties
- controversy about the label
- unhappiness with the elitism and exclusivity sometimes associated with the label
- dealing with the stereotypic views others have of giftedness
- intensified expectations imposed by oneself, by parents, or by teachers
- inflated self-confidence
- scorn and/or misunderstanding from peers
- envy and rejection from old friends

Each child and situation is unique. In addition to the educational opportunities that might result from the label, a child's personal experience can vary depending on his age, resilience, sensitivity, maturity, social competence, family support, personality, domain(s) and degree of giftedness, siblings who are (or are not) labeled as gifted, attitudes of teachers and peers, and the presence of any other exceptionalities.

Here are some other troubling situations that children experience, along with examples of their comments:

- misconceptions and misinformation about the label
  "Is being gifted like being super-smart in everything? I think they made a mistake, because there are LOTS of things I don't know!"

- ridicule or a lack of support
  "The teacher made fun of me today. She asked the class a question that NOBODY knew, and then she turned to me and said, 'Let's see how gifted you really are. What's the answer to the question?'"

- concerns about developmental issues
  "I wonder if I'll outgrow my giftedness."

- conflicting expectations
  "My teacher says there'll be a lot more work in my new class. My mom says I won't have to worry about it because I'm gifted and I can handle it. But I AM worried."

- confusion about roles and responsibilities
  "I bet I'm going to have to lead all kinds of study groups. I won't be able to do that!"

- fears that the test scores were wrong and that the child is not really gifted, or that he or she won't be able to measure up in the gifted class
  "I think they messed up when they scored my tests. I won't be able to keep up with all those smart kids!"

With the mystery model approach, some students are categorized as gifted and provided with segregated gifted programming, and this may work well for them—provided that they are given differentiated learning experiences based on their individual patterns of abilities. At the same time, however, this approach lets a lot of children fall through the cracks, and it too often ends up causing collateral damage to those who are implicitly labeled "the not-gifted," including the siblings of identified-gifted students, those with domain-specific gifted learning needs, and those who fail to meet the cut-off criteria because they were ill on the day of testing, didn't like the tester, or any of the other reasons we indicated earlier. And there is also collateral damage done to some who have been identified as gifted but do not find a good match in the gifted programming being offered, or who begin to avoid taking intellectual risks because they are afraid of being proven "not-gifted" after all.[12]

Although there are certainly many cases in which children and their parents believe that the gifted label is essential for the child to find a good educational fit, in general, it is best if a child can be in a challenging learning environment that matches her learning needs *without* the gifted label. The label's meaning and value reside only in its practical consequences. It should be pursued or accepted only when it is required for entry to the educational programming that a child needs in order to maximize her learning.

There is a simple and effective alternative to the practice of labeling students that emerges out of the mastery model approach and is consistent with current best practice in special education. This is to label *educational services* instead of students, offering a variety and range of options to those who are interested in and capable of taking advantage of them.[13]

Parents and Children Need to Know What's Happening and Why

"Now what?"

For anyone, but particularly for a child, gifted identification can convey inconsistent messages. It can be self-affirming and a source of pride. However, it can also be a problem if, for example, the gifted label causes worries about having to do well in everything, or if it evokes unfavorable reactions from other people. Sometimes it generates an inflated notion of what being smart means, and a child comes to think of himself as superior to others in a whole lot of ways that have nothing to do with what has actually been measured. For some parents and teachers, a child's identification as gifted suggests strengths and abilities that are well beyond the child's actual competence. Being labeled as gifted can be very worrying to a child, as well as an unfair burden, especially if the gifted designation is accompanied by unreasonable expectations or responsibilities. It is important that the child, his parents, and his teachers all understand in what areas the child has exceptional abilities, to what degree, and what it all implies (and does not imply) in practical educational terms.

A gifted label is often mysterious to both the child and her family, raising more questions than it answers. It is important that communication channels among the child, the family, and the school be kept open.

Adults can prevent possible future problems if they remain sensitive to the child's needs and feelings about labeling and program experiences.

Children, for their part, benefit from being informed. This means knowing what might transpire at home and school as a result of the identification process and any subsequent labeling. It also means learning to focus on their learning strengths in positive ways so that they can enjoy developing their exceptional abilities as much as possible. The bottom line is that parents and teachers should explain many things to children, including programming options and what kinds of changes, if any, to expect.

Let's listen in on a conversation between a mother, who has just found out that her daughter has been identified as gifted, and her nine-year-old daughter.

A Conversation about the Gifted Label

"So, Amber, what did you think of that test you took a while back?"

"Do you mean the gifted test?"

"Yes, the intelligence test."

"It was fun. I liked doing the block patterns. Did you get the scores yet?"

"Yes. That's why I'm asking you about it."

"SO…HOW DID I DO? DID I PASS?"

"You did very well, Amber, but it really isn't a test that one passes or fails. It simply helps with educational planning. In fact, the school is suggesting that you might like to go into the gifted program."

"WOW! Wow. Oh. Wow. That is actually sorta scary. I don't know if I want to."

"Okay. We'll talk about it later with your dad and see what he thinks about it. We don't have to decide right now. We can think about it for a couple of weeks and talk about the pluses and minuses."

"I don't want to leave Jessica and Lynn's class. Are they gifted too?"

"I don't know. Maybe we should make a chart with all the positives and negatives, and also the questions like that that we need to investigate."

> *"Does that mean I'm smarter than the other kids?"*
>
> "No, not really. It does mean that your mind works very well, that you're really good at solving puzzles and figuring things out, and that you have the brainpower you need to do lots of wonderful learning. All kids have things that they're good at and things that they're not so good at, and you happen to be good at the kind of thinking that that test measures."

For several reasons, this is an effective way to tell a child that she has been identified as having gifted learning needs. The parent is low-key, not enthusiastic or pushing one attitude or another, and this allows the child an opportunity to think about her own questions and concerns. The parent listens actively for the child's questions and then reassures her that they can work together to address them carefully and patiently. This kind of dialogue helps the child know what the test scores and any other gifted assessment indicators do and do not mean. The high scores do mean that she is particularly competent at certain kinds of intellectual tasks that help her do well at school, but they do not mean that she is superior to other kids in all things.

Now let's listen in on a conversation between another mother and her son.

> ## A Conversation about the Not-Gifted Label
>
> "So, Matt, what did you think of that test you did a while back?"
>
> *"Do you mean the gifted test?"*
>
> "Yes, the intelligence test."
>
> *"It was fun. I liked doing the block patterns. Do you have the scores yet?"*
>
> "Yes. That's why I'm asking you about it."
>
> *"SO...HOW DID I DO? DID I PASS?"*
>
> "You did very well, Matt. You scored higher than most of the kids your age."
>
> *"But did I pass? Am I gifted?"*

"It's not a test that you can pass or fail. You definitely did great in a lot of areas, but overall, you didn't quite make the score that they need for the gifted class. That does *not* mean that you aren't very capable, only that there were some things you didn't do quite as well as you'd have to do to get that label."

"I failed it."

"You did *not* fail that test—not at all! Let's take a look at the scores, and I'll show you where you did well and where you didn't do so well. Actually, there were no bad areas, and there were some amazingly good areas. Look how well you did on the verbal reasoning area! The 98th percentile! Definitely terrific in verbal reasoning."

"What does that mean?"

"What do you think it means?"

"Maybe I'm good at figuring things out with words?"

"Sounds like it. And 98th percentile means that you did better than 98% of kids your age."

"Verbal reasoning is pretty important if I want to be a lawyer, isn't it?"

"I think so! My guess is that it's pretty important in practically everything."

"So maybe I didn't do so bad after all."

"Exactly. What these scores show is that your mind works very well, and it shows some areas you are especially good at—for example, solving puzzles and problems. And you have the brainpower you need to do lots of wonderful learning. All kids have things that they're strong in and things they're not so strong in, and you happen to be good at many of the things that this kind of test measures. You are also great at all sorts of things that are *not* on that test—you're a dynamite hockey player, a fabulous big brother to your sister, a caring friend to a lot of people, and you play the piano beautifully. If there were scores for those things, I think you would have been through the roof on all of them!"

There are many things to note in this conversation, too, that make it an effective way to talk with a child about not making the gifted cut. As with the previous example, the mother has parked her own emotional responses off to one side, understanding that the child needs to process this news for himself, and that her emotions (one way or the other) will only get in the way of that. She is available and responsive but not expressing her own disappointment, if that is how she feels. As with the previous example, she is helping her son see what the scores do and do not mean. She is emphasizing his strengths, as well as the fact that people vary in how well they do on tests like this.

Unfortunately, many schools don't inform children and parents about the specific test results or their implications, let alone how to go about imparting the news. All too frequently, not enough is said about the kinds of learning or placement decisions that will be required. There are often many unknowns to confront, and children and parents may not know where to turn for information.

Everyone benefits when educators ensure that their policies and procedures are widely and easily available and readily understood. There are many ways to make this happen, perhaps by posting a gifted information page to a website or by sending information home with the request for assessment permission. Most parents find it very helpful when schools hold information sessions where they can ask questions and become familiar with gifted education policies and processes. When a teacher, principal, or school psychologist is available to discuss parents' and children's concerns, there is considerably less speculation, angst, misinformation, and misunderstanding.

There are some other benefits to schools when they make gifted education information more easily available. For example, as teachers become more familiar with the principles and practices and think collectively about how to implement them, they become even more attuned to and supportive of the need for differentiated education. As a result of their understanding the issues, policy can be refined and improved. Many schools with which we have worked through the years have found that opening up their gifted education practices for school-wide discussion, with a focus on the mastery model, has led to positive changes in other areas of the overall learning climate, too.[14]

Moving toward Mismatch Diagnostics

"I bet those tests don't really show how much kids actually know."

Program standards of the National Association for Gifted Children are clearly aligned with the mismatch diagnostics approach that we emphasize, and they are entirely consistent with the mastery model of giftedness: "Student assessment for gifted identification is an organized, systematic, ongoing process that seeks to identify student needs for purposes of matching students to programming options."[15] We have developed four general recommendations that emerge out of these standards and that reflect the mastery model perspective. Rather than being disconnected from learning and teaching (as with mystery model identification practices), these recommendations are focused and lead logically and directly to evidence-based programming.

1. Multiple Measures

The assessment process should be based on current and grounded conceptions of how competence develops, which requires using multiple sources of information.[16] The categorical gifted identification process does not take into account current understandings of competence and talent development in several important ways: (1) intelligence is domain-specific and *not* best represented by composite test scores such as IQ, (2) giftedness is dynamic, not a static attribute of a person, and (3) for educational programming to match a child's real learning needs, a range of individual, contextual, and developmental issues must be considered.

As we discussed in Chapter 4, an optimal multiple measures approach includes: (1) prior achievement in certain subject areas, as indicated by school grades and other reports, (2) scores, by subject area, on high-ceiling tests of abstract reasoning, such as the Cognitive Abilities Test (CogAT),[17] (3) children's demonstrated interest in the subject area in question, and (4) their persistence in the tasks and learning environments required to achieve expertise in each subject area.[18] This kind of thorough approach is productive because it enables teachers to target their curriculum decisions most effectively to meet individual students' gifted learning needs.

2. Assessment as an Ongoing Process

Gifted assessment should *not* be a one-time-only test. As children mature, there should be regular (perhaps yearly) re-evaluations of their emerging abilities,[19] as well as opportunities for children to be evaluated at any other time if teachers or parents notice clear changes in academics that might warrant it. Although ongoing assessment is an important part of program standards and recommended practices, it is rarely implemented in any real way in typical gifted educational practices. Instead, once a child is labeled gifted, he is usually considered to be gifted for the rest of his school career, unless serious problems develop in grades or behavior (which may then threaten programming eligibility, not necessarily the label itself). In such schools, a child who does not meet the gifted criteria at the time of testing is unlikely to have giftedness-related educational needs reconsidered unless the parents take some action, such as seeking professional testing outside of the school system. Thus, many gifted learners are lost in the very identification system that is supposed to discover them, and it can be difficult for them to get the educational adaptations they require. School districts that do offer ongoing testing and assessment opportunities are better positioned to identify high-ability learners, including those who are later in maturing or who did not test well at earlier stages.

3. Diagnostic Emphasis

Because the identification process should be used to assess individual children's learning needs or degree of educational mismatch, it should be seen as *diagnostic*—that is, test data should be used to find children's areas of weakness, as well as areas of exceptional strength, for purposes of specifying adaptations to programming.[20] It is unusual to find school-based gifted identification practices that are, in fact, diagnostic. More often, the assessment for school-based gifted identification is a summary report consisting of scores, along with a simple statement about whether or not the child has met the gifted criteria and therefore "is" or "is not" gifted, which perpetuates the "one size fits all" mystery model approach. This is in sharp contrast to the mastery model's focus on matching curriculum to an individual child's areas of strength and challenge.[21]

4. Labelling the Services, Not the Child

As the paradigm continues to shift, more educators are arguing that it is programming that should be labeled gifted (or challenging, or advanced) rather than individual children.[22] When there is a range of learning options available (including many kinds of acceleration, enrichment, and extracurricular learning) that allow educators to match an individual to a learning option at a particular point in time, the need to label children as gifted disappears.

Early Identification

> *"Our 22-month-old daughter is advanced for her age. Her vocabulary is amazing, and she prefers to associate with older kids. But the teachers won't place her in a daycare group with older children. Should I have her tested?"*

One of the most contentious areas in gifted education concerns early identification. Even in jurisdictions with gifted identification policies and practices, such policies often do not come into play until third or fourth grade. Although many children come to school having mastered basic literacy and numeracy skills quite well and may appear to need gifted programming as early as four or five years of age, there are other skills that are at least as important to their future success. Prior to age eight or nine, much of the learning going on in children's lives concerns their physical, social, and emotional development. Research on high-level development[23] emphasizes that for most children who will go on to exceptionally high-level achievement and healthy adult lives, those early years of learning are better characterized as play than as work.

Another important concern about early identification is the high degree of developmental variability and the low reliability of test scores before age seven.[24] When a gifted labeling process is begun too early, children are at risk of being inappropriately placed in a program where they may have trouble keeping up with the learning of the other students. The majority of primary-level children who obtain high scores on an ability or achievement test generally do not retain their status for more than a year or two. Each year, new children excel. Others whose accomplishments were unusual at one age may show less precocity a year later.[25]

From this perspective, parents who are anxious that their young child should be learning more are often not doing her a favor by advocating for gifted identification. As long as that child is not actively unhappy in the regular classroom, a parent's energies might be better spent ensuring that she has extracurricular and other activities that engage her enthusiasm for learning, including lots of opportunities for spontaneous unstructured play and exploration.

There are some young children, however, who, because of their advanced ability in combination with their temperament, find it difficult to handle a regular classroom and curriculum. Some are impatient with or feel insulted by a teacher's insistence on their doing work that they find too easy. If, for example, a child is already reading at a level markedly higher than other children in the class, a solution might be to provide single-subject acceleration or enrichment through more materials at the child's level of comfort and challenge, without changing anything else. In other situations, it can be appropriate and beneficial to accelerate the child to a higher grade, which we discuss more fully in Chapter 7. Despite widespread notions to the contrary, the research is strongly supportive of the benefits of early entrance to school or whole-grade skipping for certain children.[26]

The research on high-level achievement shows that when parenting or working with young children, what is most important is listening and responding sensitively to the child.[27] Three particularly sensible points to keep in mind are:

1. "Proficiency and learning come not [only] from reading and listening but from action, doing, and experience.

2. "Good work is more often the result of spontaneous effort and free interest than of compulsion and forced application.

3. "The natural means of study in youth is play."[28]

Parents' Roles

What parents typically know about their children is worth a thousand standardized tests. Parents are constantly observing their children under a variety of changing conditions and over a period of years. Testers, on the other hand, see kids in only one setting: the school.[29]

> "Parents and teachers who are at odds with one another are up to no good. As a principal, I sometimes see contentious attitudes, and it doesn't help the situation or the child."
> "I really appreciate parents who can provide input and who are also willing to help me put things in perspective."

Children display their learning progress and the richness of their individual growth experiences in many ways. Parents who work collaboratively with their child's teachers and assist in the assessment process can help teachers identify learning needs and even become involved in planning appropriate programs and instructional strategies. Many abilities and accomplishments can be demonstrated through non-testing assessment approaches that provide valuable information about a child's learning. We offer the following suggestions for parents:

- Encourage your child's teacher to use a variety of evaluation methods besides tests—methods that are diagnostic and not only provide information about mastery of subject matter, but also give information as to where your child may need help. (Examples include checklists of skills, progress charts, student-maintained journals of learning activities, questionnaires, interview and conferencing records, and work samples.)

- Keep a record of your child's learning activities outside of school, and share your concise observations with educational professionals.

- Keep a scrapbook or portfolio of photos, paintings, written material, audio recordings, etc. that illustrate your child's abilities in different areas and at different ages. Video-record and document special events, presentations, various indications of effort and persistence, and learning outcomes.

- Encourage your child to become involved in self-assessment—that is, to keep a record of learning experiences and personal accomplishments that can be shared with teachers. This is also a useful strategy to help your child develop self-confidence, solid work and organizational habits, and self-reflection skills.

- Recognize that some educational environments are toxic, and some situations require finding alternative placements. Assessment information is useful only if interpreted and used intelligently. This means *matching the educational provision to an individual's ability on a subject-by-subject basis.*

We discuss how to do this in Section III.

Section III

Being Smart about Meeting Gifted Learning Needs

Chapter 6

Adaptations: The Gifted Learner in the Regular Classroom

Many advanced learning needs can be met in a regular classroom by a teacher who is well-trained and well-supported in working with exceptionally capable learners.[1] At face value, this may sound simplistic or idealistic, and we do recognize that the required level of training and support is not a given in most schools at this time. However, this perfect-world description is closer to possibility than many people realize. The first step to getting there is an attitude shift—a realization of what giftedness really is (which we addressed in Section I). The next step requires an understanding of how gifted learning needs can be assessed (Section II). Now, in Section III, we ask, "What educational options can meet gifted learning needs?" We consider how to use these various educational options to support high-level development in *all* students on an as-needed basis.

In this chapter, we discuss some tried-and-true strategies that can be used in a regular or general education classroom. There are, however, some circumstances in which other approaches might be needed. In Chapter 7, we consider a range of alternatives, some of which take the child out of the regular classroom full time or part time.

A Flexible Range of Educational Options

> *"Our limit should be the world. Then again, it should be the stars!"*
>
> *"I love school because work is fun; work is fun because I like to learn new things!"*

From the mastery model perspective, gifted education is about matching curriculum to advanced learners' specific academic needs. Because these are so diverse, this means providing a flexible range of educational options. Before outlining what those options might be, we define some of the basic terms and concepts.

We begin by referring to the National Association for Gifted Children's guiding principles of curriculum and instruction:[2]

1. Differentiated curriculum for the gifted learner must span grades pre-K-12.

2. Regular classroom curricula and instruction must be adapted, modified, or replaced to meet the unique needs of gifted learners.

3. Instructional pace must be flexible to allow for the accelerated learning of gifted learners as appropriate.

4. Educational opportunities for subject and grade skipping must be provided to gifted learners.

5. Learning opportunities for gifted learners must consist of a continuum of differentiated curricular options, instructional approaches, and resource materials.

Differentiation

> *Differentiation is not something to do from time to time—it is a way of thinking and should pervade what a teacher does in the classroom.*[3]

"Differentiation" is a term used to describe the process of making educational expectations match individual students' different learning needs. In its application to giftedness, it is about challenging advanced learners appropriately, and it is the foundation of the mastery model's approach to gifted education. Educators wanting to differentiate can think about this on different levels.[4] For example, working with *curriculum planning* (think big-scale and broad–based, over several weeks or months), suitable modifications might entail:

- removing unnecessary or repetitive chunks of content

- enhancing existing units of study by reorganizing or intensifying content

- connecting a unit of study to other subject areas or disciplines

Working with the *program* (think smaller scale, more focused— i.e., daily instruction within a classroom), teachers might adopt one or more of these ideas:

- using flexible grouping practices, based on students' strengths, interests, and weaknesses

- increasing breadth (more choices, learning style variations)

- increasing depth (different levels of content for different ability levels)

All of these approaches come under the heading *differentiation*. When differentiating experiences for diverse learning levels, these practices can and should be combined. From looking at curriculum development to adapting daily lesson plans, the teacher's goal in differentiation is to engage students fully in their own learning as much as possible at their individual ability levels.[5]

The Inclusive Classroom

The inclusive classroom is one in which the teacher differentiates effectively for every learner. This is a welcoming and opportunity-rich environment—one where diversity is respected, where teachers respond to the needs of individual students by offering a range of instructional supports, and where students are systematically encouraged to master their individual learning objectives.[6] An inclusive classroom not only keeps advanced students engaged, but it can also meet the needs of students with various kinds of learning challenges.[7]

Before discussing some of the learning options that help teachers differentiate effectively to create an inclusive classroom, we include here Carol Ann Tomlinson's principles of a differentiated classroom:[8]

1. Learning experiences are based on diagnoses of student readiness, interest, and/or learning profile.

2. Content, activities, and products are developed in response to varying needs of varied learners.

3. Teaching and learning are focused on key concepts, understandings, and skills.

4. All students participate in respectful and engaging work.

5. Teacher and students work together to ensure continual engagement and challenge for each learner.

6. The teacher coordinates use of time, space, and activities.

7. Flexible grouping ensures consistently fluid working arrangements, including whole-class learning, pairs, triads and quads, student-selected groups, teacher-selected groups, and random groups.

8. Time use is flexible in response to student needs.

9. A variety of management strategies (such as learning centers, interest centers, compacting, contract, independent study, collegial partnerships, tiered assignments, learning buddies, etc.) is used to help target instruction to student needs.

10. Clearly established individual and group criteria provide guidance toward success.

11. Students are assessed in a variety of ways appropriate to demonstrate their own thought and growth.

Options in the Regular Classroom

It is often said that in an ideal world, special education, including gifted education, would not be necessary, because curricula would be sufficiently responsive to individual differences to make separating children into exceptionality categories unnecessary.[9]

"Have you ever spent time in a classroom? Do you have any idea how hard it is? I have kids coming to school in the morning without breakfast. They can barely function. Now you're expecting me to also think about providing a smorgasbord of possibilities for the extra bright ones?!?"

"I can't do everything! It's enough just to keep on top of the mandated curriculum and all of the paperwork. I can't individualize a program for every child in my class!"

On their first encounter with differentiation principles, teachers might express concern, dismay, dismissal, or even anger. We often hear comments like the ones above that focus on the real and difficult challenges that teaching presents, without also adding individual gifted accommodations to the burden. We are not actually suggesting that teachers provide an individualized version of every lesson targeted especially to each child's developmental level. As teachers ourselves, we fully appreciate the impossibility of that demand. However, we also know the power of providing fundamental adaptations to basic instruction as required, as well as how very doable that really is once a teacher understands what it is and how to do it. We have observed and experienced how wonderfully effective differentiation can be in practice, enlivening the learning process for both teachers and students.[10]

Foundations of Best Practice

Effective differentiation is built on and enhances solid teaching practices. In every classroom, there are certain "non-negotiables" of best practice that encourage high-level learning outcomes. We have characterized this approach as the five R's of teaching for gifted development: being *resourceful, reasonable, receptive* to changes, *respectful* of students' feelings and abilities, and *responsive* to their questions. The best activities are designed or adapted responsively to children's learning interests and levels of readiness. Expectations and goals should be clear and aligned with children's areas of strength and weakness in different domains.

No matter the level of their students, from preschool to graduate school and from developmentally delayed to exceptionally advanced, effective teachers are sensitive to their students' individual levels of competence. They open channels of communication and enable them to stay open—by listening, showing a willingness to entertain creative and sophisticated ideas, and encouraging growth in reading, writing, and the use of technology. Everyone benefits when teachers take the initiative to network, become familiar with available support services, tap into a wide range of community resources and learning provisions, and seek information about gifted education from multiple sources. Educators strengthen children's learning spirit when they are proactive, motivating, supportive, nurturing, well-informed, and attentive to diversity in all its forms.

Diversifying the Options

Perhaps our single most important recommendation for the regular classroom is that educators provide as wide a range of learning options as possible. This has been suggested by many educators over the past several decades, including June Cox, Neil Daniel, and Bruce Boston, who did a nationwide survey of gifted programs in the U.S.[11] They noted that highly visible programs (pull-out or self-contained) were most often used—programs that administrators could publicly point to—but they emphasized that the more powerful and effective programs were less visible, such as continuous progress in the regular classroom. They do not use the terms "mystery" and "mastery," but on the basis of this research, they strongly advocated the use of flexible pacing and many alternatives from which to select.

Although providing a wide range of learning options might sound formidable and impractical (and frequently, parents' and teachers' first response to this idea is that it is too idealistic), most teachers are already doing many of the things we recommend that can help differentiate curriculum to meet gifted learning needs. In fact, the best advocates for the multiple options approach are teachers and parents who have had a chance to see this approach in action.[12] Consider, for example, the reflections of Shoshana Cohen-Taitz, a teacher.

A Teacher's Program

I think that one of the most valuable things I learned from the professional development workshop is that meeting the needs of gifted learners is not as difficult as I had previously thought. Actually, many of the strategies that I've been implementing in my classroom are already providing enrichment for the gifted

---

children (and all students), helping them to achieve beyond the simple letter of the curriculum and to experience appropriate challenges. This really makes me feel hopeful and more optimistic about working with gifted children in my classroom. With this in mind, I am now able to look at the strategies that I have begun to work with, and I'm thinking about developing them further. I guess the idea that we do not have to start from scratch, that we do not have to recreate everything, but rather can work with what has already been started is a very valuable lesson that I've been able to take away from this training to work with in my classroom.

A second thing that I learned deals with the relationship between teacher and student. I have always believed that the teacher is required to offer students a range of options within a structured environment. This is what I have always done in my program. I take a lot of time developing different ideas and extensions for my lessons. However, from this session, I learned that designing the rubric and selecting activities should not be just the teacher's responsibility. Student input is valuable. Balancing what the teacher has to cover with what the child wants to cover can be tricky, but it is essential. I have begun to encourage my students to be active in developing topics and ideas based on what I need to teach. For example, I am currently working with Grade 7 students on designing a book report. I know what expectations I need to cover, but getting their input for the style of the book report and the way it will be presented allows them freedom and a feeling that they are actively involved in the learning process. They are then involved in the decision making, the presentation of work, and independent and/or collaborative effort. This strategy is effective for all students, and it helps me in my planning.

I think that the strategies we discussed (e.g., guided independent study, project-based learning, and single-subject enrichment) can greatly enhance the learning of gifted students in the regular program. Advanced learners will feel less singled out. These strategies are not threatening and do not place kids in the spotlight or set them apart as different from their peers.

Shoshana's story is similar to others we have experienced. As teachers come to understand the mastery model perspective on giftedness and acquire the tools they need to provide a flexible range of curriculum options, they are usually surprised to discover (after the initial learning investment) that their workload decreases. Like their students, they usually find themselves enjoying school a whole lot more.

In fact, many gifted needs can be met with adaptations to the basic instructional program in a regular classroom. This approach has some obvious advantages, such as being flexibly responsive to changes in a child's development, interests, and circumstances, as well as preventing most of the problems associated with labeling and elitism. It also allows for considerably more teacher creativity.

Here are nine specific strategies that we have found useful for adapting the regular classroom for gifted learners.

Curriculum Compacting

Advanced learners can often acquire the important facts, concepts, and skills of a given curriculum unit or subject area of strength with minimal instruction and practice. Carefully assessing a student's subject-area mastery and then condensing curriculum areas so that they can be covered more quickly is called curriculum compacting.[13]

Curriculum Compacting: An Example

Natasha is planning to teach a math unit on four-digit addition. She has ascertained through pre-testing that Xavier, one of her students, has already developed a reasonably high degree of proficiency in adding four-digit numbers. She compacts the assignments in the math unit for him, choosing only a representative few questions, thereby ensuring that he has a solid grasp of all of the necessary principles and skills that are covered in the unit, and yet also providing him with extra time that he can invest more happily and productively elsewhere.

Shortening the amount of time needed to cover a section of curriculum accomplishes several objectives:

- It frees up time and energy that can be directed toward other student interests and other real and relevant learning outcomes.

- It allows children time to delve further into the material and thereby intensify their content mastery.

- It reduces the boredom of unnecessary repetition for students who have already mastered the concepts and related skills.

Curriculum compacting values students' prior learning. It is a prerequisite for many of the strategies we describe that adapt basic instruction to gifted learners' needs without radically changing programs or schools. It must be done with care, however, so that important foundational skills are not omitted from the child's learning and so that children do not feel rushed in their learning. Several steps are required for successful implementation:[14]

1. Identify the essential learning outcomes of a particular unit of study.

2. Develop a pre-test to assess how much of the essential learning the students have already mastered. Pre-tests can be informal or formal, varying from a discussion with the child about what he already knows to a score on a standardized test.

3. Establish the criteria that will be used to designate mastery of the essential outcomes—that is, should the child know 85% of the required material? 75%? Or perhaps 95%?

4. Plan for the time gained by compacting or eliminating the already-mastered material.

And this is where the other options and strategies come in.

Project-Based Learning

Many learners enjoy opportunities to explore their interests somewhat independently of normal classroom constraints. Project-based learning can be done individually or in a group format and is focused on a target product (the project). It begins with identifying a real-world problem or question of interest to the child. This problem or question is then used to motivate the child to learn the skills that she needs in order to arrive at an understanding of the issues. Some of these skills might include predicting, designing experiments, researching, data management, drawing conclusions, and communicating. The child then creates artifacts or products that address the initial question or problem.

The value of project-based learning is enhanced when:[15]

- the problem is authentic (real world)

- the problem is challenging

- tasks are varied

- the students have choices

- the students have opportunities to work with others

- there is an opportunity for closure, and the students have a sense of completing something important

Authenticity is a key concept for those concerned about increasing engagement in learning, and motivation to learn is greatly enhanced by a feeling that activities have real-world relevance.[16] The following is an example of project-based learning with upper elementary students.[17]

Mr. Graham's Project-Based Learning Experience

Mr. Graham was a fifth-grade teacher who observed that his gifted students often "tuned out" during geography class. A teacher for many years, he described himself as "cynical about gifted education." In his opinion, gifted students did not "need anything extra," and he was frustrated with our perspective that he could meet the learning needs of the gifted kids in his class without compromising the time he needed to spend with the children who had learning disabilities. However, he did participate in our professional development session, and he saw some interesting possibilities in project-based learning. We worked together to design a project that ended up transforming the way he experienced teaching—and the way several of his students experienced learning.

For his project-based learning experiment, Mr. Graham asked his students to work in small groups, together choosing a country of interest and creating a list of questions to explore. He encouraged students to use any resources that they could think of for their investigation. What happened next delighted him. Using books and diverse non-text resources (including visual, electronic, and human), Mr. Graham's fifth graders discovered answers to their questions, as well as several more questions to ask. They interviewed friends, neighbors, and relatives; they found old records and were given treasured mementos to borrow, along with personal histories of what the mementos meant; they scoured libraries and the Internet for answers to their questions. The children then became interested in their classmates' histories and in their own families' histories. Geography classes went from being "ho hum, boring" for everyone (including Mr. Graham) to being an active and creatively productive hour.

As the learning continued to evolve, each group of students classified its information into four different categories and created a model of a four-room museum. Each room contained artifacts and written information about topics from the research. Groups took turns presenting their video-recorded tours of their model museum rooms.

All of the students in this mixed-ability class were involved in various interest-motivated educational activities: collecting and managing data, drawing conclusions, and communicating these conclusions in a multimedia final product. Most of the gifted students took advantage of opportunities to learn skills at levels commensurate with their abilities—levels not typically achieved in their regular classrooms. Several students who had previously shown no sign of gifted-level ability achieved exceptionally high learning outcomes. All students experienced the pleasure and sense of competence that can be gained from productive engagement in intellectual mastery—an experience that in itself can lead, over time, to gifted levels of achievement.

Mr. Graham became an enthusiastic advocate of project-based learning and lost some of his cynicism about gifted education.

Project-based learning can be used in any subject area, from history to science to mathematics to literature. For instance, it can incorporate scientific methods and concepts (involving, for example, a consideration of the activity's purpose, hypotheses, methods, observations, conclusions, and implications), which makes it an excellent way to teach science in a meaningful and engaging manner to all kinds of learners.

Project-based learning experiences like the one we have described here have many benefits for diverse kinds of learners, including—but not restricted to—those who are gifted. However, sometimes teachers assign a project and expect the student to do it, whether or not that student is interested, or to pursue it to completion without any further guidance. Sometimes gifted learners are simply sent off by themselves to the library or elsewhere to work on a project. The learning outcomes in circumstances like this are typically unsatisfactory. Project-based learning should be a rewarding, challenging, and enjoyable learning experience, accompanied by ongoing monitoring, scaffolding, and guidance.

Because portfolio assessment is process-oriented, it can be a good way to assess project-based learning. Teachers can encourage children to build ongoing connections across their learning, rather than focus exclusively on the end product. The process of developing a portfolio (as we discussed in Chapter 4) helps students to become organized, reflective, and explicit about what it is that they are learning. It gives them an opportunity to showcase their efforts, to be creative, and to use a variety of expressive and illustrative means to record and chart information (such as conferences with the teacher, interviews, and any resource material they've gathered). Portfolios can be used for a variety of independent learning activities, and they have the advantage of being flexible in design and orientation.

Guided Independent Study

Guided independent study is an umbrella term to describe project-based learning, as well as other kinds of activities in which students identify and explore interests beyond the regular curriculum while working somewhat independently of teacher instruction. Some examples are learning a foreign language or a new computer program, studying environmental issues or local history, learning the impact of certain drugs on certain behaviors, or other areas of personal interest with academic merit. For guided independent study to be successful, it is essential that a teacher, parent, or mentor be actively involved with the student in creating and monitoring the study.

Many parents and teachers think that guided independent study is for older students only, but even for younger children, it can be an exciting way to learn, as long as there is sufficient scaffolding and guidance. Ruth Morgenthau, a resource teacher who participated in a professional development program focusing on giftedness, sent us the following correspondence describing her plans to strengthen the way in which this method is approached at her school.

Ruth's Plan

I am a teacher-librarian in an elementary setting (K-8). Students in my school are often sent to the library to do independent research on different topics assigned by their teachers. Typically, the assignments are to be researched and written right there in the library, which I've found puts undue pressure on both students and the librarian. Now that I've taken the gifted development course and know more about gifted learners, I'm asking teachers to meet with me so that we can plan children's independent study assignments together.

As the librarian, I'm familiar with the material available in my facility and can guide the classroom teacher, suggesting possible topics. With advance notice, I can ensure that information will be available in the library for a student to use in his or her research. Too often in the past, students came to the library "to do research on whatever topic they wished," only to find that we did not have enough information on that topic or that the question needed a lot more consideration and planning before it could be investigated. Their time and mine was wasted, and nothing was accomplished.

Library research assignments need to have a focus and a proper structure. When I meet with teachers to plan assignments collaboratively, all of the related tasks become more meaningful for the students, and ultimately, they're much better executed.

I know that my learning resource center/library can fill many roles for gifted students. For example, independent study can provide enrichment; the resources in the library go well beyond the classroom material. The library is a wonderful setting to work in, and for a gifted child who may have social issues, the library is a familiar and safe haven. Experience has taught me that a librarian can form a special rapport with students who like to study independently, and it's always great when students are able to develop a working relationship with a trusted adult.

With the help of a resource librarian like Ruth or another interested adult, a child can pursue a topic and engage in various research and thinking activities. This is not a replacement for what goes on in the classroom; rather, it is a way to enrich a child's learning in a personally relevant and purposeful way when time has been created by compacting the curriculum. Here is a story from our case files about just such a situation.

Dynamic Assessment in the Classroom

Sean learned everything he could about dinosaurs when he was in kindergarten and first grade, so he had little motivation to study them with the rest of his Grade 3 class. His teacher, Miss Kuna, conducted an assessment of students' knowledge before beginning the unit on dinosaurs and, recognizing Sean's advanced knowledge, talked with him about what else he would like to learn about the topic. She consulted with the school librarian, who was able to find some more challenging books for Sean containing information about the disappearance of the dinosaurs and recent discoveries. Together with Sean, Miss Kuna worked out some meaningful activities that he found stimulating and that kept him happily engaged while the others in the class were learning basic skills that he had long since mastered. She encouraged him to keep everything in a portfolio folder so that he could work on his dinosaur project whenever he wanted to.

Sean began an e-correspondence with a dinosaur expert at the American Museum of Natural History and learned about some recent findings that weren't even published yet. He proudly showed his dinosaur folder to his parents, and he also shared it with some of his classmates who were interested.

Cross-Grade Resources

Schools have many enrichment resource possibilities in addition to what is contained in the regular classroom. Very often, excellent gifted programming approaches are discovered or created merely by considering as resources all locally available teachers, classes, materials, and students at all levels (pre-school through college). For example, a ninth-grade student, gifted in the area of language arts and a keen writer, might find his learning needs met by meeting once a week with an interested English teacher at his school who sets up a workshop for serious writers across several grade levels. Such a student might find that the creative stimulation, support, and discourse provided in the weekly meetings, combined with writing time that substitutes for his normal English classes, are enough to sustain his interest in writing and learning about writing. In fact, he may actually come to appreciate the fact that much of his other coursework is easy and that he has time and energy to pursue his real passion—writing.

Consider, as another example, a sixth-grade student who is outstanding in both math and science. This student might be introduced to high-level algebra by an interested math teacher in the nearby local middle school. If this student has a particular interest in, say, lab experiments, she could also be invited to work with a middle school or high school science teacher in setting up and conducting research experiments.

There are innumerable similar possibilities, each of which is embedded in the local context. These options cost little more than time and flexibility on the part of educators and parents. The best way to find what makes the most sense for a given learner is to start by identifying his learning interests and needs, and then ask the question, "What provisions might be found or developed that will help meet those needs?"

We view this as a "What are the possibilities?" approach. It provides a contrast with the more usual approaches, such as "This is the program for gifted learners. If you don't want it, we have nothing for you." Or as Mr. Graham said prior to his project-based learning experience, "If a kid is gifted, he shouldn't need anything extra." The best gifted programming often emerges serendipitously from educators working together creatively and being open to opportunities for collaborative solutions.

Single-Subject Enrichment

Very often, educators and parents think that a gifted learner requires adaptations in all subject areas. Sometimes this is the case, but for many students, focusing on just one subject area at a given point in time is a good way to encourage a (re)connection with a love of learning and meaningful engagement with school. The example above of providing writing enrichment for a linguistically gifted ninth grader illustrates this concept. So, too, does the following initiative, described by Nanci Wax Pearl, a teacher who participated in one of our professional development sessions.

A Teacher's Plan for an Enriched Math Group

Nanci's Learning Strategy

Nanci selected a small group of students on the basis of their math proficiency to participate in an enriched math program. They have been working together in the classroom on a variety of different math activities designed to extend the regular fifth-grade curriculum.

Nanci's Reflection on the Process

The students were eager to participate in the math group. They have been open to every idea and math-related subject investigation presented to them. The parents were supportive and happy that this enrichment idea was being established.

The concept is working, but I have to refine the process. I realize that some students are gifted in one area but not others, even within math. For example, some children show tremendous proficiency in number sense and numeration but not in geometry. Then, within number sense and numeration, they might demonstrate strong computation skills but struggle conceptually with fractions and percentages.

I've learned several things that I will apply to future implementations of this idea. I have to keep the group of more able learners open to constant change in order to accommodate individual strengths and weaknesses. The block of time set aside has to be flexible. I've discovered that we need a more specific set of criteria to show which students might benefit from enrichment grouping in particular units of study, because I want to choose the right students without leaving anyone out. Also, I think I need to have better communication with the parent body as a whole about the program.

Single-subject enrichment can be beneficial for students and can be implemented within the classroom or on a pull-out basis. It may be coordinated by the classroom teacher, a resource person, or another individual on staff who is willing and able to take on the responsibility.

Single-Subject Acceleration

Acceleration is a topic we discuss at greater length in Chapter 7, but we introduce single-subject acceleration here because it can be done within the context of a regular class placement. Take, for example, the case of a seventh grader who was extremely capable in many areas but who had a particular interest and exceptional proficiency in math.

Ben's Story

Ben was assessed when he was in the fourth grade. He scored in the gifted range on the WISC-III (above the 99th percentile) and in the highly gifted range mathematically, operating at that time at the tenth-grade level (six grades above his own) on tests of math reasoning. Although he was eligible for the gifted program at the local public school, his parents decided to send him to the nearby private school that his two siblings attended. Although there wasn't a gifted program at that school and no accommodations were made for his exceptional ability, things went along pretty happily for him until the end of sixth grade, when he began to be described by his teachers as a behavior problem. His parents and teachers were concerned about how he would do in seventh grade and so arranged for an updated assessment during the summer, with a follow-up meeting to be held early in the next school year.

In early October of Ben's seventh-grade year, a team meeting was held that included the school principal, gifted coordinator, Ben's parents, his homeroom teacher, and a gifted consultant, along with Ben himself for the first part of the meeting. It was clear that something had to be done; the behavior concerns were getting worse, and Ben's attitude was becoming disruptive in the classroom.

Team members listened thoughtfully to Ben's concerns, suggestions, and opinions and concluded that there was an educational mismatch. He was told that the principal and his parents would discuss any plan with him before finalizing it. Working together, the team devised an individual challenge program for Ben. In subject areas other than math, his teachers agreed to enrich and extend the curriculum and assignments for him, as well as for a small group of other highly capable seventh graders. However, Ben's mathematical ability and interests were so advanced that they knew they would need something else for him in math. His temperament was an additional complication (as temperament so often is!). His impatient personality meant that he was at serious risk of dropping math altogether if he didn't feel like he was progressing as fast as he wanted to.

On the recommendation of the gifted consultant, Ben was allowed to take the seventh-grade end-of-year exam to demonstrate his competence. Because he did well (the criterion was set at 85%), he was excused from attending all seventh-grade math classes. Instead, he was provided with a combination of independent study and tutoring help to work his way through the eighth-grade math curriculum, and he was encouraged to participate in regional and national math competitions as well. The advantage of this independent study approach from Ben's standpoint was that he was excused from work that provided no real learning for him and that he found deadly boring. He was allowed to finish the eighth-grade math curriculum at his own pace, and he was then free to move to higher-level or enriched mathematical work as he wished.

The math teacher who was tutoring Ben spent two or three hours weekly with him and mentored his progress in the eighth-grade math curriculum to ensure that everything was moving along smoothly and that he was understanding the work. Despite the additional challenge for Ben, there were a few glitches along the way. For example, for a time, Ben thought he'd been given a "spare" for math class, and he let his classmates know what a good time he was having while they were slaving away. By threatening to withdraw the privilege, Ben's parents made sure that the taunting stopped. Over the months that followed, Ben moved from being noticeably bored and unhappy at school and causing trouble both there and at home to being the happy, keen, and engaged boy that he had been as a younger child. He felt respected and became committed to making his program successful.

Postscript on Ben

Ben is now attending a highly challenging university. He has a double major in math and music, and he is flourishing. After elementary school, he went to a competitive high school where he was allowed to accelerate mathematically. While there, he participated in math classes with students who were a few years older than he was and who were also excellent math students. Although there were bumps along the way, he learned to thrive on challenge. Another interesting outcome of this experience is that the elementary school that he attended went on to make similar accommodations for other exceptionally capable learners and became known as a good school for high-ability students.

Optimally, as in Ben's case, an elementary or middle school will have enough flexibility and a strong enough relationship with a local high school that an arrangement can be made to grant high school credit for any courses that a highly competent student completes ahead of time. However, the student may need an advocate to negotiate on her behalf if the higher learning institution is reluctant to follow this kind of individual plan. For example, if a student is willing to take the Grade 9 end-of-year exam or an informal assessment given by the math coordinator in order to prove her competence, and high school administrators are agreeable, then arrangements for an individualized math program can be made, as occurred with Ben. As such a student gets older, she might be helped to find Advanced Placement courses and other university-connected high-level options that will allow her to continue to pursue her learning interests at her own pace.

In some jurisdictions, there is legislation that allows elementary school students to take high school courses when they demonstrate the necessary capability. This approach generally requires the high school principal to assume responsibility for the evaluation and recording of credits. What students gain through this process is the freedom not to be bored by courses well below their competence and the opportunity to take more courses at higher levels.

With mathematically gifted learners, subject-specific acceleration is particularly important for a number of reasons. First, the subject itself tends to build more sequentially than many other curricular areas. It is therefore harder than with other subjects to create enrichments that do not also move beyond the child's age/grade level. Second, there is solid research evidence supporting this approach, grounded in the widely renowned Study of Mathematically Precocious Youth (SMPY), conducted for more than 30 years at Johns Hopkins University in Baltimore.[18] Third, most important breakthroughs in the field of mathematics are made by individuals in their twenties. For students who are truly gifted in mathematics, appropriate early acceleration is necessary for them to build the foundation of skills and knowledge that they will need to make their contribution to the field while still young.

Career Exploration Built into the Curriculum

> *"Whenever we travel as a family, I take my children to explore the local university campus. They've seen Harvard, the University of Toronto, Berkeley, McGill, Columbia, and many others. This summer, one goes to Oxford. It helps them keep their eye on a better intellectual place than high school, reminds them that school is a long process that they have to learn to function in, and through university catalogues, exposes them to non-typical fields of study."*

Students with exceptional ability should be encouraged to explore a wide range of unconventional career possibilities. This should begin earlier in their education rather than later to increase the likelihood of their choosing the appropriate high school courses and, in some cases, to prevent dropping out of school.[19] Gifted young people who have talents in many areas will need adult help in prioritizing their interests and activities and in exploring possibilities for combining two or more strong interests—for example, learning about bioengineering as a way of combining strong interests in both math and science, or medical engineering for combining medical research, math, and science.

We include here an excerpt from a report by Laressa Rudyk. Her observations were made during her student teaching practicum in a high school computer science class.

Computing Science Class:
Self-Perception, Participation, and Gender

Initial Observations

1. Girls in the computing science class were initially very quiet compared to the boys.

2. Girls hesitated to ask for help when they were having trouble with an assignment.

Findings

I administered a questionnaire to students in September. Their responses suggested that the girls lacked confidence in their abilities in this subject area as compared with the boys in the class.

I administered a second questionnaire at the end of November, asking the same kinds of questions. Results showed increased confidence among the girls, bringing them closer to the boys' confidence level. I also noticed a change in the girls' behavior; there was more vocal participation and greater comfort with experimentation. Perhaps most importantly, however, girls' achievement levels were considerably higher at the end of November than they'd been earlier in the term, and they expressed more enjoyment and interest in the course.

Strategies I Employed from September through November

I made it a point to give the girls lots of praise and encouragement, and I kept the idea of confidence-building in mind. I asked leading questions that directed students to draw conclusions on their own. I tried to help the girls unobtrusively so that they would experience the confidence-building joy of figuring things out for themselves.

Personal Reflections

This study was relevant to me because I was the only girl in my college math and computing courses. My experience was extremely positive. I felt confident and enjoyed battling wits with the boys and my professors (all male). The idea that girls are underestimated or otherwise discouraged in math or computing was foreign to me. I was sad to discover that the girls thought so little of themselves in September when I first administered my questionnaire. I was glad to see some positive change, and hope that my conscious confidence-building efforts contributed to this.

I think the issue of whether these girls perceive themselves as "good at computing science" has broader social implications. Many careers with higher compensation levels require knowledge of computing, and girls are unlikely to pursue careers in areas where they lack confidence. The skills developed by learning programming are also valuable in their own right. Programming teaches students how to articulate (and follow) a set of unambiguous instructions to perform a task, so students learn communication skills that can be applied in other areas.

I may take up the cause of promoting computing science to teenage girls!

Laressa then set up a class forum in her practicum to discuss the experience, engaging the students in discussing the value of achievement in computing science, the kinds of careers that are open to individuals with these skills, and areas that might be closed to those without computer skills.

Another reason to encourage career exploration in exceptionally capable learners is to support their understanding of the relevance of schooling. Interest in a possible career path can sustain academic engagement in those who need their learning to feel meaningful and worthwhile. Sometimes people can endure high school better when they see that it can take them to a better place.

Peer Coaching

One of the reasons that peer coaching works so effectively is that it combines pressure and support in a kind of seamless way.[20]

"I believe that the best way to learn is to teach."

"Peer coaching gives my gifted learners a chance to see how 'normal' children think. It should make them grateful that learning comes so easily to them, rather than resentful that they have to do it."

For some students in some settings, a peer coaching experience can consolidate knowledge, encourage high-level discourse, and support the development of both intellectual and social skills. Working together with others in a group of mixed strengths can encourage respect for diverse kinds of ability and facilitate the development of alternative skills.

All too often, however, when teachers who lack training in gifted education are faced with an advanced-level learner in a regular class-room, they ask the advanced student to work with someone who is having problems. These teachers think that they are not only giving better learning opportunities to the child who is behind in his work, but they are also providing the gifted student with an opportunity to develop social and communication skills. As might be predicted, how-ever, if the gifted learner is neither a natural teacher nor unusually altruistic (in other words, a typical child), and if peer coaching is used too frequently, the gifted student becomes a resentful teacher's helper. He may come to think of peer coaching as an irritating and unfulfilling annoyance, especially if he feels neither intellectually stimulated nor enhanced in his social skills or reputation. Many excellent students are unable to explain to someone else how they "get it"—they just do. There is also a risk that the coach will end up completing the work himself rather than going to the trouble of guiding someone who is having a hard time through something that is easy and obvious to the peer coach.

Alternatively, the student who is used too frequently as a peer tutor may come to identify with the teaching role and take that as an unexam-ined career path, coming to see herself in the helper/mentor role and never comfortably stepping to the fore in other ways. She may learn to downplay or even hide her abilities out of sensitivity to those she must help. Worse still, working with struggling students may reinforce con-cerns she might have about being abnormal.

For peer coaching to work well, each participant must be gaining something from the activity and must perceive that that is the case. The teacher should have private preliminary discussions with each of the prospective participants. These discussions should include whether or not each one is interested in participating, what the responsibilities, obligations, and benefits are, and what the teacher's role will be. It is essential, too, to discuss procedural basics such as how to respond in various situations, how to recognize when the peer teaching is not working, and what to do if that should occur. In some jurisdictions, students can receive course credit for doing peer tutoring under a teacher's guidance, which can help make it worthwhile to the tutor. Peer coaches in such settings can function like a teaching assistant, helping with some administrative duties, planning and preparing materials, and working one-to-one monitoring seat work.

As with all of the strategies discussed here, and perhaps even more so with this one, peer coaching must be undertaken carefully and appropriately, with the teacher available to step in at a moment's notice if requested. Peer coaching must be tailored to individual learning needs and to the personality profiles of the students involved, as well as the learning objectives of the task. When the conditions and supports are in place to ensure that it works for everyone concerned, peer coaching can indeed satisfy many educational needs all at once.

Cyber-Learning

Every learner can, at his or her own choice of time and place, access a world of multimedia material.... Immediately the learner is unlocked from the shackles of fixed and rigid schedules, from physical limitations... and is released into an information world which reacts to his or her own pace of learning.[21]

The frontiers of learning now extend into cyberspace. Technological possibilities have advanced to the point at which different learning styles, curriculum requirements, and individual educational objectives can be met online by even a very young aspiring techno wizard, as long as he has a computer or handheld browser available for use.[22] (In fact, as most adults realize, students often surpass their parents and teachers when it comes to e-learning.) By going online, kids can navigate discussion threads, access a never-ending and far-ranging supply of resources, and supplement material that's being covered in class, thus deepening and broadening their knowledge. Students can become part of a community of learners—a community that knows no boundaries.

E-possibilities and electronic learning resources are growing almost too quickly to comprehend. There are countless homepages and links to interactive and other learning activities. Software programs and online courses continue to be developed and refined. Textbook companies have interactive materials on the web. Electronic devices are powerful and yet tiny enough to fit in pockets for easy access day and night. Opportunities abound to join a collaborative group, be a facilitator, or work independently, all at an individual pace. With a few keystrokes, one can find webforums and pathways to learning that were not available just yesterday. People around the globe use the Internet to explore interests, answer questions, develop new understandings, and motivate one another across culture, age, time, and space.

Here is one prospective teacher's experience with e-learning.

E-Learning in Action

In my secondary education English class, the professor took our whole class and put us online with a high school English class. We helped the tenth graders write by providing immediate online feedback during their writing process. It was totally interactive and gave us a solid sample of the power of the medium.

I have another, more personal, example of how e-learning works. Last summer, my ninth-grade daughter fast-tracked online through a required tenth-grade civics course. Such courses can be pretty tedious for high-ability children, especially when those kids are already clearly on a path because of their talents. My daughter did the course in one month instead of five and was able to take a Grade 11 psychology course in her Grade 10 program, giving her much more interesting content to study, plus the opportunity to complete her required course ahead of schedule.

Online possibilities hold many obvious benefits, as well as some risks. Parents' and teachers' monitoring concerns and limits should be made explicit from the start of any kind of online application. Online discussions are fine, but they should not take the place of real ones. And with so much information accessible at the mere touch of a button, the potential for plagiarism is greater. Ethical issues have to be addressed—what plagiarism is, why it's wrong, and consequences for doing it. Plus, the credibility of online sources should be checked out, as youngsters may not recognize what is reliable and accurate versus what is not.

Many high schools are developing "edlines" and encouraging students, parents, and teachers to log on regularly. For example, on one site, one might find educational resources, technical support, library catalogues, study skills and tips, a virtual reference desk, web-adventure-learning experiences, instructions for building web pages, and more. There are also e-moderating guides for those who want to hone their e-skills. We are witnessing an unprecedented range of learning and teaching possibilities, including innovative processes and far-flung connections. What was first viewed as "a potentially powerful teaching and learning arena in which new practices and new relationships can make significant contributions to learning"[23] has now become even more powerful and expansive as e-frontiers continue to grow.

Systems of Differentiation

Each of these options provides a way for a classroom teacher to differentiate programming to meet gifted learning needs, and each can expand the range of learning possibilities in a given classroom or school. A school that wants to go slowly into gifted education can make a good start by implementing just one of these options. Educators who are ready to differentiate and want to consider a more systemic approach may be interested in adapting one of the many systems of differentiation for giftedness that have been proposed through the years. We review here three widely-used schoolwide systems; each one is evidence-based and has a strong track record of effectiveness.

One of the most longstanding approaches to differentiation is the schoolwide enrichment model (SEM).[24] With SEM, a continuum of enrichment services is put into place. On the basis of a comprehensive assessment process that includes student-created talent portfolios, teachers make decisions about curriculum compacting and differentiation. Students are then encouraged to engage in enrichment activities at one of three different levels: Type I, general exploratory experiences; Type II, group learning and training activities; and Type III, individual and small-group investigations of real-world problems.[25]

For the past several years, Joyce VanTassel-Baska and her colleagues at the Center for Gifted Education at the College of William and Mary have been investigating ways to integrate differentiated learning experiences into the regular curriculum in such a way that gifted learners receive the accommodations that they require while systematically mastering the regular curriculum in alignment with educational standards.[26] One of the important contributions of this group has been the development of an integrated curriculum model for gifted learners. They have developed flexible approaches to enrichment and acceleration, as well as comprehensive field-tested curriculum resources across subject areas and grade levels.[27]

The parallel curriculum model is a third outstanding systematic approach to differentiation.[28] It layers four curriculum areas: (1) the core of the curriculum, (2) connections and relationships, (3) practice, including authentic problem solving, learning activities, and grouping, and (4) student identity, attending to individual interests and differences. Tasks, lessons, and units of study revolve around these four parallel layers, blending and modifying them in accordance with learners' needs and levels of ascending intellectual demand.

Some gifted education circumstances call for system-wide applications, and others require one or more of the other options that we have reviewed here. Still other circumstances require moving beyond the general education classroom altogether. You will see that the ideas that we have presented in this chapter interconnect and overlap with those that follow in Chapter 7. The boundaries between the various possibilities for gifted learners are not distinct, and implementing one approach almost always means incorporating important aspects of one or more of the others. Parents and educators should keep in mind that the wider the range of learning opportunities available, the more likely they are to find a meaningful educational match for a particular child.

Chapter 7

Alternative Options: Stretching the Boundaries

Although many gifted educational needs can be met in a regular classroom by a teacher who is well-trained in working with gifted learners, some children require alternative options which may take the child out of the regular classroom full time or part time. These approaches include various kinds of acceleration, full-time and part-time gifted programs, second language immersion, dual track programs, specialty subject focus, specialized and alternative schools, private schools, and finally, homeschooling.

A little creativity and a resourceful attitude can stretch the boundaries even further and lead to many other exciting opportunities for high-level learning outside of the more conventional approaches to schooling. In fact, sometimes all that is required to meet the gifted learning needs of a child at a given point in time is for a parent, teacher, or the child to take a curious look around at the world and see what possibilities are out there waiting to be explored. And sometimes the best course of action is to combine educational alternatives and/or to complement them with supplementary learning experiences.

We offer an array of ideas to consider.

Whole-Grade Acceleration

> *Whole-grade acceleration is the practice commonly known as grade-skipping.... A decision to whole-grade accelerate a student is one of the more difficult and controversial issues that educators and parents encounter.... However, a great many gifted and talented children clearly need additional educational challenge that can only be obtained by allowing them to advance at least one grade, sometimes two or more.*[1]

> *"I really don't like to hear the word 'skipping' used when referring to moving children ahead in school. It makes it sound frivolous, when in fact it's a serious decision for parents and children."*
>
> *"What on earth were they thinking when they decided to skip Jon? He may be smart, but his behavior is completely inappropriate, and the other kids don't like him. His social maturity is WAY behind his intellect."*

Acceleration enables advanced learners to move through school more quickly than usual. On the one hand, some people perceive acceleration as a controversial or suspect intervention—an approach that rushes childhood, can lead to gaps in knowledge, and forfeits the benefits of placing a child with age peers. On the other hand, when important factors are taken into account, such as a child's readiness and willingness to accelerate, her level of advancement in subject-specific areas, and of course, the necessary planning and support from parents, teachers, and administrators, then acceleration can work well and merits careful consideration for students who exhibit highly developed content mastery.

There are many forms of acceleration—for example, placement that is advanced by one or more full grades or in a single subject area, early entrance to a program, telescoping of grades (say three years across two), split grade classrooms, and mentorships. In order to make wise decisions about which option might be best in a given situation, teachers and parents need to better understand the goals and implications of these various possibilities, including potential social ramifications, the emotional aspects of tackling advanced-level challenges, and cost-effectiveness.

How do you know if an individual is a suitable candidate for acceleration? Here are some fundamental points to consider:

- the extent of the child's intellectual advancement in specific domains, as demonstrated in a comprehensive evaluation conducted by an educational psychologist or other educational professional

- the child's motivation, feelings about accelerating, and maturity levels

- the attitude and competence of the receiving teacher

- the child's social/emotional adjustment history, including a consideration of other changes happening in the child's life, the child's resiliency, and his overall health

- timing (earlier in the child's school career is generally better than later)

- opportunities for and likelihood of teamwork (optimally, the child's current and receiving teachers, parents, and other stakeholders can involve themselves in thoughtful discussions about the various aspects of the decision-making and change processes)

- the accessibility of counseling and psychological supports

The *Iowa Acceleration Scale*,[2] now in its third edition, is a research-based guide for educators and parents that facilitates systematic analysis of the pros and cons of acceleration for individual students. Its design included pilot testing with hundreds of children who skipped a grade, and the questionnaire incorporates the diverse factors that predict whether or not an acceleration process is likely to be successful with a given child. An interdisciplinary team, composed of educators and the child's parents, considers a series of factors, including intelligence and achievement test scores, grades, academic strengths, motivation, attitude toward learning, and other social and developmental factors. The answers generate scores which indicate whether or not the child is a good candidate for a full-grade skip or whether the team should consider other options. Targeted to students in kindergarten through Grade 8, the IAS includes case study examples and descriptions of key elements for decision making. It emphasizes the importance of discussion, planning, and continued monitoring of the student.

Other researchers have also weighed in on the matter of acceleration.[3] Over the past few years, there has been much discussion and research on the topic, including practical issues, best practices, and process monitoring, both during and following a grade skip. In 1992, Rogers and Kimpston conducted a meta-evaluation of research studies about acceleration forms and outcomes.[4] They concluded that when done thoughtfully and with attention to many factors, including children's physical, social, and emotional development, in addition to their academic levels, acceleration can be academically and socially effective, as well as cost efficient.

In the 2004 publication *A Nation Deceived: How Schools Hold Back America's Brightest Students*,[5] the authors explain why educators and parents have not fully accepted the idea of acceleration, in spite of 50 years of evidence that supports this practice. Based on their research into the surprising rejection of this learning option, they cite the following reasons:

- lack of familiarity with the research on acceleration
- the philosophy that children must be kept with their age peers
- the belief that acceleration "hurries" children
- political concerns about equality
- a belief that other students and their parents will be offended if one student is accelerated

Other potential pitfalls include creating a situation in which a child's less-developed social, emotional, or physical maturity might put her at risk of social isolation or rejection, or alternatively of feeling a need to conform to older social norms (such as moving into dating behavior before feeling ready). Additionally, when whole-grade acceleration has not been well-planned or well-chosen, it is quite possible that a child won't succeed at the new advanced grade level, resulting in the unhappy circumstance of a previously successful student experiencing a sense of failure.[6] Although educational placement decisions are not irrevocable and a child can go back to her original class where the teacher can try another approach, this can be disconcerting. If a child is unhappy and the acceleration process is not working out, then it's time to revisit the alternatives.

A Nation Deceived has generated lively discussion about acceleration processes, policies, and beliefs, and it provides the education community with a comprehensive perspective on what acceleration entails, its effectiveness, and why it should be seriously considered as one option in the range of viable options for advanced learners.[7] Follow-up research[8] since publication of the original document indicates that there has been a substantial increase in the number of children who are accelerating, as well as greater acceptance of acceleration practices across North America and elsewhere. The heightened awareness draws attention to the need for more research, policy initiatives, and information for purposes of intelligent decision making about gifted learning needs.

There are many indications that the research on all types of acceleration will continue to grow. Although whole-grade acceleration continues to be controversial, there is considerable evidence that acceleration practices have positive long-term effects. In fact, it is the gifted educational option with the strongest and most robust research validation.[9]

To help in the decision-making process, parents and teachers can do a cost-benefit analysis. The costs to the child of *not* accelerating may be continued and increasing boredom, frustration, alienation from school, and behavior problems, to name a few. Possible benefits include a faster and more appropriate pace of learning, less time wasted in classes where content has already been mastered, a level of challenge that is better matched to a child's capacity to learn, and a continued excitement about learning.

Generally speaking, a student who is self-directed, achieving well beyond grade level, comfortable working ahead of age peers, and socially, emotionally, and physically mature for his age is an excellent candidate for whole-grade acceleration. One or more teachers should be available to monitor and guide the process, crafting a good ongoing match between the child's ability in the different subject areas, the curriculum content, and the pace and depth of learning. It is important that both the pre- and post-acceleration teachers monitor possible problems that may later compromise the child's knowledge or skill-building. We have seen how acceleration can be done thoughtfully and well if the current teacher and the receiving teacher work together to make the process as smooth as possible. For example, prior to a grade skip, the pace of learning can be faster for a time so that the child masters grade-level content and skills systematically but more quickly than usual. This helps to eliminate gaps in knowledge once the child is placed in the higher grade. As we emphasize throughout this book, children's learning trajectories are highly individual, and even the most exceptionally advanced learners can have gaps in foundational knowledge or skills that, if not addressed, can cause difficulties down the road.

Schools can facilitate a successful whole-grade acceleration experience by providing teachers with the professional development and support options that they need to make the process successful, as well as by creating a school climate that respects individual differences. Some schools choose to develop non-graded or multi-grade classes which allow for a seamless kind of acceleration where appropriate, with children moving along through the curriculum at their own pace. However, if this is not the case, then there are some issues with whole-grade acceleration that merit consideration. There are certain times in a child's life when acceleration is simpler and less disruptive, such as early entrance to kindergarten or first grade and early entrance to college. In addition, whole-grade acceleration works best and the problems associated with it are minimized when arrangements are made for a group of students to go through the process together. An obvious advantage of the group approach is that, as students move quickly through the curriculum, they do so with a network of peers. This is beneficial in every way, from academic support and discourse to friendship-building. School factors to consider include the nature and degree of support provided, as well as the school's culture and respect for diversity.

> *The goal of acceleration is to position the student where there is appropriate challenge on what is being learned with the possibility of enhancing the student's work ethic and reducing the time necessary for traditional schooling.... This means that the student is not wasting time with curriculum he has already mastered and supports moving toward arenas with more satisfying and long-term academic involvement.*[10]

In the end, acceleration may or may not be the best option for a particular child. However this approach represents a respectful recognition and addressing of individual learning needs, and it certainly warrants careful consideration.

Gifted Classes

> *"Finally, I found a class where I can learn what I want to learn with others who want to learn cool stuff, too!"*
>
> *"By the time I get home and finish all my work, there's hardly any time left to relax or do other things, like skating or swimming or playing the piano."*

> *"Betsy used to be what her teachers called a 'lazy learner.' But once she joined the gifted class, she began working harder and enjoying it more."*
> *"It seems as if the gifted class has revved Ryan's learning a few notches, but he doesn't seem any happier. He's just more...I don't know...driven."*

Full-Time Gifted Classes

Many parents and teachers believe that self-contained classrooms are the best way to provide gifted learners with appropriate intellectual stimulation, as well as opportunities to meet and interact with others of like mind and interest. In some cities, there are entire schools for gifted learners, sometimes affiliated with university campuses and teacher education programs. There is considerable support for this option in the gifted education literature. Nancy Robinson describes self-contained classes as "singularly inexpensive and...probably constitut[ing] the easiest and most effective way to meet the needs of many (certainly not all) gifted children."[11]

At the same time, there can be problems with full-time segregated gifted classrooms. One particular concern has to do with labeling, as we discussed in Chapter 5. In a self-contained class, the gifted label is made explicit on a daily basis, exposing the child to possible experiences of social ostracism from students who don't have the gifted label, former friends, siblings, other children's parents, and sometimes even teachers. Another potential problem is transportation. Participation in gifted classes may require commuting to a new school outside of the home neighborhood, which cuts into the time and energy a child has available for other activities, including before- or after-school or co-curricular programs. It also reduces the time available for sleep, play, and leisure, all of which are essential to optimal developmental outcomes.

There are some additional concerns. When considering a self-contained gifted class, parents and educators should remember that within each such class, half of the students will be below the class average. A child who moves from being routinely at the top of her class to being below average can suffer serious blows to self-esteem. On the other hand, such challenges, when accompanied by the necessary understanding and support, can also provide students with opportunities to learn about the resilience and persistence that are needed for high-level achievement.

Another possible social/emotional problem identified with participation in full-time self-contained gifted classes has been called the "hothouse effect."[12] A segregated gifted class is an artificial environment in many ways and may not provide sufficient opportunities for children to learn to cope effectively with the broad variety of people and situations that they will have to learn how to interact with sooner or later. In order to address this concern, some schools organize their self-contained gifted classes so that academics occur in the self-contained format, but co-curricular activities are organized more heterogeneously, encouraging more diverse kinds of interactions among students. Diverse interactions can also occur through school activities, clubs, teams, etc.

An academic concern with full-time gifted classes is that individual domain-specific learning needs are not usually taken into account unless the teacher has the necessary training and support. For example, a child who is exceptionally gifted in math is unlikely to be provided with a mathematics curriculum appropriate to his ability, which is highly advanced relative to his classmates, whose areas of advancement may be in language or science or other areas. Another often-overlooked fact is that sometimes exceptionally gifted learners are deeply disappointed to discover that they do not fit in even within the gifted class, that their interests and methods of discourse are still not understood, and that their exceptionally advanced learning needs are still not being met. This can increase the burden of feeling different and somehow wrong.

In spite of these concerns, many children find that full-time placement is both socially comfortable and academically stimulating. Some important benefits of this option include the greater probability that the teacher has had more training in gifted education than many professional colleagues, and the increased likelihood of students finding intellectual peers. A child's learning needs may be better met on a consistent basis in a self-contained gifted class, facilitating a higher level of motivation to learn and subsequent personal achievement. Many parents have told us that the full-time class is a very good way for their children to receive the kinds of challenges that they need, as well as the depth, breadth, and pacing of learning experiences that make school more enjoyable for them. As with all placement decisions, the emotional, social, academic, and motivational implications of joining a full-time gifted class—where one is available—have to be weighed carefully by parents, teachers, and students working together during the decision-making process.

Part-Time Gifted Classes

> *"I'm not gifted—just on Tuesdays from 2-3 P.M."*
> *"I can teach Cassie perfectly well! My strongest math students do*
> *not have to leave my classroom in order to be challenged."*

For a number of reasons, part-time gifted placements are rarely a good option.[13] Children's gifted learning needs are not restricted to the day on which their pull-out gifted class is scheduled. Some children tell us that their regular classroom teachers penalize them for their absences by planning for treats and fun activities during the time when the kids have gone to the gifted program, or by giving tests or assigning work that they are expected to make up later.

An additional problem with part-time programs is that the homeroom teacher can resent the pull-out teacher taking the strongest students out of class. Most problematic, perhaps, is that typically, the work in the pull-out program is not differentiated for individual learners' special needs, nor is it well-integrated into a child's other learning experiences. Too often, such programs do little to meet gifted-level learning needs other than reduce boredom for a few hours a week and bring together for short periods of time those who are more likely to be intellectual peers.

Second Language Immersion and Dual Track Programs

> *Opportunities to learn more than one language should*
> *be provided to all students in an increasingly smaller*
> *world with the concomitant need for communication*
> *across languages and cultures.*[14]

> *"Miguel is able to talk fluently with his grandparents now!"*
> *"I had hoped that the immersion program would challenge*
> *Zoe. Instead, she became even more bored than before."*

Opportunities to learn about other cultures and languages can enrich a child's life immeasurably, and dual track and language immersion programs can provide interesting ways to do that. In dual track programs, students learn to speak two or more languages over the course of many years. Typically, such programs provide a compacted version of the regular age-appropriate curriculum in one part of the day, with a separate course of studies for the rest of the school day. For example, the students might spend the morning on the general studies curriculum of math, language arts, science, and history and the afternoon working on various aspects of religious studies or humanities, as well as on alternative language learning. In both immersion and dual track programs, most or all subjects may be taught in the second language, beginning at the preschool level and continuing on through high school.

Canada is officially bilingual, and all children are provided with both French and English language instruction, although the age at which second-language instruction begins and the extent of that instruction varies widely. In some jurisdictions in Canada and elsewhere, parents can choose to have their child enrolled in a language immersion class starting at kindergarten, and many parents of high-ability children choose such classes as a way of enriching their child's learning.[15] Sometimes learning part or all of the core curriculum in a second (or third, or fourth) language provides sufficient additional challenge to keep a gifted learner interested in school, while at the same time developing another area of skill (the language itself, such as French, Hebrew, Chinese, or Spanish).

Such programs, however, are not always good choices for meeting gifted learning needs. Consider, for example, a child whose strengths are her reasoning skills and conceptual mastery and who thrives on high-level discourse. In a French immersion program, it will take years before her knowledge of the French language is well enough developed to keep pace with her ideas and concept formation. She won't be able to have meaningful discussions with her teacher or classmates until she achieves fluency in the new language. This can make her school experience frustrating and boring rather than stimulating and challenging, especially for the first few years in this kind of program.

When instruction is being provided in a foreign language, the general conceptual level is typically significantly lower in science, geography, history, etc. than what is provided in first-language classes. With children whose reasoning skills are exceptionally advanced, it is often best to provide second-language instruction as a subject area on its own rather than as a medium for learning in other areas, at least until a high level of second-language proficiency has been acquired. This is particularly true for those children who are not really interested in second- and third-language acquisition.

Another concern with using language immersion to address gifted educational needs is that it may put the child at a disadvantage in standardized testing, at least for a few years. Because he will not have the same depth and breadth of discussion in his first language as he otherwise would, his test scores are unlikely to be as high. While this disadvantage evens out over time and is eventually converted into an intellectual advantage, this can be an important consideration if a language immersion program is being considered as a temporary enrichment measure until the child is old enough to participate in another program that requires high scores on standardized testing.

Educators in dual track and immersion programs often argue against additional provisions for gifted learners, suggesting that the programs themselves are challenging enough to meet gifted learning needs. Also, because of the time pressures involved with such an intensive curriculum structure, these educators usually question the practicalities of adapting instruction for gifted learners, even if it is deemed desirable or necessary.

A dual track program can work very well for those children who are keenly interested in the particular focus of the second track and who don't mind spending less time on other subject areas. However, for those who are less interested in the second-track focus or who experience some difficulty with it, such programs can be seriously problematic. The sheer breadth of the curriculum leaves little room for in-depth study of areas of interest (math, science, English literature, etc.). Similarly, creative and intrinsically motivated learners often experience frustration due to the narrowness of focus necessitated by the amount of material being covered. However, when teachers are given the professional development opportunities and support they need to learn how to effectively implement adaptive instruction, they may be well able to meet gifted learning needs in these programs. We discuss teacher development approaches in Chapter 12.

Specialty Subjects

"Joey amazed everyone when he joined the Drama Club. Up until then, he hadn't been doing particularly well at school and was having trouble with reading. But once he discovered drama, he had a reason to become an excellent reader. Now, English has become his best subject."

"Last year, Collin joined the school band. Previously, he had no friends and no interests outside of academics. Now he has discovered a talent for music, and he's got a much broader set of interests, as well as a group of kids to do things with."

Throughout this book, we concern ourselves primarily with students who are so advanced academically that their time will be wasted in school if little or no accommodations are made for their exceptionality. Not only is there tremendous diversity in patterns of gifted development within the core academic areas, but also there are many children who have gifted learning needs in one or more of the specialty subject areas such as art, music, drama, leadership, or alternative language study.

In much the same way that differentiated programming can be developed for the more traditional academic subjects, gifted programming can be designed in subjects such as drama or dance. It can be used both to support gifted development in those who show evidence of talent in certain specialties and also to provide high-ceiling learning opportunities for those whose academic giftedness is not otherwise being addressed.

Consider, for example, a highly accomplished young pianist who is interested in challenging herself musically. Such students can be given opportunities to hear, play, and perform advanced pieces, to compose their own work, and to incorporate music into school projects and activities. They can be encouraged to participate in extracurricular bands, orchestras, and other musical venues. There are myriad possibilities for parents and educators interested in finding challenging learning opportunities in the arts. We know of one student who played a violin solo with the local orchestra when still a teenager. Another had a featured part in a production of *The Nutcracker Suite* ballet. Others may find vehicles to develop their talents, interests, and love of learning through community-based theatre organizations or festivals rather than in traditional classrooms.

Children who might otherwise focus too narrowly on their area of expertise can be encouraged to explore their abilities and interests more extensively. For example, someone who is advanced in and passionately engaged by science but unremarkable in the arts might enjoy dramatizing a scientific discovery in drama class, drawing an invention in art class, or researching physical responses to athletic activities in physical education classes. Developing a cross-curricular attitude that invites children to bring their enthusiasms into their learning helps to broaden their scope, discoveries, and understandings.

Other strategies that work well in specialty subject areas that are useful for supporting talent development more broadly include:

- flexibility in program design, allowing for individual differences

- open-ended assignments that encourage high-level exploration

- student participation in planning and choosing learning options

- children not being pushed to operate at the gifted level in every subject area

- availability of a variety of resources, with openness to finding more

- authentic collaborations that are carefully planned, guided, and facilitated

Specialized and Alternative Schools

Many jurisdictions establish schools or programs within schools that specialize somehow—maybe in the performing arts, applied sciences, technology, languages, or the International Baccalaureate. Sometimes, alternative schools are established in which the approach to learning is more flexible and individualistic, or more structured and traditional, than is usually the case. These kinds of schools vary greatly across jurisdictions. Most are aimed at the high school level, although some have specialized and alternative programs for younger students, too.

These facilities frequently operate on a magnet school basis, attracting those who are interested and can demonstrate their ability to participate in the programming offered, independently of any prior official designation as gifted. There is almost always some kind of audition or application process involved and/or other prerequisites for admission. We have seen many cases in which a particular alternative school has provided exactly the right kind of educational match for a particular student. New York City has many such schools, such as the Bronx High School of Science and the LaGuardia High School for the Performing Arts (featured in the movie *Fame*). Many communities have similar kinds of schools.

Although specialized and alternative schools can be wonderful for addressing gifted learning needs and supporting high-level development, there are concerns that require consideration. One is the possibility of prematurely narrowing a child's interests and focus. For a child with diverse intellectual enthusiasms, a challenging traditional school may be the best learning environment in which to hold open as many options as possible for as long as possible. Also, while specialized or alternative schools may provide a high level of challenge and stimulation in the targeted areas, they are not always as strong in others. Schools for the performing arts, for example, are sometimes less demanding in the traditional academic subjects, which can pose problems for intellectually gifted learners. And while some students thrive on the competition that is part of many specialized schools, others find that they do better in a more collaborative atmosphere. Finally, extra travel time and other commitments are almost always required.

Private and Independent Schools

> "I won't send my child to a public school. She'll get a much
> better education at a private school."
> "Tyrone didn't need some kind of gifted label in order to get into
> the program at The Alliance Heights School. He loves it there."

A private school that provides academic support and values achievement and excellence in a wide variety of areas is a fine choice for some children. For example, good Montessori or Reggio Emilia-type schools can work very well for independent, intrinsically-motivated young learners.[16] These kinds of schools encourage and respect children's unique learning needs and interests within a context of independence and structure. Children are given many opportunities for sensorimotor experiences, manipulative play, social skills development, and leisurely pursuit of learning activities. The theoretical framework of these methods provides excellent foundations for nurturing children's individual and developmental diversity, including supporting gifted-level abilities, but it should be remembered that the actual schools vary considerably in how well they translate theory into practice.

A word of caution applies to any school that bills itself as a learning academy or institute. Sometimes these schools publish attractive brochures or develop high-tech websites and promote exciting or unusual learning opportunities, such as theater outings, rock-climbing excursions, ski trips, archeological digs, museum visits, and so on. Experiences like this may sound enticing. However, as with any major purchase, parents will want to investigate marketing pitches carefully and not take glossy brochures or fancy homepages too seriously. For example, what does a "global curriculum" or "child-centered approach" really mean in a particular context? What exactly is a school promising when it claims to provide a curriculum that encompasses "a wide body of knowledge and range of experiences that all children need in order to develop into successful, happy, and self-confident individuals?"

Many independent schools *do* provide supportive learning environments, but parents must do the necessary research to find out if a particular school will actually be a good fit for their child. (We discuss this in more detail in Chapter 11.) We suggest that parents take the time to visit the schools that they are considering; ask lots of questions; be attuned to what is happening in classrooms, schoolyards, and hallways; and find out what kinds of programming adaptations are available for children with the kinds of needs, interests, or abilities that are of particular concern to them.

Regulations concerning teacher qualifications in independent or charter schools are often different than those governing teachers in the public sector. Therefore, parents should also inquire about teachers' certification and experience, including specialized training in gifted education, gifted consultation and support network availability, and professional development opportunities.

Homeschooling

Homeschooling seems to require the same formula for success as parenting, which is to say, it can work when the parents are loving and open-minded and dedicated.[17]

> *"We'd like to homeschool our son because we don't think the educational system can provide him with the kinds of opportunities we can offer by teaching him at home. But how do we design a curriculum?"*

Thomas Edison, Florence Nightingale, and Agatha Christie were all taught at home, as were countless others who have achieved at very high levels in one or more areas. Some children are too advanced or otherwise unsuited to the learning environments of the classrooms available locally. If parents are willing and able to invest the necessary time and effort, and if they have the inclination to provide homeschooling, then this can be a viable alternative for some children. However, there are a number of factors to consider.[18]

According to a recent consideration of the research on homeschooling,[19] there are no reliable comprehensive data on homeschooling gifted learners. This is primarily because there are few systematic data available for homeschooling at all, much less for the curriculum and pedagogy that is being employed.

Although homeschooling is widely practiced in the United States and Canada, regulatory practices vary from place to place and (as with education generally) are under constant review and revision. Parents who wish to teach their own children, or who plan to hire an education professional to do so, should investigate government policies in their jurisdiction. In order to meet local requirements, parents may simply have to inform local educational authorities of their intent to homeschool, or they may have to provide extensive evidence of curriculum development and evaluation processes, and perhaps educational attainment levels for themselves.

There are many active support groups and online networks across North America that provide information about all aspects of homeschooling—from establishing goals, expectations, and limits to legislative issues, curriculum, and extracurricular options, as well as providing a way to interact and share resources with others.

As might be expected, there is a continuum of approaches to learning in homeschooling practice.[20] It ranges from mirroring what might go on in a typical classroom and runs across the spectrum to extremes of various kinds. For example, homeschooled children might learn about llamas by doing book or Internet research and then going to the zoo, or they might be involved in buying and caring for a llama. What goes on in a homeschooling program is as individual as the children and educators or parents who design it, which can be the biggest advantage of this educational approach, as well as its biggest drawback. "On the one hand, parents frequently will have deep insight into the educational strengths, weaknesses, and needs of their child. On the other hand, their lack of specific expertise in gifted education may result in them overlooking useful pedagogical strategies and curricular resources."[21]

Many parents who homeschool choose to do so because of their objections to practices in public schools, which they view as too permissive or constraining. According to recent figures, about 30% of those Americans who choose homeschooling make that choice for religious reasons.[22] Additional parent concerns revolve around safety in school, frustration with the educational system, wasted time, and children's special learning needs. Depending on parents' values, teaching expertise, and personality, a homeschooling program can be nurturing, motivating, and directly targeted to a child's domain-specific strengths and weaknesses, or it can be rigid, narrowly focused, and authoritarian.

Homeschooling advocates are increasing in number, and heightened technological possibilities are making it more attractive today than ever.[23] Curricular flexibility, direct parental involvement, and academic effectiveness are also draws. Parents of children being homeschooled often work collaboratively to develop meaningful programs and to advocate on behalf of their children. The barriers that traditionally have existed between homeschooled students and public schools are now far fewer than was previously the case. In many districts, homeschooled children can participate in public school band, sports, clubs, and other activities.

Homeschooling concerns include financial implications, record keeping, goal setting, progress assessment and evaluation, academic credentials (important especially as children get older, if they hope to attend postsecondary education), and social development. Children may benefit from opportunities to attend a local school part time, taking one or more classes or participating in extracurricular activities so that they can interact regularly with age mates. Homeschooling support groups also often provide opportunities for social interaction, and students can become involved in community and volunteering pursuits as well.

Sometimes parents opt for homeschooling because of their child's boredom or waning motivation. Such learners "may exhibit exceptional motivation to learn at home, especially if the homeschool environment encourages self-efficacy, self-pacing, enjoyment of learning for its own sake, challenging explorations in the areas of strength, and consistent hard work in areas of weakness."[24] On the other hand, motivation problems may persist or even be exacerbated if parents take too much responsibility for keeping their children challenged, thus robbing them of the chance to become self-sufficient and intrinsically motivated. A little bit of boredom can be a very good thing if a child learns to become accountable for his own learning and intellectual stimulation.

Parents who homeschool also need to pay attention to their own needs and to monitor whether they are becoming too stressed by the responsibilities of managing and implementing an educational program in addition to the other responsibilities in their lives. On the other hand, with some children, homeschooling is actually easier than one might expect because these children can become self-directed learners. Consider the following letter, sent to us by a parent.

Homeschooling: A Mother's Perspective

Homeschooling is going very well for us. There are days when I feel like pulling my hair out, but then I had days like that when Derek was still in school! The real difference now (so positive!) is that if something isn't working, we can just sit down, talk it through, and try something else.

I've found a discussion group under my district's educational services umbrella. It is very interesting to read and exchange emails with other homeschooling parents. There is something quite refreshing about the "been-there-done-that" advice and comments, even when you know each kid is unique. The group is also extremely useful for getting advice and evaluations of book and curriculum alternatives, since there is almost always someone who has had some relevant experience.

We are still having some of the behavioral issues with Derek that we experienced while he was in school. I believe that they are largely the result of the poor socialization and emotional "hurt" he suffered while at the private school. We certainly aren't completely blameless in that. With 20/20 hindsight, I recognize that we were more lenient with Derek than would have been optimal. However, I am reasonably hopeful (most of the time!) that we will get through this behavioral phase.

On the educational front, Derek is soaring ahead. He really loves the ability to focus on topics in as much detail and for as long as he wants (at least until he has exhausted his mother for any single sitting). We quickly evolved an approach that is quite eclectic. I think the "classical education approach" is often too rigid, so we are relying on the basic framework for guidance with a flexible structure for day-to-day planning. One of my biggest challenges is how to find the appropriate balance of a predictable schedule and routine for a kid who loves many things, while at the same time letting him pursue a specific topic for as long as he wants to, rather than shutting it down simply because it's time to do something else. My feeling is that getting a well-rounded education is something like eating a well-balanced diet: you don't have to have something from each food group every meal to remain healthy, so long as you don't go for too long without spending some time with each group.

Derek wants to keep on homeschooling until he is ready to go to college. I'm keeping a more open mind, although I must confess that I'm not sure if a school exists that can accommodate his wide range of skill levels.

Casting the Net Farther Afield

> *We should no longer even be thinking about "a program" in gifted education for which testing is required to "get in." Rather, we should be thinking about how to collect a variety of information on individual children in order to best match their demonstrated needs with any of a variety of options our particular setting can offer.*[25]

Thanks to current technology, educators and parents can readily learn what's happening in classrooms close to home and far afield. School walls no longer constrain students; the innovative options of yesterday are part of schools' basic repertoires today, and who knows what will be accessible by tomorrow?[26] Students in North America can take part in online math, science, and language arts programs offered at facilities elsewhere in the world, such as the Weizmann Institute in Israel, the Virtual School for the Gifted based in Australia, and the International Writers Project in Florida.[27] We know adolescents who have networked and participated in summer learning programs in Greece (archaeology), the United Kingdom (English literature), Italy (art), Costa Rica (biology), and elsewhere. Some of these programs are affiliated with universities. Students find that these can be great ways to learn—and to acquire school credits. When educators and parents work together to take advantage of what's new, interesting, and potentially useful, they greatly increase the likelihood of keeping gifted learners engaged. The supplementary learning activities that we propose in this chapter are only a sampling; there really are no limits to the possibilities!

Extracurricular Enrichment

"How can I supplement what's going on in my daughter's school?"

Extracurricular enrichment activities can help keep children intellectually challenged and developing.[28] There are many extracurricular options:[29]

- *Music:* playing an instrument and/or participating in a choir, band, or orchestra

- *Theatre:* costumes, makeup, acting, script development, sets, lighting, clowning, puppet plays

- *Dance:* ballet, jazz, modern, ballroom, ethnic

- *Performance appreciation:* professional concerts and showcases in different artistic media

- *Art:* painting, drawing, sculpture, photography

- *Crafts:* woodworking, sewing, pottery, model-building, knitting, jewelry design

- *Recreational reading:* anything of interest

- *Writing:* stories, poems, articles, for pleasure or submission for publication

- *Classes or tutoring in a second or third language:* also, summer language-learning experiences

- *Math and science:* business, engineering, or other specialized programs

- *Computers:* advanced web-related activities, interactive media networks

- *Community service:* health-related associations, youth organizations, global causes, political affiliations

- *Leadership opportunities:* tutoring, interest groups, cultural activities, religious and community organizations

- *Competitions:* local, regional, national, and international levels in many different areas[30]

- *Clubs:* chess, astronomy, cooking, photography, photojournalism

- *Summer programs:* talent development programs of many types run by museums, other cultural organizations, universities, and talent searches[31]

- *Camps:* summer and/or weekend recreational or specialized by area of interest, such as sailing, dance, or language immersion

- *Sports and physical activity:* gymnastics, martial arts, other sports

- *Distance learning:* unlimited possibilities and options[32]

There are countless possibilities for extracurricular involvement. At the same time, however, it is important to remember that children and adolescents also need time to do nothing, to find out more about who they are, and to discover what it is they want to do with their time and their lives. Because over-programming kids can be counterproductive, the key is to find a healthy balance that also affords opportunities for relaxation and enjoyment.

Mentorships

> *Mentoring makes a difference in lives. In their simplest form, mentoring programs can begin with one child working with one adult. From that simple beginning, the possibilities are endless.*[33]

> *"Our 14-year-old daughter had an incredible mentorship experience working with a doctor who helped her design an experiment on pediatric testing for chicken pox. She learned how to structure a research study, and her results were compatible with findings from other studies. Her work is being sent to a medical journal for possible publication."*

Understanding Mentorships

The term "mentor" comes from Greek mythology; Odysseus' son Telemachus was entrusted to the care of Mentor, a wise advisor. Mentoring is a supportive relationship that can be established wherever there is a learner and someone with more experience who has the time, patience, and willingness to support, challenge, and guide the learner to greater knowledge and understanding.[34] It is a dynamic interaction that can include the transmission of values, attitudes, and passions, as well as knowledge, skills, and practical connections. History and literature from classical times to the present abound with examples of mentorships in politics, business, science, the arts, and education. Aristotle benefited from his mentorship under Plato, as Mickey Mouse benefited from his (with some interesting resistance and turbulence from time to time) in *The Sorcerer's Apprentice.*[35] Mentorships aren't always smooth sailing and do require work.

Mentors can have many different roles in students lives and "may serve as intellectual sparring partners, emotional supporters, or providers of professional contacts."[36] Strong mentorships are built on foundations of shared interests and are mutually respectful, responsive, and gratifying.[37]

Mentorships offer potential benefits for both parties. Benefits to students include:

- enriched perspective on a topic or area of interest
- increased competence
- encouragement and guidance for self-directed learning
- new connections between one's learning and the real world
- discovery of resources beyond the classroom
- personal growth (confidence, persistence, empowerment, self-efficacy, autonomy)
- career path awareness
- respect for expertise
- relationship-building experiences
- model for enjoyment and accomplishment in the chosen area
- introduction to other individuals who might provide insight and support
- increased exposure to and visibility within a field of interest
- preparation for taking on roles within society

Benefits to mentors include:

- continued learning
- rejuvenation of spirit
- sense of fulfillment
- sense of respect and being valued
- fresh perspective
- involvement and enjoyment
- vicarious satisfaction through accomplishment of the protégé
- contribution to skills and expertise of those entering the field
- connection to the educational system

There are many models for and levels of mentorships. For example, they can take the form of job-shadowing programs, in which students prepare for the mentorship phase in school classes and then spend a certain number of hours in the career setting of their mentor. Alternatively, mentorship programs can consist of visits to the school from community experts who increase the depth of programming that classroom teachers are able to provide. Under the guidance of the teacher, a mentor and student can co-create an individualized program. Students can be assisted in finding individuals in the educational or broader community who are (or have been) actively engaged in working productively in areas of interest. Mentorships also work well in elementary schools, although they require careful monitoring.

To encourage the formation of such learning partnerships, teachers and parents can network with one another, asking for nominations for possible mentors. We have seen such collaborations recruit both actively working and retired musicians, actors, doctors, chefs, professors, business people, artists, artisans, architects, and others, each of whom was willing to help a keen and able student explore and develop particular interests and abilities. Ideally, the mentor is someone who possesses good communication skills, is comfortable working with young people, has a flexible attitude, and is prepared to invest the time, effort, and patience required to make the mentoring relationship work.

Structuring Mentorships

Though the format of mentorship programs vary, all involve a student in some kind of relationship with an adult whose work she respects and who can inspire and guide the student in her own development. In any mentorship arrangement, expectations should be clarified and agreed upon by both the mentor and the student. In formal academic situations, it's a good idea to prepare a written agreement that specifies the intent and responsibilities of each party, including the right to withdraw from the arrangement. Periodic review of this written "contract" helps to ensure that expectations are being met by both parties.

When developing a framework for a mentorship arrangement, there are a number of questions to consider:[38]

- What is the student's current level of expertise? What can the student do independently, and where does he or she need help?

- What is the student interested in?

- Is the student receptive to the learning opportunity and willing to commit the necessary time and energy?

- How does the student learn best?

- Are there any special issues to be aware of (for example, with respect to personality, resiliency, or emotional or social issues)?

- Does the student demonstrate a high level of motivation? Self-management skills? Task commitment? Responsibility?

- Is there a safe and comfortable space available for learning, or can such an environment be created?

- What community resources have already been accessed and used wisely?

For those who are thinking about implementing a mentorship program in a school, there are important time and energy factors to consider. Organizing, maintaining, and monitoring mentorships is time-consuming. Teachers who want to support mentorship activities must think about the form that they want these experiences to take and what their own roles will be in the context of their other duties. School mentorship programs often work best when the major responsibility for coordinating them is assumed by a member of the special education or administrative support staff working in collaboration with teachers, parents, students, and mentors.[39]

Mentoring should not stand alone. The arrangement will be successful and mutually rewarding if it is embraced and valued as an integral component of the individual student's overall educational plan. It can be even more effective when academic credit is granted.

Mentorships are an excellent way of providing students with gifted-level challenges, and they are one of the most highly and frequently recommended—though under-utilized—practices in gifted education.[40] They can be particularly important for students from culturally diverse and economically disadvantaged backgrounds, providing positive role models and contributing to an understanding of the components of and pathways to high achievement.[41] Female and minority mentors do triple duty; they challenge gender and cultural stereotypes and serve as alternative role models, in addition to providing the mentorship experience itself. Bringing nontraditional minority professionals such as female Black and Hispanic mathematicians, scientists, and other experts into the classroom as mentors is an excellent approach to enriching and accelerating education while also providing authentic connections to important domains of competence, and simultaneously expanding students' understanding of diversity and possibility.[42]

In the end, after finding and happily settling upon one another, the student and mentor select a suitable learning environment and then shape that environment to their particular situation. They develop a shared focus for the mentorship activities and, in the most successful mentorships, experience many rich and mutually productive hours.

Career Exploration

> *"Last fall, a lady from the Humane Society came to our school and described how they look after all the animals. I've been volunteering there twice a month ever since. I want to become a veterinarian when I get older."*
> *"A forensic diver told us all about his underwater diving job. It was awesome!"*

As learners discover and develop their talents, they will also need support in exploring career opportunities and information, and in learning how to deal effectively with rapid change and the uncertainty of the future.[43]

In our rapidly changing world, students with diverse exceptional abilities can derive great value from learning about wide-ranging and atypical career possibilities.[44] The learning can take many forms, both in the classroom and outside of it. Some ideas that work well include:

- career days, in which representatives from various occupations address interested students and are available for discussion

- a career resource center located in the school library or elsewhere, providing a place for students to access information and discuss ideas with others

- student visits to career sites (also known as job shadowing)

- career exploration options infused into coursework

- internships, mentorships, co-op placements, and other opportunities for authentic exploration

- informal discussions with people engaged in diverse kinds of pursuits

- skills-based personal growth plans, designed in consultation with guidance counselors, parents, mentors, or teachers

- critical analysis of occupation-related media stereotypes built into curriculum

- biographies of eminent people in different career paths

- simulations and role playing

Students can be encouraged to participate in these kinds of activities and to perhaps devise other ways to learn about career options and pathways.

Books

> *"With a book, you're never alone."*
> *"Other kids don't realize that books are way better than TV."*
> *"It only took me two days to read the last Harry Potter book. I wish there were more!"*

People who grow up loving to read are at an obvious advantage. Through reading we can develop and expand our interests, whether they are related to work, hobbies, families, ourselves, or the world around us. Reading is a great way to learn about almost anything, and books can nurture, inform, stimulate, and soothe. They can be used as a basis for sharing, thinking, learning, dreaming, inspiring, and exploring.

Why is recreational reading important for children? According to current understandings of teaching, learning, and brain development, reading:[45]

- stimulates reflection and high-level thinking

- increases engagement in relevant, self-directed learning

- broadens and extends one's knowledge and understandings

- contributes to a feeling of connection to different communities and cultures

- alleviates loneliness, especially for those who feel different or who experience social isolation

- provides an escape from stressful or troubling circumstances

- inspires and motivates

- provides models for experiences in various circumstances and contexts

- stimulates thinking about values and life choices

- provides relaxation

Reading is a fundamental aspect of many kinds of learning and can also be a compelling way to enrich people's lives. Some children prefer fiction, but most also enjoy at least some kinds of nonfiction. There are books of every type on every topic to capture children's attention and imaginations. Good books also challenge and expand young readers' minds and vocabularies.[46] Reading can lead to greater knowledge, deeper understanding, changed attitudes, increased motivation, and altered behavior. Books can also help children think about what matters to them and how they want to live their lives.

Some books are particularly useful for helping children come to terms with their problems (such as friendship issues or feelings of different-ness). *Bibliotherapy* refers to a specific therapeutic process whereby selected reading material is used to help in dealing with personal problems. A modified version of the same concept can be applied developmentally (rather than therapeutically), whereby books are used to encourage children's awareness, empathy, and emotional development.[47] Given the right book, a young reader can identify with a character in a story and experience a sense of kinship by following that person through a difficult situation and toward a successful resolution. In this way, a child can gain insight and learn how to handle similar kinds of circumstances. As he interacts with a literary character, he can learn about himself and achieve insight into his own difficulties, if only to feel that he is not alone.

Educators and parents can use books as a foundation for shared exploration and discussion. Books can help address children's concerns related to their giftedness and other aspects of their lives, such as adjustment to changes and challenges, personal growth, values, identity, social and cultural concerns, and family issues. Reading can also be useful as a preventive measure to anticipate and solve problems before they occur. Optimally, the adult is familiar with the book that the child is reading and is prepared to engage in discussions about the child's observations and questions. The adult should choose the book carefully, avoiding poorly written material and stories that might make the child feel too exposed or uncomfortable. Like any therapeutic technique, however, bibliotherapy should be approached thoughtfully, with care and caution—children's problems can be exacerbated rather than solved or soothed by reading about someone going through something troubling that they, too, are encountering. Mental health professionals are the right people for addressing deeply rooted problems.

A final word about books for avid readers: librarians are often the richest and least used of our available resources. They know so much about books and where to find really good ones. They are usually pleased to offer suggestions based on what someone has read or might enjoy reading, and they will discuss both new books and the classics on their shelves. Reading can provide an endless source of intellectual and creative stimulation for people of all ages and should be encouraged (and modeled) whenever possible.

Travel

...it was a beautiful map, in many colors, showing principal roads, rivers and seas, towns and cities, mountains and valleys, intersections and detours, and sites of outstanding interest both beautiful and historic. The only trouble was that Milo had never heard of any of the places it indicated, and even the names sounded most peculiar.... He closed his eyes and poked a finger at the map. "Dictionopolis," read Milo slowly when he saw what his finger had chosen.... Suddenly he found himself speeding along an unfamiliar country highway.... "Welcome to Expectations," said a carefully lettered sign on a small house at the side of the road.[48]

> *"MOM! I just looked up the route from Rome to Paris on Mapquest. I found out that it's only 875 miles and that the total driving time is 13½ hours! I'm going to plan a trip, in case we ever want to go!"*

Travel is another horizon-stretching approach to learning—a springboard for extending and supplementing more conventional learning methods. Whether it is actual, factual, virtual, or whimsical, travel is one of the best ways to learn. Although long trips to foreign lands are not possible for most families, any kind of travel stimulates children's intellectual development and broadens their horizons. Family excursions can cover short or long distances and may last a few days, a semester, or a full year or more, depending on individual circumstances and constraints.[49] For example, a short trip might be a one-day hike in the mountains, a weekend in a nearby city, or a visit to a museum or historical site. The learning accrues much more from the attitudes and perspectives of family members than from the duration, cost, or destination.

Although travel can be expensive, creative families with a limited budget can also experience the benefits. There are many ways to encourage children to get the most out of travel-related experiences The ideas that we mention here can be implemented by a family touring a faraway continent, taking a day trip to a town a few miles away, exploring their own hometown, or embarking on a "virtual vacation" on the web.

Before You Go

- Include everyone in family decision making regarding places to visit.

- Encourage all family members to spend some time looking at atlases, maps, or travel websites, tracing possible routes.

- Buy or download travel guides.

- Discuss information, observations, and ideas.

- Spend time online, or browse travel magazines or newspaper travel sections, investigating what might be interesting and what each person might like to explore. For example, if one child is enthused about a particular sport or art, make sure there will be opportunities for some kind of exploration of that interest while away. (And if new interests are found, these can be followed up back at home.)

While You Are Away

- Encourage everyone to notice and discuss differences that they find in food, buildings, scenery, and other sights, sounds, and influences.

- Think about what captures your own interest in the new environment. Act as an authentic model of engagement in learning and exploration.

- Ask questions that stimulate higher-order thinking about the experience and environment. For example, if a family spends a weekend at a cabin on a lake, discover what everyone likes best about this new place. What do they like better at home? What aspects of life in the new environment would they like to take home?

- Encourage everyone to keep a diary or sketchbook (or both) to record their impressions.

- Look for ways to make the experience productive. For example, during or after the excursion, write articles for a website, a local newspaper, or for a school assignment.

- Create a collaborative travel document or scrapbook. Consider compiling a photo journal. Perhaps one or more members of the family can take pictures of personal interest (not necessarily the usual tourist sites), while someone else takes responsibility for writing, and another person puts together the final product. This can be assembled upon returning home to be shared with friends and other family members.

Travel offers a world of opportunities to learn and acquire fresh perspectives on other places, cultures, and languages. Some children love the detailed organization of actually planning a trip (doing the research, planning the itinerary, thinking about the budget, and so on). And for those who think creatively, planning a virtual foray into another era or into space or beneath the seas is yet another way to "go." Just planning a get-away can be a wonderfully motivating and invigorating learning experience—and if you actually take the trip, well, so much the better!

Do-Nothing Times

"Mom, I've got way too much to do!"
"I never have time just to think anymore."

These comments are typical of children who may need some down time. In encouraging optimal long-term development in children, it is important that they experience periods entirely free of scheduled stimulation. We all need some unprogrammed time and space in our lives to explore the scope and shape of our interests and pleasures, figure out what we enjoy doing, and consider and reflect on our experiences, successes, failures, and preferences. If we don't invest in this kind of reflection, we will eventually find ourselves quite out of touch with our goals, our hopes, and our dreams. One of the most important tasks of childhood and adolescence is discovering a sense of self, and this requires an investment of time that is not otherwise required for homework or participating in scheduled activities.

"Mom, I'm BORED!"

From another perspective, parents should try not to rescue their child from boredom. Figuring out what one wants to do with one's discretionary time can be a valuable learning experience in and of itself. Children need unscheduled time in order to develop time management skills and learn to set priorities. Many conscientious parents, in an attempt to provide appropriate stimulation, take full responsibility for keeping their children engaged, happy, and organized. However, too much programming can deprive children of something vital—it can prevent them from learning what it is they enjoy doing and who they really are. As with adults, children whose lives are micromanaged lose their zest and enthusiasm, and those who are over-programmed can get stale and stressed.[50]

And So...

> *No matter where you've come from or where you're*
> *headed, your thirst for adventure never ceases.*
> *It's an insatiable desire to experience the unknown,*
> *to test your own limits, to explore further than*
> *your imagination has ever ventured.*[51]

The number of approaches that can be used to nurture high-level development is enormous. Some approaches can occur in regular classrooms, while others are designed to be implemented in different kinds of special learning environments. What works well for one child will not necessarily work at all well for another. When selecting or constructing a program from so many possibilities, the main task is not to find the fullest slate or even the right or the best option, but to find what is most appropriate for a given child at a particular time in his or her development, given the constraints of the particular situation and context. The objective is to find a good match between the learning needs of an individual child and the range of learning opportunities available in the child's particular circumstance. And so, having considered many of the learning options available for high-ability students, it is now time to think about motivation, social and emotional issues, and other developmental considerations.

Section IV

Being Smart about Gifted Development

Chapter 8

Motivation and Achievement Issues

Motivation is the art of getting people to perform necessary tasks they might not otherwise do.[1]

Motivation is the study of why people think and behave as they do.[2]

There are almost as many theories about what motivates people as there are theorists to think them up.[3]

Motivation: The Heart of Learning

"I try to encourage my students to learn by capturing their interest in the subject being taught, showing why it's important and how it'll be useful to them."

The question of motivation is at the heart of gifted-level learning. By understanding what motivation is and how to sustain students' motivation to learn, we understand a lot more about how to support gifted-level learning outcomes. Data from a major longitudinal study on gifted development[4] indicate that some children show evidence of "gifted motivation" at an early age, and that motivation is more important than cognitive ability in achievement outcomes, both short-term and long-term. Obviously, then, it is important to do as much as possible to support students' motivation to learn.

One urgent question asked by educators is how they can stimulate and sustain their students' motivation to learn. When they think about it constructively, teachers can generate both creative and practical ideas. As expressed by teacher Chris Healey:

> *Students need to know where they stand relative to expectations.... Teachers must effectively set goals for their students based on their individual needs and motivation levels.... This may require creativity and resourcefulness on the part of the teacher, but consistent, constructive feedback is especially important for maintaining interest, keeping [the students'] situation in perspective, etc.*

Motivation is tied not only to an individual's valuing of the task at hand ("Do I want to do it?"), but also to an expectation of success ("Can I do it?").[5] A student who believes that math is important but also believes that she cannot do it may behave in a variety of self-defeating ways. She may skip class, avoid doing homework, or give up very easily when asked to solve a difficult math problem. All of these behaviors will contribute to poor performance, which in turn will reinforce her low expectation of future mathematical success. Similarly, a student who does not value the achievement of the assigned learning task can be expected to invest very little effort, if any, in doing it, even if she feels fully competent to handle it. However, a student who feels confident about her ability and who also values a particular activity is likely to persevere and gain at least a measure of success. Academic expectations are much more readily met, and even exceeded, when students experience the motivation that results from a combination of self-confidence and personal engagement in learning.

The theory and research on academic motivation point to three major recommendations for motivating high-ability students' continued engagement in learning:[6]

1. Teachers and parents should try to *match tasks to each child's ability.* Tasks should be both challenging and manageable.

2. Learning opportunities should be *perceived as valuable and authentically relevant* to the individuals engaged in the learning process.

3. Adults should *encourage a growth mindset* so children learn that intelligence is incremental and that failures are opportunities for self-knowledge.

In a recent study, 100 high school students were asked, "How can teachers motivate their students?"[7] From the students' many interesting answers, three distinct themes emerged. The best ways for teachers to motivate students, they said, are by: (1) encouraging their expectations of success, (2) facilitating their understanding of the value of learning and relevance of the tasks, and (3) maintaining and enhancing their self-esteem. These three perspectives align very well with the research on motivation. They provide organizers for our discussion (which follows) of 10 ways that teachers can motivate learning, which are consistent with research findings on the instructional methods of effective teachers.[8] Examples of the students' actual comments are included.

Encouraging Students' Expectations of Success

1. Facilitating Accomplishment

   "A sense of accomplishment makes us feel like we're really good at something, so we try to keep up great grades."

   Content mastery provides a sense of accomplishment, which is a powerful motivator for learning. Students who become competent in subject areas that they value (and who recognize their growing competence) are motivated to continue the learning process at a higher level.

2. Teacher's Confidence and Expectations

   "A motivating teacher makes us feel that we can do anything. A teacher needs to believe that we are competent and never underestimate us."

   Teachers' confidence in their students translates to students' increased confidence in themselves. Students who sense that their teachers have faith in their ability are more motivated to work toward academic success.

Facilitating Students' Understanding of the Value of Learning

3. Use of Relevant and Authentic Examples

   "It helps when the teacher tells real-life stories to illustrate a point."

   Personal connection to a topic area is a potent motivator for learning. Students are far more likely to want to master and apply complex concepts when, at least part of the time, success or failure is determined by their actual performance in a real-world situation. Teachers can motivate students by structuring learning experiences that involve direct interaction with authentic experiences and objects in their natural context.

4. Teacher's Enthusiasm for the Subject

   "It won't work if a teacher who hates chemistry has to explain about carbon dioxide. When a teacher loves what he or she is teaching, students are likely to be motivated, too."

   A teacher's enthusiasm is infectious. When students perceive that a teacher finds the content interesting and worthwhile, they are more likely to take the course seriously and be motivated to learn.

5. Variety in Teaching Methods

   "A teacher can keep students motivated by doing different things and not always using a textbook or the board or talking on and on."

   By changing things up and incorporating group work, lectures, visiting experts, discussions, hands-on learning, games, field trips, and other kinds of learning options into their teaching, teachers can bring the content to life and motivate student engagement.

6. Explicit Discussions of Why the Learning Is Important

   "Talk about the importance of what we're learning. How will it affect our future?"

   It is important that students understand how the learning is relevant in their lives. Teachers can discuss why they think the learning is valuable, and they can initiate discussions with their students about how it might be valuable for them.

Enhancing Respect and Self-Esteem

7. Respect and Rapport

"Try to remember that some of us have things on our minds. Take the time to get to know us. And please remember our names!"

Students are more motivated to learn when they perceive that their teachers are caring, respectful, available, and willing to help.

8. Classroom Atmosphere

"I find that I always pay more attention when the teacher talks in a good-natured way, like we're real people."

Both learning and teaching should be enjoyable. A teacher's patience, attitude, and sense of humor are important components of a classroom climate, and also ways of showing respect for students.

9. Positive Reinforcement

"If a student gives a wrong answer, a teacher can still say, 'Nice try.'"

Praise, when it is earned, increases confidence, involvement in learning, and risk-taking. Positive reinforcement and constructive feedback enable children to recognize their accomplishments and to feel proud of them. When adults praise children's worthy performances and do not overreact to mistakes, they inform and enhance the children's perceptions about their developing capabilities. It is important, though, to make sure that praise is targeted and genuine and that there is solid evidence to back it up. In other words, keep it honest and make it matter.

10. An Atmosphere that Allows Autonomy

"Be nice. We won't take advantage of you. It's one thing to be in charge, but if you're too strict, I'll skip class."

When students are allowed and helped to make their own meaningful choices, as well as to feel that they have some control over their activities, they tend to perform the given tasks better and to experience more joy in getting them done. They are also more likely to be engaged by the topics and to feel more committed to their decisions and more responsible for any consequences. Other ways of encouraging autonomy include giving students opportunities to evaluate portions of their own work, choose personal goals with the guidance of their teachers, and help decide classroom rules.

In summary, "Encouragement, acceptance as a person, sharing of interest and excitement—these are critical to the healthy development of a person's sense of self-worth and to his obtaining a life-long desire for learning and creating."[9] Although developed with teachers in mind, this information applies to all adults who work with children, including parents, grandparents, coaches, mentors, and others.

Motivators: Practical Strategies

How can parents and teachers implement these recommendations? Here are some ideas for parents and teachers who want to motivate children's learning.

Suspense, Intrigue, and Curiosity

Give children opportunities to connect uncertainty and effort with the joy of discovery. This is particularly effective if the question is an authentic one for which you don't have a ready answer. For example, you might observe, "It's a hot summer day, and all of a sudden, the weather turns nasty. Big hailstones and ice pellets start to fall. Ice! On a hot summer's day! How can this happen?" Your children might not know the answer, but if the question is asked at an opportune moment, they may become curious about it and begin to generate hypotheses. Together you can think about how to find the answers.[10]

Guessing and Feedback

Guessing (or, in more scientific language, hypothesis-generation) and feedback are complementary partners in high-level learning. Suppose you start a science investigation with the question, "What are the basic human survival requirements?" Children's guesses and their responses to each other's guesses can whet their appetite for knowledge and motivate further learning. Your appropriate and timely feedback can guide and stimulate their further inquiry, ensuring that it is channeled productively.

Use of Previous Knowledge

When introducing new ideas, draw links to what children already know. By connecting new learning to already consolidated knowledge, you increase the likelihood that it will be meaningfully accessible later. Perhaps you want children to learn about a particular historical event. You might start by talking about circumstances that are similar in one way or another and that are familiar to them. For example, most children have experienced peer pressure and perhaps criticism when they have challenged school or family traditions. Leaders of various social movements, such as women's right to vote, civil rights, and environmental causes, have prompted similar backlash when these advances were first implemented. Using students' previous knowledge in this way will help them to understand the dynamics of these movements and put the situations into a meaningful perspective.

Controversy and Contradiction

There are almost always several points of view on any given topic. An awareness of what those controversies are can be great motivators for learning. A teacher or parent might ask a child to consider the relative importance of one thing as compared to another. For example, "Which is a better form of transportation, a car or a bicycle?" Or ask whether a certain regulation should be reconsidered, such as allowing dogs in restaurants. Adults can help children gather information and engage in reasoning, critical listening, and refutation. By encouraging students to give serious consideration to alternative perspectives, controversy and contradiction can be motivating and stimulating.[11]

Conducive Learning Climate

A learning environment that is unwelcoming, dull, and full of distractions will not usually be as motivating as one that is accepting, richly stimulating, and well organized. Children are more likely to be motivated to learn in an atmosphere of challenge and support, in which parents and/or teachers encourage persistence and goal-directed activity, respect the children's interests, and foster curiosity. Children work best where they have opportunities to participate responsibly in program planning and evaluation processes, where expectations and timelines are reasonable, and where they feel safe enough to risk making mistakes.[12]

Innovative and Expansive Approaches

A discussion of ways to motivate learning would not be complete without mentioning innovative educational approaches. Countless creative educators nurture children's confidence, generate excitement about what's happening in their classrooms, and try out new ways to engage their students in learning. We address only a few of these, and we encourage our readers to explore other innovative possibilities.

One example of a promising innovative project is arts-based learning, in which meaningful collaborations between classroom teachers and artists (including songwriters, musicians, writers, fabric artisans, and others) serve to inspire students to do their own creative work. Different programming designs use art or music or drama to complement various academic subjects, including (depending on the teacher and the artist) math, language, science, and social studies, in all cases incorporating creativity and interactive thinking into the curriculum.[13] Children and teachers participating in these experiences report that they enjoy integrative approaches in which the arts are not peripheral but are woven into the curriculum's foundational subjects.

Many innovations of the past began with educators' attempts to address gifted learning needs, and an exciting recent example of this is the Renzulli Learning System,[14] a computer-based program used to augment and individualize children's learning, enabling every teacher to do a better job of matching their students' gifted learning needs. In other situations, computer-based software is used to support students in constructing knowledge, building on concepts and questions, and connecting with others around the world. These programs motivate students to become part of a global community of learners and to experience the joy of sharing ideas, as well as the fulfillment of greatly expanded content mastery.[15]

Another promising innovation is "slow schooling," in which it is argued that education is not a race and that more information and intense rapid-paced instruction is not necessarily the best way to educate children. Many people are afraid that too much pressure on children to perform or to acquire facts and figures can be counterproductive and can take the joy and motivation out of learning. Educators in countries around the world are thinking about how to infuse excellence *and* enjoyment into the learning process, and many are advocating taking a slow route. Slow refers to a different way of learning: "exploring something deeply and thoroughly, learning how to learn, how to ask questions, how to understand, how to apply that understanding to other areas of study."[16] Students use nonstandard textbooks, seize moments and opportunities to learn without curricular constraints, take time to think about matters, experience learning rather than study facts, and are given ongoing support so as to sustain their enthusiasm and engagement.

Research findings on motivation emphasize the importance of social and emotional development,[17] and in many important ways, learning motivation is more about emotion than it is about cognition. An approach that intentionally integrates cognition and emotion is Teaching for Intellectual and Emotional Learning,[18] in which teachers help students make connections between qualities of character—appreciation, mastery, ethical reasoning, empathy, and reflection—and thinking operations—cognition, memory, evaluation, convergent thinking and production, and divergent thinking and production. Teachers who use this approach use many different techniques for helping students become aware of the connections among their various cognitive and emotional processes—between their learning motivation and their achievement, for example, or between their esthetic appreciation of a piece of music and their ability to learn to play it.

Finally, emerging from the living theory approach,[19] some innovative educators are advocating a gift-creation approach to gifted education, whereby educators assist students in finding and developing their own talents and abilities.[20] The emphasis shifts away from identifying a select few students as gifted, and toward fostering giftedness much more diversely—in teachers as well as students. This approach is a strong example of the mastery model of giftedness, as well as the growth mindset.

In their focus on engaging students in the learning process for its own sake, each of these innovative approaches puts the emphasis squarely on helping children discover an intrinsic motivation to learn.

Extrinsic and Intrinsic Motivation

The importance of intrinsic motivation, persistence through good and bad times, and responsiveness to extrinsic rewards remains constant [across stages of talent development].[21]

> *As they explore and learn, very young children are the most nearly perfect examples of intrinsic motivation— the type of motivation that encourages them to ask and answer questions without worrying about the "One Right Answer"—and the kind of motivation that often goes to sleep when the thrill of learning is replaced with classroom regimentation and rote learning.[22]*

Intrinsic motivators are internal to the person experiencing them and a natural part of the learning process. They include feelings of competence, pride, autonomy, self-actualization, and the satisfaction of internalized values (such as persistence and perseverance).

Extrinsic motivators include factors that are external to the task itself, factors put in place by the individual or by others to encourage the completion of a given task. They include grades, scholarships, praise, money, gifts, trips, and many other kinds of treats, awards, and prizes. In order for an extrinsic motivator to be effective, the student must value it, and he must believe that he can be successful in attaining it.

We have to use caution when providing extrinsic rewards because there can be unintended and counterproductive consequences to using them. For example, grades are used regularly to motivate learning and are highly valued by most parents, students, and teachers. Say that a certain child wants to earn high grades and the praise that goes with them but doesn't believe that she has the necessary ability. She might choose to take easy classes rather than more challenging ones, or she might decide to achieve the high grades that she wants (or feels that she needs) by cheating. Rewards are two-edged swords; they can stimulate behavior, but paradoxically, they can work to undermine rather than motivate effort, achievement, and real learning.

In spite of these problems with extrinsic rewards, when parents or teachers use them wisely, they can facilitate intrinsic motivation to learn. Although extrinsic motivation is generally short term (that is, once the reward disappears, the desired behavior may cease), an extrinsic reward can act as a bridge to intrinsic motivation. For example, a child who is told that he will earn some kind of outing if he does all of his piano practicing for the week may, in addition to collecting the prize, find himself pleased with his musical achievement and wanting to continue his practicing the next week, whether or not he gets an extra outing. Extrinsic rewards can provide opportunities to experience the pleasures inherent in a sense of growing competence and mastery and so support a movement toward intrinsically motivated learning. Parents support a powerful form of intrinsic motivation to learn when they encourage children and adolescents to think about who they uniquely are, and then guide them in finding good pathways to advance their enthusiasms.

Once a value like honesty, diligence, kindness, or integrity has been internalized, it becomes an intrinsic motivator, and extrinsic rewards or punishments are no longer needed in order to sustain them. A child who internalizes the value of diligence may find pleasure in working hard at school and become intrinsically motivated to read and study. It should be noted, however, that valuing hard work is unlikely to sustain itself through self-reinforcement alone, and it usually needs to be supplemented by other motivators, such as feelings of competence and mastery.[23] This usually happens naturally, but parents and educators should be careful to pay attention to it.

Increasing competence leads to experiences of success, and it enhances self-esteem. By providing children with opportunities to experience the pleasures inherent in developing competencies, from proficiency with mathematical calculations to mastery of a second language to computer keyboarding skills, we can encourage their intrinsic motivation to learn.[24] If a task is perceived as being too easy (that is, the individual already knows the material or skill very well), then it will have little value, and there will be little or no intrinsic motivation to complete it. On the other hand, if a task is perceived as being too difficult, then the individual will not expect to succeed and so once again will not feel intrinsically motivated to attempt it. The research on motivation to learn shows that students learn best when the level of challenge is calibrated to match their learning needs.[25] If a student is not responsive to a task, a teacher should reconsider the design and intent of the task and check to make sure that it is appropriately targeted both to the student's interests and to her prior learning.

There are several other issues that can have a direct impact on student motivation and achievement. We consider them one at a time.

Achievement Issues

> *It's about joy. Joy is what gives us achievement.... We need a curriculum that makes kids happy to go to school.*[26]

> *To truly understand motivational problems and triumphs, we must realize that gifted students find themselves in contexts that are supportive and not so supportive of their learning and motivational needs.*[27]

> *"Rae used to LOVE school. Now she refuses to do her homework and is getting C's and D's when all her friends are getting A's."*

Many parents who consult with us have serious concerns about their children's grades. These concerns might center on a recent drop in interest in a particular subject area, but sometimes they are broader and more pervasive. There are many reasons why students do not do well at school.

Highly capable learners do not always learn more quickly, nor do they automatically get high marks on their report cards. And low achievement does *not* necessarily mean laziness, willfulness, or lack of ability. Neither do low grades always indicate a problem; sometimes they simply reflect the temporary and intentional disengagement of a self-directed learner who finds himself in a boring classroom environment, is otherwise preoccupied, or perhaps is experiencing peer pressure not to excel. There are times, however, when gifted learners, just like other exceptional learners, require educational or psychological interventions. Here are some of the issues and considerations relating to gifted learners' achievement problems.

Cultural Differences

> *Several recent studies with minority populations both at elite universities and in working-class public schools have shown that simple motivation-relevant interventions can significantly boost school engagement, grades, and achievement test scores.*[28]

A great deal of effort has been invested in exploring differences in achievement levels, and in particular the under-representation of cultural minorities in gifted education.[29] We address cultural differences in more depth in Chapter 9. We will highlight here, though, that supporting the development of a growth mindset and a feeling of acceptance and belonging can make an enormous difference for minority students who have had problems with peer pressure or with achievement, including increasing their engagement in academic learning or experiencing academic success.[30] Recent perspectives on motivation provide some of the answers to addressing these concerns.

Underachievers

Student performance that falls noticeably short of potential, especially for young people with high ability, is bewildering and perhaps the most frustrating of all challenges both teachers and parents face.[31]

"There are two ways to think about gifted underachievers. The first is to focus on the tragedy of the wasted intellect, and the second is to re-examine the labeling process."

"To what extent are some of these students set up to fail by their placement in gifted programs where there's increased competition and task-orientation?"

There are problems with the term "underachiever," as well as the political implications and personal repercussions that sometimes go with it. People typically use the term to describe a child who is doing poorly at school and who is perceived as very capable (the "smarter" student), but not to another who is achieving similar grades and perceived as not so capable (the child of whom less was expected to begin with). The designated underachiever often feels confused and criticized by this designation. Frequently, such a child actually wants to do well and, when told that she is "not working up to her potential," feels even more pressure than she did before. Conversely, for the student in the same school environment who is *not* given the underachiever label but who has similarly poor grades, it is an implicit assumption that low grades are the best she can do, and a cycle of low expectations is thereby reinforced for her.

This selective designation of some children as requiring attention as underachievers while others are just fine because they are inherently low achievers is problematic for two reasons. First is the assumption that school grades are relevant to all learners. There are times in a healthy and capable child's life when he wants or needs some down time or distance from studies or from having to prove himself to others, in the same way that sometimes an accomplished chef wants to order in pizza for his family and friends, or a poet creates a watercolor picture on canvas instead of using words to express herself. For various good reasons, schoolwork and grades may not be the most important things in a child's life at a given point in time. Some of the most capable learners, and some of those children who go on to become the highest achieving adults, couldn't care less about report cards because they're more interested in other things, including extracurricular or real-life learning. More important than school grades is whether the child continues to be excited about learning.

Secondly, this categorical approach of designating some children as underachievers assumes that methods of assessing intellectual potential are sufficiently reliable to distinguish the underachiever from the low achiever. In addition to the fact that these assumptions are questionable, neither the underachieving nor the low achieving student benefits from them. The underachiever often feels confused about what is expected of him and why, as well as being unsure about how to meet the higher expectations, and the low achiever feels that he is not expected to achieve academic success, so why bother to work harder?

Although we are uncomfortable with the use of the term "underachiever," we acknowledge that there are many children who do not do well at school, and it is important that parents and educators try to understand the reasons for this. Linda Edwards, now a secondary school teacher, was once described as an underachieving gifted learner. She has since designed a learning strategies program for teachers and field-tested it with a group of advanced high school students whom she wanted to motivate—students who "regularly arrived in a disheveled manner, flopped into their seats, and read novels, regardless of what was requested of them." The program that Linda created may be helpful to other teachers.

Linda's Program for Gifted Underachievers

Program Design

In order to entice the students to participate, I developed three separate activities for the classroom teacher. Each program featured content that met the following criteria:

1. relevant, current, and significant in the students' outside-of-school life

2. not traditionally presented in schools

3. technology-based

4. immediately accessible, but offering challenging breadth

5. targeted to development of effort and specific skills rather than achievement or evaluation

Briefly, the three projects involved:

1. listening to and interpreting the song lyrics of twentieth-century music *(auditory note-taking skills)*

2. decoding text-messaging poetry *(literacy skills)*

3. looking at cell-phone copyrights and product specification documents to make detailed descriptions and diagrams of these communications devices *(observation, language, math, drawing skills)*

The Results

These were all very successful projects. The students were engaged and cooperative. The "cool" factor was way up, and the output blockades were gone. Students have since returned to more traditional activities such as web quests on study skills, personal surveys on time management and learning styles, readings on study habits, and traditional homework help. Their motivation and engagement has dramatically increased.

Reflection

As teachers, we should offer non-motivated, underachieving students acceptance and patient friendship, gently leading their education by exposing them to relevant, concrete subject matter that connects to their own lives and current interests. In a relaxed, nonjudgmental environment, intellectual sparks fly, and students willingly engage with challenging material. We need to provide smaller student-teacher ratios, content that focuses on unlearning negative attitudes and behaviors, and as much student choice and freedom as possible. Teachers have to be creative because standard rewards and motivational tools are not potent enough for students who reject achievement-based rewards like praise and grades.

Adults often lecture underachieving students to work harder and to rise to their intellectual potential, but clearly that doesn't work. Some of these kids endure school bitterly but opt for invisibility by skipping classes or dropping out. (I know; I did that.) In the classroom, they drain motivation from their peers and teachers and spark frustration and anger as others try to motivate them. These students reject things that others value (e.g., education, direction, goals, rules, evaluation). The challenge to educators is to avoid personalizing this rejection, which in turn can lead to rejecting or ignoring these students. Rather, we must make ourselves available for patient personal connection and support, and we must be flexible about the non-essential elements of education. Their low motivation and achievement do not need to be terminal.

By confronting underachievement in creative ways like Linda describes, teachers can sometimes engage students who have temporarily lost the drive to learn. There are other strategies, too, some of which we have discussed already in this chapter and others which we discuss next.

Academic Mismatch

If unchallenging scholastic environments produce underachieving gifted students, then providing intellectual challenge and stimulation at all grade levels should decrease underachievement.[32]

> "I think Sonia should take full responsibility for her poor grades. She blames the teacher, the school, the system— everyone but herself."

The simplest and most obvious reason that a capable learner might get low grades is that there is a mismatch between the curriculum being offered and the child's learning needs.[33] In some instances, the child is being asked to do work that is so easy that she's not learning much, so she sees no point in doing it. In other situations, the teacher's demands entail more work or harder work with no attendant benefits, and again, the child sees no point in investing the necessary effort to do it. In yet other situations, the work may be targeted reasonably well to the child's ability, but she sees no connection with her life and interests.

When curriculum match and relevance are addressed as carefully as possible and a child is still not doing well at school, there may be other reasons for his academic problems. The possibility of cognitive processing problems (such as a learning disability or problem with attention) should be considered. Other reasons for low achievement can include learned helplessness, frustration, boredom, or academic overload, all of which we describe below. In still other situations, children may not do well at school due to one or more outside factors, including environmental, physical, and psychological stressors such as isolation, poverty, physical or mental illness, minority issues, linguistic barriers, problems at home, or power struggles with parents or a teacher. When a child is both academically advanced and experiencing serious outside stressors, it becomes even more important that parents and teachers consider the perspectives that we address in this book with flexibility, sensitivity, and attention to the individual situation.

Learned Helplessness

> *"The work is too hard. I can't do it."*
> *"Lavonne will not accept anything less than perfection within herself. She hates failure."*
> *"Our daughter has trouble dealing with pressure, disappointment, or big challenges."*

Sometimes a child decides to avoid work that is causing her trouble and chooses to tackle only work that is "safe." Children who are uncomfortable with open-ended tasks, who demonstrate a lack of initiative in problem solving, or who will only put effort into safe learning activities may have acquired learned helplessness. These children believe that they might as well not try something that appears at first glance to be difficult because failure is probable.

Learned helplessness is characterized by an avoidance of anything new or challenging. It becomes a self-fulfilling prophecy and increases the likelihood of mediocre performance and failure. When confronted by an unfamiliar or challenging task, the child who has developed the learned helplessness pattern shuts down and says to himself, "I can't do this," and then finds a reason why he cannot learn or will not try the new skill. He might complain of a stomach ailment, explain that he is already working too hard, or state that he can't do math or isn't athletic or is otherwise incapable. You might recognize the fixed mindset at work here.[34]

On the other hand, individuals with a growth mindset, or mastery orientation to learning, tend to welcome and even thrive on challenge. Like the brave little engine in the children's story *The Little Engine that Could*,[35] they can take on big challenges and are far more likely to risk failure. They look for opportunities to expand their range of skills and knowledge, expecting to encounter difficulties along the way. However, they tend to see problems as opportunities for growth rather than as blocks to further progress. In general, they feel much better about themselves and are more successful, regardless of their actual ability.

Those with the learned helplessness pattern tend to believe that people are either smart or not smart and that each of us is born with a fixed amount of ability or intelligence (fixed mindset), while those with a mastery orientation tend to believe that learning is incremental and that intelligence develops systematically over time through effort (growth mindset).[36]

Many intellectually competent children (particularly girls) develop the learned helplessness pattern. One effective approach to eradicating this pattern is to help children challenge their beliefs. Students can combat learned helplessness by:

- learning to define success in terms of improvement and progress instead of grades and prizes

- viewing errors as a normal and essential part of the learning process rather than as unacceptable embarrassments to be avoided

- orienting themselves toward the process of learning rather than the products that are a result of it

- finding pleasure in learning itself rather than in doing better than others

Three aphorisms illustrate the growth mindset in action:

1. "When life gives you lemons, make lemonade."

2. "Some people see stepping stones where others see stumbling blocks."

3. "You can see the glass as half full or half empty."

All children should be encouraged to welcome errors, false starts, and failures as constructive learning opportunities, remembering that learning happens incrementally, one step at a time, and that no one is exceptional in everything. Mistakes help us understand something about what we need to learn. Children suffering from learned helplessness need help putting these ideas into practice.

Frustration and Boredom

> *"My daughter does well in school, but she says she dislikes it. I want learning to be exciting for her, not some kind of heavy task that weighs her down."*
>
> *"He seems to resist learning, and he acts willfully. I know he's smart, but why isn't he a better student?"*
>
> *"I just can't be bothered. It's all so tedious! It tires me out! It's boring."*

Academic instruction that is far above or below a student's ability/challenge level induces frustration, boredom, and alienation. When students are allowed to demonstrate their competence and are given appropriately targeted learning opportunities, they are more likely to stay engaged by school and learning. As we have mentioned in connection with several other themes, when previously keen learners show signs of being bored or frustrated, the first thing to determine is whether or not there is an appropriate educational match for their ability. Allied with this is the question of relevance. All too often, authentic learning experiences are absent from academic programs, and it is up to teaching professionals to bridge the gap between the official school curriculum and the vitality of real life.

Another consideration when dealing with frustration and school boredom issues is whether the degree of a child's exceptionality might actually be outside the realm of a given school's capacity to address the child's learning needs.[37] Considered to be a genius as an adult, Albert Einstein found much of his schooling deadly boring. He failed courses, was considered a mediocre student by most of his teachers, and was not accepted into the university program of his choice. The nature and degree of his giftedness was almost certainly a major reason for his lack of engagement in class. A school would need to be truly extraordinary to recognize and address the degree of giftedness of such a person.

In addition to creating a better educational match, sometimes the best way to address boredom, frustration, and alienation is to help the child find engaging extracurricular activities. It can be motivating for a child to participate in extended learning opportunities with other kids who are as keen about particular areas of interest as she is, no matter what those are. Examples include high-level music or dance classes, chess clubs, community outreach, career exploration, homeschooling, and mentorships. We can speculate that the only thing that might have made school interesting for Einstein would have been opportunities to explore his interests with experts and mentors. Finding one area of shared enthusiasm can infuse other areas of life with renewed vibrancy, improving a student's feelings about learning, herself, and life itself, as well as leading to improved school engagement and achievement.

Study Skills and Work Habits

> *"Nobody ever taught me how to properly organize notes or how to write a composition. Now I'm in high school, and even when I know the subject matter, I can't put together a decent essay!"*

Capable learners often have trouble with study skills and work habits.[38] When learning comes too easily for too long, children can manage to get by with minimal effort, and they acquire little in the way of good work habits. At some point in their education, however, they will almost certainly find that they have to invest some effort in acquiring those habits and skills (organization, time management, note-taking, etc.) that less capable learners have long since mastered. It's easier sooner than later, but that is not always how it happens.

When the day comes that a lack of study skills catches up with a student, there are many avenues of exploration. As with everything else, what works for a particular student depends on his age, temperament, and context, as well as other individual factors. For some, it is best to work with a private tutor who can help in a one-on-one relationship in an environment conducive to learning. The tutor can teach the student how to address his particular issues and concerns, adapting instruction to meet changing needs over the school year. The tutor might be an older student with expertise in the necessary skills, a retired teacher, or a professional tutor.

For other students, a peer study group works well. The group can be organized according to what members think will be most beneficial. Participants might choose to structure their collaboration in this way:

1. Do a preliminary read-through of assigned text material.

2. Organize material into themes.

3. Devise conceptual frameworks.

4. Take turns analyzing and synthesizing what has been read.

There are many other ways to design study groups, but some kind of structured approach is helpful in the process of acquiring study skills. Students can meet more or less formally, weekly or as desired, depending on circumstances. Study sessions may include teachers, parents, relevant experts, or other students from time to time.

Some students prefer to devise and develop their own approach to studying and then to work independently, perhaps with some guidance from parents or teachers. They might work with study skills workbooks or other resources, many of which can be found on the Internet.[39] "How to" books on developing organizational skills and study techniques can also be found in libraries and at reputable bookstores.

Teachers can show students how to attack difficult work by breaking it down into more manageable portions. They can explain ways of designing simple frameworks that enable students to follow tasks through to completion, and they can encourage students to set achievable standards for themselves when they are first learning new material. Teachers should guide effort, facilitate collaborative learning, and help to scaffold work appropriately by involving the learner in the task, offering tailored assistance, encouraging goal-directed motivation, and providing constructive feedback that promotes self-monitoring and persistence.

Academic Overload and Gifted Programming

We had many voices to choose from about the prickly topic of overload and gifted programming, but we finally settled on six. The first three are from students, and the rest are from parents:

> *"Watch out for the homework!"*
> *"It's a lot of pressure. Everyone expects so much of me. I HATE IT! And if I make one mistake, I never hear the end of it."*
> *"I've got way too much work! The pile is as big as a chair!"*
> *"He was expecting <u>different</u> work in the gifted program, not <u>more</u> work."*
> *"Complete tension. I feel like tearing the pages out of the books and throwing them out."*
> *"I see her struggling with the amount of work. I wonder if it's fair."*

Schoolwork should be engaging and appropriately challenging, but it has to be balanced with other activities in a person's life. Just as for adults, there can be negative consequences if a student's work becomes too burdensome or all-consuming. Increasingly, even normal academic expectations are so arduous in some school settings that kids and parents are stressed, and the quality of family life is adversely affected.[40] A differentiated curriculum for gifted learners sometimes requires them to produce more work and at a more sophisticated level than that required of their age mates. When academic overload results, it is imperative that teachers and parents pay attention to a child's balanced development and adapt the demands accordingly. For example, teachers can stagger due dates and encourage interim goal setting so that students can pace themselves more comfortably.

Sometimes it is not the academic program itself but rather a child's extracurricular commitments that are causing overload. Some children juggle school with commitments for lessons, practicing, games, and social, family, community, and religious activities. One way to address this is to pare down the extracurricular commitments so that the child has some breathing room—time to enjoy the learning that is her education.[41]

Academic stress can sometimes be caused by the expectations of others. For example, parents who derive a sense of pride and accomplishment from their children's achievements may have very high performance expectations. These expectations may enhance a child's achievement, especially if parents are appropriately proactive and provide good opportunities for the child's learning and development. On the negative side, however, the child may experience an overwhelming burden of having to achieve in order to continue to please his parents, enhance their self-esteem, and thus earn their approval. Parents must seriously consider what the child can reasonably achieve, as well as how much he wants to achieve.

Undue stress can also result from the demands that some children impose upon themselves. Accomplishment can be risky if doing too well leads to feelings that one has to do well all of the time. Some children tend to be too self-critical or to search too relentlessly for complexity, perfection, and/or order. Others have learning problems so that they experience academic overload in situations where their classmates might not. Children and adolescents need help from the adults that they trust in order to put the demands in their lives into a healthy perspective. "One can celebrate the fact that the individual has high standards and recognize that life is an existential struggle to reconcile the discrepancy between 'what is' and 'what ought to be.' The key is to try to move forward each day to reduce the discrepancy."[42]

Although it can be rewarding to pursue excellence, it is unhealthy to pursue it to extremes of overload or to the point of disillusionment. Students with oppressive workloads may begin to procrastinate, lose initiative, or even become alienated from school altogether. These avoidance behaviors can reflect a personal response to a number of circumstances, including, for example, the quest for heightened achievement, worry about task completion, stress about making mistakes, and a sense of doubt about one's capabilities.[43] Sometimes children choose to avoid challenge in order to concentrate on activities that showcase their areas of strength, thereby lightening their load and circumventing disappointment, mediocrity, or tasks that might expose their areas of weakness. Helping students develop a growth mindset is an important step in helping them to feel good about themselves and to experience productivity and success.[44]

In addition to scholastic problems, children who are wrestling with academic overload may also find themselves experiencing social problems, as their anxieties and concerns interfere with their ability to relax and interact with classmates and friends. Parents and educators who live or work with children who feel overwhelmed by work or who push themselves too hard or avoid their responsibilities must be sensitive to the signs of overload. Some things to watch for include:

- a drop in grades or markedly lower levels of academic achievement

- procrastination, reduced initiative

- tension, stress, short temper

- anxiety, worry, nervousness, sleep problems, lack of communication, change in appetite

- fear of failure, fear of success

- academic burnout, which may include giving up and extreme exhaustion

Like children who are low achievers, those who exhibit learned helplessness, and those who are disenchanted with learning because of boredom or frustration, children who are distraught due to heavy workloads can learn to regulate their response to the demands of school and home. Parents and teachers can assist these children and adolescents by showing them how to pace themselves, set learning priorities, relax, break tasks down into smaller parts, and establish reasonable goals—all of which will enable them to feel more comfortable about whatever learning demands come their way.[45]

Here is an example of one teacher's approach, shared by teacher Linda Edwards.

Motivation and Context

I had a bright student who was always tired in class because he worked the night shift in order to help his family pay the rent. I think that in cases like this, we obviously have to modify classroom requirements as much as possible. But beyond that, we can reward the value of a student's work experiences in class. I praised this young man's work ethic and expressed that I was impressed by his attitude amid tough circumstances. After I had given an assignment, I always went over to him to make sure he had heard and understood it, and I made a point to show him ways to work smarter rather than harder. I showed him shortcuts and how to be precise with his effort. Efficient and effective time and work management will help him get through the very heavy load that he has to carry.

Other coping strategies for students for addressing academic overload and sustaining motivation include the following:

- Try to pause and step back from work now and then in order to get a healthy perspective on what really has to be done, to what extent, and when. [46]

- Work with teachers and/or guidance counselors to manage, reduce, or rearrange academic loads.

- Think carefully about what can and cannot be accomplished within a given timeframe.

- Maintain a sense of humor, especially when things get tough.

- Develop better organizational and study skills.

- Create a personal system of guidelines and strategic work plans (such as checklists, periodic rewards, or interim "finish lines").

- Increase emotional intelligence in order to learn about ways to handle stress. [47]

- Choose one or two areas of perfection; try not to be perfect at everything.[48]

- Talk to someone about plans and concerns (parents, teachers, a guidance counselor, or a psychologist).

Good communication links between teachers and parents are very important; informed home and school support systems that work cooperatively are most effective in helping children overcome academic difficulties. Parents and teachers should be ready to intervene as necessary, and sometimes professional counseling is warranted.

Practical Ideas

There are risks and costs to action. But they are far less than the long range risks of comfortable inaction.[49]

"The curiosity level for each student varies, and it can be a race for a teacher to keep up with the demands of individual students."

"It is far better to focus on process and improvement because that's where achievement can be seen, measured, and felt."

Some approaches for motivating high-ability learners seem to work especially well. Here is a list of practical strategies,[50] many of which we have touched upon elsewhere. These ideas, primarily directed at teachers, can be easily adapted for use at home by parents.

Ideas for Maximizing Motivation

Nature of Tasks

- Engage students in considering the purpose and real-world significance of all new learning.

- Assign work that is appropriately challenging and achievable.

- Assign tasks that are multidimensional and open-ended.

- Provide learning opportunities that invite active participation, exploration, and experimentation, including hands-on activities that involve substantive learning.

- Design tasks that are novel and incorporate an element of surprise or wonder by linking learning to children's interests, curiosities, and experiences.

- Value children's perspectives.

Student Involvement

- Provide opportunities for children to make choices in their day-to-day work.

- Invite individuals to express their opinions or respond personally to content.

- Provide enriching activities for those who have completed their work.

- Make it safe to ask for help.

- Give help in a way that facilitates children's own accomplishments.

- Connect new or abstract concepts to familiar or concrete ones.

- Give children opportunities to collaborate with each other and with others outside of the classroom.

- Include problems and questions that challenge those with the highest levels of mastery.

- Give children as much discretion and autonomy as they can handle.

- Maintain a realistic pace.

Evaluation

- Where possible, base grades on effort, improvement, and achieving a specified standard rather than on performance relative to others.

- Make sure that grading criteria and timelines are clear and fair.

- Provide timely and constructive feedback.

- Allow children to participate in the design of their tasks, in choosing the level of difficulty of assignments, and in self-evaluation throughout the learning process.

- Involve students in personal goal-setting—short and long term.

- Monitor learning and understanding.

- Hold children accountable.

- Treat errors as a natural and important part of learning. Emphasize the information value of mistakes, and incorporate "wrong answers" into discussions as productive contributions to the learning process.

The Teacher as a Model for Learning

- Create a community of learners, in which teachers and students model using resources, sharing ideas, taking courses, and reading books.

- Convey to children that not knowing something is not a reason for embarrassment (for example, many teachers seek help from students with expertise in technology).

- Be enthusiastic.

- Attribute successes to effort and perseverance, not innate ability.

- Give tasks that can be completed at different ability levels.

- Convey the value of different kinds of skills, that there is variation in skill levels, that skill development builds over time, and that it is domain-specific.

- Evaluate, fine-tune, and re-evaluate your practices.

At the risk of reducing a complex set of ideas about sometimes troubling topics down to something too simple, we want to end this chapter with a succinct summary of our approach to motivation and achievement: "Let's try to teach each child each day something he or she doesn't know already and really wants to learn."[51]

Chapter 9

How Does Giftedness Develop?

Nature or Nurture? Back to Origins

Even highly gifted children have to learn the hard way. Mozart still had to learn and work very hard for an extended time (more than 10 years) before he was able to produce his first masterpiece.[1]

From a neurobiological standpoint, giftedness is a type of neural plasticity that we do not understand.[2]

"Where does intelligence come from?" This is a question that researchers, the popular media, and the rest of us have been debating for at least a century. Current findings in the neurosciences, as well as in developmental and cognitive psychology, show that we cannot effectively separate inherited from environmental influences and that it is the dynamic interaction between nature and nurture that leads to intelligence.[3] It makes little sense to assign percentages to the relative influences of innate inheritance (nature) and environment (nurture) on an individual's intelligence. Who we are and what we eventually become, including our intelligence, is a result of all that we experience, shaped by *how* we experience it and influenced by myriad genetic predispositions. A person's intelligence is a result of early nurturing experiences, the various environments experienced, the surrounding cultural milieu, educational paths and circumstances, life events, and other factors, all interwoven with inherited genetic patterns and organized by the individual as an active agent in creating his or her own intelligence.[4]

Because one's intelligence is a result of dynamic interactions over time, it is considerably more mutable than it was once thought to be. Several noted researchers have conducted and analyzed comprehensive studies of high-level linguistic development, for example.[5] Based on their work, it appears that linguistic giftedness develops where it is systematically encouraged, nourished, and nurtured; environmental differences in children's opportunities to learn from their earliest days can be critical. Where language use is valued in the child's home, community, and/or scholastic experience, *and* where time, attention, and opportunities are provided for its ongoing development, then, barring major biological or psychological constraints, a high level of linguistic competence (or even, perhaps, linguistic giftedness) can be seen as a logical, predictable developmental outcome.[6] This is not to say that genetic predispositions for certain kinds of intelligence are trivial or nonexistent, but rather that the human brain's capacity for learning is much greater, much more amenable to learning and growing, and much more plastic than most of us realize.

Developmental Pathways

Inherited influences on people's achievements are not direct, not reversible or immutable, not inevitable, and not inescapable.[7]

It may be that genes and environment work together to create not simply the ability itself, but also the psychological factors that are prominent in geniuses and that foster the development of talent over time, such as specific fascinations, sustained attention, the love of challenges, the enjoyment of effort, and resilience in the face of setbacks.[8]

Simply put, each child's developmental pathway is unique, and it may or may not be smoothly paved. All children have strengths and weaknesses that vary from a lesser to a more profound degree in one or more areas at any given point in time. Whether or not the strengths manifest themselves at the highest levels depends on a great many factors, including culture, family values, supports, and suitably targeted opportunities to learn and explore,[9] as well as extracognitive factors like effort, resilience, persistence, and motivation.

The developmental pathways that lead to the individual differences that characterize giftedness remain complex and fascinating scientific puzzles. The more exceptional a person is in one domain, the more likely it is that there will be wide discrepancies across domains and over time.[10] For example, picture an 11-year-old boy with advanced physics and biology texts in his knapsack but giggling at a silly joke. Imagine the nine-year-old girl who can sing intricate musical passages but whose fine-motor skills are impaired. Or think about a first grader who can solve complicated math equations but has trouble mastering multiplication tables. Differences across areas of ability—also called *developmental asynchrony*—are far more common than most people realize.

Now consider children's development over time. What are we to make of a 10-year-old girl who appreciates the complexities of Shakespeare yet fails to do well in high school, or the boy who barely passes middle school but goes on to become an extraordinary graduate student? How do we account for such disparate patterns of development?

Two of the most vulnerable periods in human development are early childhood and early adolescence, and what happens during these periods can influence whether individual differences will develop into gifted-level achievement or not.

Gifted Development in Early Childhood

"Steve is only in Grade 1 and already has a lot of trouble sitting still and doing his work."

"Mae-Lin came home from her first day in kindergarten in tears. She said that all they did at school was play. She is ready to work hard, and she feels insulted when the teacher treats her and the others as if they were babies."

The problems pertaining to early identification arise because of questions about whether giftedness can be reliably identified during infancy and early childhood.[11]

Up to and through the primary years (from birth to about age seven), most of a child's learning is about the pleasures to be found in exploring and understanding the world in her family, playgroups, classrooms, and community. Whether or not a young child is formally identified as gifted is not usually relevant to that child or her developmental outcomes. What does matter is that the adults in her life respond to her individual interests, respecting her, listening to her, playing with her, and providing opportunities for her to learn what she can do and wants to do next, all in a context of predictable stability and support.[12] The most important achievements of the early years are the construction of a foundation of secure self-confidence, enthusiasm for learning, and resilience, all of which can usually be accomplished without a formal gifted identification or assessment process.

Parents naturally look to the future and may wonder if their children will grow up to be proficient, high-achieving, or even eminent in one way or another. If a young child is advanced for his age or seems to be exceptionally creative, does that signify great things to come? Increasingly, experts are saying, "No, not necessarily."[13] One's destiny depends on many factors, not the least of which are environmental influences, learning opportunities, temperament, motivation, and good old-fashioned hard work mixed in with a little bit of luck.

Early Childhood: A Sensitive Period

> "I'm curious about a lot of things. I must have a million questions."
>
> "Parenting a child like mine is like attempting a jigsaw puzzle when someone keeps throwing in extra pieces and you've never seen the finished product!"

What transpires before a child enters the educational system is not just a prelude to real learning; in fact, there are good reasons to think that the most important learning in a person's life occurs before she starts her formal education. Language acquisition, motor development, social interaction, and play are just a few of the early learning activities that shape a child's future. However, whereas all infants have potential to learn, not all young children receive the kind of nurturing and learning opportunities that are likely to optimize their healthy overall development across the years.

Although there is considerable debate about developmental timing constraints (also referred to as critical or sensitive periods or optimal windows of opportunity for certain kinds of learning), the scientific community generally agrees that the early years are tremendously important in an individual's development. At least for some competencies, there are periods when a child may be more sensitive to certain influences—times when neurological development best supports specific kinds of learning.[14]

One of the ways that exceptional learners are exceptional is in their maturational timing—they experience the sensitive learning periods earlier, later, or differently than other children. In the case of gifted learners, they tend to be advanced relative to average timelines, with some (but not all) aspects of their development occurring earlier than normal. Because learning happens according to highly individual schedules, parents should recognize that from infancy on, and regardless of age-normal sensitive periods, it is important to respond to children's curiosity and encourage their engagement in learning.

Children thrive when they have access to a variety of learning possibilities and when they are encouraged and empowered to gain competence in various domains. Self-confidence, a positive attitude toward learning, and the drive to achieve are all strengthened when parents encourage their children's curiosity, creativity, and emerging needs to know and experience more about themselves and the world.[15]

Young Children: Recommendations

Here is an overview of some of the ways to support gifted development in young children. It is written for parents but is equally applicable to educators:

- Listen to your children.
- Be as flexibly responsive as possible to children's interests.
- Encourage an attitude of playful exploration.
- Create an environment of predictable stability and support.
- Respect each child's personhood and right to have feelings and opinions.
- Provide opportunities for them to learn what they can do.

- Provide opportunities for them to learn what they want to do next.

- Be proactively available to offer guidance, support, and encouragement.

- Help your children set reachable goals.

- Play with your children.

- Provide a variety of age-appropriate play materials, thinking about as many domains of development as possible (including physical, musical, social, mathematical, linguistic, and visual/spatial).

The Importance of Play

The truly great advances of this generation will be made by those who can make outrageous connections, and only a mind which knows how to play can do that.[16]

Schoolwork, most notably test preparation, has now eclipsed play from preschool onward. The growth of structured work times for American children has been accompanied by a drop in the hours apportioned to play.[17]

Think about the times in your life when there has been too much work and too little play for too long. Not good. As unhappy and unhealthy a situation as that is for an adult, it is an even more troubling when it becomes a chronic reality for children. In many of the families we work with, children's schedules are so full that they have very little time for unstructured, invent-it-yourself, imaginative play. In addition to school, which can sometimes involve long commutes, children may participate in various organized activities that require practicing, performances, and homework. This leaves little discretionary time for play—very few hours when kids have the time and energy to think about what it is they want to do. Then, in those moments when play might be possible, they may find it easier to turn on a television, computer, or electronic game than to invent their own play activities or engage in play with others.

In addition to meaningful opportunities for engagement with learning, giftedness develops with ample unstructured time. Time is a basic requirement for the kind of play that leads to self-discovery and skill development. Although parents and educators of high-ability learners often feel a sense of responsibility for keeping their children entertained, occupied, and stimulated, it is sometimes better to let children be bored so that they are motivated to create their own fun. The child who is bored is in the right place to discover who he is and what he wants to learn next.

Play is not only a pleasurable activity engaged in for its own sake, but it is also an essential part of children's development. It serves many purposes in people's lives,[18] including friendship-building, tension release, cognitive stimulation, sensorimotor development, and the exploration of possibilities. Children learn the mechanics and specifics of social interaction through play. They learn about possible ways of being and the consequences of different ways of behaving. Through play, they practice the various roles that they will assume later in life, and they have opportunities to imagine and try out possible roles. In play, children practice and exercise their social, cognitive, and physical competencies and skills, and they test their limits with less anxiety than is associated with many other pursuits. Imaginary play encourages the development of creative habits of mind.

One writer makes the point succinctly: "There is plenty of evidence…much of it from the arena of science, which increasingly shows that children who are stuffed full of factoids and expected to perform don't do as well as children who are allowed to play. By a dreadful irony, trying to make your child smarter can backfire."[19] Too much emphasis on academic drilling and intensive attempts to hasten children's education are detrimental when they erode play opportunities or compromise the important aspects of social, emotional, and cognitive development that play affords.

Children whose parents encourage their imagination are lucky indeed. They are free to explore and consider alternate realities, roaming through the regions of their minds and figuring out who they are, what they care about, and how they like spending their time. However, although we are emphasizing here the importance of play and plenty of do-nothing times when children are free to invent their own play, we don't want to encourage a tyranny of playtime in which children are forced to play games or participate in activities that *adults* think are fun and playful. Every child and every developmental pathway is unique, and one child's play can be another child's misery. Some children so love to acquire academic skills that school learning really is play to them. We know children who spend countless hours inventing play-school games in their free time; it would be counterproductive to take away their books and chalkboards and insist that they play with dolls or trucks instead. What is important is to strike a happy and respectful balance with the type and amount of play in children's lives, making sure that they have enough time to figure out what it is that they love doing.

Play is particularly important in the early stages of the development of any talent, whether it is mathematical, linguistic, athletic, artistic, musical, spatial, or something else. Gifted-level outcomes in all areas start with playful exploration and proceed through skill acquisition, then through increasing mastery and expertise to creative performance or outstanding productivity.[20]

Early Adolescence (Sigh)

> *"I got through my own adolescence, but I'm not sure I can make it through my daughter's."*

> *How do we manage to survive the anxieties, the heartache, the worry, the exasperation? Well, I've repeatedly asked my husband to knock me out with a blunt, heavy object and then wake me when it's all over, but he refuses.[21]*

> *Adolescents may not want to practice as much as before, their peers may disapprove of academic effort, or students who had coasted along before may be afraid of the new challenges and turn away from school.[22]*

People are more vulnerable to environmental influences and experiences at some developmental stages than at others.[23] Early adolescence is second only to early childhood in its volatility and sensitivity, as well as in its possibilities both for developing and for suppressing giftedness and talent. Eleven- to 14-year-olds are engaged in the complex and sometimes overwhelming experience of dealing with puberty. Everything in their lives is changing all at once: their body shapes, voices, hormones, sexuality, emotions, and cognition, to say nothing of their changing relationships with parents, siblings, friends, and others. Some children experience this period in their lives more easily than others. This might be because they are "on time" relative to their peers, because they have strong social support networks and resources, or because they have few other stressors operating simultaneously in their day-to-day existence.

Early adolescents are also moving from predominantly concrete to more fluid, abstract thinking. This shift might have started earlier for them, but it becomes more solid at this time. With the development of stronger abstract reasoning abilities, early adolescents become more cognitively flexible and more capable of simultaneously considering several dimensions of a problem. This sounds like a good thing, and in the end, it usually is, but in the process of giving up the naïve but comforting certainty of childhood, with its clearly defined notions of right and wrong, good and bad, early adolescents tend to undergo a period of doubting almost everything. They frequently come to believe that reliable conclusions cannot be drawn about anything. This has been described as "rampant relativism,"[24] in which nothing seems trustworthy or dependable, including, and perhaps especially, their parents' statements and ideas.

Complex changes in identity also occur during this period, including sex-role orientation and gender identity.[25] Identity formation is a lengthy process which involves moving toward an eventual separation from one's parents. To facilitate the separation, children initiate stronger peer affiliations, experiencing a need to be like their peers and to be liked by them to fit in with what is considered typical for their age at that time and place. This is when being cool, or conversely, being a dork, can mean everything. Peer relationships are very important to the developing self-concept of an early adolescent.[26] Very often, school is significantly less salient either than peer relationships or than it previously was.

Given the complex and interacting changes occurring at early adolescence, a variety of problems becomes more prevalent at this time.[27] Life stress increases steadily through childhood and into early adolescence, which is a time of heightened risk for a number of social and psychological problems—for example, heightened self-consciousness; greater instability of self-image; lower self-esteem; reduced conviction that parents, teachers, and same-sex peers hold favorable opinions of them; and greater likelihood of depression. Parents who have survived their children's adolescence are usually not surprised to hear that this is a time when parents, too, are at increased risk of stress, insecurity, feelings of inadequacy, and diminished marital satisfaction. And, as if all that weren't hard enough, all too often, children's early adolescence happens to coincide with their parents' midlife reappraisals.[28]

Early adolescence, then, tends to be a difficult phase in a young person's life, and in her parents' lives. Everything is changing; it is a period of social and emotional vulnerability. Somewhat surprisingly, however, most children do not experience serious problems at this juncture, and many young people really enjoy this time in their lives.[29] Nevertheless, there are factors associated with giftedness that can combine with early adolescence to heighten the risk of problems for gifted learners going through this period.

Giftedness: A Risk Factor at Adolescence

Identity formation is a major challenge during the adolescent years.[30] At early adolescence, there is a strong need to be just like one's age peers. Yet there is an equally powerful need to be unique—a desire to be completely and unmistakably oneself. These conflicting pressures are demonstrated in the conformist nonconformity of young people who see themselves as expressing their individuality through their clothes and music but who dress just like their chosen peer group and who listen to the same songs. Students who have been identified as being academically exceptional (such as gifted) can experience more anguish than others in their attempts to identify with their age peers.[31] Some of them experience more pressure to be just like everybody else because there's an official designation—"gifted"—that indicates otherwise.

Being different in an important peer-interactional area such as the way information is processed can give added weight to the usual cognitive distortions of this age. A young person who really *is* different from his peers in such a basic way as how he learns and understands might be expected to see himself as truly different than others and therefore as the subject of uncomfortably intense scrutiny. An added burden of loneliness and ostracism can ensue from the self-consciousness that results from this kind of real differentness from one's peers.[32]

Early adolescence is when developmental asynchrony can become particularly difficult for the adolescent herself, as well as for those around her. Strengths are sufficiently well-developed at this stage that gaps between areas of ability are getting noticeably wide. The emotional maturity of the 12-year-old who expresses herself like an 18-year-old is usually closer to her real age than to her intellectual age, but that doesn't stop her from making an excellent 18-year-old argument for privileges that her 12-year-old emotional maturity really can't handle. "Often gifted children will have critical and analytical skills that exceed their judgment and restraint."[33]

Although early adolescence is a critical developmental juncture, it is certainly not the case that every exceptional learner has serious issues during this period. However, when the risk factors of early adolescence and educational exceptionality interact with other risk factors, such as gender identity issues, cultural conflicts, or family disruptions, they create a situation of greater potential for problems.[34] In such cases, it is more important than ever that the principles we discuss here of active listening and support be solidly in place.

Differences between Boys and Girls

When each gifted boy is free to create his unique masculinity, and each gifted girl is free to create her unique femininity, they will also be liberated to fulfill their dreams.[35]

Adolescent boys and girls differ dramatically. It is important to remember, though, that gender differences in characteristics and behavior do not mean that all males are one way and all females are another.[36]

Developmental pathways are highly individual and diverse. Broad categories such as *gifted* and *female* and *Black* can sometimes assist parents and educators in thinking about how to proceed with a child's education and development, but it is critically important not to lose sight of the unique person behind any label or grouping. In the next section of this chapter, we discuss diversity within giftedness and ways in which uniqueness can influence individuals' lives. In other words, we consider how to optimize many different kinds of "circumstances gone right—the powerful combination of mixing ability with preparation, opportunity, and timing."[37]

In recent years, it has become a little more politically correct to discuss sex differences in ability, and there are many interesting findings to consider in this regard.[38] Although the gap is narrowing in many dimensions of academic and career success,[39] the research continues to show males ahead of females in some aspects of mathematical reasoning ability, particularly spatial reasoning. On certain mathematics and science tests, at least in the U.S., boys tend to score higher than girls, and the more competitive the test in its construction and administration, the truer this is. And the higher the ability level, the greater the difference.[40]

At the same time, girls tend to do better at school as compared with boys, particularly in verbally-oriented tasks and tests, right through to the end of high school. Girls begin to read at an earlier age, and they tend to be smarter in areas of social and emotional intelligence.

Exceptionally capable children (both boys and girls) tend to be more androgynous in their interests, incorporating elements of both the feminine and the masculine stereotype into their preferences and activities.[41] They are more likely than others to choose interests without regard for traditional gender stereotypes. One caveat when considering sex differences in giftedness: most of the research findings apply to mainstream rather than to minority populations. There is considerable evidence that the findings vary across cultures and depend on cultural values.[42]

Girls and Giftedness

Wholeness is shattered by the chaos of adolescence. Girls become fragmented, their selves split into mysterious contradictions.[43]

Historically, it is only relatively recently that females were seen as deserving of the same opportunities in learning as males, at least in Western society.[44]

"She used to be much more enthusiastic about her schoolwork. She's still doing well, but she doesn't seem to care about it anymore. Now it's all about her hair and her clothes and her friends."

Typically, girls start off their school careers doing better than their male peers. They mature at a younger age and are better able to sit still and do what teachers want them to do. When they are young, they tend to be more interested than boys in typical school tasks like reading and writing, and in fact, more girls than boys attend gifted programs in the United States.[45] Girls' academic advantage over boys disappears, however, as they enter adolescence and gender identity becomes important.

Although some girls go through adolescence apparently oblivious to the feminine stereotype that excludes high intelligence and ambition, others "dumb down" their academic performance or behavior for the sake of social acceptance or popularity or because they see themselves as less capable than they really are.[46] This has serious consequences because choices made early on can influence the availability of subsequent choices. If a girl decides not to take trigonometry, calculus, or physics, she cuts off many future careers, such as medicine, engineering, architecture, and the sciences. Alternatively, for some girls, participation in gifted learning opportunities and commitment to authentic self-discovery gets them through an otherwise painful adolescence.

One explanation for sex differences at the highest levels of math achievement is that there are sex differences in coping with setbacks and confusion; recent findings show that when the environment supports girls in acquiring a growth mindset, they perform as well as males.[47] Another explanation concerns cultural attitudes; in many countries outside of the United States, there are no sex differences in math and science test scores, or the differences favor girls. In the United Kingdom, for example, the gender shift, with girls now outperforming boys even in the hard sciences, has been attributed to gender equity policies and practices.[48]

Boys and Giftedness

> *Gifted boys are often held to rigid stereotypes of masculinity.*[49]

> *"Jared is busy with chemistry, photography, and computer graphics. He doesn't want to socialize or participate in sports, and he has no close friends. I worry because he seems to be more interested in products than people."*

> *"I'm not sure what to do about Zack. I know I should let him*
> *play with dolls if that is what he wants to do, but really....*
> *That's his favorite activity, and it worries me."*

As with girls, boys can experience several varieties of giftedness-related problems. Active, curious boys who are enthusiastic hands-on learners often have trouble in the first few years of their schooling. They do not like to sit still and do what the teacher asks them to do, and some decide that they hate school when they are very young. Another problem stems from the cultural pressure placed on boys to develop their independence, self-reliance, and responsibility, all of which help to facilitate high-level academic and career achievement. But for some boys, this can be too much of a good thing; the challenge of learning can be more rewarding than the rigors of socializing, and so they opt out of their social and emotional development, which causes problems in relationships and career development. Alternatively, the pressure to conform to cultural stereotypes of masculinity can be overwhelming; exceptionally capable boys are more likely than their female peers to have problems with low academic achievement and dropping out of school.[50]

Although much more research has been done investigating problems with female achievement (because of men's domination in high-paying and high-status occupations), there is also reason for serious concern about minority males:[51] "It is evident that ethnic minority males (i.e., African-American and Latino) are faring more poorly than are females [regardless of ethnicity]."[52] This has been shown in high school graduation rates, as well as enrollment in and completion of college.

Although stereotypes for women have relaxed considerably over the past 30 or 40 years, stereotypes of masculinity regarding acceptable interests and behaviors for boys and men remain troublingly rigid. There is still a belief that boys should not consider professions that are associated with stereotypically feminine attributes of artistic sensitivity and caring about others. Gender stereotypical views like these can undermine boys' motivation to explore and develop their gifted abilities.[53] At the present time, it may actually be tougher for boys than for girls to be true to themselves.

Gender Stereotypes and Encouraging Gifted Development

A home or classroom climate that is conducive to optimal development for children of both sexes is one in which parents and educators are aware of the nature of differences between boys and girls but are also unbiased in their expectations and values as children mature.[54] Adults who realize that it is normal for boys to be delayed relative to girls in their ability to sit still, for example, will be patient with primary school children who are restless, and they will offer plenty of opportunities for them to exercise and explore. They will provide all children with opportunities to choose stereotypically girl-friendly activities and resources (such as books and dolls), as well as stereotypically boy-friendly ones (such as trucks and building toys). All of this becomes more interesting and difficult at early adolescence, when gender stereotypes are at their strongest.

Here are some suggestions for supporting gifted development that can help young people excel and also transcend the damaging effects of stereotyping:

- Bolster children's development in subject areas that they perceive as weaker.

- Provide opportunities for competitive as well as collaborative learning.

- Engage children with authentic learning—hands-on activities with a real-world focus.

- Discuss and illustrate the importance of math and science to subsequent career choices.

- Create academic and career development workshops and speaker forums, ensuring that nontraditional and non-stereotypical choices are explored and encouraged.

- Provide job shadowing and mentoring opportunities with accomplished people who enjoy their work and who are from a wide range of demographic backgrounds.

- Encourage young people to be themselves and to explore who they really are, not who others think they should be. Support girls in their achievement-oriented behaviors and activities. Help them see that it is possible to be feminine, attractive, popular, *and* intellectually curious and competent. Help boys discover that it is possible to be masculine, respected, tough, *and* sensitive and aesthetically engaged.

- Provide access to counseling when needed.

Parenting Adolescents

> Parent: *"That's it. I quit! We used to discuss things, and I was able to reason with her. Now we barely communicate."*
> Adolescent: *"They won't quit! We used to discuss things, and I was able to reason with them. Now we barely communicate."*

The same parenting skills that foster gifted-level development in early childhood can become problematic in certain situations and at other times. Parents who are very involved in their young child's life—parents who are aware, caring, stimulating, and responsive, and who provide lots of opportunities for learning—may experience developmental challenges of their own as their child becomes an adolescent. Parents of pre-teens and teens have to learn to back off—to become reactive instead of proactive. They have to trust that their children have the necessary resources, including parental support and guidance, to deal with the consequences of the wrong decisions that they make. They have to find ways to understand that decision making is a skill that must be acquired, like all others, through practice, including some trials that result in errors. This kind of developmental challenge is not an easy one, particularly if a parent has concerns about a child's development or well-being. Although mothers tend to have more trouble letting go of their children than do fathers, we have certainly seen fathers challenged in this way, too.

One way to put this in perspective is to think about adolescence as an opportunity for a young person to acquire and practice the skills and habits conducive to a successful and independent adult life. By the time a teenager is ready to leave home at age 18 or so, it is best if he does not need someone else to take care of his room, clothing, and food; to make sure he gets up on time; to tell him how many hours of homework he has to complete; or to make other kinds of decisions about what to do and with whom. Having achieved puberty, then, it is time to practice being an adult. If he is lucky, he will be able to have this opportunity in the context of a safe, supportive, and caring environment in a home with adults who love him and are able to provide respectful and helpful guidance as he demonstrates that he needs it.

With all of this in mind, we offer a few pointers for the parents of gifted adolescents:

1. *Decision Making.* An adolescent's ability to handle sexual intimacy, decisions about drugs, and other potentially dangerous peer pressures is not improved because of her intellectual or reasoning ability, no matter how persuasive she is.

2. *Power/Conflict Issues.* These cannot always be avoided, and that's all right. In fact, the best long-term developmental outcomes occur in families characterized by lots of warmth, as well as lots of intergenerational discussion, much of it heated and conflictual in nature.[55]

3. *Parent Development Issues.* Learn to relax and let go while providing backup support. Let the child make mistakes. Your holding the reins can prevent him from achieving the independence that is an important developmental task at this stage, or from learning from those setbacks.

4. *Rules.* Make rules only about those things that really matter. You will likely be spending a lot of time defending the rules that you establish, and this is easier to do if you really believe that they are necessary.

5. *Identity Issues.* Work on relating to the *person* she is underneath the costumes and mannerisms. Trust that she will become herself again once she's tried out all of those foreign identities and alternate personas.

6. *Gender Identity.* Continue to support your children in their intellectual endeavours while accepting their gender identity explorations (for example, your daughter's yearnings to be attractive and to develop her own sense of style, or your son's realization that he is gay).

7. *Cultural Issues.* When the family background is different than the surrounding culture, recognize that the child is growing up in that surrounding culture and that his healthy identity development

depends on peer identification. Try to minimize his problems with conflicting cultural values.

8. *Academic Engagement (or lack thereof).* Encourage the adolescent to find something that she really wants to learn about and to keep as many educational and career options open as possible. Understand that school may not be at the top of her list of what matters for a few years, and that's okay. It's more important that she figures out who she is and feels good about it; everything else builds on that.

9. *Unpredictability.* What a gifted adolescent needs is predictably unpredictable and changing all of the time. This means that a parent's job is a challenging balancing act, requiring constant vigilance and flexibility.

10. *Cultivation of interests.* Adolescence is the ideal time to explore and discover interests and abilities. Adolescents benefit from wide exposure to various subjects, activities, and people.

Being Smart and Being Funny

While students with musical aptitude may be shown to the music room, students with humor ability are often sent to the principal's office.[56]

The quick and cutting remark is a special skill (of dubious value) that often accompanies verbal giftedness and, if not controlled, may imperil relationships with peers and adults.[57]

The pleasure which I cause them tells me that at least for a short moment they love me.[58]

As with play, humor can be critically important to children's healthy development, no matter how intellectually capable they are. Humor can provide an essential outlet for difficult feelings, a way to cope with stress, or a means to connect with others. It can also be a way of masking or handling anger, unhappiness, bitterness, or loneliness, or of taking charge of a difficult situation.

Being humorous helps initiate social interactions and establish friendships. In a study of sixth- to eighth-grade students in a gifted program,[59] one sixth-grade boy explained, "When you're funny, people like being around you." Some interviewees discussed how their talent for humor had facilitated the move from their neighborhood school to the special gifted class at a new school. Humor had helped ease them into a new social group, as well as deal with the sense of loss experienced by leaving old friends. According to one girl, "Being funny breaks the ice since people can't hate you if they're laughing with you." A funny child is also less likely to be classified as boring, which is a dreaded designation. Once a friendship is formed, that same humor serves to solidify and enhance intimacy, particularly when private jokes are shared.

Some of the gifted humorists in this study[60] admitted to deliberately using humor for manipulative purposes to achieve social control or power. Making a joke can help extricate a young comedian from a difficult situation, especially with peers, but also with parents. Several interviewees complained that these techniques weren't usually so effective with teachers. "Teachers don't want you to be funny. They think you're making fun of them or trying to disturb the class." Many of the children saw humor as a potent force that can be used to change both circumstances and people. They knew that they could change the atmosphere in a classroom by employing humor.

These children recognized humor as a way to irritate, cajole, empower, change, help, or control others. Students who are gifted humorists need opportunities to exercise and develop their special talent. Teachers can recognize the contributions that class comics are able to make by encouraging their leadership and creativity. When educators and parents appreciate children's humor and comprehend its possible meanings and functions instead of punishing them for their distracting behaviors, they simultaneously take advantage of a wonderful, enlivening resource at home and at school, and they support the optimal development of those who bring smiles to so many.[61]

What's Love Got to Do with It? The Role of Passion in Gifted Development

Neither a lofty degree of intelligence nor imagination nor both together go to the making of genius. Love, love, love, that is the soul of genius.[62]

Zeal seems to be a characteristic common to all the prodigies described here. They are obsessed with numbers, treat them as familiar friends, and actively seek closer acquaintanceship with them.[63]

People are at their most productive when they are doing what they love to do. Ellen Winner identified one common characteristic across the otherwise highly disparate prodigies that she studied. She called this characteristic a "rage to master"—an intense desire to take learning as far as possible—and she argued that the passionate drive to learn more is an essential component of all extraordinary accomplishment.[64] This same quality has been called other things—for example, the zeal that Butterworth describes when studying mathematical prodigies[65] or the intellectual overexcitability that Dabrowski discussed.[66] But no matter what it is called, it appears that an intense motivation to understand and learn more and more is an important driving force in all gifted-level achievement.

Parents and educators who want to support their children in achieving gifted-level outcomes help them find what they love to do and give them the opportunities and the support that they need to do that learning.[67] Over time, it is the love of one's work that drives the effort, discipline, and perseverance that is required for productive achievement.

Effort, Persistence, Perseverance, and Practice

In the beginning, wide exposure and playful exploration are appropriate, but as a child develops competence in a domain, he or she needs more challenge, instruction and disciplined practice.[68]

Students must learn to view setbacks as normal.[69]

Extraordinary scientific accomplishments require extraordinary commitment both in and outside of school.[70]

Although playful exploration opens up the possibilities for talent development, what is needed next is more like work than play: persistence, perseverance, and plenty of practice. In every domain, gifted-level outcomes are built on many, many hours of practice in a context of scaffolded support for learning.[71]

Mindset as it influences one's attitude toward failures and setbacks—and therefore one's likelihood of persisting—is one of the most potent predictors of whether or not a child is likely to invest the necessary effort in gifted-level achievement. The way in which a child approaches challenges, failures, and setbacks has a powerful influence on how successful he will become. Those with a growth mindset think of ability as developing incrementally, one step at a time, with effort and practice and engagement, and they are not fazed by setbacks. In fact, they see failures as a predictable part of the learning process—opportunities to figure out where they need to concentrate. Children with a growth mindset are much more likely than others to persist through the tough times and, in fact, are measurably more successful in the academic, career, and psychological dimensions of their lives.[72] However, those with fixed mindset beliefs—who think that intelligence is fixed and innate and that smart people don't have to work hard—tend to interpret failures as shameful indicators of intellectual shortcomings. No wonder those with a fixed mindset have a harder time persisting through obstacles and are far more likely to avoid tough challenges.

Parents and educators can encourage the development of persistence, practice, and perseverance by fostering a growth mindset and by looking for opportunities for children to work hard in areas of interest with the enthusiastic support of the adults in their lives.

Cultural Differences

The ideal culture is one in which there is a place for every human gift.[73]

Gifted and talented students come from all cultural, linguistic, and economic backgrounds.[74]

Racial inequalities in the identification of gifted students have been a constant throughout our history, and they persist today.[75]

Around the world, students from some cultural minorities are under-represented in gifted programs, as are students from lower socio-economic backgrounds.[76] Donna Ford, an expert in the area of diversity and giftedness, describes American schools as "places of inequity and barriers to talent development."[77] She has suggested that there is a "pervasive deficit orientation,"[78] in which group differences are interpreted as shortcomings of minority group members rather than as opportunities to enrich society through embracing diverse ways of being. Ford and others have made many recommendations about ways to address these concerns, and we review some of those recommendations here.

Supporting Gifted-Level Development More Broadly

The under-representation in gifted programs of certain groups is a thorny problem that has proven highly resistant to change. Many solutions have been proposed, tested, and discarded through the decades since this under-representation was targeted as problematic. The *Jacob J. Javits Gifted and Talented Students Act*, passed by the United States federal legislature in 1988, has provided funds to promote research and demonstration grants to increase the inclusion in gifted programming of students in under-represented populations.[79] Since the passage of this Act, tens of millions of dollars have been spent addressing issues of access to gifted programs, support for minority learners, and appropriate opportunities for *all* students to learn.

Many who have worked with students in minority populations recommend comprehensive, multi-factored assessment approaches that attempt to discover minority students' strengths, especially when these diverge from mainstream notions of intelligence.[80] Another suggestion is to provide those who show promise of being exceptional (in the absence of meeting gifted cut-off criteria) with "pre-gifted" programs that foster their talents and enable successful transitions to gifted programs.[81]

An innovative way to address cultural, racial, and linguistic equity concerns is to spend less time finding ways to label more minority students as gifted and work instead to ensure that every child has the kinds of opportunities to learn that research shows lead to gifted developmental outcomes.[82] Rather than worrying so much about underrepresentation of minority students in gifted programs, many of the experts working in this field are advocating that we put more effort into ensuring high-level outcomes for all learners. Other recommendations made by experts in diversity issues in gifted education (and that are also consistent with the mastery model of giftedness) focus on the need to provide flexible grouping and choice within a wide range of programming options.[83]

A final but important recommendation is to ensure that all teachers receive the professional development and ongoing support that they need.[84] By learning how to implement inclusive and flexible giftedness policies and practices, and by opening up a wide a range of options to as many students as possible, educators can support high-level development and work to rectify some of the historic inequities in education.

Prodigies and Extreme Giftedness

Even in prodigies, talent is accompanied by a tremendous zest for the skill domain and by sustained engagement in it.[85]

Most prodigies do not become major creative contributors to their fields; their distinctive characteristics are very rapid mastery of existing knowledge and skill, but relatively rarely does a prodigy transform a domain in a significant way.[86]

> *The further students deviate from the norms for their age,*
> *the greater is the differentiation in curriculum and learning*
> *environment they require in order to learn optimally.[87]*

Child prodigies provide the most extreme example of developmental asynchrony; they have extraordinarily highly-developed skills and exhibit professional adult-level ability in one area but are closer to average in others. The domains that tend to produce the most prodigies are music, chess, and mathematics, in that order. These domains share several characteristics, including that they are highly rule-bound, can be learned in relatively straightforward and obvious progression, use technology to demonstrate knowledge, have accessible criteria for excellence, and can be adapted to the capabilities of very young children.[88] While some prodigies go on to adult renown in their area of expertise, it is rare that they go on to be innovators.

When people talk about extreme or high levels of giftedness, they are generally basing this characterization on intelligence test scores rather than on adult levels of competence in a particular domain.[89] Traditionally, the gifted designation has generally referred to those who score two or more standard deviations from the mean—that is, above 130 IQ, or above the 98th or 99th percentile. The major reasons for concern about those who score in the top 1% to 2% of the population relate to their special educational needs, as well as the increased likelihood of difficulty in finding social peers and the possibility of emotional and behavioral issues. For those who are even more exceptional, who might be called "extremely" or "profoundly" gifted and who score above IQ 145 on intelligence tests, or at the 99.9th percentile, these educational and other concerns can become even more pressing.

Scores above 99.9% indicate that these children have scored higher than 999 people out of 1000. They are exceptional even within the gifted exceptionality. In terms of their intellectual ability (at least as measured by IQ), they are as much out of step with other gifted learners as gifted learners are from the norm. In a gifted program, such children can feel even more alone and different than they did before, finding that they *still* have to restrain their minds and communication, that the so-called gifted learning opportunities are nowhere close to meeting their needs, and that neither the other kids nor the teacher understand their thinking unless they "dumb down" their communication. Since adults and other children rarely have any prior experience to draw on when dealing with extreme giftedness, they may in fact be intimidated or confused by these exceptional learners and so very often respond to them with alarm or rejection.

As with prodigies, extreme giftedness is almost always accompanied by a high level of developmental asynchrony; more than 95% of extremely gifted learners show a strong disparity between mathematical and verbal competencies, and extraordinarily strong mathematical and spatial capability often accompany average or even deficient verbal abilities.[90] Because they are so asynchronous in their development, if they receive "globally gifted" instruction, such children can experience frustration both in their weaker and in their stronger subject areas. It is especially important that such children receive domain-specific learning opportunities adapted to their particular strengths, as well as any possible weaknesses.

Extreme giftedness brings with it a risk of social isolation, as well as the potential for problems with anxiety due to heightened self-expectations in combination with the extreme asynchrony, and a sense of alienation and differentness which is sometimes interpreted as something being wrong with them.[91] They also often need quite unusual educational modifications. Just as those who work with profoundly developmentally disabled learners must tailor their expectations and attitudes, so also must parents and educators of extremely gifted learners work hard to be sensitive to these children's extreme exceptionality and high-level learning needs. This means allowing them opportunities for content mastery and higher-order thinking, as well as supporting them in using their abilities productively.[92] Some strategies to consider:

- radical acceleration, in which the child is advanced more than one grade level, either subject-specific in the area of extreme advancement or globally across grades

- mentorships in areas of special interest and ability

- project-based learning that involves independent guided study on topics of interest

- self-directed learning

- diverse and flexible learning possibilities, including acceleration; in-school, cross-subject, or cross-grade learning; and extracurricular enrichment activities, such as university-affiliated, community-based, or business-sponsored programs

- opportunities to develop other skills, such as athletic, artistic, or leadership abilities

- involvement in community, regional, national, and international contests and programs

- the luxury of time and space to explore their curiosities and passions, both in the area of extreme giftedness and elsewhere

Because of the degree of their exceptionality, profoundly gifted learners have highly individualistic schooling needs. In some circumstances, homeschooling is the best possible option for a certain time in their lives. In other cases, a child may go through reasonably normal school pathways until college and then diverge widely from the norm. In yet other situations, there may be a variety of approaches tried through the years, including radical acceleration, special projects, contests, and extracurricular activities, with some options and some years working out better than others. It is important to provide as wide a range of learning options as possible, helping children balance their needs for both autonomy and support while staying responsive to their changing needs over time.

Twice Exceptional: Learning Problems and Gifted Development

"She's so bright, but she can't read!"

Twice-exceptional students require dual differentiation in order to meet their often-contradictory sets of needs.[93]

As important as it is to help twice exceptional students overcome their weaknesses, it's even more important to maintain the primary focus of their education on their strengths.[94]

Many experts on learning problems are as tentative about the use of the term "learning disabled" as we are about the term "gifted."[95] The position we take on the subject of learning disabilities, which is consistent with our approach to giftedness, is that there are naturally occurring variations in all aspects of all children's development, and to be successful learners, different children need different teaching strategies at different times in their schooling. Just as with the gifted exceptionality, for a variety of reasons, some children have serious learning difficulties if instruction is not adapted to meet their needs.

The most prevalent learning problems that co-occur with gifted learning needs concern attention and so might be diagnosed as Attention Deficit Hyperactivity Disorder (ADHD); cognitive processing, which might be labeled as a Learning Disability (LD); and social processing, sometimes resulting in the label of Asperger's Syndrome or Nonverbal Learning Disability (NVLD).[96] As we note throughout this book, children vary tremendously in the maturational timing of their development, their degrees and domains of advancement, their interests, their study skills, their test-taking skills, their environments, and their social/emotional development. These variations are both interpersonal (between and among children) and intrapersonal (within a given child). It is the intrapersonal variations, or developmental asynchrony, that we address in this section, noting that it is not unusual to find children who have gifted learning needs and yet also have trouble (whether diagnosed or not) with one or more aspects of schooling.[97]

Children who find learning much easier in some academic areas than others are sometimes called paradoxical learners because "they demonstrate inefficiency with basic types of cognitive processes, yet function intellectually at very high and even superior levels of skill and expertise."[98] For example, some children have highly developed reading and verbal reasoning skills but closer-to-average fine-motor skills. They find that their thoughts come much faster than they are able to write them down, and they are unhappy with how their ideas look on paper. Not surprisingly, children with this profile tend to hate writing, and they find ways to avoid tasks that require it. Over time, this can become a serious problem that can undermine their learning and achievement.

It is best if this sort of concern is addressed sooner in a child's academic career rather than later, starting with the recognition that everyone has areas of strength and weakness, and the more exceptional a person is in one area, the more likely that person is to experience a wide gap across areas of competency. Learning to enjoy developing the strengths while mastering the challenges is an important achievement, and one that is essential to high-level accomplishment over time.

Parents and educators can help children accept their disparities across ability areas. For example, when a child is advanced in reading but closer to age-normal in penmanship, adults can make sure that she has access to a computer from a very early stage and that she has a chance to acquire effective word processing skills. In cases like this in which there is no real disability, it is not the discrepancy itself that is the problem, but rather the child's (and/or adults') reactions to it.

Identification Issues with Twice-Exceptional Learners

Identifying gifted learning needs becomes complicated when a child has learning problems because the different exceptionalities can mask one another. A child might exhibit his strengths in oral contributions to class and in conversation but not achieve very well in his schoolwork. His teachers might describe him as lazy, tuned-out, or as a disturbance in class. All too often, parents or teachers will assume that the child is not working hard enough and insist that he try harder, when in fact, he is already trying as hard as he knows how. Quite predictably, the child may begin to have emotional or behavioral problems. Not infrequently, the reason for gifted/learning disabled children coming to the attention of school psychological services is because of emotional or behavioral problems, with neither giftedness nor learning disabilities suspected.[99]

Depending on the nature, severity, and extent of the problems that the child is experiencing, as well as how entrenched her sense of frustration or even despair is, such a child may not achieve the necessary test cut-off scores to qualify for gifted identification, even if she does come to someone's attention for possible giftedness. This is sometimes a problem of psychometrics and test interpretation practices when scores are averaged across several ability areas.[100] Although all too widely employed, this tactic is clearly ludicrous. Would we say that Tiger Woods is an average athlete because, although he is a great golfer, he doesn't swim or play hockey very well? Yet this is exactly what is done when IQ (or some other score that represents a combination of several abilities) is used to identify giftedness. Thankfully, there are indications that, increasingly, professionals are paying attention to a breakdown of separate scores, particularly when those scores are widely discrepant.

There are three common patterns of giftedness as it combines with learning problems:[101]

1. *Learning problems are masked by giftedness.* The child's gifted-level abilities are evident, and he is able to use his giftedness to compensate for his problems.

2. *Giftedness and learning problems mask each other.* Neither giftedness nor learning problems are evident.

3. *Giftedness is masked by learning problems.* The child appears to have learning problems, while giftedness is not evident.

Which of these patterns applies to any given child will depend on her personality and coping skills, as well as on the nature and degree both of the giftedness and of the learning problems. Sometimes children move across these categories, with the problems getting more apparent as they get older and interfering increasingly with gifted-level functioning. The twice-exceptional pattern is almost always characterized by a high level of frustration and unhappiness. It can lead to serious problems with self-esteem, depression, and behavior, often spilling over into other aspects of the child's life and later into adulthood.

Recommendations

> *Use…materials rich in ideas and imagination coupled with a focus on higher level skills.… Both self-concept and motivation are in jeopardy if prolonged use of compensatory strategies and basic level materials are used in the educational process of these learners. Challenging content with a focus on ideas and creative opportunities are essential to combat further discrepant performance.*[102]

As with all children, but particularly those with extreme patterns of strengths and weaknesses—whether diagnosed as exceptional or not—it is essential that parents and educators emphasize creative and imaginative possibilities and that they encourage the development of individual strengths. This helps to create a strong foundation of learning, confidence, and self-esteem.

When children's weaknesses are addressed in the context of their strengths, learning is far more pleasurable, motivating, and successful. For example, if a child has difficulty reading but enjoys art, that interest can be used toward developing his reading skills. The child can create books, illustrating others' words or his own, if necessary enlisting the aid of someone else (a parent, friend, older child, or teacher) to write the words or the captions for his pictures, which are collected and assembled in story format. He can dictate the story to a parent or older child and read it back. He can look at beautifully illustrated books for children on topics that he finds interesting. He can draw, trace, copy, and/or design letters, words, names, and signs. These kinds of activities can be encouraged in the classroom and at home. Dramatic enactments of plays and stories are another way to encourage a child's development of more fluent reading skills. Trips to bookstores and libraries can be planned as enjoyable and exciting excursions.

Becoming a Reader: A Library Expedition

Stacey's favorite time of the week was Thursdays after school. Her Aunt Lena would come over, and they'd go to the library. Stacey used to feel that the library was a stuffy kind of place. "There are too many fat books, and I'll never be able to read them in a million years!" she told us. However, she soon learned that reading could be a wonderful adventure. Each week, on the way to the library, Lena would ask Stacey what topic she wanted to explore. One time it was sea turtles, another day it was clowns, and on one particularly cold afternoon it was hot chocolate. Lena and Stacey enjoyed the time they spent together researching the chosen topic, reading about it, and making a shared journal entry. Stacey would select a book to take home. It was always her choice, even though Lena would make suggestions.

Stacey's teacher, who was helping her with reading problems, encouraged Stacey to bring her library books into class. Stacey would read a book (or parts of it) over the weekend. Then on Mondays, she would share ideas from it with her teacher, creating a link between reading activities happening inside and outside of school. Stacey was enthusiastic about the learning experiences, felt pleased with herself and her reading progress, and told us, "I might get through those fat books after all!"

There are many kinds of pleasurable reading activities that involve the child spending some time with another reader, usually an adult, who is willing to encourage her selections and share reading-related pleasures. Seeing others enjoying books and hearing them talk about their reading with one another encourages a child to further develop a love of reading, which is so important to learning. Another approach is to encourage a child to help someone who is younger and whose reading skills are not as well-developed. By helping a younger child with reading, a child can consolidate her own skills and learn where some of her own reading problems might lie.

The following strategies can benefit all children but are particularly useful for those with dual exceptionality learning needs. These ideas work well for both parents and educators.

Emotional and Motivational Ideas

- Pay attention to the emotional and motivational aspects of learning.

- Ask the child to think about what might help him learn.

- Seek out and celebrate success.

- Incorporate the arts as an outlet for furthering creativity and expression and as a way of integrating experiences.

- Encourage the child to take pride in her accomplishments.

- Help the child to design "escape valves" by fostering self-awareness and self-modulation.

- Show the child how to handle stress, to vent in healthy ways, and to make time to unwind.

- Help the child create strategies of self-reminders.

Details for Instruction and Learning

- Break large tasks into smaller, more manageable ones.

- Repeat directions in different modalities (spoken instructions, written notes).

- Emphasize quality rather than quantity of work.

- Monitor progress, and give frequent feedback.

- Teach outlining and underlining.
- Simplify.
- Color code.
- Structure learning activities so that they include previews, reviews, limits, and reminders.
- Take advantage of technological advances.
- Teach memory aid strategies (such as mnemonics).
- Teach test-taking skills.
- Reduce or eliminate timed tests.

Environmental Features

- Create a home office or workspace for independent work time.
- Promote and model collaborative activities and idea sharing.
- Teach social cues.
- Model prioritizing.
- Make rules and expectations as explicit as possible. Post them in clear view.
- Set boundaries, maintain a predictable schedule, and minimize variance.
- Encourage structure.
- Introduce novel concepts and approaches, but don't over-stimulate.

You'll see that these strategies take into account the individual's affective and social development, as well as cognitive concerns. It is important to think of the child as functioning within a particular context and to remember that the best interventions capitalize on all of the available strengths and resources, including those within the home, school, community, and the child himself. When parents and educators work together to find and implement the appropriate and necessary supports, it increases the likelihood that children with diverse learning needs, including those with dual exceptionalities, will thrive.

Career Counseling and Gifted Development

> *Career education is on nearly every list of program advice in gifted education.*[103]

> *Giftedness is not a problem to be solved but a unique challenge to be nourished.*[104]

We began the discussion of career exploration in Chapter 7 in reference to curriculum adaptations for gifted learners. We come back to this topic once again as an important issue in gifted development. The fact of exceptionality generally prompts those giving career guidance to simply suggest jobs that require a longer time in school, such as engineering, medicine, or law. While this adaptation is excellent advice for some, it is not appropriate for others. As is true in so many other areas, academic and career guidance for exceptional students must be tailored to the unique interests, strengths, possibilities, aspirations, and constraints of their highly individual situations.

Another reason to consider career education and counseling is that unfortunately, few guidance counselors have the training or experience required to consider the ways that giftedness impacts career development. Published materials (such as career interest inventories and career decision-making guidelines) do not have a wide enough range to encompass the needs of those who are exceptional in their abilities—on both ends of the ability spectrum. Because of this, it is incumbent on adults who live or work with exceptional children and adolescents to pay special attention to career education.

Multipotentiality

Multipotentiality is the name given to the situation in which a child has many areas of high-level ability and interest that, with development, might provide interesting and successful careers.[105] Although it sounds like a wonderful bonus to be able to select from several possible areas of high-level achievement, multipotentiality can cause real confusion and unhappiness as a multitalented adolescent or young adult contemplates which of her favorite pursuits she will continue to focus her energies on and which she will have to let go or develop only to a mediocre level.[106] Some gifted learners are keen to be involved in a host of activities. They may opt to participate in band, choir, chess club, and writing, while at the same time taking a few Advanced Placement classes. However, multipotentiality can sometimes result in burnout from trying to do everything well, and other times it results in rustout from doing nothing very well.

With a little creative thinking, two or more disparate areas can sometimes be combined. The student who is gifted athletically and loves science might become involved in sports medicine, or the student who is advanced in mathematics and has heightened social awareness might become a psychologist, sociologist, or demographer. In other situations, one interest can be developed into a vocation while another continues to be developed as an avocation, as in the lives of the many doctors who play instruments in community orchestras, or the professors who write fiction or poetry in their spare time.

Certainty, Uncertainty, and Time Out

> *"I'm going to be an astronaut. For sure."*
> *"I wish I had a better idea of what to study. Everyone else in my class seems to know what they want to be when they get older, but I really have no clue yet."*

Some children decide on a future career when they are very young and never deviate from that. For many others, this kind of early commitment forecloses other possibilities and leads to an unhappy sense of being trapped in a career without ever having fully explored other options. Early commitment reduces uncertainty and anxiety, both for the child and his family, and it enables him to move smoothly through his schooling. However, it can also carry a heavy price later.

Uncertainty can last into early adulthood, and although it can feel uncomfortable and worrying, it is not necessarily a bad thing. Rather than going through uninterrupted schooling from kindergarten to graduate studies, it is sometimes healthier for these children to take some time off somewhere between 17 and 25 years of age.[107] The "time out" can be spent working or traveling, while simultaneously engaging in active self-exploration, reading, thinking about society, observing oneself in interaction with others, and figuring out how to be independent, interdependent, and happily productive. Ideally, this career and self-exploration period should be a time of learning about various kinds of responsibility, including financial, emotional, and social. Once a young adult has worked out some of these issues of self and society, choosing a career usually becomes a little easier.

Recommendations

Adults involved in supporting exceptionally capable students through academic and career decision-making processes should recognize not only these students' exceptional thinking ability, but also other potentially complicating factors, such as interests, values, habits of mind, and temperament. Educators can encourage understanding and thoughtful reflection by inviting people who work in different fields to speak to students about their work. Parents, as well as friends, neighbors, acquaintances, and relatives, can be asked to discuss some of the issues that they have experienced in making career and life decisions. On a larger scale, teachers and parent volunteers can work together to plan a "Career Day," in which various speakers come in to talk to students about their careers. Considerations in planning such events include making sure that a range of representative possibilities is explored, including both conventional and unconventional occupations and that the speakers (both men and women, as racially and culturally diverse as possible) are asked to discuss how they became interested in what they ended up doing in their lives and what kinds of paths they followed to make it happen. When students hear about the educational requirements for various careers, they learn that their career interests can be supported or damaged by the choices they make. Not taking advanced levels of high school mathematics, for example, can compromise a student's ability to pursue careers in technology, sciences, medicine, and architecture.

Other methods for facilitating career exploration include job shadowing that starts by asking students to investigate occupations that interest them. They can conduct interviews with practitioners and share information with classmates. Activities like these make good topics for social studies and other subject-specific assignments and can be used to stimulate meaningful classroom discourse that benefits all students, while supporting exceptional learners in thinking about a wider range of possible futures than they might otherwise have done.

Further activities that can help diversely gifted learners consider alternate career paths include mentorships, extracurricular camps and clubs, and contests or fairs at local, regional, national, and international levels that enable students to engage intensely for a short period of time in areas of strength and of possible future interest.[108]

Additional ideas for those who may be struggling with academic and career decision making include:

- Think about what you're good at and what you enjoy doing.

- Think about what you're good at and what you enjoy doing that might be useful to others.

- Do not restrict yourself to established professions or careers or jobs. Many of the most interesting jobs are created by the person doing them and are frequently custom-made patchworks of activities rather than easily defined occupations.

- Remember that loving your work is an enormous bonus if you want to be happy and successful in your career. Seek what promises to be enjoyable learning.

- Finally, people are changing jobs more frequently today than used to be the case. Whatever you decide now is just the starting point for your future career, not its final destination.

Chapter 10

Emotional, Social, and Behavioral Considerations

The affective and social-emotional needs of students should not be overlooked in the talent development commitment. Students must be able to develop a healthy perspective about their own talents and limitations, and those of others; a positive self-image; a positive regard for the processes of learning and inquiry; and a commitment to a guiding set of moral and ethical values.[1]

Emotional, social, behavioral, and academic factors are not separate from one another in people's lives, but rather are intimately interconnected in myriad complex ways. Our intellect and emotional perceptions influence our social experiences and behavior, as well as our effort and achievements. How we think about ourselves affects what we do, as well as what we perceive that others think about us. We begin this chapter by addressing some of the emotional, social, and behavioral considerations that are associated with being very smart, and then we bring them together and provide recommendations for promoting children's well-being.

Gifted Labeling

> *The gifted label that many students still receive, and that their parents relish, may turn some children into students who are overly cautious and challenge-avoidant lest they make mistakes and no longer merit the label.*[2]

"Why do I have to be gifted? I was happier when I was normal."
"Being gifted is like getting in a serious car accident. I mean, you get two points off your driver's license, your insurance rate goes up, and you have a broken car."

Emotional well-being promotes healthy learning and development; conversely, emotional turbulence and anxiety can short-circuit it. A child's sense of self and emotional balance is affected by many different factors, and gifted identification and placement processes (which we discussed in Section II) can have an impact on the child and her family. These experiences can be emotionally charged, leading to reactions such as excitement, anxiety, pride, self-doubt, or confusion, and it is important for parents, teachers, and children to be as informed as possible about potential emotional responses and concerns.

The gifted label can cause children to question not only what lies ahead, but also their identity and abilities, asking, for example, "Am I really different than other kids?" and "Do I want to be different?" It can trigger introspection, self-questioning, and even worries that someone has made a mistake about their abilities. Some children react to the label by working hard to prove their intelligence; some worry about their ability to manage the unknown academic expectations ahead or the potential for uncomfortable social situations, such as being teased or left out. The identification process and all that goes with it can be daunting, and so it is important that trusted adults take time to talk with children about their hopes and fears, discussing specific circumstances and implications and offering truthful reassurances. An open, honest, and careful response to a child's questions, made with sensitivity to his level of understanding, can be helpful—even essential—to his self-acceptance, self-awareness, and healthy self-concept.

Children are not the only ones with concerns. Parents also have concerns about giftedness:

"Does this mean that my daughter is smarter than I am?"
"Now that Jesse is officially gifted, I guess that means we have to sacrifice everything for him, right?"
"I was never a good student. The gifted gene must come from my husband's side of the family."

And here are some comments we've heard from teachers:

"I'm not nearly as intelligent as some of the kids in my class."
"I have two children in my class who are so smart, it makes me nervous."
"If he's really gifted, why do I have to give him special help? I have kids to work with who need a lot more help than he does."

If parents and educators don't pay attention to their own self-doubts, questions, and concerns, their underlying unresolved issues can hinder the task of supporting the children in their lives. Adults should keep in mind that every child is unique and needs lots of help growing into a healthy adolescent, and ultimately into a happily self-sufficient adult. No matter how apparently smart or confident, each child is still a *child* first and foremost, with all of the difficulties and anxieties that go with being young, vulnerable, and inexperienced in life. Giftedness does not define a child.

Caring adults can increase their chances of making good decisions for and with children by learning about giftedness, networking with others to enhance their understandings of key issues, and considering a variety of strategies for addressing them. For example, one way to avoid the problems associated with labeling is to encourage exceptionally capable learners to participate in activities that interest them with others who are as keenly interested as they are. With mentorships, high-level music classes, chess clubs, or other extracurricular activities, these children can often get their learning needs met without labels entering the picture. Challenging activities that do not carry a gifted label as a prerequisite are an excellent way to provide the learning opportunities that a child needs without the problems associated with the label.[3]

It may seem that attending both to a child's giftedness and to her well-rounded ability to fit in with what is typically perceived as "normal" involves irreconcilable opposites. However, social/emotional health depends on finding a way to reconcile those apparent opposites, to respect and support the development of each, and thus find a balance where the child can accept both her unique strengths and her weaker areas.

School Change: Social Concerns

"Why won't they be friends with me? I'm, like, yanking my hair out!"

"He wants friends more than anything, but he doesn't know how to go about it."

"The children in Megan's class are VERY hard to handle. They tend to form cliques, and lately she's been the odd one out."

As noted earlier, we believe that the best learning environment is one in which students are allowed to move at their own pace. In some situations, this means gifted programming that is at least partially separated from other school activities. Thus, one social concern for parents and educators dealing with gifted learners is a transition to a special gifted program, especially if this involves changing schools. This can go very well or very badly. To begin with, we want to state what may be obvious but is not always given enough attention: humans are social animals. Our needs for social acceptance and belonging are hard-wired, a survival adaptation that continues to stand us in good stead. For children, peer pressure, neglect, or rejection can be particularly brutal. Although giftedness signifies cognitive strengths, it is not a predictor of social competence, and it can sometimes interfere with peer acceptance.

Social competence varies as much as mathematical or linguistic competence. As with adults, some children attract friends like magnets, easily and effortlessly, while others seem to repel them. Some children have trouble socializing in certain situations and yet manage fine in others. And some children try very hard to get along with their peers but just can't seem to make it work, and so they decide that they don't want or really need friends after all.

Take a moment to think about a child's social milieu: the classroom, the playground, the places he goes outside of school, and the people he encounters each day. Is he a valued member of his social group? Does he have a sense of belonging, or does he feel like an outsider or at odds with others? Over the years, many children have talked to us about their social experiences. We've listened to them discuss ways of maintaining friendships, as well as confide their concerns about relationships, adjustment problems, and how their giftedness can separate them from others. Many of their voices can be heard in the comments that appear throughout the rest of this section.

Transition Experiences

The following comments, first from children and then from parents and teachers, illustrate how variable children's social experiences are in their move to a full-time gifted class:

> *"It was really bad for me in my old class. They pretended to be my friends. They're no longer my friends."*
> *"Mean kids from your school who aren't in the gifted class tease you and bug you more."*
> *"I'm definitely more open now, and I have way better friends."*
> *"My friends are my friends, and I don't care if they're gifted or not."*

Parents' views are also variable and sometimes disturbing:

> *"She's gained personal confidence in social situations."*
> *"It wasn't cool to be smart, so they started to ridicule my daughter in the regular class. She was always miserable when she came home from school. Always."*
> *"Even now in the gifted class, he still doesn't have a close friend at school."*

Teachers' comments confirm the need to pay attention to children's social concerns:

> *"I have a whole class of gifted learners, and it's a real jumble, emotionally and socially."*
> *"I have three really smart students who don't want to participate in group activities. They're kind of isolated. It's sad, and it's frustrating for me, but it's their choice."*
> *"The kids in my gifted class don't socialize much with kids in other classes. There's not a whole lot of opportunity for that, I guess."*

It is important for teachers to establish a supportive classroom culture in which individual differences are accepted, diversity is seen as a strength, and students are helped to understand themselves and others. In such a classroom, all children feel welcome, respected, and appreciated and have ample opportunities for positive interactions with others in the school.

It is not always possible to predict how a child will respond to a new social milieu. However, it *is* possible to enable children to collaborate and engage in satisfying social interactions and to learn some guidelines for building relationships. Even children who purposely distance themselves from others (for example, by immersing themselves in music, books, or computer activity) can learn to feel good about their roles in the social fabric.

Adapting to a Gifted Program: Short Term

> *"We really had no idea it would be this hard. He left his school, classmates, teachers, and a set of rules that he knew to go to a distant neighborhood into an already established pecking order with no support."*
>
> *"After viewing the gifted class, we came out frazzled. Are we doing the right thing?"*
>
> *"I felt like I could start fresh at a new school because I had no friends at my old school."*

Parents are sometimes surprised to discover that adapting to school-related change can involve social and emotional challenges that are harder to manage than the changes in curriculum. Many children feel uncertain, confused, or anxious when they are invited to join a full-time gifted class in a different school. Parents may feel this way as well.

Most people who enter new learning or work environments try to figure out how to be *a part* of things, rather than *apart* from them. They assess the new social landscape and try to adjust to it—that is, they learn how to behave in the new milieu. School culture and attributes that are valued (such as looks, social skills, family wealth or social status, clothes, intellectual abilities, or athletic prowess) vary from one school setting to the next. Fitting in can require a child to work on adjusting her "likability." For example, she might need to adjust her vocabulary, or take more (or less) care with her dress or personal grooming, or think carefully about volunteering answers too often in class. Some children find these adjustments difficult, or they don't perceive the need to adjust and do not understand why they are suddenly less popular than they were before. Others perceive the change in culture and expectations but refuse to conform. Still others see social adjustments as temporary inconveniences, or even interesting challenges. It is wonderful for all concerned when a child quickly makes herself at home in a new environment. At the same time, it is not the end of the world when this doesn't happen.[4]

Changes in educational programs bring with them hidden and unexpected social adjustments. By being aware of this ahead of time and by being responsive to children's concerns and observations, adults can help children anticipate and manage change in ways that increase their resiliency and sense of competence rather than undermine them.[5] We discuss this further in Chapter 11 when we address parenting issues.

Adapting to a Gifted Program: Long Term

"She prefers the new classmates, and she is much happier."
"She's part of a whole group of kids who think like she does. They seem to feed off of each other's talents."

There are wide differences within the population of gifted students; it is a fallacy to think that one kind of program or provision will meet the educational and affective needs of all gifted students.[6]

Taking a longer view, in the whole scheme of things, change can be a positive learning experience. Sometimes a change works out so well that everyone wonders why they worried about it in the first place. Sometimes it proves to have been a mistake, in which case wise parents and educators begin to problem-solve in order to decide how to proceed from there, a situation we also address in more detail in Chapter 11.

For many children, well-chosen new classes, programs, or peer groups represent a kind of beginning *and* an end—a timely conclusion perhaps to what was, and a fresh start toward what might yet be. Children, like adults, have a need to feel accepted, to be affiliated with others with whom they share something, and to be recognized for their accomplishments without being socially disadvantaged as a result. This can take time, effort, acquired social skills, support, compromise, and self-confidence, all of which can be encouraged and reinforced by parents and teachers who care.[7]

Social Skills

> *"I don't know why, but I don't seem to have friends over at my house anymore."*

Many children have trouble with social activities because the nature and degree of their exceptionality is such that their age peers do not understand their particular enthusiasms or language use. This can be misdiagnosed as a social skills deficit, but it isn't, and no amount of social skills training will fix that. When a person's interests are profoundly different and his communication skills are several years ahead of his grade-mates, it can be very difficult to forge a meaningful friendship with an age peer. In these situations, it is best if the child's individuality is respected and he is allowed to find interactions when and where he can. Children like this often find it relatively easy to interact with adults or older children—others who are engaged by their areas of interest.

Many well-meaning educators and parents exert pressure on socially awkward gifted learners to take socials skills training so that they can learn how to behave more "normally" or so that they can "fit in better" with their age peers. This can be a dismal failure or even traumatic—an experience in which the child's perception of herself as some kind of hopeless misfit is only reinforced and her social skills further eroded rather than enhanced. It is usually more productive to invest that energy in ensuring that the child's learning needs are well met and that she has opportunities for high-level engagement in areas of interest and strength. Consider the following email exchange.

Developing Social Skills

Parent

Our son Ahmed is eight years old. Are you aware of any resource groups or programs to help gifted children deal with social skills issues? Any ideas would be appreciated. Thanks.

Our Response

To be honest, one should be leery of social skills training programs which may focus on "niceness" by trying to fit wonderfully individualistic square pegs into conventionally round

---

uncomfortable holes where children may come to think that there is something wrong with them. Our recommendation is to ask these questions: "Does Ahmed experience social skills as a problem area? Whose problem is this?"

When children have trouble getting along in social circumstances, sometimes it is because they need extra help figuring out the rules of social interactions, just like some kids need extra help learning to read. For these children, a well-run social skills group can be beneficial.

If, however, the problem is about a parent or teachers' notions of Ahmed's need to have (more) friends, it might be because his age peers do not understand or share interests with him, and this is not something that will be rectified by social skills training. It may instead be resolved over time or with opportunities to engage with intellectual peers. If it is about Ahmed's own desire to make and have friends, well, there might be something gained by participation in such a group, as long as there is a good personality fit with the group leader, and as long as the group leader respects and values your son's individuality (which is not always the case).

If Ahmed seems satisfied with his social situation, then social skills groups can cause more discomfort for him than he's already experiencing, and they can be seriously counterproductive.

There are many strategies for building social skills that you can use at home. Here are a few ideas to help make Ahmed's social experiences more positive and reaffirming:

1. Consider his social preferences and tendencies (some children do not need or want more than one friend).

2. If he has no friends at all, help him find one person with whom to share a common interest. It doesn't matter how old, how young, or how unlikely that person is. It could be his grandfather, the librarian, or the younger next door neighbor.

3. Assure him that feelings of differentness are often a function of age and school program and will probably improve over time.

4. Reinforce positive social behavior whenever you see it. Be sure to do this privately, however, as it is essential not to embarrass him publicly.

5. Look for ways to increase his self-confidence in social situations in and out of school by helping him find promising opportunities for successful interactions. Look for clubs or interest groups in which he has some interest or expertise to share and that will engage him intellectually.

6. Encourage him to participate in extracurricular activities, cooperative play and learning, and shared activities within the community.

These suggestions are good for children who are very smart and have trouble fitting in. In situations in which children have more serious social skills deficits, such as Asperger's Syndrome and Nonverbal Learning Disabilities, other approaches may be required.[8]

Self-Concept

"When they told me I was gifted, I felt sort of funny. I don't know why."
"I've had people tell me I'm too smart for my own good. What's that supposed to mean?"

> *Contrary to stereotypes, gifted students are not socially isolated misfits. Their social self-concept is similar to that of their peers.... Attempts to enhance self-concept will require examining an individual's communication with significant others, comparisons with reference groups, experiences of success, and perceived ability across various domains.[9]*

A person's sense of self is constructed in an ongoing and complex process.[10] It emerges from a dynamic interaction of:

- the perceived opinions of others

- available support mechanisms
- personal history
- developmental maturity

How we feel about ourselves greatly influences how we approach people and situations in our lives. Those who feel confident about their competence are more likely to experience successes than those with troubling self-doubts.[11]

As with intelligence, there is considerable evidence demonstrating that self-concept is at least somewhat domain-specific—that people generally see themselves as competent in some areas but not as competent in others. Children have different levels of self-concept in the academic, social, behavioral, appearance, and athletic dimensions of their lives, all of which come together in different weights to inform their global self-concept.[12] Global self-concept, which reflects the level of self-concept in the dimensions that are most valued by the individual, is the most important predictor of emotional well-being. This is very much affected by a person's age and developmental history. For example, early adolescent girls tend to care most about the social and appearance dimensions of their lives. This means that, in general, if a girl between the ages of 11 and 14 feels good about her social life and her appearance, she is likely to feel pretty good about herself. If she doesn't feel competent in those areas, it is usually harder for her to achieve a healthy and strong global self-concept.

Although there is considerable research on giftedness and self-concept, the results are not consistent.[13] Some studies demonstrate that gifted learners are at serious risk for low self-esteem, to the point of being vulnerable to depression and suicide; others show that high-ability learners feel better about themselves than others and are at higher risk for an inflated sense of their own worth than for low self-esteem.[14] A synthesis of the research on social/emotional development and giftedness suggests that, generally, gifted learners are no more or less likely than others to experience problems with self-concept and other social/emotional dimensions.[15]

However, giftedness can be both a *risk* factor and a *resiliency* factor when it comes to self-concept. Children are at risk of self-esteem problems because of their exceptionality from the norm—their differentness from others. Being exceptional increases the likelihood of feeling isolated, as well as being rejected by peers because of that difference. This can have a negative impact on a person's social self-concept. In addition, academic self-esteem may be reduced when a child goes into a full-time gifted program; in the new program, when comparing himself with others who do just as well as or better than he does academically, a child who was previously the best student in his class can feel a lot less capable and become unsure about his intellectual ability. At the same time, however, giftedness often generates respect and positive behaviors from others, conferring advantages and heightened self-respect. Giftedness is also associated with higher academic self-concept, particularly for children who are not in full-time gifted programs.[16]

How these various possibilities play out depends on individual circumstances and situations, as well as on the social and other supports that are in place to help a child adjust and figure herself out. We provide several suggestions throughout this chapter for parents and educators who want to support resiliency and positive self-concept in the children in their lives.

Perspective and Attitude

It is a psychological truism that what matters in our lives is not so much what happens as the way we *experience* what happens. What are some of the perspectives and attitudes that can cause problems for gifted learners?

Fear of Failure

> *"There's no way I'm going to enter that Math Olympiad. What*
> *for? Just because I'm good in math? I'll have to work myself*
> *to death, and I won't win anyhow."*
> *"I don't need to study. Only nerds study."*

Somewhat paradoxically, high-ability learners who experience consistent successes can develop a fear of failure. It is human nature to fear the unknown, and people who never learn how to recover from failure come to fear it. Conversely, those who've fallen flat on their faces several times and who've had the support and resources to pick themselves right up again discover that they can not only recover from failure, they usually learn something, too.[17]

You know that a child is becoming afraid of failure if he doesn't want to try new activities or if he stops looking for challenges and selects only safe tasks that will lead to easy victories and successes. Children who opt out of challenging opportunities and competitions are showing signs of developing a fear of failure. If not remedied, this fear can be debilitating. Although this kind of attitude can nevertheless result in a child being able to achieve strong academic grades for many years, it minimizes real learning and reduces the likelihood of subsequent successes at higher academic and professional levels.[18]

A key to high competence in any area is purposeful and meaningful engagement over time in that area, with an understanding that risks, explorations, and failures are essential to the learning process. Children who purposefully tackle challenges and who welcome setbacks as learning opportunities can achieve successes that those who are afraid to fail cannot.

Fear of Success

> *"Once I get the basics of something, I move on to something else. I enjoy a new challenge."*
>
> *"He does his homework so beautifully, and then he forgets it or loses it or doesn't hand it in. It's almost like he's afraid to excel."*

Doing well leads to ever-increasing expectations from others and (often worse) from oneself, perhaps even to ridiculously high or unachievable expectations. Sometimes it feels easier to just not try. Not infrequently, highly able learners pre-empt their own possibilities of success, for example, by not submitting their work, not studying for a test, investing little effort in a project, or not applying for an award that they might win.

Although fear of success might appear to be the other end of the spectrum from fear of failure, it is actually oddly similar. Successful experiences can lead an individual to doubt that she's actually merited the achievements with which she's been credited, or whether she will be able to achieve at that level in the future (sometimes called "the imposter syndrome"). In cases like these, success can be more anxiety-provoking than average achievement so that, over time, people develop a fear of doing very well that is just as debilitating as the fear of failure.

A fear of success usually shows itself in self-sabotage. This can be in the form of procrastination, pessimism, forgetting essential tools or deadlines, or laziness. At its root, it is usually an unconscious fear of future possible changes. Parents and educators who are worried about a child's fear of success can encourage his healthy self-awareness and self-acceptance so that unconscious barriers and defense mechanisms do not impede his optimal functioning. Sometimes fear of success (as with fear of failure) becomes so debilitating as to require professional help, a topic we address in Chapter 11 in connection with other parenting matters.

Perfectionism

> *"Sylvie always has to get a 100 on every assignment. Last week, she got 98% on a test and asked if she could retake it!"*
> *"How can we foster growth and high expectations without it leading to anxiety or perfectionism?"*

There is no empirical evidence that the incidence of perfectionism is greater among gifted individuals. To be precise, there is no evidence supporting the psychological construct of perfectionism as currently conceptualized as a characteristic of gifted individuals....[19]

The desire to get things right and to do them well is conducive to high achievement. Some children, however, establish unrealistically high standards for themselves and become anxious, dissatisfied, and discouraged when they don't meet them. As with all dimensions of physical, cognitive, and emotional well-being, the objective for children who have perfectionistic tendencies should be to find a healthy balance in which there is enough challenge that there is growth, but without undue and debilitating stress.

Perfectionism is associated with an emphasis on order, precision, and perseverance, all of which are also associated with healthy achievement motivation. When there is an overemphasis on these tendencies, however, or when individuals focus too hard on their deficiencies or even on their strengths, it can become problematic or counterproductive.[20] Some high-achieving students are vulnerable to perfection-driven underachievement (for example, not completing or turning in assignments unless perfect) or emotional turmoil (such as feelings of worthlessness when they cannot meet unrealistic expectations). However, for the most part, gifted learners exhibit healthy levels of perfectionism, marked by high personal standards and organization.[21]

Perfectionists tend to overwork, invent excuses if they cannot accomplish what they set out to do, and feel tremendous pressure to succeed. To address these tendencies, parents and teachers can help children understand that their worth is not dependent on their achievement, and criticism need not be devastating; it can, in fact, be productive. Adults can assist with goal-setting, monitoring, and matching timeframes to the scope of tasks. They can also help children to examine the lives of eminent people,[22] looking at the obstacles, setbacks, and accomplishments of others —recognizing that achieving at a high level is not easy, even for individuals who are held in very high regard.

Sometimes highly able students who exhibit signs of perfectionism simply need extra reassurance and encouragement, including friendly, clear delineations of realistic expectations, in addition to consistent and supportive modeling about when to say, "This is good enough for now; it's time to stop and let it go." Other times, however, perfectionism can be a sign of deeper problems requiring professional attention. When the suggestions we provide here (both in connection with perfectionism and throughout the book) are not enough, it is time to seek professional help.

Arrogance

> "*Everyone* knows that Mesopotamia was the cradle of civilization."
> "That question was too hard. Nobody could get it right. Or maybe you didn't ask it right."
> "Mrs. Bell, I know that 'success' has two c's. You wrote it on the blackboard with one."

One of the stereotypes about gifted learners is that they are intellectually arrogant—that they think they are smarter (and, by implication, better) than others. Neither research on gifted development nor our clinical experience supports this position. In fact, it is quite the reverse; many children who are annoyingly superior in their manner have serious self-doubts underlying their apparently inflated self-regard.

Rather than thinking that they are better than others, some exceptionally capable learners are actually afraid that they are not as smart as others might think, or they feel that they are valued only when they are clever, and therefore, they need to constantly prove how smart they are.

Such children usually have trouble admitting that they are wrong, and they are embarrassed when they cannot understand something quickly. This embarrassment may be masked by blaming someone or something else or by anger, impatience, or annoyance, all of which look and feel like arrogance to the recipient. In situations like this, it is particularly important that the child feel respected. She should be helped to learn how to welcome failures and mistakes as opportunities for learning and to see them as something that everyone experiences.[23]

There is another very different reason for apparent arrogance. It is that children who are passionate about learning and want to know everything may assume that other people (including classmates, siblings, parents, and teachers) also want to be made aware of their personal errors. Such children are particularly likely to get into trouble with peers who are not receptive to having their mistakes pointed out to them, as well as with teachers who have control or self-esteem issues of their own. Arrogance here lies in the other person's perception, of course, rather than in the child's attitudes or perceptions; the child does not see himself as superior but rather is making the possibly erroneous assumption that the other person is as hungry for knowledge as he is. At the same time, this kind of child does need to learn something about social skills. He has to understand that people do not always appreciate having their errors identified.

Similarly, impatience can sometimes get the better of a child when certain tasks come easily to her but when other people take a long time to complete them or find the work difficult. This impatience can also translate into what appears to be arrogance. Learning to be more accommodating of others can be a challenge, but eventually, most children do learn it and manage to get along better as a result.

Excessive Computer Time

> *"If only people would get it! I can work as fast as I like on my laptop, and I can choose whatever connections I want without any hassle."*
>
> *"I've been called a 'geek' and a 'brainer.' Yes, I enjoy working on the computer, but I like doing other stuff, too, you know."*

One stereotype we encounter is that of the nerd who is hopeless at social skills and spends a lot of time peering at a computer screen. Not having any friends can be a problem, but spending a lot of time on a computer is not necessarily a problem. Whether or not it ought to be of concern depends on the context and the balance.[24] A key question is, "What else is going on in the child's life?"

For some children, the Internet and e-friendships provide opportunities for positive social interactions that they would not otherwise have. These relationships can be good ways for these young people to learn enough about relating to others that they become interested in applying their knowledge to real human contact. In such cases, virtual experiences are productive, and the amount of time spent on a computer keyboard is a good investment in healthy, long-term development. In a situation like this, parents and educators can ease up on their concerns about computer time. (They should, of course, pay attention to which websites and chat rooms are being visited.)

Sometimes, however, children retreat farther and farther into a virtual world. By consistently choosing electronically mediated interactions over real-world social activities, they can become increasingly isolated and less comfortable interacting with real people. For such children, it is essential to think about ways to intervene. A good starting point is to find a social activity that uses the child's interests and strengths—an activity that: (1) is intrinsically motivating for the child, (2) provides opportunities for success, and (3) requires at least an element of human interaction. For example, a young person could join a computer club, or work collaboratively on a team that is building software, or act as a computer trouble-shooter or mentor. Although each of these suggestions requires the individual to spend more time in front of a computer screen rather than less, such activities can also act as the thin edge of a wedge that opens the child to positive social experiences that lead over time to increased real-world social engagement.

As with other potential concerns, it is important that adults do not overreact to the heavy use of computers, that they consider computer-related activities in the context of what else is occurring in a child's life, and that they ask themselves how these activities are meeting the child's needs. If the problems obviously outweigh the advantages for a particular child's development, the adult can consider how to use the attraction to computers to motivate the child toward healthier activities, remembering that those who are online with others are at least putting themselves into a quasi-social situation, which, with patience and appropriate support, can often be channeled productively. As with the other social/emotional concerns that we address here, however, excessive computer use can also signal more serious problems that require professional help.

Suicide

There is no compelling evidence that being gifted places a student at risk for suicidal ideation, gestures, attempts or completions.... Claims in the literature are speculative at best.[25]

Suicide rates in children and adolescents have been climbing alarmingly over the past two decades.[26] While giftedness certainly can bring emotional risk factors, there is no reason to expect suicide more frequently among gifted learners.[27] There is some controversy in the field about this, but at this time, there is no research evidence that giftedness is itself a risk factor for suicide among children and adolescents. We should be concerned about the social and emotional health of all children, including those with exceptionally advanced cognitive abilities.

Risk factors associated with suicide that are independent of giftedness include "psychiatric disorders such as depression and anxiety, drug and alcohol abuse, family loss or disruption, being a friend or family member of a suicide victim, homosexuality, rapid sociocultural change, media emphasis on suicide, impulsiveness or aggressiveness, and ready access to lethal methods."[28] There are some basic strategies that schools can implement to lower the risk of suicide (again, irrespective of the cognitive competence of students). These include promoting positive social relationships; creating a school environment where students feel safe talking about their problems, as well as their hopes and dreams; and providing opportunities for children to develop their strengths, interests, and abilities. For families grappling with suicide concerns, the most potent resiliency factor is a network of social support.[29] "Communication and intervention by schools, parents, and friends thus seem the keys to preventing the loss of life to suicide.... In the end, the old standbys of communication, care, and involvement are the foundational principles."[30]

Other Behavioral Concerns

"I'm fed up with all of the disciplinary problems in my daughter's class. Some of the kids are off the wall!"
"Rafe has been the class clown since he started school. He gets bored quickly and loves to make things happen."

Adults who encounter badly behaving children usually begin by wondering what is wrong with the child, even going so far as to look for some kind of pathology. However, when thinking about behavior issues and giftedness, it is important to distinguish real behavior problems or conduct disorders from high-spirited attempts to make school more interesting and relevant. Many creative, well-adjusted, and intelligent students are charged with the former when actually engaged in the latter, seen most prototypically in the class clown.[31] Teachers who are inflexible in their attitudes are more likely to be troubled by this kind of activity. It is sometimes the teacher who should be identified as needing assistance with classroom management strategies, developing programming that is suitable, facilitating well-planned groupings, and setting parameters and consequences, rather than the child, although the child may also need to learn to appreciate the teacher's point of view.

However, there are children who exhibit serious behavioral problems of one kind or another, and these should not be dismissed. Sometimes there are circumstances that are beyond a parent's control and require professional attention, but in other situations, there are elements of the environment that exacerbate or even foster bad behavior—elements that can be changed. When a child's learning demands do not match his developmental level, for example, we can expect him to be bored, frustrated, and unhappy, and perhaps to misbehave—a situation that can lead to a misdiagnosis of attention or conduct disorder problems.[32] Learning problems can also contribute to negative behavioral patterns and should be investigated by adults who are trying to understand the causes of a child's misbehavior.[33]

A child having difficulty adjusting to special programs, peer groups, or increased academic demands may exhibit inappropriate behavior in class. This might involve, for example, incessant calling out or disobeying classroom rules. An additional complication is that kids with behavioral problems are not usually tolerated by their peers for very long, especially if they repeatedly disrupt classroom activities or compromise their class-mates' learning. When badly behaved children are ostracized, it tends to increase both their emotional and their behavioral problems.

Behavior problems can become aggressive and serious, such as when a child hurts or intimidates peers or causes property loss or damage. Conduct that is persistently disruptive and aggressive can indicate serious underlying problems. When a child is violating the basic rights of others, breaking fundamental rules, or ignoring major age-appropriate societal norms, it is time to seek professional help.

Parents and teachers who are sensitive and responsive to social and behavioral problems can minimize the likelihood that such problems will escalate. As we outline later in this chapter, there are many strategies that can be implemented preventatively and proactively, ranging from listening attentively to a child's concerns to acquiring professional assessment and support. When an intervention is required, success depends on collaborative efforts by parents, teachers, and the child her-self—and of course, time, patience, and commitment.

Bullying, Anger, and Conflict Resolution

> *"Being bullied really traumatized her."*
>
> *"Ryan was suspended yesterday for kicking a classmate. The other kid had been ridiculing him all year, and the teacher refused to do anything about it, so he had to do something to put an end to it."*
>
> *"I'm not sure why exactly, but Lateesha seems to get picked on an awful lot."*

People disagree all the time. They often see and value things differ-ently, and they have different expectations, ideas, manners, and mores. Conflicts occur as a result of our differences and are, in fact, a natural part of life. Children need to learn how to prevent and handle conflict, including managing their feelings of anger and annoyance, learning to respect and understand others' feelings and views, and thinking about how to attack problems, not people.

Aggression

The term "aggression" refers not only to physical attacks on others, but also to verbal attacks, including gossip, ridicule, slander, harassment, and personal insults. Boys and girls tend to handle their negative feelings differently. Whereas boys are more prone to externalize their difficult feelings and be physical in their attempts to deal with anger, impatience, frustration, disappointment, embarrassment, and sadness, girls are more likely to internalize their feelings and become depressed and withdrawn or verbally or indirectly aggressive.[34]

Whenever bullying or victimization shows up, it is a warning signal that children do not feel safe, and this must first be addressed at both school and family levels. Parents and educators can do a lot to prevent bullying and to minimize its impact.[35] Safe environments are inclusive and respectful of diversity. People in healthy, nurturing environments feel that their strengths are recognized and that they are valued for who they are. When children are being bullied because they are different than others, they need our protection, and the best protection we can give is to work to change the culture of the environment in which the bullying is taking place. It is important that everyone knows that there is no tolerance for mocking, insulting, or mistreating people.

We have worked with children who have been labeled by adults as aggressive, as a chronic victim, and as both bully and victim in different circumstances or at different stages, and we have observed interesting patterns of adult behavior that can unwittingly sustain the antisocial behavior that they are complaining about. We understand why adults might take a morally superior tone of righteous indignation when they confront what they interpret as aggressive behavior, as well as a tone of caring, protective empathy for those they perceive as victims. However, neither of these attitudes is likely to yield the best possible outcomes for the children in question. For example, those who are chronic victims are sometimes unjustly victimized because of their differences from others, but sometimes they are really good manipulators who have learned that they will get attention if they appear to be vulnerable and poorly treated. It is important to know the difference and not to become complicit in reinforcing unhealthy social patterns.

Bullies and Victims

There is a complex connection between bullying and victimhood. What appears to be bullying behavior is very often the so-called bully's response to real or perceived earlier victimization, reflecting a choice now to be the winner instead of the whiner. There are many variations of this. For example, an independent, sensitive, and intelligent child feels that he is being bullied by another child, when in reality he has taken another person's actions or words too personally or misinterpreted their intent. Perhaps a classmate has said something in jest, and the child has perceived this as aggressive or hurtful. This seems to him to justify a defensive but aggressive reaction on his part (which others see as bullying), because the only other alternatives that he can identify are sadness and victimization, and he does not want to give that kind of winning power to others. Threats, blame, bossiness, or antagonistic or aggressive behavior can be used defensively, even though they may appear to be bullying.

Getting past the destructive and downward-spiraling aspects of circumstances like this—on both the giving and receiving end of aggressive behavior—means that the child must learn to feel safe. She must be protected by a secure environment and come to recognize that she has the necessary resources to make herself safe without resorting to aggressive or submissive behavior. The next step is for the child to learn to reinterpret the actions and words of others. This involves looking for what is helpful, positive, or useful in what others say and do and not taking offense too quickly. Many of the recommendations made throughout this book are designed to help children develop a sense of security and appreciate that they have some control. This can smooth the transition away from bullying and from being the victim of bullying.

Cyberbullying

"Our daughter is being harassed online just because she's smart. How can we track and deter the aggression?"

Over the past few years, cyberbullying has become an increasingly pervasive form of harassment. It involves the use of information and communication technologies such as cell phones, pagers, instant messaging devices, websites, email, blogs, and online social networks such as Facebook and MySpace as means to engage in hostile action. Bullies often cannot be traced, and because their identity is protected, there may be no tangible consequences for their actions.

This form of aggression is an easy way to be intrusive and to lash out any time of day or night. Feelings of hatred or intolerance can be harsh when expressed in this disconnected way and can inflict serious harm. Moreover, because cyberbullies can act anonymously, they can inflict greater damage than might take place face to face.[36] This is an area of complex and evolving knowledge, but nevertheless, parents and teachers must make it their business to be aware of what children are doing online, learn to be more Internet savvy themselves, and become informed about cyberbullying and its potentially devastating effects.[37]

Strategies

A child who has been involved as a bully or a victim (or both) needs to learn how his actions and reactions might be contributing to his problems. This learning is best when it happens in a nonjudgmental, unemotional way and when it is provided as exploration and education rather than as punishment. In order to encourage bullies and victims to take a positive look at others' words and actions (a crucial first step in moving past this behavior), it is imperative that they feel they are being listened to and that their words and actions are being seen in the most positive light possible. When a child has a bad social experience or behaves poorly, it should be viewed by the adults in his life as an opportunity to learn something together about how he is processing his experiences. Very often, this means reviewing the circumstances (including the environmental safety factors) and asking what else the other person might have meant by his actions or words. Could there be a possible innocent or even acceptable motivation behind them? If not, then it becomes a matter of learning how to recognize what those actions and words mean in the broader scheme of things and how to be tolerant.[38]

Children can be encouraged to think constructively for themselves by taking the following steps:

- Focus thoughtfully on the various aspects of the problem.

- Try to separate the key issue(s) from the personalities involved.

- Keep an open mind, being respectful of others and tolerant of diversity.

- Take responsibility for their own actions.

It is obviously helpful if one or more of the adults in a child's life models these attitudes. Moreover, children can be supported in developing a new set of habits that gets them out of the bully/victim/aggression loop. Whether the child's problems have been as a victim or a bully or both, parents and teachers can help her maintain dignity and build positive relationships. A strategic approach might involve encouraging the child to recognize when she is making a negative attribution of another's actions or words and to refrain from responding immediately. For example, she could take a deep breath or count to three before saying anything, and then move that up to two deep breaths or counting to 10, and so on. She could also ask herself if there is an innocent or reasonable motivation underlying the other person's behavior. Adults can suggest that she think of whether there might possibly be good intentions rather than bad ones, as well as how she would respond if the intentions were friendly instead of aggressive.

Children begin to feel good about themselves as they implement this reflective and positive pattern. They enjoy surprising their peers, parents, and teachers by their more mature actions and their reactions. The learning process is even more effective if the conflict resolution skills are developed and practiced on a wider scale, as the following vignette illustrates.

A Justice League for Children

From his youngest days, Jack's parents noticed in him an intense concern for issues of justice and fair play. Jack felt things very deeply when he perceived an injustice, either against himself or against others who might have trouble defending themselves. Partway through fourth grade, Jack was given a three-day suspension from school because he used physical means to defend himself against a teacher he thought had intervened unfairly and aggressively. Jack felt that the teacher had not listened to his point of view and had used undue force against him.

Jack decided to take advantage of his suspension by inventing what he called a Justice League for Children. He designed this as a school grievance court to ensure that children got a fair hearing from a panel of their peers and a teacher, should there be similar cases in the future in which a teacher and student disagreed about something or in which two students had a serious disagreement and wanted to be heard. His mother helped him write a manifesto for the Justice League for Children, and when he got back to school, he set up a meeting with his teacher to discuss it.

Jack's teacher was impressed at Jack's preparation and idea. After the meeting, she announced in class that there would be a lunchtime meeting to discuss forming a Justice League for Children.

She said that Jack had a very good idea and that it was an opportunity for the fourth-grade class to take some leadership in the K-6 school. Over the next few days, Jack's teacher made time in class for Jack and a few of his classmates to work together to figure out the details and write a serious proposal to present to the principal.

The group of five fourth graders who worked on the proposal met with the principal, who loved the idea, and before long, Jack and his team were going into each of the classrooms in the school to discuss their concept.

Simultaneously, Jack's parents were working with him (with the help of a counselor) to help him learn some better anger management and conflict resolution skills. By the end of the school year, Jack was feeling much happier about himself. The teacher reported that the school had benefited in all kinds of unexpected ways by Jack's proposal and that many parents had observed some subtle and not-so-subtle changes in school culture, as people (including the primary children!) were talking more openly about how to solve problems together. By the end of fifth grade, Jack was perceived as a leader and was looked up to by many of the other students in the school. Children across all of the grades often went to him when they had problems that needed solving, and he willingly shared ideas to help them learn how to resolve matters themselves.

With some help from his parents, teacher, classmates, and principal, Jack had converted what started out as a terrible situation into an opportunity for learning and growth.

We have seen other circumstances in which a school climate became friendlier and fairer because one family responded creatively and thoughtfully to ensure a healthy, school-wide approach to conflict resolution. Interestingly, when these kinds of situations are addressed constructively, students like Jack who have had problems with aggression often become much better than others at resolving situations collaboratively and productively.[39]

Solutions: Emotional Intelligence

> *"I'd like to be in the 'cool kid zone,' but I just haven't found the way to be cool."*
>
> *"Most of my students are happy and productive, but I have a few who are very intense and won't mix, and a couple who are loud and bossy and don't get along with anyone."*

Several years ago, Daniel Goleman wrote a bestseller called *Emotional Intelligence*[40] that provided a foundation for understanding problems that people can face in their emotional lives. In this book, he discussed how cognitive and emotional intelligences affect each other, and he described how emotional competence in different areas (for example, self-motivation, mood regulation, and hope) can be learned. Goleman described windows of opportunity when certain emotional skills and habits can be more readily taught or encouraged. He also reviewed emotional literacy programs. These predominantly school-based programs consist of curricular and extracurricular activities designed around children's and adolescents' experiential issues so as to help them acquire and consolidate emotional competence in a number of different areas. Since then, the focus on emotional intelligence has mushroomed, and today there is considerable evidence that programming that enhances emotional functioning can help students understand and manage their feelings about issues such as adjusting to a new label, classroom setting, or peer group.[41]

An emotional literacy program can be used to support children in thinking about the gifted identification experience, how they feel about social difficulties in the schoolyard, or uncertainties that they have about their ability to meet academic expectations. Within a mixed-ability classroom, teachers can design emotional literacy experiences that foster increased understanding and social interaction among diverse kinds of learners. A discussion or role play about a hypothetical collaborative learning activity whereby everyone contributes something personally relevant can be helpful.[42] Other promising suggestions include a focus on the arts[43] and fostering self-understanding through biography.[44]

The roles of curiosity, persistence, and motivation in high-level development are increasingly being emphasized from a variety of standpoints, including Dabrowski's work on positive disintegration,[45] Subotnik's work in talent development,[46] Dweck's work with mindsets,[47] and Ericsson's work on expertise,[48] among many others. We discussed the role of these factors in Chapter 8.

At a time when social support networks are fragmenting, people's sense of security is threatened, economic stability is compromised, and rapid change is a too-constant companion, it is more important than ever that adults support and reinforce the development of children's emotional intelligence. There is much at stake, including children's abilities to relate to others, to cope with uncertainties and insecurities, and to make wise decisions in their lives.

Well-Being, Benevolence, Wisdom, and Leadership

> *The hope for the future lies in the global recognition that as individuals we are not just developing from dependence to independence—we are also growing to appreciate that we are interdependent in a global community, with responsibilities to the community, and, consequently, rights earned within the community.*[49]

> *In addition to talented performance and achievement, the ultimate goal of learning should be self-cultivation and self-transformation to attain* <u>ren</u> *(benevolence).*[50]

There is an increasing focus in gifted education on the importance of social and emotional intelligence. This is taking many interconnected forms, including an emphasis on wisdom;[51] community involvement, connection, outreach, and service;[52] social context;[53] psychosocial strength training;[54] and social/emotional development.[55]

Somewhat counter-intuitively perhaps, leadership activities can be particularly important for those with emotional, social, or behavioral concerns. Sometimes (as we discussed in connection with computer use, for example) concerns in these areas emanate from a child's advanced understandings that are not well-matched by available relationship opportunities or activities, and once a young person finds a good fit, he blossoms. When well-chosen to match an individual's abilities, leadership activities can provide authentic outlets for children and adolescents to apply their abilities, affirm their competence, develop a sense of responsibility, enjoy contributing to the greater good, and learn to behave in socially acceptable ways, all of which enhance their self-esteem.

There are many opportunities for personally rewarding and socially beneficial leadership activities and community service. Such activities can:

- provide ways to put an individual's competencies to practical use
- allow children to test and further develop their skills
- offer a chance for them to acquire leadership experience
- enable them to experience a sense of responsibility and fulfillment
- foster productive and meaningful interactions with others
- provide preparation for future work endeavors
- help with the career selection process
- lead to references and networks that may prove important later on

There is usually more social support and understanding for the "disadvantaged different" child than for the so-called "over-advantaged" child, but the inner reality can be similar: differentness and rejection don't feel good. Parents and teachers should watch for these feelings and respond to them with understanding and acceptance. Counseling about the normalness of those feelings under the circumstances, and the likelihood that they will change as a child moves forward in her education and life, can also be beneficial. At the same time, parents and teachers should help high-ability learners to understand that everyone has variable strengths and weaknesses and that, in fact, others are more like them than they are different.

Parents and educators who work together are in a much stronger position to help children become more emotionally knowledgeable and secure, as well as more socially responsible, competent, and caring. An attitude of nurturing the whole person as a unique, valued, and valuable individual is essential. And it should be combined with sound instructional methods that help children to acquire an understanding of themselves and others, relationship-building, and ways to manage their feelings and behaviors.

With all of this in mind, we offer parents and teachers the following suggestions for supporting children's emotional health and their social/behavioral competence:

1. Consider the whole person. Remember that a label is an arbitrary and artificial category, but the child or adolescent is a unique individual whose sense of self is affected by many different interacting factors.

2. Learn to be a good listener. Work toward positive, open, and engaged communication so that the child feels respected, safe, and secure and has someone to trust and in whom to confide. This means listening carefully to what the child says without interruption or judgment, and it also means keeping it confidential as requested.

3. Be tolerant, patient, and flexible, remembering that the child or student (like the rest of us) is doing the best he can to be the best he can be.

4. Encourage positive interaction between home and school.

5. Model and foster a growth mindset.

6. Encourage and model personal resilience.

7. Be available. Make your relationship a priority.

8. Try to reduce sources of anxiety in the family, in the classroom, and in the child's life. Consider the causes, nature, intensity, and duration of any current stressors. Work together to minimize or eliminate those that impede healthy functioning.

9. Understand that it is healthy and normal to experience failures and setbacks in one area or another of development. Generally, such experiences need not be damaging to a child's sense of self and emotional well-being if understood and mediated by a trusted adult.

10. Regularly send positive messages that affirm the child's ability to learn and succeed at school and beyond. Tell the child what you appreciate about her. Encouragement, attentiveness, responsivity, and guidance are fundamental to optimal development and should not be compromised by the demands of daily life.

11. Remember that some situations require professional help and that there are people who have the necessary training and expertise to assist with more serious problems.

Ways to Love a Child

Finally, we would like to close this chapter with the following advice, which arrived in the mail from the Kids Help Foundation without author attribution (unfortunately, because we would very much like to acknowledge the writer):

Give your presence. Laugh, dance, and sing together. Listen from a heart space. Encourage. Understand. Allow them to love themselves. Ask their opinions. Learn from them. Say yes as often as possible. Say no when necessary. Honor their no's. Apologize. Touch gently. Build lots of blanket forts. Open up. Fly kites together. Lighten up. Believe in possibilities. Read books out loud. Create a circle of quiet. Teach feelings. Share your dreams. Walk in the rain. Celebrate mistakes. Admit yours. Frame their artwork. Stay up late together. Eliminate comparison. Delight in silliness. Handle with care. Protect them. Cherish their innocence. Giggle. Speak kindly. Go swimming. Splash. Let them help. Let them cry. Don't hide your tears. Brag about them. Answer their questions. Let them go when it's time. Let them come back. Show compassion. Bend down to talk to little children. Smile even when you're tired. Surprise them with a special lunch. Don't judge their friends. Give them enough room to make decisions. Love all that they do. Honor their differences. Respect them. Remember they have not been on earth very long.

We invite you to consider making additions of your own to this list.

Section V

Being Smart about Families, Advocates, and Educators

Chapter 11

Parenting Matters

> More than 80 years of research and experience
> demonstrate that the education of any child is made
> more effective by sustaining and increasing the role
> of parents at home and in partnership with the
> schools. Because high ability children require
> academic interventions, parents and teachers must
> work together each year of the child's school life.[1]

Making Decisions about Programming, Placement, and Change

"My son's school just doesn't know what to do with him. What do you suggest?"

It is an unfortunate but predictable reality that education systems designed to meet the learning needs of most children are often less effective in meeting the needs of those who are exceptional. Even the most highly competent educators do not always have the knowledge or support that they need to work effectively with gifted learners, including checking their progress on an ongoing basis.[2] This means that parents have an important role as advocates for their children, and they must remain flexibly open to changing needs in both cognitive and emotional areas.[3]

Most parents prefer to make decisions that work for several years, rather than having to revisit them on a regular basis. With planning, flexibility, and good luck, it sometimes happens that one schooling approach will work well for several years, but sometimes this is not possible. In general, it is wise for parents (as with educators) to approach decision making for exceptional learners as an ongoing work in progress.

Before altering or challenging a current situation, however, it makes sense to address the following questions:

- Why is change needed?

- What are the advantages and disadvantages of each of the educational options under consideration (including those of maintaining the current situation)?

- If changes are made, how will the process be supported by the parents and the school administration?

Some factors to consider when analyzing the options available are short-term and long-term goals, assessment issues, social/emotional concerns, extracurricular interests, and the anticipated fit between the individual and any proposed changes. Many other factors, too, relate to a family's particular circumstances, including health, finances, travel schedules, and parents' work schedules.

A school-change decision may involve moving a child from a school where there are no gifted programming provisions to another school where a better learning opportunity exists, but where travel to and from school means that the child will not be able to play the sports that he loves. It may mean moving a child from an environment where she has lots of good friends, but that offers no targeted programming, to one where she worries about not knowing anyone. It may involve transferring a child from a good-enough learning situation to one that appears to be better but has unknown elements or perhaps financial ramifications. Parents may be considering homeschooling but are concerned about the time demands for themselves and the social dimension for their child. Or if they are looking for a mentorship, there will be decisions to make about structuring that relationship.

Change takes many forms. It can be comfortable and smooth, or it can be a bit rocky.

Change-Related Considerations

> *"We want her to stay with her age group, but she is pretty far ahead of her classmates in most subjects, and her mind never seems to take a break. And now she has started telling us that she feels different from other kids. How do we strike a balance?"*

Being smart about educational change means staying attuned to children's learning needs and well-being, as well as providing the necessary supports, charting their educational courses, and helping them adapt well to the changes. It is of utmost importance that parents remain available to respond to their children's questions and allay their concerns so that school-related choices and changes are as positive and affirming as possible.

Children's attitudes and adjustments to change, whether at school or at home, with peers or with siblings, vary from one person or situation to the next. Although parents are the first line of support, there are many other possible sources of support too, both for parents and for their children, including extended family members,[4] teachers, neighbors, community members, faith-based contacts, classmates, and friends.

Understanding and talking about change from a mastery perspective involves emphasizing the naturalness of exceptional ability within the context of education and human development. Adults can demystify giftedness by focusing on practical matters, which include the need to find a good learner-learning match. This can help a child understand the nature of his exceptionality and accept the changes that it may bring with it.

Helping Children Adapt to Change

> *"We're thinking about changing schools, but I know Jenna will have a really hard time making that adjustment. What should we do?"*

During times of change, how can adults support a child in feeling as self-confident, motivated, engaged, and content as possible? The best supports depend on the way in which the individual child experiences the particular situation. For example, a child about to begin attending a full-time gifted program might express concerns about being viewed differently or making new friends, or about the amount of work that may be required, or about finding her way around a new school. Her parents can try to learn about the specific circumstances involved in the change process, get a sense of the social milieu, familiarize themselves with the teacher's expectations for learning, and in general become as knowledgeable as possible. They can reassure their daughter that experiencing change is part of everyone's life, and they can remind her of changes that she has already successfully navigated (such as when she first entered school or began a new activity or conquered a challenge that she had worried about). They can also remind her that she demonstrated enough competence to qualify for the new program. They should remain patiently attentive throughout the change process and be ready to respond supportively as their daughter makes the change, reminding her as necessary that there is more in her life that is *not* changing than *is* changing.

Because change, by definition, upsets the status quo, it is usually controversial in one way or another. It helps if everyone involved (teachers, administrators, parents, and students) feels that they are a part of any proposed changes. Those likely to be affected by it are usually a lot more accepting if they are kept informed and given a chance for input. The best change processes include dialogue, clarification of expectations, collaboration, and regular monitoring and reflection. Although there are always people ready to criticize unfamiliar approaches, change is likely to be viewed more favorably when all participants are engaged in the process.

Talking to others going through the same kind of experience can help. Many local parent associations provide support groups, information, and opportunities for parents of exceptional learners to network with one another. Other information sources include books, journals, websites, and professionals experienced in working with gifted-related issues.[5]

Choosing a School

> *"In a large city like Toronto where there are lots of options, how*
> *does one determine which are the best ones?"*
> *"We live in a rural setting, and the only school nearby is not*
> *working out for our son."*

Mapping out a child's education means a lot more than selecting a program. It's also necessary to think about the school itself—the advantages and disadvantages, as well as the larger picture. Some families live in communities where there are many possible choices; others live in areas where there are limited options. Either way, there are schooling decisions to make.

Generally, a good choice to consider for young children is the regular classroom in a local publicly funded school. Such a placement facilitates children finding nearby friends to play with informally and casually on their own initiative. Going to the local school encourages a sense of belonging to a neighborhood, and it assists in a feeling of autonomy and mastery to be getting to school on one's own. These factors continue to be important as a child matures, and at the secondary level, extracurricular sports, drama, music, student government, and other school-based activities make proximity important as well.

Public school classrooms tend to be diverse and provide a wide spectrum of experiences of people and life. These settings encourage a child to consider and develop his own way of being in the context of lots of possibilities, with fewer predetermined boundaries than may be experienced by children in more select or exclusive circumstances. On the other hand, sometimes a student needs more challenge or a differentiated curriculum that is not available in a particular classroom. The educational matches that we envision in neighborhood schools may be ideal, but in some situations, it does not happen that way.

When a family is lucky enough to have a choice between two or more possible schools, they have to consider many factors, including proximity, affordability, after-school options, stability, and the needs of others in the family, to say nothing of the highly variable and often unpredictable needs of the learner herself. This is complicated by the fact that it is very difficult to know exactly what kind of education a given school really provides and how that might change over time; decision making can sometimes feel like a nightmare. Some parents become immobilized with worry in their deliberations over selecting schools.

When parents ask us for help with this kind of decision making, we suggest that they consider the following questions.

Looking at Teachers

- Is there support for teachers' ongoing professional development, including gifted development and learning needs such as differentiation?

- Is teachers' content mastery valued? For example, do any hold graduate degrees in their subject areas?

275

- Do teachers display intellectual curiosity? Do they welcome and implement innovative approaches?

- Do teachers focus on diagnosing and addressing children's abilities and strengths, as well as on any learning problems that need to be addressed?

- Do teachers display a sense of humor?

- Do they listen? To parents? To children? To each other?

- Do they respond promptly to children's questions and behavioral issues with patience and understanding?

Looking at Programs and Classroom Settings

- Are academic standards high?

- Are expectations clear?

- Is programming both flexible and challenging? That is, does it accommodate and support children's diverse abilities, interests, and learning preferences?

- Are students given ample opportunities to interact with intellectual peers, as well as with age peers?

- Is there an emphasis on classroom activities which encourage creative expression?

- Do problem-solving activities allow for many possible answers and lots of exploration?

- Do children have sufficient time and opportunity to muddle through problems and work them out by themselves and/or with others?

- Do teachers and students appear to be engaged and stimulated by what they are doing?

- Do teachers and students display mutual respect?

- Are there open channels of communication across grade levels and subject areas?

Looking at the Administration

- Are the priorities of the program's administrators consistent with your needs and concerns?

- Do the administrators have accepting, respectful, and appropriately nurturing attitudes and program flexibility toward high-ability and other special needs learners?

- How does the administration support teachers in becoming more knowledgeable about theories of child development, instructional methods, and course content?

- Does the administration encourage parental involvement in the school?

There are always unknown elements when choosing a school, and no facility or teacher can be expected to meet *all* of the criteria that we discuss here. However, if parents do what they can to become well-informed about the various aspects of the possible learning environments and the associated teaching professionals, the decision-making and change processes can be smoother for everyone.

Ten Things that Make an Exceptional School

In order to help parents think about school excellence, a national newsmagazine conducted a reader survey. They asked parents to nominate schools that they thought were exceptional. The magazine's editors then consulted 60 experts about the parents' selections and asked them about the most important criteria in school choice. We include here the top 10 criteria of the experts, all of which are essential when it comes to meeting gifted learning needs.[6] Parents may find this list helpful when evaluating schools.

1. High-quality classroom teachers

2. Principal's leadership skills

3. Teamwork

4. Parent communication and involvement

5. A caring, respectful, orderly, and secure school environment

6. Community involvement

7. High student expectations

8. Student engagement and leadership

9. Academic excellence

10. Excellence and innovation in non-core programs

Parents can think about the advantages that one school might have over another by considering these factors, as well as the range of academic facilities, extracurricular programs, and the way in which the system accommodates children with special learning needs. Another important variable is the "personality" of the school (the social atmosphere and the learning environment, taking into account a range of people's perceptions and observations).

Making the Decision

> *"When does school choice become more the child's decision? I know some families who seem to give far too much weight to their kids' opinions at a very young age."*
> *"I'm not sure if the decisions we make are binding or if there's a grace period. What if Emma hates the new school?"*
> *"Is there anything special we need to know for this school meeting that we've been summoned to?"*

The best educational program is one that provides learning opportunities that are appropriate to a child's mastery level and pace in a context that supports his optimal development. The objective should be to find the best-fit program on an ongoing, year-by-year basis, taking into account both the available options at that level and the child's educational, social, and emotional needs at the time.

Each programming approach and situation has its own goals, content, problems, and advantages, and academic advancement is not always the most important factor when making decisions about what's best for a given learner. Consequently, choosing the most appropriate plan at a given time for a given child can be a complex process that involves research, advocacy, and collaboration between home and school.[7] Finding the best-fit program requires flexibility from parents and teachers, often involving deciding on a combination of options and/or changing programs from time to time as circumstances dictate.

School-based team meetings, whether formal or informal, can be useful for monitoring the learning process and for working through programming decisions. In many jurisdictions, there are official processes in place for such purposes. In school-based team meetings, parents have an opportunity to consider the child's needs with the help of teachers, the principal, a school psychologist, and other consultants as needed. In some cases, the child is also included. Everyone gives input during a discussion that is structured and led by the team leader, who is usually the principal.

A meeting such as this might involve samples of the child's work being reviewed, the psychologist presenting test results, educators describing their views of the child, and parents (and possibly the child) expressing their concerns and suggestions. Such a meeting can help to identify and clarify issues and provide a multidimensional consideration of a child's educational programming needs.[8] We have learned that one of the best techniques for keeping the discussion focused and productive is to keep in mind that the real question on the table is not, "Is this child gifted?" or "Is the child eligible for the program?" but rather, "How do we create the best possible learning fit for this particular child?"

An Individual Education Plan (IEP), or a similar type of approach, can help to pave the way. An IEP typically consists of student profile information; a description of the child's needs and areas of strength based on current and appropriate assessment data; a program description including the student's current level of achievement in different domains, recommended annual program goals, and specific skills or learning expectations; special strategies and accommodations required; and recommendations for evaluating student progress.[9]

When determining how to create a learning fit, the child's opinions matter. She should feel a part of the decision-making process, but at the same time, this should be monitored wisely. A child may prefer a school simply because the playground or computer lab looks better—not a trivial reason, but probably not the highest priority in making the decision. The older the child, the more input she should have and the more her preferences should be considered, including her areas of strength and weakness, favored learning modalities, interests, and personal preferences.

Parents who feel bewildered by all of the learning options and placement possibilities available should remember to take their time when making decisions. For further insight on what the school decision-making process entails, we invite you to read about Jeane and her family's experience, described in Appendix II.

Making the Choice Work

"We've chosen a new school. Selena starts next week. I hope she'll be happy."

Once they've made a choice, how can parents help their children stay challenged, engaged, learning, and secure? We present our "A" list of strategies for parents, each with a few examples for getting started. All of them can be used at home to complement schooling situations.

Activities for Rainy (and Not So Rainy) Days

- Collect a "bag of tricks." Replenish it frequently so that it always contains fresh surprises such as books, games, discussion starters, puzzles, art supplies, writing journals, costumes and props, paints, crafts supplies, ideas for outings, experiments, and so forth, for use whenever your child feels bored, anxious, discouraged, or needs time alone.

- Read for your own pleasure and learning. Read with your child. Read to your child. Explore sports, the arts, politics, business—whatever looks interesting.

- Bring into your child's life activities and people that are as diverse as possible. This may include sharing the pleasures of visiting art galleries, libraries, bookstores, museums, concerts, and/or participating in other cultural activities.

- Take virtual vacations together, enjoying the spirit of adventure and the possibilities for learning.

Augmented Learning

- Cultivate your child's interests and areas of strength. Be creative in finding ways to use them as springboards to other learning.

- Provide guidance appropriate to your child's questions and interests. When you don't have the answer to a question, try to find it whenever possible, searching together with your child. Use various resources—a newspaper, dictionary, thesaurus, atlas, or the Internet.

- Demonstrate the value of learning in your own life. Discuss current events and ideas that you hear about. Include children in the discussion when they're interested.

Accounting

- Keep track of learning activities that your child enjoys. Take note of how he likes to learn, and share information with others who might benefit from knowing this.

- Keep a log, scrapbook, video, or written journal.

- Encourage your child to keep a record of positive learning experiences and personal accomplishments, and/or create this kind of record together with her. This type of portfolio encourages habits of self-reflection and can be good on down days, serving to motivate and boost self-confidence.

Achievement

- Set realistic expectations of success.

- Reinforce feelings of accomplishment. Look for opportunities to praise and honor authentic achievements.

- Show faith in your child's ability to do well. A child who senses that his parents have confidence in him is more likely to be self-confident and will be more motivated to take on challenges.

Autonomy

- Respect your child's need for autonomy. Kids thrive in relaxed settings where they are given a chance to explore, play, and create on their own terms, independently as well as with others.

- As much as is safely possible, respect your child's desires for independence and privacy.

- Don't work too hard to keep your child busy and engaged in activities that you think are worthwhile; let her figure out what *she* is interested in.

Attitude

- Ask questions that matter.

- Work together to find ways to overcome problems and concerns.

- Lighten up. Maintain a sense of humor. Don't be overly serious, demanding, or critical.

- Be enthusiastic about the things that you do.

- Welcome challenges and setbacks as opportunities to learn.

- Model perseverance.

- Model sensible risk-taking.

- Advocate on behalf of your child.

Advocacy: Helping Schools Meet Children's Needs

> *Five ingredients for success…passion, preparation, inspiration, perseverance, and the ability to take advantage of serendipity.*[10]

"Gifted programs are easy targets for spending cutbacks."

Advocacy is also on our "A" list of strategies for parents, and it is particularly important in the lives and education of exceptional learners. An advocate is a person who notices a problem and works to solve it, often on behalf of someone unable to advocate for him- or herself. Concerned parents, teachers, and students often find themselves in advocacy roles, especially in the face of changing educational policies, changing legislation, and funding cutbacks in many schools and jurisdictions.[11]

The Advocacy Process

> *Advocacy can be compared to bridge building…. Advocates look to the future, nurture relationships, design a new vision.*[12]

Advocacy works on many levels, from an individual parent getting his own child more appropriate educational programming to a concerned group improving the way an entire district or jurisdiction deals with gifted education. In order to be effective, advocacy requires patience, attention, and respect for all participants, including the realizations that one need not function alone and that advocates can often learn a lot from those who seem to be their adversaries. Successful advocacy can be thought of as a problem-finding and problem-solving process characterized by a commitment to actively listening to all stakeholders.

Informed parents are the best advocates for their children, and the first step in the process is information gathering—not only about what the parents consider to be a problem, but also about processes, players, relationships, goals, and commitments. There will be many questions to ask and answer. For example, what are the school's governing rules, principles, and politics? What are the costs of current programs? What are the costs of proposed changes, and how will they be funded? How and when will changes be implemented? Who will be in charge? Who will monitor the changes to see if they're working? What is the timeline? What are some possible unplanned implications of the change?

We have been involved in many types of advocacy situations, working with parents to ensure that an individual child's learning needs were well met, principals to help a school move toward better learning provisions for all students, gifted consultants to help a board move toward more inclusive giftedness policies and practices, and parent groups to address needs for system-wide changes. In all successful cases, there was at least one keen, patient, and persistent advocate who had a flexible vision of the way things could be and who was willing and able to become informed, actively listen to all stakeholders, and see the advocacy process as a long-term collaborative endeavor.

Unsuccessful or counterproductive advocacy attempts often involve an adversarial or self-righteous attitude on the part of the would-be advocate. We have observed that one of the biggest challenges for an advocate is to find a way to respect other perspectives. It is only by understanding others' points of view that one can develop one's own views in a meaningful, targeted, and sophisticated way and then communicate this persuasively. If an advocate is successful, it is often those who initially appear to be adversaries who will be in charge of implementing the changes—and who will be able to sabotage them if they disagree. Sometimes those who appear to be an advocate's enemies later turn out to be important friends. Nevertheless, we do recognize that there are some situations that cannot be rectified by advocacy, and it may be necessary for the parents to advocate in a different way, namely by finding a new educational alternative for their child.

Advocating for Your Child

"I think teachers should use different ways to assess kids' learning. But how can I actually make this happen in my son's school?"

Assume that parents, teachers, and administrators all want what is good for the children.[13]

Advocacy can take tremendous time and energy. Here are four points to think about before you get involved:

1. Become informed about gifted assessment and programming practices in your school or community.[14]

2. Learn all you can about available educational opportunities.[15]

3. Arrange onsite visits.[16]

4. Investigate alternatives.[17]

If you conclude that action is necessary, you will want to do some forward planning. A comprehensive plan is critical if a change is not going to be a jump-start to a dead-end. The following basic guidelines can help:

- Before setting out to advocate for any changes, define specific needs to be met.

- Be practical and realistic about what can be altered.

- Prioritize. You cannot change everything at once.

- Try to define a sensible timeline, fair tasks and responsibilities, and workable parameters. Then show flexibility.

- Because a school community is a complex and interdependent workplace, strive for collaboration and mutual respect. Work to maintain open communication channels among children, parents, and teachers. Aim for free-flowing dialogue.

- Remember that change is an emotion-laden process. Optimism, pessimism, anxiety, grandiosity, and confusion are some of the many feelings that can be experienced by those involved—all feelings that can interfere with people's ability to be reasonable. Try to be patient and to monitor and regulate your own emotions.

- Maintain your resolve.

Successful change depends on the interaction of many complex and dynamic variables, including the educational setting, teacher commitment, administrative support, parent-teacher collaboration, and children's ability to cope. It's best to find others with similar concerns and work together. Members of an advocacy group can broaden the circle of awareness and fine-tune perspectives and plans. As concern widens and builds, it can generate a growing momentum toward change through recognition, commitment, and compromise. By publicizing the positive aspects of the process toward change, expressing appreciation where it is due, and developing sound policies, parents and other advocates can sustain this momentum. Ultimately, action can be taken to rectify the problem or concern.

Advocates should think carefully about focus and relevance, making sure that their driving principle is to find or create a better fit between children and the schooling situation. Remember that advocacy processes and change almost always take longer than anticipated. Be patient.

Advocating for All Children

Parents have a great deal of power. They can advocate for students and the program in ways that a teacher cannot, such as talking with administrators about specific needs and concerns.[18]

Very often, a parent advocating for one child makes a bigger difference than she would ever have anticipated because the child's teacher may become better able to meet many other children's learning needs as well. If that one teacher happens to be an enthusiastic practitioner who is a leader in her school environment, and if the school culture is ready for change, there can be a dramatic shift in the way student learning needs are met throughout the school.

There are many worthwhile advocacy causes that can benefit all students.[19] Parents can advocate for increased professional development opportunities for teachers that will enable them to better recognize and address diverse needs. Parents can also help to promote a wider conception of talent development by tapping into community resources in order to build rich, multidimensional, and collaborative learning environments. Many sectors of society, including business, industry, media, professionals, and seniors, can help extend the range of learning options for children.

Parents who are involved with their children's schooling enhance the likelihood of their children's academic engagement and success. Teachers who listen to and respect parents' views can find their teaching enriched and their professional satisfaction greatly increased. Children who are involved in self-advocacy learn important skills of reflection, cooperation, negotiation, self-respect, and independence. Administrators who support positive change may find that they have a school that is better attuned to and respectful of the values of teaching for depth, breadth, and individual learning needs. When working together in a spirit of collaborative advocacy, parents, teachers, students, and administrators can create a school culture that supports high-level learning in many more students.

Supportive Parenting

"Some children are handicapped by their giftedness."
"How do I support my daughter? Once your child is labeled gifted, you're walking a different path."

A common misconception is that the best way to foster high-level development is to provide children with sophisticated learning tools, structured educational activities, and more and more lessons and schoolwork. However, as we have discussed elsewhere in this book, a busy and highly structured agenda is not always the best learning environment. One of the most important supports that parents can provide is encouragement of their children's social and emotional development, including their enthusiasm for learning. Kids are not robots. Even those who are most capable are *children* who will be happier and more successful as adults if they experience plentiful opportunities for play and exploration during childhood, and if they have easy and natural opportunities for interaction with adults who love and respect them and whom they respect and trust in turn.

Parents can fan the inner spark that motivates and sustains learning, but it must be done carefully and lovingly.[20] They should protect their children from situations in which learning becomes a heavy, stress-filled burden of relentless duty and loses all its joy. Well-intentioned parents can become frustrated and disconnected from their children and caught up in a web of failed expectations and misunderstandings, or instead, they can take the same strands of challenges, strengths, and opportunities and weave with their children a circle of trust, growth, fulfillment, and understanding.

Top Ten Strategies

These 10 strategies echo approaches that we have discussed elsewhere in this book. We bring them together here in the context of supportive parenting:

1. *Listening.* Be an active and attentive listener.

2. *Respect.* Respect your child's thoughts, feelings, ideals, interests, and goals.

3. *Perspective.* Maintain a healthy perspective on the ups and downs of daily life. A sense of humor goes a long way.

4. *Attunement.* Pay attention to the factors that might be affecting your child's emotional, social, behavioral, and/or academic functioning. Whether your child's special needs relate to temperament, gender, ethnicity, disability, or specific talents or abilities, be aware and prepared to offer support as needed.

5. *Information.* Seek information about high-level development. Pay close attention to sources that provide insight into the particular kinds of support that your child requires.

6. *Exploration.* Expose your child to a wide range of extracurricular opportunities for play, exploration, and learning in response to his individual abilities, interests, and needs.

7. *Consultation.* Consult with professionals and other parents to explore alternative learning opportunities in your child's school, within the community, and beyond.

8. *Advocacy.* Advocate for appropriate learning options that will suit your child's individual needs and levels of advancement in different areas.

9. *Cooperation.* Work with educators, other parents, and members of the community to create as rich and engaging a learning environment as possible for your child and others.

10. *Clarification.* Clarify expectations—your own, your child's, the school's, and others,' such as extended family members'. Are the various demands being placed on the child well-defined, fair, and flexible? If not, think together about ways to improve the situation.

Parents can strengthen a child's learning spirit and help sustain her drive to mastery by respecting her choices, nurturing her independence, and allowing that sometimes the most valuable learning of all is what happens serendipitously through the many experiences of daily life with friends, neighbors, classmates, and family members.

Finding Reliable Information

"I found this great website.... I just kept wandering through it.
I found an article written by a mother of gifted children,
and I was sitting there crying, going 'I know! I know!'"

Although there are many sources of information about gifted development and education, it is not always easy to distinguish thoughtful, evidence-based material from that which is inaccurate, overly simplified, or even misleading. A library or bookstore with a well-staffed education or child development department is often an ideal place to find useful resources, and school librarians, counselors, and teachers may also have helpful and relevant suggestions. In addition, there are advocacy organizations that post online lists of recommended reading material,[21] where you may also find announcements about regional or national conferences, contests, updated booklists for avid readers, and so on.

The rapid expansion of e-technology offers opportunities to contact experts in the field, which can be another great source of information and support. Articles in journals and periodicals can also provide excellent and current information.[22] You can subscribe to these different publications or find them at university libraries, or you may be able to borrow them from the education office within your school district. Many publications run pieces on a variety of gifted-related topics, such as educational programming, gender issues, developmental stages, at-risk students, school reform, and so on.

Although there are more topics of interest to parents than we could possibly mention here, one of the most controversial has to do with supportive parenting of siblings.

Sibling Relationships

One Gifted, Another Not

> *"My brother was a math whiz. When we were growing up, my parents said they couldn't afford summer camp for me, but somehow they could always afford special trips and contests and all kinds of activities for him."*
>
> *"My dad was never too busy to do stuff with me. He used to love quizzing me, and we'd have long philosophical discussions. It made me feel sort of embarrassed, though, because it was obvious that he thought I was more interesting than my sister."*
>
> *"My sister is the smart one, I guess, and I'm just average. She was identified as gifted, but when I took the gifted test, they said I didn't quite make it."*

When one child is identified as gifted and another is not, what are the implications for the family? Parents should anticipate the possibility of different reactions and responses. Jealousy, annoyance, embarrassment, sibling rivalry, and provocation can all be minimized if parents use their anticipatory antennae. They should try to ensure that all of their children feel valued, competent, and supported, and they should be prepared to act quickly at the earliest sign of trouble. Just as in families in which only one of the children is an accomplished athlete, the "ungifted" siblings often resent the implication that they are less capable. They may feel a need to prove their worth, sometimes by challenging the ability of the designated gifted one(s) in the family, and sometimes by choosing another domain of achievement for themselves. An unlabeled sibling of a child designated as gifted can feel incompetent or stupid, even though he may be highly capable himself.[23]

Some parents take academic (or athletic, or other) giftedness far too seriously and give it more weight than it deserves. Yes, it is important to recognize and address exceptionality where it occurs, but no, a child who scores above a certain IQ (or demonstrates gifted learning needs in some other way) is not more deserving of parental time and other family resources than her lower-scoring siblings. "Look for each child's unique abilities and gifts, and reinforce those strengths by stating your belief that the child is worthy and capable and that you are proud of his abilities. It is important for children's self-esteem that they feel loved, accepted, and capable, and that they believe that each child is equally valued within the family."[24] Emotional and behavioral problems can be expected when one sibling is given more recognition, special opportunities, or attention than another.

Julie Stoyka, a teacher, studied the long-term effects of gifted labeling on a set of fraternal triplets, only two of whom were identified as gifted. At the time of their independent interviews, the sisters, whom she calls April, May, and June, were 31 years old. This is an excerpt from Julie's transcript, and it includes her own reflections as well.

Triple Threat

April

I remember that May and I were told, "You are going into a special program." It was a big deal for my family. I was excited. I think I was proud—I was one of those kids who liked to do well in school. But there was a torn feeling in my family of, "Should we do it, should we not do it?" because of what it would indicate to June if we went into a gifted program and she didn't. In the end, I remember that we had to do things right—treat the individual, rather than think of ourselves as a group. So I remember it being a pretty complicated decision at my house.

May

June always reveled in being different, so she took it as a positive—like, "I'm different than you guys"—and purposely made sure that she seemed different than us and tried to make us feel that she was better than us. And she tried to find other ways to be superior in school.

June

I was the only one who wasn't smart. Now I can say that I have a more positive view of it, but it was really hard back then, especially because we all went to the same school, and we had a lot of the same friends. So I think, for me, it came up a lot more as an issue. It took me a lot longer to do my work, and I sometimes felt that everyone else was feeling sorry for me. So I started doing different things.

Julie Writes

There are some important findings from these comments and others made by the sisters. First, June claims to now view the experience in a more positive light. Second, all three sisters make reference to being "different" or being individuals. Third, June managed the experience. Fourth, they all got along then, and cohesiveness has prevailed over the years. Although June did have some negative feelings, she chose to overcome them. When June was diagnosed with a learning disability in high school, everything seemed to fall into place. "I suddenly realized that it was my learning disability that was holding me back, not that I was stupid," she recalls. June then made what she feels was a tough decision: she chose to go to a different university than her sisters. Free of her gifted sisters and labels, she finally began to achieve academically.

Interestingly, April also speaks now from the perspective of having acquired teaching experience. As an educator, she believes that in gifted programs, "Too much emphasis is placed on the fact that you're good at school. I don't know how to surpass that, but I think it's about getting involved in things that are bigger than school. I think it's true—a lot of people are good at school, but they're not good at putting it all together. So emphasizing life skills, communication skills, presentation skills, thinking skills, and entrepreneurial skills is more important than the marks."

This is where parental encouragement and support are very important! Parents have a lot to do with reinforcing and maintaining a strong and healthy family dynamic.

All three of the sisters are happy, stable women with at least one undergraduate degree, wonderful home lives, and fulfilling careers. They are close with each other and their extended families. Overall, they feel good about their past and current relationships with their siblings.

Having known these women for nearly 25 years, I have watched each one grow as an individual. Each has forged a separate identity for herself, and today, all three excel in different areas, regardless of whether they were labeled gifted or not. As adults, they have independent interests and pursue different activities. While all three proudly proclaim their individuality, they are extremely proud of being part of a warm, loving, and supportive family group.

Parents who create a healthy home environment where each child feels loved and valued reduce the likelihood of problems from destructive sibling comparison and rivalry. Here are some strategies for parents to consider:

- Look for ways to show that you value each child's strengths and abilities.

- Help children know and appreciate their unique strengths and areas of weakness.

- Avoid comparing children's abilities.

- Provide each child with opportunities for learning that are consistent with his interests and abilities.

- Look for activities for each child that will allow her to shine. Each child needs her own area(s) of special competence.

- Don't allow the pursuits of one child to take precedence over another's or to consistently disrupt family leisure time.

- Don't refer to one child as *being* gifted (and others not), but rather put the emphasis on the mastery model and growth mindset perspectives of different people having different learning needs.

- Be sensitive to the stressors that children may experience due to the gifted exceptionality.

- Be alert to signs of a child feeling inferior or superior relative to his siblings.

- Consider family counseling if necessary.

Environmental Response Differences

"When they were little, Josie needed me to be a traditional mother, making rules and enforcing them consistently and dependably. It was important for Diana, though, that I give her some leeway and bend the rules from time to time."

"Maleke welcomes almost any change as an adventure, an opportunity for learning and exploration. My other two need lots of preparation and advance warning."

Members of a family living in the same household can respond very differently to the same environments. Siblings do not react in the same ways to parental pressures to perform or to other aspects of home life or parenting styles. Factors influencing children's responses include their birth order, birth spacing, sex, relationship to one parent or the other, perception of parents' treatment relative to siblings, personality, interests, ability, and temperament. Parenting approaches that work well with one child do not necessarily work well with another, and although it is important to try to be fair, it is sometimes essential to treat children differently.

What must be consistent for all children in a family is that their parents provide support in the form of love, discipline, nurturing, respect, communication, provision of a variety of stimulating learning experiences, and encouragement for responsible independence. How parents provide this can vary across individual children in the same family. When parents manage to do a good job with these factors, children are free to thrive in distinctly individual and self-fulfilling ways.

Differences of Opinion

How siblings relate to each other differs from one family to the next, as well as among siblings within the same family. Consider, for example, those children trying to keep pace with an older brother or sister, or those who feel under-appreciated in light of their siblings' accomplishments. It can be difficult to stand by while someone else receives accolades, special learning opportunities, or extra parental attention. Parents should try to ensure that *each* child has opportunities to extend her learning reach, regardless of how far that might be.

Consider the following reflection, written by Laressa Rudyk, a teacher.

On Being a Gifted Sister

I was identified as gifted in Grade 4, but my sister Taryn, who is exactly one year older than me, was not identified as gifted.

Recently, I remembered with worry and guilt a conversation that Taryn and I had three years ago, during which she said, "Nobody understands how hard it was to have a sister like you." I recalled my extreme sensitivity to Taryn's feelings when we were kids. I remember deliberately "dumbing down" my abilities as early as age five in front of our parents to protect her feelings. Our father was particularly insensitive and treated my sister and me differently. Our mother, a psychologist, was aware that I was scared of hurting Taryn's feelings, and we discussed it in private regularly.

Taryn and I have the same birthday. On my fifth birthday and her sixth, our father gave each of us a book: hers was *Cinderella* and mine was a Mensa puzzle book. When Taryn saw my book, she started crying, dropped her book, and ran out of the room. I guiltily dropped my book, picked up her book, and went after her. Ever since, our father has given us exactly the same thing for our birthdays, probably at my mother's insistence.

On my tenth birthday and Taryn's eleventh, our father made us a birthday cake and put the numbers 10 and 11 on the cake—in binary. He put the cake down in front of us and told us to try to figure out what the candles represented. I recognized the numbers immediately but pretended that I didn't. He eventually said to me, "Come on. It's binary. You know that." Last week, I asked Taryn if she remembered the binary birthday cake incident. She most certainly did. "It was so mean to put the candles on *our* cake in binary when he knew that I didn't know it. I asked him to explain it, and he just waved me off, telling me not to worry about it. That was pretty awful because it was supposed to be my cake, too."

Of course, conflict happens from time to time within all families. Although it is difficult for many people to handle conflict well, it is an important part of a healthy family dynamic.[25] Children need examples, guidance, and instruction in order to find ways to settle things constructively, responsibly, and creatively. Adults who can express their opinions honestly and can disagree with others productively and respectfully have assets that are valuable in personal and professional relationships. Such skills are best acquired in a safe and loving environment, and the family is the best of all places to learn these and other conflict resolution skills.

A good way to reduce unnecessary friction among siblings is for parents to help their children support and learn from one another. Optimally, each child contributes positively to the family dynamic, buoys up the others' weaknesses, demonstrates his own strengths, and celebrates each family member's success as a shared success. Parents can model this behavior and make it explicit as appropriate. Although differences of opinion are healthy, the overall family climate should be one of fostering, not festering—one of warmth and generosity to each other, not one of ill will. When there are giftedness-related issues or when family dynamics become chronically strained, supportive parenting strategies become particularly important.

Talking to Children

Life has a way of confusing us, blessing and bruising us....[26]

Discussing giftedness with a child is tricky. Such conversations should be handled carefully, with the emphasis on high cognitive ability as a difference from others, but not a superiority. It helps if parents see giftedness as associated with differences in learning needs, just as they should with a child who has a learning problem of one sort or another. This becomes a necessary conversation when a child receives the gifted label, is feeling different or odd somehow, or is having trouble with social interactions.

Rosa's Question

Parent

Should we tell our child that he is gifted? I am sure that my son knows—he certainly feels different—but we don't know whether to talk about it or not. How do you suggest we broach the topic?

Our Response

It sounds like it would be a good idea for you to discuss with your child how his mind works. You might say something like this: "You will probably find that there are lots of things that you learn more easily or more quickly than others. This doesn't mean that you necessarily learn it better or that you don't have to work to learn things, but that you've got some advantages in some situations. Other kids have other kinds of strengths. Josh is really good at basketball, and Melanie is good at word games."

If everything is going well and there is no need for any kind of official labeling process because individual learning needs are being met in the course of day-to-day schooling without labeling or compartmentalizing individuals, there may be no need to have this kind of conversation. However, parents should remain alert to the possibility that it may arise at some point.

Seeking Professional Help

Grant me the serenity to accept the things I cannot change, the courage to change the things I can, and the wisdom to know the difference.[27]

Wise professional guidance can help parents learn the difference between the qualities in their children that they should accept or even cherish as assets and those that they should work to change. Parents may, at times, know what needs changing, but they may need some advice on how to do it. Just as very few of us have the expertise required to set a child's broken bone, or even to know that a bone is broken, few parents have the training in child development and exceptionality that is sometimes required to make it happily through a child's growing-up years without some professional help from time to time. Finding the right person at the right time can be difficult.

Who to Consult?

"Are there people who specialize in counseling gifted kids? If so, how do I find them?"

Yes, there are people who specialize in working with gifted learners and their families, and the best way to find such experts is by networking in person or online. You might find the right professional by talking to other parents or by asking educators and doctors. Sometimes the right professional can be found through contacts at organizations such as the Association for Bright Children or the National Association for Gifted Children, or through parent advocacy groups, such as those found in many states in the U.S. Parents can also call a school district office, university, or clinic. Other sources include *careful* Internet searches, including tuning in to other parents' referrals in online chat rooms.[28]

There are many possible avenues of professional help, depending on the nature of the problem that a family is experiencing. Fees vary considerably, as do health plan coverage and availability of professionals. In general, as with other areas of specialization, the more exceptional the situation (for example, the highly gifted learner with emotional problems at adolescence), the more likely it is that appropriate specialists will be found only in larger urban areas.

If the problem requires tutoring or educational advocacy, parents can contact an educational consultant with experience working with gifted learners. This person might be an educator with graduate training in special education, or it might be a psychoeducational consultant with a master's degree or doctorate in some aspect of educational psychology or special education, working either within or outside of the child's school system. Ideally, it is someone who understands giftedness issues and has a successful track record in dealing with them.

If a psychoeducational assessment is required, the best consultant is usually a psychologist with training and experience in giftedness, or a psychoeducational consultant (someone with both educational and psychological training, as well as expertise in assessment). This professional should have an earned doctorate in psychology or education. If it is a matter of taking a test for the purpose of meeting gifted identification criteria, the services of a psychometrist may be sufficient. This is someone with a master's level certification in test administration but not in interpretation or synthesis of findings.

In situations requiring counseling help for family dynamics or emotional issues, there are counselors with graduate degrees in counseling psychology or social work who have experience working with high-ability learners. When there are serious emotional or psychological problems, a psychiatrist with expertise working with giftedness may be the right professional to consult. Psychiatrists are medical doctors specializing in psychiatry, and they can prescribe medication if needed. However, parents and educators should be aware that very few physicians or psychologists receive any training in the needs of gifted learners, and behaviors that actually arise from educational and/or peer mismatch may be diagnosed incorrectly as an behavioral disorder such as ADHD, Asperger's Disorder, etc.[29]

With such a wide range of possibilities, in combination with a scarcity of gifted specialists in each category, it is no wonder that so many parents find it daunting to figure out where to find someone who will be able to help their child and their family. However, by finding one professional with expertise in working with giftedness, you have a very good chance of tapping into a larger local network. At the very least, if you discuss your concerns with one of these professionals, you should be able to get a better sense of what kind of help you need, and you may get some ideas about where to look for a more appropriate referral, if necessary. In fact, about half of the parents who contact us, after discussing their situation with us, have a plan for proceeding without further help, have decided to postpone action for the time being, or have the names of other professionals to consult. Parents who increase their knowledge on giftedness issues and act upon some of the suggestions that we provide here are in a good position to make sense of their child's exceptionality and thereby prevent some of the problems that parents of gifted learners often experience.

When to Consult?

Many of the parents who consult professionals about gifted issues feel the same kind of uncertainty that the parent in the following vignette expresses.

A Parent's Request for Help

Luke's reading is coming along slowly; he is showing no great interest in it. This would not concern us very much at this point except that the school has made it abundantly clear that acceleration is impossible unless his reading and writing skills keep pace with his math reasoning skills. I must admit that at times, I wonder whether Luke's learning ability is as advanced as the test results indicate. I'm worried because most of the literature I've read suggests that he is likely to encounter difficulties if the school does not respond more appropriately to his needs.

We have sought the assistance of a psychiatrist because of Luke's argumentativeness. Things seem to be improving, but my husband and I wonder whether boredom at home and at school contribute, at least in part, to his acting out. Would it be helpful for Darren and me to meet with you once again before Luke's spring identification, placement, and review committee (IPRC) meeting? When we met with the principal, the special education resource teacher, and Luke's teacher last December, the school administration clearly stated that they would not consider acceleration or out-of-level instruction—at least not yet. I am concerned that Luke's academic needs will not be adequately addressed at the IPRC. Would it be possible for you to contribute your opinions and interpretation of his assessment results to the hearing? I think we'll need an advocate!

This message illustrates the confusion and turmoil that many parents feel as they try to navigate their way through the circumstances of a gifted learner's childhood. In this case, we had previously done a psychoeducational assessment in which Luke had scored exceptionally well on an intelligence test and extremely well on mathematics achievement tests, but he had scored in the average range in both reading and writing. We responded to this parent's message by affirming the school's current position on full acceleration, pointing out that it is quite reasonable and sensible not to do a whole-grade acceleration at this time. We wrote, "If Luke isn't reading and writing at least at a moderately high level in the grade into which he would be going, we would not be helping him by accelerating him there."

We also affirmed the parent's concerns about Luke running into difficulties if his giftedness needs were not met, while at the same time cautioning a need for a balanced perspective, saying, "School is not the only place where a child's learning needs can be met. There are extracurricular and other options that we can discuss." We agreed with the parents about the importance of working with the school, and we set up a meeting to discuss ways to facilitate that.

Luke's vignette illustrates a situation in which it is a good idea for parents to consult with experts. These parents had some concerns about their son's development in a number of areas, including problems with boredom, anger management, and argumentativeness, as well as his exceptional educational needs. They understood that the social/emotional concerns and giftedness needs might be interacting and reinforcing each other, and they had chosen to try to combat them both at the same time. They were seeing a counselor for the social/emotional needs, in this case a psychiatrist, and they were consulting us for help with educational planning. Other parents in similarly complex situations may choose to tackle one problem at a time (and in fact, this would be our usual recommendation) in the hope that as one problem area is solved, others will lessen. In many cases, once a child's learning needs are being well met, the argumentativeness (or boredom, or frustration, or other problematic behavior) does in fact diminish. In more serious cases, however, it can be a good idea to address several issues simultaneously, as this family was doing.

Giftedness is truly an individual developmental differences phenomenon. Each story is unique, and therefore each situation must be looked at in its own context. The simplest answer to the question of when or why to look for professional help is to try to pay attention to the child's development and to seek sound advice when things aren't going well.

When families have to deal with exceptional circumstances such as parenting a gifted learner, they often find that "common sense" approaches fail them. They discover that what they read about child development, what their friends and family tell them about parenting, and what educators recommend based on experiences with other children and adolescents do not apply very well to their particular situations. Often, they just need some help understanding the exceptional developmental needs of their children. Sometimes they simply require reassurance that their sense of the situation is right and that they *do* know how to proceed with the current and next stage of parenting.

Very often, consulting a giftedness expert means having one's parenting instincts confirmed. It can also mean finding support, strategic approaches, and targeted assistance for sorting things out and responding to the unique challenges that a child presents.

Being Pre-Emptive

One of the problems with seeking professional help is the risk of pathologizing a situation that is not pathological—that is, making a child feel that there is something wrong with her when in reality, everything is "exceptionally right." Depending on the circumstances, there are ways to provide counseling help that will not make the child feel that she is somehow defective or deficient. Many experts on giftedness recommend that educators and parents pay routine pre-emptive attention to gifted learners' possible counseling needs. For example, regular small group and individual counseling mentorships and consultations can provide close attention to affective and cognitive development. Similarly, a focus on the arts can be used "as a therapeutic intervention as well as a creative and expressive outlet."[30]

Career counseling is another recommendation for gifted learners. This can provide a forum for self-discovery and can open up interesting possibilities for current and future investigation. If this is not offered at an adolescent's school, parents might consider looking for outside assistance.

Parents might want to talk to a giftedness expert when they have concerns that their child is unhappy, is hiding his giftedness, is being singled out as a behavior problem for acts of mischief or boredom, or is not making good academic or career decisions. Just as there are medical specialists available to deal with specific physical problems, parents can take comfort in knowing that there are professionals who can help them if they run into trouble with parenting or gifted-related issues.

Chapter 12

Teacher Development

Perhaps there is no intervention more completely researched and confirmed in the field of education than the efficacy of teacher preparation and professional development.[1]

Without exception, there is a need for training of teachers globally which in turn will prepare them to recognize and meet the needs of children from all cultures who exhibit gifted attributes.[2]

Because gifted learners are diverse in their talents and abilities, teachers need access to a wide range of possible educational options. No one option can do a good job for all high-ability children within a particular classroom, much less within a whole school. If teachers are to provide both the challenge and support required to meet diversely exceptional gifted learning needs, they need access to support for themselves, as well as readily available learning options and resources for their students. Where teachers are provided with the necessary training and support, they can create a challenging climate of learning for all students. Unfortunately, the vast majority of teachers do not receive the training they need in gifted education.[3]

Teacher Development

> *I've come to a frightening conclusion that I am the decisive element in the classroom. It's my personal approach that creates the climate. It's my daily mood that makes the weather.... I can humiliate or humor, hurt or heal. In all situations, it is my response that decides whether a crisis will be escalated or de-escalated and a child humanized or dehumanized.*[4]

"*Teachers are not properly prepared to teach the range of kids identified as gifted.*"
"*Children are languishing in programs that just don't work for them because there is nothing else available.*"

Most educators who train teachers acknowledge a lack of professional development programs that prepare new teachers for working with special needs learners. Generally speaking, teacher candidates are expected to learn about teaching their "general education" students, including the basics of child development, pedagogy, classroom management, and planning and implementing instruction. It is only as they move along in their careers that teachers are encouraged to acquire some additional qualifications, including teaching strategies in special education.

The problem with this approach becomes apparent when a new teacher arrives in her first classroom on the first day of class. She soon realizes that her students have many different learning needs. Addressing the diversity of learners in a classroom requires considerable know-how, even for experienced educators. Moreover, although the needs of students with learning difficulties are obvious to most teachers, in many cases, teachers can be unaware that they may have students with gifted learning requirements.

Unfortunately, the situation is usually not much different in designated gifted programs; in most jurisdictions, teachers of gifted students have little or no special training—perhaps only one or two introductory courses on giftedness. They have limited theoretical understanding of exceptional development and little experience in adapting curriculum to meet exceptional learning needs. Most teachers in gifted programs find themselves working alone or perhaps with one or two colleagues to invent a curriculum. As a result, what is offered to students in gifted programs varies tremendously, ranging from an extra amount of work, with no time or attention paid to divergent thinking or to students' abilities and interests, to a laissez-faire emphasis on "creativity activities," with little in the way of content mastery, rigor, or higher-order thinking.

What Do Teachers Need?

Educating teachers about gifted development and related issues is not something that should be provided piecemeal, nor is it a frill.[5] It should be coherent, well-targeted, and strategic, focusing on giving teachers the knowledge and skills that they require to support effective learning outcomes for their students. It should be provided by those who have advanced knowledge and skills themselves and who are able to communicate well with teachers.

We've spoken with many teachers about what they need in order to feel better prepared to work with gifted learners, and their perceptions closely match our own observations. We have organized their ideas into three general areas in which they express a need for further learning.

Assessment Information and Support

- report interpretation skills

- information on applying assessment results and individual education plans to classroom practice

- professional support in connecting children's individual learning profiles to learning processes, achievement, and evaluation

Curriculum Information and Support

- better understanding of how official curriculum guidelines apply to gifted learners, including how much leeway they have to deviate from mandated content and expectations

- practical strategies for modifying lesson planning in order to differentiate for individual differences

- information about and access to possible placement options

- information about and access to community-based learning options

- access to resource materials to support gifted learning needs

- support for learners with dual exceptionalities
- information about models of teaching for gifted learners[6]

Information and Support on Other Topics of Interest

- motivation and engagement
- self-confidence
- identity development
- creativity
- higher-order thinking skills
- flexible grouping practices
- gender issues
- emotional, social, academic, and cultural dimensions of giftedness
- study skills and work habits
- classroom management techniques
- cognitive/developmental issues
- developing technology (e.g., electronic portfolios, data collection, tele-mentoring, simulations)
- mentorships
- addressing misconceptions about giftedness in the school and parent communities
- leadership and community service opportunities
- cooperative learning
- and many more, depending on the context, age of students, teachers' interests, etc.

Like their students, teachers usually have good ideas about what it is that they need to know, particularly as this reflects their changing classroom circumstances and demands. The most effective learning happens when teachers feel that they are an integral part of the consultation and planning process, as well as when they feel that their learning experiences are personally relevant.[7] When teachers are directly involved in needs assessments and development planning, they are more likely to be engaged in their own learning. An enormous additional benefit of teachers' involvement in this kind of authentic consultative process is that it provides them with an excellent model for facilitating the same kind of process with their gifted learners.

Teachers need to have the tools and support necessary to adapt educational programming for exceptionally capable learners. They should also be encouraged to participate in creating their own professional development (PD). To this end, teachers can work together to prepare a needs assessment with respect to themes or topics that they would like to have addressed, and they can speak to administrators about the possibilities of this, including perhaps having regular workshops, brown bag seminars, cyclical question-and-answer sessions, or resource reading and sharing sessions. There are, of course, logistics to providing PD (dates, times, location, goals, format, presenters, materials, assessment and follow-up aspects, and so forth);[8] however, these service delivery matters can be readily addressed if everyone contributes to the effort and if administrative support is in place.

These are some of the ideas that teachers have given us about the ongoing high-level professional development that they need:[9]

- regular and frequent opportunities for collaboration with colleagues

- opportunities for action research (that is, teacher-directed research embedded in classroom practice)

- ready access to a gifted consultant or coordinator who can provide information, support, and resources as needed

- leadership and networking opportunities within the district and beyond

- access to a gifted resource center for information, connections, and support

- access to advocacy networks

- administrative support for trying out different programming applications

- opportunities to attend conferences and workshops

- opportunities to suggest and choose areas of focus for staff development

Administrative Support

Professional learning is at the heart of teacher professionalism.[10]

Valuable and meaningful professional development does not occur in a vacuum. It requires the involvement and support of principals and other members of a school's administrative team. By becoming familiar with the issues in gifted education alongside their teachers, principals are better able to support them in planning and implementing well-designed programs.

The National Association for Gifted Children stipulates four guiding principles for principals and others in positions of responsibility who want to implement effective professional development:[11]

1. A comprehensive staff development program must be provided for all school staff involved in the education of gifted learners.

2. Only qualified personnel should be involved in the education of gifted learners.

3. School personnel require support for their specific efforts related to the education of gifted learners.

4. The educational staff must be provided with time and other support for the preparation and development of differentiated education plans, materials, and curriculum.

Teachers can fine-tune their ability to work effectively with gifted learners if they have access to compelling and affirming teaching experiences, as well as ongoing encouragement from their administrators. The following vignette illustrates one middle school principal's blueprint for helping teachers meet gifted learning needs in his school. After attending one of our professional development programs on giftedness with classroom teachers and other educators within his district, Jerry Rosenfield, a school principal, wrote about the importance of collaboration and decided to implement a multi-grade program to support gifted learners in his school. Here is a condensed framework of his action plan.

A Principal's Initiative

Objective

To facilitate collaboration among teachers sharing ideas and materials for children who are advanced relative to their age or grade.

Target Subject Areas and Population

Collaboration and sharing of materials and ideas will occur for core subjects in Grades 6, 7, and 8, with a focus on enrichment materials and extension activities for in-class use with individuals who demonstrate readiness.

Approach

We will conduct a teacher workshop to increase appreciation of giftedness. We will then arrange for departmental meetings to formalize: (1) collecting age-appropriate and grade-appropriate enrichment materials and activities, (2) organizing these materials, and (3) open sharing, in which teachers will discuss how the materials might be best used.

Implementation Process

1. Meet with program leaders to have them buy in.

2. Arrange departmental meetings facilitated by program leaders and staff resource teachers to establish a mechanism for sharing enrichment materials and for collaborative activities among teachers.

3. Invite the board's gifted education consultant to work with separate groups of teachers (by department) to encourage dialogue and to help plan strategies for classroom use.

4. Facilitate teacher observations of other teachers' classes, by invitation, so that teachers can see how individual students in other classes are involved in meaningful enrichment activities.

> 5. Maintain contact with the consultant for ongoing support as required.
>
> 6. After a few weeks, solicit evaluations from all participants.
>
> 7. Continue to build from there.

After developing this plan, the principal put it into action. Since then, the district gifted education consultant has provided professional development to small groups of teachers by subject area. Teachers are encouraged to examine their own practice in serving high-ability students and to adopt some suggested strategies for differentiating their instruction.

Administrators who understand gifted learning needs and who think creatively can find context-sensitive ways to support teachers in enhancing learning options for the high-ability students in their schools. Effective staff development processes focus on specialized know-how, encourage collaborative endeavors among professionals, and facilitate meaningful discussion and sharing of ideas. Administrators can take an effective leadership role by strengthening staff cohesion and best practice through such initiatives.

Formats

At its best, *preservice* training (teachers' college courses) provides the fuel and thrust needed to become an effective teacher. *Inservice* training (professional development of teachers already engaged in practice) replenishes the source and sustains the momentum.

Preservice Teacher Education

> *Universal pre-service and in-service teacher professional development in gifted education is essential.*[12]

There are many ways to provide the kind of education that teachers need if they are to work effectively with their gifted students and incorporate the basic principles of special education—including giftedness—into initial teacher training programs. To be prepared to work with students with exceptional learning needs, aspiring teachers need appropriate resources and educational experiences, as well as solid grounding in pedagogical theory.

In a perfect world, the principles of gifted education would be a mandatory part of preservice teacher education, but this is not the case at the present time. Only one state in the United States—Washington— requires coursework in gifted education for regular classroom teachers.[13] Most of the training and support that teachers receive comes in the form of inservice or professional development learning experiences.

We offer the following recommendations for preservice teacher education:[14]

- facilitating communication skills, such as active listening

- working with paraprofessionals, specialists, volunteers, administrators, support staff, teacher aides, mentors, and other support personnel

- fostering students' self-regulatory abilities

- individualizing instruction and pacing

- modifying instruction and monitoring students' progress

- selecting and developing materials that address the diverse needs of students

- interacting with parents of special needs students and determining how they can be effectively involved in their child's education

- assessing, managing, and preventing problem behaviors

- balancing group and individual needs

- promoting social development of students, particularly those who are experiencing difficulty with their peers

- being aware of changing technology and potential benefits in meeting student needs

- developing a foundation of information pertaining to assessment practices, materials, curriculum approaches, and identification and placement procedures

Inservice/Professional Development

> *"I've learned that teachers must learn to resist the temptation to make their students fit the curriculum. Rather, the curriculum must fit the students' needs. In this way, students will be less frustrated and more fulfilled."*
>
> *"After taking the course, I'm being more flexible and less afraid to try new teaching strategies in the classroom. The ideas will take time and effort to implement; however, I'm patient and determined to make things work."*

Along with special courses on high-level development, teachers need ongoing access to someone with expertise in gifted development and education so that they can consolidate and refine their understandings as they encounter challenges and situations, as well as learn about emerging options for the students in their classrooms. As with anyone acquiring expertise in any area, teachers need support as they work to implement the appropriate strategies.

In our experience, professional development can provide lively and dynamic opportunities for teachers to work collaboratively to enhance their ability to facilitate high-level learning. Such workshops can include interested teachers from within one school or from several schools, and they work best when delivered in a coherently organized series, with opportunities between workshops for ongoing interaction, support, and consultation with one another and with experts.

Here are two perspectives from teachers who work in different schools who participated in a professional learning program on giftedness.

Teachers' Perspectives on Professional Development

Edison: Fifth-Grade Teacher

I learned to be flexible about who might be gifted. Perhaps a child will shine in new areas, and I'll have to be prepared to offer support. The ideas we discussed made me think about social, behavioral, and motivational issues. I want to promote learning experiences that will enable my students to be proud of their abilities. I'll be open to their feelings and provide a positive emotional setting to support the gifted children in my class.

> Deidre: Remediation Specialist
>
> As a remediation specialist, I don't get to know my students in the same way as the classroom teacher. This presentation highlighted the fact that I have to make an extended effort to discover exactly what interests the gifted student and where his or her talents may lie. I learned that a teacher who tries to provide an extension activity might be completely off target unless she has prior knowledge of the student's interests, hobbies, personality traits, abilities, concerns, and experiential background. Knowledge is power. A teacher with insight into how a student functions and what interests him or her is better able to implement meaningful and motivating programs.

Teachers who understand how to work effectively with gifted learners find that they are better able to meet other kinds of special learning needs as well. By understanding the principles and practices involved, teachers get better at recognizing and addressing special needs in a variety of students in their classrooms. As a result, the classroom culture becomes more engaging and inclusive, a place where diversity is welcome and each child's abilities are respected and nurtured.

When teachers are provided with opportunities to think constructively about giftedness and acquire sound strategies for working with high-level learners, *and* when they are supported in their implementation of these understandings, the school and all children in the system benefit tremendously. Whether they are teaching exceptional students in regular or ability-grouped classrooms, teachers should be given both the training and the support they need in order to provide their students with an education commensurate with their abilities. Ideally, inservice programs for teachers should incorporate information on how to identify, understand, and plan for individual learning differences. We offer the following recommendations for inservice teacher education:

- intelligent approaches to interpreting assessment information

- ways to recognize and address individual learning needs in a timely manner

- flexible instructional strategies

- well-targeted curriculum adaptation

- appropriate evaluation models

- ways to work cooperatively with the parents of special needs learners, other educators, and other professionals

This is not a comprehensive list. It cannot be comprehensive because the best professional development is flexible and fluid, taking its shape from the questions, concerns, and needs of the participants.

Consider, too, that teachers who work with high-ability students, whether identified as gifted or not, also need guidance in understanding and facilitating high-level development. This involves knowing how to create a classroom climate that addresses domain-specific giftedness, facilitates engagement and participation, incorporates an emphasis on higher-order thinking, and provides opportunities to acquire solid work habits and study skills. Gifted learners who are on the leading edge in one area or another and able to spot out-of-date information can be challenging to teachers. Teachers have to have to stay on top of their subject area, or develop a growth mindset[15] and realize that they cannot know everything—and that's okay.

Professional development should include a focus on understanding affective issues associated with giftedness, providing strategies for fostering children's social and emotional development, as well as their cognitive development. There is increasing concern about educational outcomes for all learners, and with the perspective on giftedness changing from mystery model to mastery model, this is an ideal time for educators to be proactive and constructive, ensuring that they have the requisite skills to support high-level development in their students.

The National Association for Gifted Children lists competencies that teachers should possess:[16]

- a knowledge and valuing of the origins and nature of high levels of intelligence, including creative expressions of intelligence

- a knowledge and understanding of the cognitive, social, and emotional characteristics, needs, and potential problems experienced by gifted and talented students from diverse populations

- a knowledge of and access to advanced content and ideas

- an ability to develop a differentiated curriculum appropriate to meeting the unique intellectual and emotional needs and interests of gifted and talented students

- an ability to create an environment in which gifted and talented students can feel challenged and safe to explore and express their uniqueness

In order for this level of proficiency to become a *reality* and not just a *reach*, administrators should ensure that a range of staff development opportunities are readily available, not only because these skills have a direct impact on children's learning, but also because they can enrich a school community and help to energize the collaborative spirit.

What Can Parents Expect?

"What can I expect my child's regular classroom teacher to know about addressing his specific needs and levels of advancement in different subject areas?"

There are established standards of practice for the teaching profession, and some relate specifically to special needs learners. In the province of Ontario, Canada, for example, the standards are set forth by a self-regulatory body,[17] and they are incorporated into all accredited preservice and inservice teacher education programs. They include the following commitments, all of which are important to students with exceptional learning needs:[18]

- *support for student learning*, such that teachers understand and use a range of teaching methods to address learning, cultural, spiritual, and language differences, as well as various family situations

- *equitable and respectful treatment*, such that teachers accommodate the differences in students and respect their diversity, help students to connect learning to their own life experiences and spiritual and cultural understandings, and provide a range of ways for students to demonstrate aptitudes, abilities, and learning

- *knowledge of the student*, such that teachers recognize the strengths and weakness of students and know that teaching those with exceptionalities requires the use of specialized knowledge and skills

- *professional development*, such that teachers understand that teacher learning is directly related to student learning, and they engage in a variety of learning opportunities, both individual and collaborative, that are integrated into practice for the benefit of student learning

- *knowledge of teaching practice*, such that teachers know ways to shape instruction so that it is helpful to students who learn in a variety of ways

- *planning for instruction*, such that teachers respond to learning exceptionalities and special needs, adapt teaching practices based on student achievement, and apply teaching strategies to meet student needs

The National Association for Gifted Children states, "Gifted learners are entitled to be served by professionals who have specialized preparation in gifted education, expertise in appropriate differentiated content and instructional methods, involvement in ongoing professional development, and who possess exemplary personal and professional traits."[19] Although this may seem like a tall order, it provides a good starting point for thinking about appropriate standards.

As we discuss throughout this chapter, educators can participate in various kinds of learning experiences. They can:

- enroll in academic courses offered at universities or colleges or in distance education programs

- partner with professional networks (business, industry, committees)

- form study groups and network with colleagues

- participate in conferences and workshops that focus on specific areas of interest (such as giftedness or high-ability learners)

- plan and implement action research or job-embedded research activities

- develop innovative curriculum materials

- read and contribute to journals and educational publications that focus on aspects of teaching and learning

- arrange opportunities to observe exemplary practice

- increase their levels of competence in computer technology

- collaborate with consultants in areas in which they wish to gain expertise or acquire additional support

Professional opportunities like these not only help teachers remain current in their practice within an ever-changing educational environment, they also serve to enhance the teaching profession as a whole. Teachers who grow professionally and who contribute meaningfully to the learning community in which they work become stronger, more effective teachers and raise the bar for others.[20] At the same time, they reinforce the importance of ongoing and collaborative learning for their students.

The Dynamic Scaffolding Model (DSM) of Teacher Development[21]

"I need some practical ideas for the classroom. But I also need some help figuring out how to put them into place for individual kids."

"It's important for me to be able to indicate what I would like to learn about in professional learning sessions."

We have developed an approach to teacher training—dynamic scaffolding—that involves interested educators working with a gifted education consultant,[22] and we have integrated into our model many consultation specifics that teachers have identified as being important to their work with gifted learners. In the dynamic scaffolding model of teacher development, the gifted education consultant acts as a catalyst for helping classroom teachers acquire knowledge about giftedness, learn to address special learning needs, and obtain ongoing access to peer collaboration and professional expertise. By providing ways for teachers to consolidate and build upon their understandings, the consultant helps teachers target learning for their students.

Based on research about how learning happens (which applies to teachers as well as to their students),[23] we have developed a three-tiered model of teacher support:

1. appropriate professional development in collegial settings

2. ongoing and targeted individual consultation opportunities

3. diverse kinds of liaisons and networking

A competent and readily accessible gifted education consultant can serve as a catalyst for a large number of schools, providing teachers with increased know-how, the tools necessary to support highly capable learners, and the ongoing help and encouragement required to ensure that it all comes together well. One such consultant can effectively help educators at all levels in many schools provide flexible, lively, and challenging learning environments designed to meet individual students' interests, needs, and domain-specific strengths. Although the planning of teacher development initiatives and new programming components for high-ability students requires some revisiting of beliefs and structures,[24] a gifted education consultant in a position of responsibility within a board can act to oversee, steer, and champion a variety of exciting development efforts.

How the Model Evolved

> *"I'd like to have more specific hands-on information about exceptional learners—the ones who are having difficulty <u>and</u> the ones who are excelling."*

The dynamic scaffolding model of teacher development that we describe here and elsewhere[25] was developed in response to current realities and concerns about meeting gifted learning needs. A board of education that had emphasized the importance of providing challenging education for all of its students for many years (without a formal system of identifying gifted learners) wanted to provide better opportunities for its teachers to meet exceptionally capable students' learning needs in its approximately 80 affiliated schools. We suggested that a gifted education consultant with the necessary expertise, working under the auspices of the board's Special Education Department, would be ideally positioned to begin helping teachers become more knowledgeable about giftedness and guide them in finding good ways to program for their gifted students. The concept of a scaffolded approach for teacher training was adopted, and the initiative took off from there.

There are numerous ways to conceptualize scaffolding, but its essential components can be characterized in these eight steps, designed to provide learners with support and underpinnings needed to reach higher performance levels:[26]

1. Engage the learner in the task.

2. Establish an individually relevant shared goal.

3. Actively diagnose the learner's needs, including assessing and addressing misconceptions.

4. Provide tailored assistance.

5. Encourage goal-directed motivation.

6. Provide ongoing feedback that encourages self-monitoring.

7. Create an environment where the student feels free to take learning risks.

8. Assist internalization, independence, and generalization to other contexts.

A consultant can use scaffolding to facilitate teachers' learning, as well as to provide a model for them to use with their own students.

The Consultant in Action

> *"I'm a middle school teacher. I have lots of questions about gifted kids, but I'm not sure who to ask, or even what to ask."*
> *"I think a class's advancement can swing according to the individual teacher's strengths and interests. In other words, if you give exceptional math students to a teacher with an English degree, or vice versa, the enrichment won't be where the students need it."*

Throughout this book, we have emphasized the importance of matching a student's education to his individual abilities. This is not always easy to do, and teachers need both training and support. They benefit from opportunities to learn more about engagement, relevance, and matching learning opportunities to individual students' levels of knowledge and understanding. Generally speaking, the more exceptional a particular student, the more challenging it is for teachers to stimulate that student's engagement in the school-based learning process and to provide relevant learning opportunities that match his specific ability levels. One difficulty is that the more exceptional a particular learner's profile is, the less likely it is that a teacher will have had experience working with such a profile. In addition, most teachers do not have the support and resources in place to assist them in developing the necessary expertise.

In some jurisdictions, there are special education consultants who circulate among schools, offering support and addressing programming needs across the full spectrum of special education, from the very low-functioning students, through those with behavioral, sensory, and learning problems, to those who are gifted. These general specialists are often spread thinly, and their focus on gifted learners is limited by constraints of time, available resources, and the extent of their own expertise. Some school boards offer self-contained gifted classes but demand little from its teachers by way of credentials in gifted education, and they provide neither expertise nor resources to support the teacher's work with diversely exceptional students. In such systems, not only is the so-called gifted education problematic, but also, too often no attention is paid to high-ability children who do not participate in such programs.

When a school or board of education has a designated gifted program coordinator, that person typically handles administrative functions (such as chairing identification and placement meetings), responds to parents' queries, and checks curricular issues, but she rarely has the time to offer extensive professional development in giftedness or consultation to regular classroom teachers. However, this scenario may be slowly changing. We have encountered some determined district coordinators who recognize the value of offering extended consultation opportunities in schools, planning mini-courses, and organizing small conferences, and who now see these initiatives as part of their job descriptions.[27] Unfortunately, massive funding cuts in many places have a detrimental effect on such initiatives.

Other schools have neither special programs nor gifted education consultants, and they have few, if any, learning options designed to encourage gifted-level development in children, or support for the teachers to help them develop and implement appropriate programming.

Fortunately, we know that some schools and boards or districts of education provide students with excellent learning opportunities that are well targeted to their special educational needs. This occurs most frequently in situations modeled on adaptive instruction approaches, in which there is an explicit commitment to respecting and attending to individual differences generally.[28] It also occurs in some special schools and programs that are designed for high-ability learners and that provide their teachers with the support necessary for matching their students' individual learning needs.

There are three key aspects of the dynamic scaffolding model:

1. *A series of workshops.* When professional development workshops are offered by an expert in gifted development and education, teachers can share their understandings about the nature of gifted development, as well as learn practical methods for facilitating high-level learning.

2. *Availability and support.* Following a teacher's participation in a professional learning program, and consistently from there on, the gifted education consultant is available to help teachers apply what they have learned in their classrooms and stay apprised of resources that become available in the community and beyond.

3. *Effort.* All participants remain committed, collaborative, and resourceful.

Learning how to meet the educational needs of exceptional students gives teachers skills and understandings that help them create a more dynamic classroom climate for all of their students. Teachers find that their own engagement in the teaching process is enhanced, and they become more enthusiastic supporters of their students' optimal development. For educators who work together to consider the nature of high-level learning and appropriately responsive teaching, there is an added bonus of becoming part of a network that offers peer support and a rich sharing of resources over time.

In our workshop discussions and ongoing pre- and post-workshop communications, we discuss this model with participating teachers. They have told us that the professional development support that they value most includes understanding and using assessment information, implementing curriculum adaptations, finding out more about high-level development, and learning how to support the development of giftedness in their students.

The consultant has another important role—that of liaison. This involves promoting outreach opportunities and networking with education leaders and consultants elsewhere. The consultant can also address the concerns of parents by offering them support and information about gifted development, including providing open-panel discussions or forums on specific issues, resources, educational practices, and other relevant concerns. These discussions give parents an outlet for their ideas, suggestions, and questions pertaining to giftedness. A particularly valuable way to encourage ongoing networking and liaison activities is for the consultant to create an interactive website where participants can discuss matters of interest, provide mutual support in problem solving, and share resources and effective techniques. Technology has opened the door to electronic chat rooms and other online possibilities for PD.

Of course, the success of the dynamic scaffolding model is directly linked to the competence and commitment of the specialist who is responsible for making it happen.[29] Ideally, the consultant will have a rich background of understanding and expertise in gifted development and education, be able to provide lively and meaningful inservice training activities, enjoy working with teachers, demonstrate leadership skills, and be approachable and encouraging in attitude so that teachers feel comfortable about the process. The consultant needs to be enthusiastic about building a strong conceptual foundation for learning, as well as building bridges among stakeholders in the learning process—parents, administrators, policy-makers, teachers, and students.[30]

Because of the highly political nature of education in general, and gifted education in particular, being responsive to individual differences and to changing circumstances and contexts (the *dynamic* part of the scaffolding model's name) is essential for those who are interested in enacting any kind of change in gifted education. By taking a proactive role in gifted education consultancy and by opening up a wide range of dynamically responsive and scaffolded support mechanisms to teachers, it is possible for schools, districts, and boards to enhance their commitment to the learning needs of all of their students, increasing opportunities for gifted-level development in as many students as possible.

Engagement in Teaching and Learning

The conventional wisdom is that we can't find enough good teachers.... The truth is that we can't keep enough good teachers.[31]

"I'm thinking about how individual development actually is. A student who is advanced intellectually might not be so advanced morally or emotionally. We need to be tightly tuned to the progress of all aspects of the individual."

"Should students be rewarded for learning? How do I know which is the right instructional strategy for gifted students?"

New Teachers

One of the most overlooked resources in the teaching profession is the entry every year of new teachers who are trained in inquiry-based, reflective processes and, in some cases, in high-level development of children. What can experienced teachers learn from the kinds of questions and issues that prospective teachers raise and hope (or fear) to address in their work with gifted learners? How can we best support—and learn from!—new teachers as they enter the field?

We find that many teacher candidates who are enrolled in pre-service education programs are deeply engaged by educational concerns and issues. They often ask important questions, and they have fresh and valuable perspectives, insights, and action research ideas, showing a remarkable breadth and depth of inquiry and insight into the teaching process. Their concerns are profound and show tremendous dedication to meeting the needs of their future students.

We like to foster prospective teachers' collaborative questioning and reflective processes by working hard to provide them with the resources they need to address their questions, in addition to guiding their learning as opportunities arise for doing so. It is important for the teaching profession and for us all that these educators-to-be sustain their spirit of inquiry and concern. Those of us already in the field can be good models of teaching and learning by helping to nest their inquiry within a supportive and responsive milieu—we can appreciate their views, allay their concerns, and engage them in collegial learning. We can also

323

benefit from their enthusiasm and inquisitiveness if we use their questions as building blocks to stimulate our own thinking and exploration.

Tapping preservice teachers' curious and engaged attitudes toward the learning process can enrich gifted education and foster dynamic and lifelong professional development among both new and experienced educators. We can encourage new teachers to:

- continue to reflect on their practice

- enhance their professional growth through involvement in ongoing professional development dialogues, active learning, and job-embedded research initiatives

- motivate their colleagues' engagement in learning so as to create a more knowledgeable professional community

- plan and implement new ideas and innovative practice

- engage in action research

Guiding Principles

Schools are revolving doors that spit out teachers as fast as they are hired.… It seems that a third of new teachers quit after three years, and nearly half are gone after five years.[32]

"Teaching is wonderful, but it's draining!"

Sadly, we are experiencing a time when many new teachers feel burned out and make a choice to leave the profession. We offer here two guiding principles for enhancing new teachers' experiences and for encouraging their engagement in their work.

Principle #1: Support Reflective and Collaborative Efforts

We can help new teachers feel empowered and stay engaged in learning (for example, about gifted education) if we solicit and use their ideas and perspectives and if we facilitate their involvement in collaborative endeavors with more experienced educators. An administrator or gifted education consultant can act as a facilitator or help to coordinate professional development sessions and offer support for this kind of interactive learning process among educators of varying experience.

Principle #2: Embed Teachers' Learning within a Supportive Milieu

Too often, good teachers are overworked and underpaid. They will persist with focused engagement in teaching and learning only when it has meaningful applications in their practice, when they feel supported in a community of like-minded lifelong learners, and when they see a solid return on their investment of time and energy. By nurturing their development and providing opportunities for them to participate in co-creating their own professional growth, we empower new teachers and increase the likelihood of their sustaining their initial engagement in education. We have observed firsthand the motivating effect of learning experiences that act as springboards to better gifted education.

Gifted Education at the Preservice Level

Based on our own experience in teacher education and recommendations for best practice in the field, some preservice gifted education activities to consider include:[33]

- case study analyses, in the form of problem-based learning

- dialogue on relevant issues pertaining to gifted education, such as assessment; social, emotional, and motivational implications; and differentiated programming

- web-forum discussions

- practicum experience with teachers who have expertise in adaptive instruction

- collaborative problem-solving activities

- reflection on learning experiences

- action research on self-selected topics of interest

Teacher candidates we have worked with have indicated that each of the learning experiences listed above is effective for a number of reasons, including that it:

- engages them personally in authentic problem-solving activities

- enables them to feel respected as competent thinkers and professionals

- encourages them to recognize the expertise of their colleagues as essential to their own thinking, teaching, and learning
- helps them discover their own resourcefulness and the resources available to them
- allows them to experience firsthand the scaffolded and incremental nature of learning
- models best practices for their own teaching
- emphasizes the value of inquiry-based learning
- broadens their knowledge about gifted education
- facilitates an understanding of the paradigm shift from a mystery to a mastery model of gifted education

Much can be culled from preservice gifted education experiences, which is then extended or reconfigured as valuable inservice education. Many course components from initial training programs are excellent sources of information for professional development purposes. Educators can reflect upon these and then take the initiative to personalize or tailor the material to use collaboratively for their professional growth.

Chapter 13

Optimal Learning for All Children

Sharing Resources in a Changing World

> *Talent is often very specific, it can wax and wane over time, and one of the most exciting questions facing researchers today is how to encourage and sustain talent—across cultures and across the life span.*[1]

We are living through a time of unprecedented and accelerating change in the ways in which people live their lives, a situation that is creating uncertainty and stress for many people and for the communities in which they live. As individuals experience unpredictable changes, including, at the point of writing our book, a global recession, their health and prosperity depend increasingly on having acquired effective coping, communication, and decision-making skills.[2] In many ways, we are reaching a crisis in education—the very milieu in which individuals learn these skills—at a time when too many students have more needs than teachers have resources to meet them.[3]

This predicament poses some particular problems for exceptionally advanced learners and their parents. Although giftedness is generally perceived as a strength (and of course, in many ways, it is one), it can also be a liability. In a context of many urgent and competing needs, gifted learning needs can be assigned a low priority and become more or less ignored, such that being exceptional constitutes a risk factor.

When exceptionality is not addressed appropriately, it can lead to feelings of differentness, loneliness, boredom, frustration, and other developmental problems. One factor that increases the risks associated with gifted-level development is the acute sensitivity that can accompany advanced cognitive ability. Highly sensitive children and adolescents who perceive more of what is happening around them and throughout the world do not necessarily have the psychological maturity to manage their increased knowledge. They need adults with whom they can relate— adults who can answer their questions, respect their feelings, understand their concerns, and help them cope with difficult and troubling circumstances.[4]

In spite of political forces working toward educational standardization, educators around the world are increasingly realizing that they must target instruction to individual patterns of interest and ability in order to be effective.[5] This requires vision and courage, and many schools and school systems are implementing flexible and responsive approaches to individual learning needs.

One solution to the problem of educational resources that are stretched to (and sometimes past) the breaking point is to look past the school walls for whatever else can be tapped. There are countless examples of how educators and parents have worked together in stressful circumstances to create enriching learning experiences for children. One that comes to mind is the remarkable successes chronicled in the book *The Power of Their Ideas: Lessons for America from a Small School in Harlem.*[6] Wonderful things can happen when parents, educators, and students work cohesively, reaching out to the community and even further for relevant and authentic learning opportunities.[7] It is possible to solve many of the most intractable problems in gifted education when people share their perspectives in collaborative problem-solving forums, which Deborah Meier and her colleagues did, working together with students and parents to ensure that there were many learning opportunities across the ability spectrum.

In order for school-community partnerships to succeed, everyone has to be involved. It is important that the *student* feels engaged in and responsible for co-creating her own learning. In the process of contributing meaningfully to her education, she is also reducing the burden on the teacher to find ways to differentiate effectively. The *teacher's* role can become that of a flexible expert—someone who can facilitate productive problem finding and problem solving; be knowledgeable about and responsive to individual, developmental, and cultural differences in learning needs; and guide students intelligently through the learning process. As with the other roles, the *parent's* role varies across situations. Parents can provide the necessary supports, including day-to-day nurturing, as well as investigating learning opportunities in the community and beyond. The *administrator's* role is one of facilitation, network-building, and coordination. This can be on an individual or systemic basis, but it demands buy-in, as well as practiced negotiating and leadership skills.[8]

All of this may sound like an intensive investment of time and effort directed at each student in a situation in which there is a limited cadre of professionals working to educate many students in large, growing, and increasingly diverse classrooms—and it is. However, this kind of collaborative approach to solving gifted-related learning problems is almost always worthwhile. It prevents further problems with each student and helps them realize their capabilities both at school and beyond. This, in turn, has obvious benefits for the school as a whole and for society at large. Advantages to the collaborative approach include shared resources and creative problem solving; mentorship, apprenticeship, and community service opportunities; and authentic and extended community-based learning opportunities.[9]

We have seen this kind of cohesive effort in action.[10] As positive outcomes happen for one student, teacher attitudes begin to change, and then, through a process of osmosis and infiltration, or through professional development and a spirit of sharing, the school climate improves. Teachers begin to realize that they have excellent curriculum development allies and resources in their students, parents, and administrators and that there are opportunities available outside of the school that can supplement the increasingly stretched resource situation within its confines. Parents are relieved that their child can be academically challenged and successful. In our experience, even the busiest parents are glad to help make that happen. They discover that a relatively small investment of their time has big payoffs in their child's engagement in the learning process. This, in turn, enhances academic achievement and makes an important contribution to school attitudes and practices that can benefit all students.

The three basic tenets of this kind of collaborative approach involve facilitating: (1) each student's engagement in his own learning, (2) partnerships between the school and the family, and (3) community involvement in students' learning.[11]

By encouraging collaborations across individuals, families, schools, and communities, we find and create the best educational responses to a rapidly changing world, gaining access to resources and reducing burdens. Educators find themselves professionally re-energized when they realize that they do not have to do it alone anymore, and in fact, it is better if they do not.

Teacher education is one of the best catalysts for bringing together all of the pieces of a collaborative approach to gifted education. And when preservice, graduate, and inservice teacher education occurs in the context of a vibrant university-based gifted center that acts as a central information clearinghouse, it provides a range of support for students, parents, administrators, and others so that change can begin to happen rapidly.

University-Based Gifted Education Resource Centers

> *"I read with interest about the proposed center for gifted education. What I wouldn't give to have a place where I could learn more about my daughter's special needs!"*

Some universities have developed gifted education resource centers that are active, inclusive, vibrant places of learning, support, and interaction.[12] Most such centers are involved in developing curriculum, providing and evaluating programs for high-ability students, conducting research on gifted development, disseminating information, reaching out into diverse communities, and supporting teacher development. However, each one has its own focus and areas of specialization. We have been involved in initiatives to create such centers and have consulted with people at many others. We provide here a synthesis of our experiences and their suggestions.

Objectives of a Gifted Center

Gifted centers can:

- provide information and support for parents, educators, and academics interested in understanding and meeting the needs of exceptionally capable learners

- act as a catalyst for gifted program development, evaluation, and improvement
- foster gifted-level outcomes in diverse kinds of learners
- forge local, national, and international connections
- stimulate professional networking opportunities
- create local libraries for information resources and expertise
- generate interest in and knowledge about gifted education
- act as a clearinghouse for information about professional services
- promote educational liaisons and collaborative networks at all levels
- stimulate research on high-level development and education

A well-planned, well-funded, and well-run gifted center can work to bring together teacher development and support; student and family support; research and dissemination activities; and access to a wide range of local, regional, national, and international learning opportunities. It can create the invigorating confluence of activities, energies, and expertise that underlie authentic exploration and discovery.

Components of a Gifted Center

Teacher Development

- expertise and resources for teachers, from initial teacher training, through inservice workshops and ongoing professional development, to graduate courses, programs, and degrees
- access to a network of resources and opportunities for best practice and gaining knowledge about high-level learning

Teacher Support and Networking

- connections with others interested in research, seminars, workshops, and conferences on giftedness issues
- clarification of identification and assessment issues
- suggestions for instructional models and approaches

- resource bank of material at different grade levels and in various subject areas for use by those who work with children who are advanced in particular domains, exhibit asynchronous development, or have multiple exceptionalities

- support for action research

Student Support and Networking

- support for learning and other gifted-related needs

- access to diverse extracurricular learning enrichments

- information on counseling and mentorships, including access to university mentorships[13]

- connections to other children and adolescents with similar interests and concerns

Family Support and Networking

- opportunities to connect with other parents with giftedness concerns and ideas to share

- access to reliable information about programs and professional services

- opportunities for networking with educators

- help for siblings of gifted learners who may have issues and special learning needs of their own

- place to acquire a stronger sense of community

School Support

- support for administrators in fostering school cultures where gifted learners are challenged and high-level ability is nurtured

- access to teacher development programs and experts in the field of gifted education

- support for action research

- access to practical information and resources

- networking possibilities

- support for interschool collaboration locally and across districts

Collaborations within the University

- coordination of resources within the university across programs, departments, and disciplines
- collaborative explorations of high-level development in different disciplines

Community and Global Outreach

- connections to local museums, dance companies, music schools, and other cultural institutions that support talent development
- collaborations with parent groups, business partners, government connections, and educational relationships of many kinds, local to international in scope
- interschool mentorships
- teacher seminars
- advanced technological services for networking purposes
- parent awareness workshops and activities on a variety of gifted-related topics
- proactive inclusion of at-risk students in high-risk neighborhoods
- connections to other gifted centers around the world

Research, Publication, and Dissemination

- support for collaborative investigations
- symposia for shared learning
- research on high-level development and education
- a nexus for information for the community, including media and policy-makers
- active and dynamic learning and sharing of material

In many of its components, a gifted center can be virtual, but it should also be a real place—where people can find someone to talk with about their concerns, have a cup of coffee, and put their hands on actual books and journals. Its virtual dimension should include a comprehensive website where parents, educators, and students can find current information on gifted development, educational options, and the latest research findings. A gifted center can make a significant and lasting difference for children, teachers, and parents, as well as for the community as a whole. In our opinion, anywhere that teacher training is happening, there should be a gifted center.

Different communities have different priorities and resources (financial and otherwise), and a gifted resource center has to be designed within that context to meet local needs. If you live in a place that has such a center, use it and work with it to help make it stronger and enable it to better meet your needs. If you do not have a facility like this available in your area, you might think about linking to one or becoming involved in advocacy efforts to support the establishment of such a resource in your community. A university-based center can provide a link among existing activities and programs related to higher education, including coordinating resources for students, families, and teachers; stimulating real understanding of the nature of giftedness; and optimizing learning and life experiences for many people.

Questions and Answers

In this book, we have addressed many questions about how giftedness develops and how parents and educators can support that process. This is only a starting point. For readers wishing to explore particular areas more deeply, we have provided references to resources for further consideration. Although we addressed gifted education internationally in the first edition of this book, we have not included it in this edition. Other sources address global happenings in gifted education much more fully than we can do justice to here, reflecting the complexity, richness, and diversity of people's experiences in other countries.[14]

We recognize that there are important questions posed by parents, teachers, children, and others for which answers are not yet known. Sally Reis has identified five turning points of current reality that can be used as springboards for future research in gifted education:[15]

- expanding conceptions of the multidimensionality of giftedness and talent development

- eradicating the absence of challenge from too many students' school experience

- addressing the needs of underserved populations

- moving from identifying gifted students to developing competencies instead

- applying gifted education pedagogy to talent development, with an emphasis on strengths

Other important information is emerging from new directions and current findings in developmental psychology. These include better understandings of extracognitive factors in talent development (such as psychosocial factors and the environmental supports and constraints that can influence the development of giftedness) and links among creativity, competency, and productivity across contexts and domains.[16] Additional areas of focus that have been targeted as promising for future research include the systematic study of diverse kinds of intelligences, information about transitional periods in maturation and development, explorations of multiple pathways to gifted-level development and expertise, and studies of developmental variability over time.

In short, the questions that researchers and others are asking most urgently concern discovering ways to develop a generation of learners who are competent, enthusiastic, resilient, and self-directed and who can find joy and fulfillment in personal growth. Promising answers are emerging. We are happy to see research moving forward, tapping into such realms as technological advances to enhance gifted education,[17] the effects of brain development on teaching and learning, and vice versa,[18] creative productivity,[19] curricular models,[20] and collaborative partnerships.[21]

In thinking about questions and answers for today and tomorrow, we recognize that we are not the last word on the complex topics covered in this book. We enthusiastically welcome our readers' inquiry and responses, including any comments, suggestions, observations, requests, or critiques.

The Importance of Staying Up to Date

> *Positioning our efforts within the best possible education for all and acknowledging that we do not know the limits or scope of human potential gives us a conceptual framework for the future.*[22]

Many parents and educators who are interested in giftedness also want to understand how current findings in developmental psychology and the cognitive neurosciences apply to teaching and learning. There are many reasons why keeping up to date with changing understandings is particularly important when living or working with exceptionally capable children. One reason is to ensure that children have access to the best learning opportunities. A second is to be better equipped to address and support their emotional, social, motivational, and other needs. Another is the desire to encourage gifted learners to consider possible careers in cutting-edge fields. If they don't know about emerging career opportunities in the neurosciences, for example, they are unlikely to think about preparing themselves for this area of specialization.

It is difficult for professionals to stay apprised of the latest research findings in their own fields, and it is considerably more difficult to know much about research findings that might be pertinent but that are being reported in other fields. Current findings concerning the brain, for example, have a direct and important impact on many aspects of teaching and learning, as well as on parenting.[23] Certainly, it can be daunting for laypeople to discern dependable, well-supported findings from well-marketed misconceptions concerning the way in which children's brains develop. As Internet resources continue to evolve, they will help to provide increasingly sophisticated possibilities for connectivity and access to information, but there continue to be traditional ways to keep up to date, too. By reading newsletters, journal articles, and books like this one, attending education conferences where experts and practitioners share their research and ideas, and talking with one another about concerns, questions, and experiences, individuals can acquire useful information. Keeping up to date is increasingly vital as we all work together to support high-ability learners at home, school, and beyond.

Being Smart about Tomorrow

The most important task facing us today is how to develop and sustain talent by fostering a love of learning, a zest for challenge, and resilience in the face of setbacks.[24]

Although we confront many challenges in our lives, our communities, and globally, there are also indicators that it is a time of unprecedented opportunity for making a difference. In this book, we provide evidence-based suggestions for supporting the development of those who are exceptionally capable in one or more domains, as well as for fostering optimal development in all children. We emphasize that giftedness is domain-specific and highly diverse and that it is not easily measured or always even recognized. We are excited about the paradigm shift in the field of gifted education, as the mastery perspective gains momentum and provides an impetus to foster gifted-level outcomes in more and more children.

We have given you many tools in these pages, not only for coping with the challenges of teaching and parenting gifted learners, but also for enjoying the process. We hope that you will continue being smart about the wealth of opportunities available for encouraging and supporting gifted level development in those children with whom you work, live, and share the richness of life.

Test Scores: The Nuts and Bolts of Assessments

We have already covered many basic concepts surrounding tests and assessments. Our intention with this Appendix is to dig a little deeper into the numbers so that teachers and parents can better understand the process and appreciate how test scores can be helpful when tests are professionally administered and interpreted. Testing and test documents are, in the words of one parent, "the nuts and bolts of assessment that parents have to deal with. Test results may be all we've got to advocate for our child, and we need to understand them." As we have discussed throughout this book, there are many other sources of information that can (and should) also be used to inform good educational decisions for children, but often the case for appropriate programming is made most easily and compellingly through test scores. Wise parents and teachers will invest some time in understanding tests and scores so they can help ensure that decisions based on them make sense.

Interpreting Test Scores

> *"We had the testing done, and the report came, and there weren't any scores. The psychologist said that she never includes the scores—that scores just confuse people."*
> *"Ethan got 135 on the IQ test. What a smart boy!"*

In a psychoeducational assessment, many different kinds of scores are generated—subtest scores, scale scores, and composite scores from academic achievement tests, intelligence tests, self-esteem measures, and more. All of these test scores can be confusing to parents, as well as to teachers, and can even distract parents and educators from the report's key findings and recommendations. Some psychologists respond to these problems by omitting test scores from their reports entirely, providing only a written description of the child's strengths and weak areas. This may avoid placing too much focus on the numbers, but—like a non-graded anecdotal report card—it can leave parents, teachers, and children wondering about the nature and degree of the exceptionality. After reading a report with no numbers, parents and teachers may find that they are even more confused about the child's ability than they were before the assessment.

In some circumstances, such as when an assessment has been done specifically to address a question of categorical identification ("Is the child gifted?"), the report might include the scores but very little interpretive information other than score classifications such as "significantly above average" or "average." In such cases, the report may be short and succinct (one to three pages). In addition to the basic scores, this kind of report includes only a few relevant observations and programming recommendations, unless there is some variability across subtest scores or test behaviors that the psychologist thinks should be noted.

When parents or educators want a more detailed understanding of a child's learning needs, a full psychoeducational assessment can be conducted. This typically includes:

- an individually administered intelligence test

- a battery of high-ceiling academic achievement tests, including various aspects of mathematical calculation and reasoning, reading decoding and comprehension, technical writing skills, and other skills as indicated

- an assessment of school functioning through an analysis of report cards, classroom observation, and interviews with teachers as necessary

- measures of self-concept and attitudes to learning

- interviews with the child and parents

- observations of the child's response to different test situations, including areas of strength, errors, and learning challenges

The resulting assessment report is designed to be as informative as possible to parents and teachers about the child's learning profile, and it includes not only an indication of the scores, but also detailed descriptions of the child's strengths and challenges, as well as recommendations for both home and school. Typically, a psychoeducational report is followed by a discussion with the educational psychologist responsible for the report.

Table A.1 shows a somewhat modified version[1] of the categorical descriptors used to designate ranges of scores on standardized tests of intelligence in which the mean is 100 and the standard deviation is 15 (which describes almost all tests in wide use). Earlier classification systems included terms such as "borderline," "mentally retarded," "mentally deficient," and "very superior," all of which have been criticized as evaluative. This classification system is more descriptive and less judgmental.

Table A.1. Standard Score Classification

Test Score	Classification
130+	Significantly above average
120-129	Moderately above average
110-119	Above average
90-109	Average
80-89	Below average
70-79	Moderately below average
69 and below	Significantly below average

Although the top scoring range includes test scores above 130, what actually constitutes giftedness is contentious. In some school districts, a score of 120 leads to gifted consideration; in others, scores have to be at least 140; and sometimes (in very rare cases), the gifted criterion can be even higher than that.

Translating Standard Scores into Percentiles

> *"These numbers don't make any sense to me! Why can't psychologists just use plain English?!"*

For most people, the best way to understand test scores is in percentiles.[2] Percentiles provide the clearest and simplest explanations of a person's actual functioning relative to others. Knowing that a child has scored at the 50th percentile in some areas (that is, at or higher than 50% of people her age) and at the 99th percentile in other areas (at or higher than 99% of people her age) has clear implications for her learning needs. A student who scores at the 99th percentile in a test of language reasoning, for example, is clearly exceptional in some aspects of her linguistic abilities and learning needs, in a way that might not be as obvious if it was reported as a standardized score (that is, 135 or higher). When parents or educators are provided with assessment information, and the standard scores do not seem to make sense, they should ask for the percentile equivalents. It is a very reasonable request to make. Alternatively, they can do their own score conversion using the chart in Table A.2.

Table A.2. Translating Standard Scores into Percentiles

Score	Percentile
155	99.99
150	99.96
145	99.87
140	99.62
135	99
130	98
125	95
120	91
115	84
110	75
105	63
100	50
95	37
90	25
85	16
80	9
75	5
70	2
65	1

Tables A.1 and A.2 apply to scores that are computed with a mean of 100 (that is, the average score is 100) and a standard deviation of 15 (a measure of scores' variation around the mean which indicates that 68% of the population's scores fall between 85 and 115).

Score Conversion

> *"I am trying to convert my daughter's WPPSI-R scores into an IQ score so that I can understand some of the material I've been reading. I have no idea when I'm reading these articles if they apply to my child."*

Standard scores such as those provided for the Wechsler Preschool and Primary Scale of Intelligence (WPPSI-R) are already IQ scores and do not need to be converted. Sometimes when people ask questions like these, what they really want to know is, "How well did my child do on the test?" In these cases, knowing the score classification and how to convert a standard score into a percentile gives them the answers they need. Tables A.1 and A.2 can be helpful in making sense of most of the scores.

Composite Scores

> *"What is a composite score actually made up of?"*

A composite score, as its name suggests, is a single score that summarizes several other scores. For example, the full scale score for an intelligence test (which is often called an Intelligence Quotient or IQ) is a composite of several subscales, each of which is itself a composite of several subtests. When a child has scored fairly consistently across subtests, his composite score can provide reasonably good shorthand communication for understanding his abilities.

However, when there is a large discrepancy across the scores on the various subtests, the composite score may be more harmful than helpful. In fact, we would go so far as to say that combining highly disparate ability scores to create a single score yields more *misinformation* than *useful* information. For example, a child who scores 140 (99.6th percentile, significantly above average) on the verbal scale of the WISC-III, and 80 on the performance scale (9th percentile, bottom of the below average range) is a child who should be considered both for gifted programming in verbal areas, as well as remediation of problems with some aspect(s) of abstract/visual processing. However, her overall IQ will be computed to fall just into the above average range (a full scale IQ of 110), which reflects neither her giftedness nor her learning problems. In cases like this in which there are wide discrepancies across scores, it is best for test administrators to omit the composite score—or, at the very least, explain thoroughly how it has been derived and what the implications are—as it can be more misleading than informative.

Interpreting Lower-than-Expected Scores

> *"We were surprised. Cindy's test scores were lower than we thought they'd be."*

There is no way for a child to do exceptionally well on a test other than to know the information and demonstrate the skills being tested. High scores always reflect a high level of competence on whatever is being tested. However, when test scores are lower than expected, that does not necessarily mean that a child does not have the knowledge and/or skills being tested. When scores do not seem to reflect a child's actual ability, there are many possible reasons for it—in addition to the possibility that the child is not as competent as he otherwise appears to be. Some of the reasons for test scores underestimating a person's ability include illness, distraction, depression, test anxiety, fatigue, environmental conditions such as noise or heat, and a lack of rapport with the tester.

Language is another important consideration. If a child's first language, parents' language, or language of schooling is not the language of testing, the child is at a serious disadvantage in an assessment for giftedness. She has not had the same opportunities as others her age to learn some of the facts being tested or how to communicate that knowledge effectively and succinctly in a test situation. Moreover, she has not had the same opportunities to think through, discuss, and work out complex problems in that language. In such cases, scores should be seen as a low estimate of the child's actual ability. This is most obviously true in linguistic areas of an assessment, although there is a second-language impact on quantitative and spatial reasoning areas, too.

Similarly, culture is an important factor in interpreting test scores. For example, some children grow up in families and cultures where the achievement that is valued is practical rather than intellectual, or where individual or unusual opinions are prized over "getting the right answer," or where abstract reasoning tasks are considered a waste of time. Moreover, some children do not see the point of doing a puzzle for its own sake or just because a stranger has asked them to do so. These children will not function as well on standardized tests as they might in more applied settings, and they won't do as well as children who grow up being encouraged to participate in challenging intellectual games, tasks, and puzzles.

Temperament is another reason why children may perform more poorly on tests than they do in their lives. Some highly capable children have very little interest in sitting through a test in which the examiner seems to have all the fun figuring out the activities, asking all the questions, and giving the orders. Children who are independent, curious, individualistic, or creative and who have strong ideas about what they do and do not like to do are hard to test, particularly when they are young.

Test scores, therefore, do not always accurately reflect an individual's actual ability, and many circumstances can impair a child's ability to demonstrate his competence. When trying to make sense of low scores that appear not to make sense, there may in fact be one or more explanations other than lack of ability.

Understanding Scoring Patterns

An assessment often contains many different findings that at first glance may seem confusing or even as though they contradict each other. There are, however, some scoring patterns that can help parents and educators understand assessment findings as they come together. We describe four of these patterns here.

Global Giftedness

Some students who achieve extremely high scores across all or almost all of the subtests of the measures administered might be understood as having "global gifted learning needs." The clearest example of such a case is a student who scores consistently above the 99th percentile on all intelligence and academic subtests on an assessment, across the full spectrum of subject areas. This student would be a candidate for a range of acceleration and enrichment opportunities, supplemented by interest-based extracurricular learning options.

Domain-Specific Giftedness

There are students who show clear domain-specific trends across subtests—for instance, those who can be considered mathematically or linguistically advanced—but who function more closely to average in their other abilities. In such cases, educational adaptations are required in certain subject areas only and might not be appropriate in others.

Multiple Exceptionalities

Some students show different extremes across different tests, or across kinds of items on the same test, with patterns that indicate learning and/or attention problems along with gifted-level development. Some of these students need differentiation both for giftedness and for learning problems, and they can be frustrated with school if their needs are not addressed. It is cases like this in which it is most important that an assessment be interpreted by someone with expertise in multiple exceptionalities that include giftedness.

Anomalous Scoring Patterns

Not all assessments yield consistent results that fit into a particular scoring pattern. Some students have very high scores in some subtests in a certain domain but not in other subtests that appear to be measuring similar kinds of ability. This requires attention to the details of the items administered, including error analyses, especially on the lower-scoring subtests. Parents have the right to a clear interpretation of the test results in straightforward language.[3] Parents and educators who have concerns about an assessment report should ask about the discrepancies between their sense of the child's ability and the scores obtained. Sometimes anomalous findings can only be understood by doing further testing or retesting.

Looking for the Anomaly

Sam was nine years old in Grade 4 in a regular classroom program when we met him. Although he loved math and was always looking for opportunities to develop new and related skills, he hated math at school. He had stopped doing his homework or complying with his teacher's requests to complete math activities. Naturally, his math grades started slipping badly. His parents brought him to our office for an assessment.

Sam participated enthusiastically in the assessment, enjoying the intellectual challenges and, in particular, the mathematical puzzles. He did very well generally, and there were no indications whatsoever of any cognitive processing or other kind of learning problem. He reported that math was his least favorite school subject. Although he scored well into the significantly above average category (above the 99th percentile) on the two mathematics achievement subtests that were administered and on one of the two quantitative subtests on the Stanford-Binet Intelligence Scale, 4th Edition (SB-IV), he scored in the average range on a second SB-IV quantitative subtest. This put his overall SB-IV quantitative area score in the high average range. It was clearly not representative of his exceptional mathematical ability as demonstrated elsewhere in the assessment, and it weakened the likelihood that a recommendation for gifted math programming would be followed up by the school.

Upon inspection of the SB-IV mathematical subtest where Sam scored in the average range, it became obvious that there had been an interaction between the test design and his knowledge base. The lower score on the problematic subtest reflected a lack of *specific content knowledge* rather than any lack of exceptionality in his mathematical reasoning ability—although the much broader assessment provided by the academic achievement tests demonstrated that his content mastery was exceptionally strong. By excluding the anomalous SB-IV subtest from consideration, programming recommendations could be made for Sam, including advanced work in mathematics that fit his learning needs.

Sam's teacher responded favorably to the recommendations. She received administrative support and implemented changes thoughtfully and creatively, which led to a much improved academic situation for Sam. After a few weeks, his parents reported that for the first time in years, he was looking forward to going to school and was actually enjoying doing his homework because, as he said, "I'm learning stuff now!" Had the assessment scores been reported without considering the subtest scoring patterns, Sam would not have been identified as having special educational needs. It is likely that he would have continued the slide into the academic apathy and behavior problems which had brought him in for testing in the first place.

A Case Study with Excerpts from a Psychoeducational Report

In the following vignette, we present some excerpts from a psycho-educational report in order to illustrate the kinds of information contained in such documents.

Paul's Story

Paul, a Grade 7 student, was one of those kids who people think of as a "computer nerd." His hair was lanky and unkempt, his glasses were always slipping down his nose, his posture, clothing, and gait were ungainly, and he appeared oblivious to the world around him. He looked as if he had never seen the sun, and you couldn't imagine him playing any kind of sport. In class, he was lost in his own world. He often asked the teacher to repeat questions, and sometimes he laughed aloud at inappropriate moments.

Paul was not achieving particularly well at school, and he had certainly never been identified by a teacher as having special abilities in any area. Even in kindergarten, he found school a waste of time. He often asked his mother if he could stay home and do something useful, like teach himself a new computer program. Paul's parents vacillated, valuing school but seeing how miserable he was and recognizing that he seemed to be a misfit among his age peers.

Paul's social oddness never really troubled him. He was not interested in what most of the other kids did or said, and he did not appear to notice that he was not included in their activities. He never liked it when teachers tried to help him fit in better, and he truly hated the social skills group he was forced to attend in Grade 4.

Paul's mother wondered if he might be intellectually gifted, in spite of the fact that he had not been recommended even for the gifted screening tests in their school board. She had been an excellent student, her husband had a Ph.D. in philosophy, and there were several eminent scientists and musicians in the extended family. Given the family history, Paul's individualistic temperament, and his intense interests, she thought that his differentness might be a reflection of exceptional intelligence instead of the "weirdness" and "social problems" that people had been suggesting through the years. She felt that if Paul were in a more intellectually challenging milieu, he might find school more interesting.

Paul's mother arranged to have him tested on the IQ test that her school board recognized for gifted identification. The results follow:

Wechsler Intelligence Scale for Children, 3rd Edition (WISC-III)

Area	Standard Score	Percentile	Classification
Verbal Scale	140	99.5	Significantly above average
Performance Scale	106	66	Average
Full scale (IQ)	126*	96	Above average

A psychometric note to the mathematically observant or curious: The full scale IQ is not an average of the other scale scores, but rather a reflection of the deviation from the mean of the sum of all of the subtest scores. The farther from the mean, the higher the score, and so if most or all subtests are above the mean, the full scale score will be higher than the average across scale scores.

The psychologist's comments included these observations:

Paul was serious, focused, intense, and attentive throughout the testing session. He demonstrated excellent task commitment and an interest in working with abstract intellectual concepts. The WISC-III Verbal subtest and scale scores demonstrate his exceptionally well-developed verbal reasoning abilities and conceptual mastery of many areas. His very high scores on the information and comprehension subtests in particular illustrate his exceptional knowledge of a very broad range of areas. He answered in some depth and with considerable assurance and accuracy questions on science, history, geography, and politics. For example, when asked why it is important to have freedom of speech in a democracy, he replied, "If we didn't, no one could ever say anything against the government. The government could then do what it wanted, and no one could stop it."

> On the performance scale, Paul's scores were considerably lower than on the verbal scale. This was not because of any kind of cognitive processing problem that was observed (he did all subtest tasks very well, frequently getting all items correct), but only because of the timing factor. When he was asked about his lower performance on these kinds of tasks he said, "I prefer not to make mistakes and do it slowly rather than to make mistakes and get it done really quickly." He then described his work with programming computers, where, if he makes an error, he only realizes it later, and then it is costly in time and effort to recover it. So he has learned to work very carefully. Although this approach does not lead to scoring exceptionally well on subtests like those on the performance scale of the WISC-III, it is a very intelligent way to approach many real-world tasks.

Paul's story illustrates the need to be very careful when interpreting test scores. Paul had appeared to be an average student at school, and his overall IQ score would not be considered high enough to give him the gifted designation in most jurisdictions. Some psychologists would have interpreted the discrepancy between the verbal and performance scales as evidence of a learning disability. However, thoughtful observation and discussion with Paul, in combination with a careful analysis of the scores, led us to realize that he is not learning disabled at all. Rather, he is a highly competent learner who has taught himself to be discriminating when completing certain kinds of tasks—and who requires gifted programming if he is to benefit from school.

By the way, Paul's story has a happy ending. His mother took the report to her school principal. He, then, became proactive in ensuring that Paul was identified as a gifted learner and offered a placement in a full-time gifted class. Paul actually started to like school, at least most of the time. He found people he enjoyed talking to, and he won some major contests and awards for his computer science activities. He may never be a social leader, but as he has gotten older, he has been able to find groups where he can fit in and where his idiosyncrasies appear "normal."

Educational Decision Making

"I hear lots of talk in the neighborhood; people seem to think that enrichment is not necessary at private schools but that it is necessary at public schools. Is that true?"
"We've narrowed it down to three possibilities. How do we know which school is the best one for us?"

With so many programming possibilities and learning opportunities from which to choose, how does one decide? To begin with, in most cases, it is not a one-time-only decision, and an educational decision is not irrevocable. The more exceptional the child, the more likely it is that parents and educators, as well as the student, will find themselves in an ongoing process of educational rethinking and decision making. It is both good news and bad news that regular (at least annual) monitoring is required. It reduces the pressure attached to any one decision, but it also adds to family uncertainties because the question stays open about how a child is doing and what aspects of her education require changes or, at the very least, some thoughtful tinkering.[1]

Consider the following email that we received from Jeane. At the time of this first note, it was clear that her older son, Thomas, who was in kindergarten, was going to need accommodations for his exceptional curiosity and advanced interests and abilities in science, math, and other areas.

Jeane's School Choice Experience: Part One

Here are our latest thoughts on schools for next year in Grade 1. I'd love your comments.

Idea #1: We keep Thomas at Boxwood, the nearby public school, and I make a special effort to supplement his studies through my own form of teaching, such as trips to the library with his little brother Edward on a regular, scheduled basis to study different things and then have him do projects on them. Also augment the math, etc. I'd do this in conjunction with what he's learning at Boxwood, and I'd talk to his teacher about appropriate topics. I'd also have study times for Thomas every day at home, and Edward could color or do something else. And then he'd have some time during the week for play dates and other extracurricular activities. Also, we'd schedule family trips to the Science Center, etc.

My husband wonders if this is too much for me to take on, but I'd be doing most of it right after school, when I'd be carpooling anyway if he was at a school farther from home. I think this might challenge Thomas enough, while giving him a nurturing home and neighborhood environment. I've heard that the Grade 1 teachers at Boxwood are excellent. They have different styles, but both run good, organized classes.

Idea #2: The other option is Lancaster, the private school, along with programs which augment the curriculum, maybe a form of enrichment once a week after school. What do you think? I continue to hear terrific things about Lancaster. It apparently has a lot of individual attention for the kids, they work hard, etc. But will he get tired of the same small school in the later grades?

Right now we're talking to a few people, both with kids at Boxwood and at Lancaster. But all in all, I think we're spending far too much time on this! When Thomas is in college, we'll laugh about how much time we spent worrying about his Grade 1 education! I mean, he's only five!

It almost makes one's head spin to think of all the variables and issues here, and as Jeane wrote, we are talking about a five-year-old child who has not had any problems with school. Jeane's analysis of how to supplement the education at the public school is excellent, including her description of spending time with her children doing interesting things instead of carpooling. One of the themes running below the surface of this correspondence is the differences that parents often have with each other. In this case, both parents love their children and are seriously committed to their well-being; any conflict reflects the complexities of the decision-making process and the fact that no school is likely to be perfect. In this case, the conflict is a minor problem that the parents resolve (as you will see). In some families we've worked with, it can take on larger proportions and become a problem much bigger than the school choice itself.

The most important thing in children's lives, especially at this early stage, is not which schools are chosen, but that the children feel loved, encouraged, and respected, particularly by their parents. Generally speaking, the more traditional the school environment, the less likely it is to accommodate a highly capable child's independent spirit and love of learning. However, as long as the child is not being harmed by her school environment (which does happen sometimes but is rare), extracurricular activities can often supplement what might be missing from the formal curriculum. Knowing this can help make the decision-making process less anxiety-provoking for parents. It is also helpful to remember that much of a child's important learning does not happen in classrooms. Most of the people who go on to interesting gifted-level achievement did not have exemplary or unusual early schooling experiences.

In the end, Jeane and her husband decided on Lancaster (a private school with an excellent academic reputation), which they thought would be better suited to Thomas' creative, intense, and intrinsically-motivated learning style. An interesting postscript to the story is that Thomas spent two and a half years at Lancaster (with his little brother Edward joining him for the second year and a half, and a third child having been born into the family in the meantime). However, sometime in first grade, the teachers began to express concerns about Thomas' poor handwriting and his troublingly enthusiastic behavior, which was described as a problem with impulse control and following school rules. He had a hard time restraining his curiosity when he had a question, for example, and found it very difficult not to blurt it out in class—something frequently seen in primary school children, particularly boys.

These concerns did not disappear in second grade, and Thomas' parents were informed that Thomas might not pass into third grade. Told by the school that he might have learning problems and worried about their son's academic ability, Jeane and her husband had him tested by a private psychologist. The psychologist discovered no learning problems whatsoever and concluded that Thomas' only "problem" was high-level development in some areas. After sharing the assessment results with Lancaster and working with the Grade 3 teacher to implement the educational recommendations, including various differentiation strategies, his parents still felt that Thomas' learning needs were not being well met. The school's position continued to be that he needed to work on his penmanship and social maturity and that he might fail the grade if his printing did not improve. So Jeane and her husband decided to move both boys to Boxwood Public School. The next year, we received this message from Jeane.

Jeane's School Choice Experience: Part Two

Boxwood Public School is great—in lots of ways, it's better than I'd anticipated; in some ways, the same as I'd thought. As for Edward, he is in his element. The kids love him and find him funny, and the teacher can see that he's very clever.

Now for the really interesting part. I could go on and on about this, but in a nutshell, here it is. The Lancaster School must have an amazing public relations person to have developed such a great reputation for itself as being so academically advanced and challenging. Parents believe that only the brightest kids are accepted and do well. But this just isn't the case. Both Thomas and Edward are being challenged *more* at Boxwood. They are asked to do more stimulating and harder things while using the same textbooks as Lancaster in a lot of cases! Plus, they have the huge advantages of being able to get up an hour later in the morning, come home for lunch when they want, and they don't have the drive at both ends of the day. All in all, they're learning as much as I'd hoped while also having a lot more free time. It's ideal! The funniest part is that Thomas is asking us to let him go back to

> Lancaster, even with the longer days, because the work is too hard at Boxwood! Ha! With his scores on the assessment, I think he can handle it!
>
> Anyway, I find this most interesting in light of the fact that a lot of parents around here assume that private schools have better academics, the kids learn more, etc. Yes, they often have better art programs, and some have better sports programs, but $16,000 a year is a high price to pay, not to mention the lack of neighborhood feeling!

Jeane's story is a true one, and we have heard many different versions of this same story over the years. Not surprisingly perhaps, the parents of exceptional learners often discover that the experiences of other parents cannot be directly applied to their circumstances. Yet there is much to be learned from the decision-making experiences of others. In Thomas' case, he was clearly not well-understood or appreciated at the traditional private school, where the focus was on his learning problems (his penmanship and exuberant curiosity) rather than his exceptional intelligence and his love for learning. By switching to the local public school (which happened to be an unusually good one at the time), Jeane and her family gained many advantages, including a more relaxed lifestyle, a better educational match, and considerable financial savings. This story illustrates the flexibility required and the need to see educational decision making as an ongoing work-in-progress when dealing with gifted learners. The school choice experience should work to include *everyone's* best interests and aspirations. It is vital that parents and children talk about the possibilities and listen to one another.

Remember also that educational placement decisions are rarely irrevocable. Families can make their best effort at a decision, try it out for long enough to be able to distinguish between adjustment problems and problems with the actual setting (should problems occur), and if it isn't working, change their minds. There is no magic formula for figuring out how long should be given to the trial. This can vary tremendously from one situation to the next, but a family usually knows within the first six weeks whether a change is going to work or not. Although Jeane and her husband did all of their homework (and then some!), they made one decision that they later realized was probably a mistake. By being flexible and paying attention to their children's learning experiences, they rectified it. Yes, it cost quite a lot of time and money, but it appears that there was no permanent damage. In the end, they gained a lot of information about educational services, and they all learned the very valuable lessons that everyone makes mistakes and that with thoughtful attention, these mistakes can be rectified.

Although Jeane and her husband found the local public school an appropriate choice for their family, we do not want to suggest that public schools are always the best option for high-ability learners. We work with some remarkable independent and private schools that deserve their strong reputations for excellence, and we have enormous respect for many private school administrators and teachers who work collaboratively with parents to accommodate children's special learning needs in innovative ways. We include this story to make the points that: (1) private schools are not necessarily better than public schools, in spite of popular misconceptions about this, (2) parents and children need to challenge commonly held assumptions and think about their own situations with fresh eyes, asking what works best for their families, and (3) parents whose budgets cannot be stretched to cover private school costs should not worry that they are letting their children down. For more on the merits of different kinds of schools, see Chapter 7.

Poem

Note from Dona: Joanne wrote this poem many years ago. It was her way of capturing some of the questions she was pondering about children's experiences of being labeled as gifted, and being Joanne, she was whimsical, relentless, and methodical in the writing process. As she kept asking herself more and more questions, she realized that they were urgent and that the answers were important for parents and teachers. We had discussed the idea of collaborating on a book, and this was just the catalyst I needed. Over the next year or so, we wrote what later became Being Smart about Gifted Children, *and we have worked together on many other projects since then. Here is an abridged version of Joanne's questions in poem form. We continue to look for answers.*

They Tell Me I'm Gifted…

They tell me I'm gifted… What does this mean?
Is this something new, or have I always been?

> *They tell me I'm gifted… Congratulations!*
> *But I am uncertain about expectations.*

They tell me I'm gifted… I'm lucky, I'm blessed.
But how do they know that from one written test?

> *They tell me I'm gifted… I'm not quite sure why.*
> *But everyone thinks my "potential" is high.*

They tell me I'm gifted… With increased understanding.
I wonder, will this make my life more demanding?

They tell me I'm gifted… Although I'm not sure
If it's something I'm meant to enjoy or endure.

They tell me I'm gifted… Where do I belong?
They say it's all right, but it sometimes seems wrong.

They tell me I'm gifted… It must be for real.
But it doesn't explain all the things that I feel.

They tell me I'm gifted… New school, new friends…
Is this a beginning, or is it an end?

They tell me I'm gifted… What should I conclude?
Is this why the other kids sometimes seem rude?

They tell me I'm gifted… I wish I were wise
'Cause then I might know what the label implies.

They tell me I'm gifted… And if this is true
Does this signify I have more "gifts" than you?

They tell me I'm gifted… I've so much to learn!
But sometimes I just don't know which way to turn.

They tell me I'm gifted… Who really knows?
Is it something unseen, or something that shows?

They tell me I'm gifted… Can this be outgrown?
What's in my future? It's all so unknown!

They tell me I'm gifted… Yet they don't explain
If it's <u>all</u> of me, or just a part of my brain.

They tell me I'm gifted… Is that a fact?
Do I have to change how I think, feel, and act?

They tell me I'm gifted… From whose point of view?
Does this mean that I am no longer like you?

They tell me I'm gifted… Could this be a blessing?
Who knows for sure, and who's only guessing?

> *They tell me I'm gifted… What should I do now?*
> *Do I shrug? Do I laugh? Do I cry? Do I bow?*

They tell me I'm gifted… They say I'm unique.
Do I have to show strengths? Can't I ever be weak?

> *They tell me I'm gifted… Now I'm in a jam.*
> *Do they think I'm smarter than I really am?*

They tell me I'm gifted… Is it destiny?
Controlled by what's inside or outside of me?

> *They tell me I'm gifted… I don't really see it.*
> *And if that's the case, then how can I be it?*

They tell me I'm gifted… I think that means able.
I hope others know they should look past the label.

> *They tell me I'm gifted… What do I need?*
> *Love and support that will help me succeed.*

They tell me I'm gifted… And so it must be,
But I know deep inside that I'm still only me…

> *~ Joanne F. Foster*

Endnotes

Chapter 1

1 Tannenbaum, 2000, p. 23

2 Matthews, Subotnik, & Horowitz, 2009; Renzulli & Reis, 2009; Worrell, 2009

3 Renzulli & Reis, 2009; Treffinger, Nassab, & Selby, 2009

4 Borland, 2003; Hymer, 2009

5 Callahan & Reis, 2004; Rogers, 2002; VanTassel-Baska & Brown, 2009

6 The Marland Report (Marland, 1972) addressed discrepancies between children's abilities and actual gifted programs, stating that children who are exceptional in one or more designated categories should be provided with special educational services. We discuss this further later in this chapter.

7 Julian Stanley was a pioneer in developing programs to identify and address mathematical ability in young people. The SMPY remains one of the strongest examples of the value of domain-specific conceptions of giftedness (Stanley & Benbow, 1983; Stanley, Keating, & Fox, 1974).

8 Robinson & Robinson, 1982

9 Gardner, 1983

10 Borland, 1989

11 Borland, 1989, p. 2

12 Howe, 1990

13 Keating,1991; Feldman, 1991

14 The talent development approach (Jarvin & Subotnik, 2006; Tannenbaum, 1983) focuses on supporting the development of domain-specific talent (e.g., music, mathematics, language) as it becomes evident in young people.

15 The integrated curriculum model, developed by Joyce VanTassel-Baska and her colleagues at the College of William and Mary (VanTassel-Baska & Brown, 2009; VanTassel-Baska & Stambaugh, 2006), emphasizes the importance of integrating gifted differentiation strategies into the regular curriculum, ensuring developmental sequence and coherence in gifted education programs.

16 The enrichment triad model (Renzulli & Reis, 2009; Reis, 2009) specifies several levels of domain-specific gifted learning needs (from early exploration of a domain

through serious investigations of that domain) and is broadly inclusive, expanding the categorical distinction between "gifted" and "not gifted." As it is further developed, it is becoming closer to the mastery model in its practical implications, but early descriptions did specify that a certain percentage of the population would fall into the "gifted" category.

17 Assouline, Colangelo, Lupkowski-Shoplik, Lipscomb, & Forstadt, 2009; Colangelo, Assouline, & Gross, 2004; Smutny, Walker, & Meckstroth, 2007

18 Butterworth, 2006; Ericsson, Charness, Feltovich, & Hoffman, 2006

19 Dweck, 2006b

20 Dweck, 2009a, 2009b

21 Balchin, 2009; Borland, 2003; Feldhusen, 2003; Horowitz, 2009; Hymer, Whitehead, & Huxtable, 2009; Rogers, 2003; Subotnik, Olszewski-Kubilius, & Arnold, 2003

22 Feldman, 2003; Treffinger & Feldhusen, 1996

23 Feldman, 2003, p. 15

24 Gottfried, Gottfried, Bathurst, & Guerin, 1994, p. 183

25 Horowitz, 2009; Keating, 2009; Nelson, 1999

26 Howe, 1999

27 Gottfried et al., 1994, p. 183-184

28 Gottfried, Gottfried, & Guerin, 2009

29 Simonton, 1994

30 Birren, 2009

31 Bloom, 1985; Howe, 1999; Simonton, 1994

32 Schoon, 2000, p. 21

33 Gould, 1981; Guilford, 1967; Spearman, 1927; Thurstone, 1938

34 Gardner, 1983

35 Gardner, 1998

36 Keating, 2009; Webb, Gore, Amend, & DeVries, 2007. Prodigies (which we discuss in this chapter in the section on other terms for giftedness) are an extreme example of asynchronous development.

37 Keating, 2009; Matthews et al., 2009

38 Matthews et al., 2009; Rimm, 2007; Webb et al., 2007

39 Dweck, 2006b; Ericsson, 2006

40 Howe, 1990

41 Goertzel, Goertzel, Goertzel, & Hansen, 2004

42 Haeys, 1989, cited in Dai & Renzulli, 2008, p. 119

43 Dweck, 2006b; Simonton, 1997

44 Horowitz, 2009

45 Dweck, 2006b; Ericsson, 2006

46 Luc Kumps, personal correspondence, 2008

47 The National Association for Gifted Children established a terminology committee in 2008 to examine this issue and to come up with terms that are more accurate and that carry fewer unnecessary negative connotations.

48 Feldman & Goldsmith, 1986; Winner, 1996

49 Howe, 1990

50 Winner, 1996, 2009

51 Gardner, 1983

52 Borland, 2003; Subotnik, Edmiston, & Rayhack, 2007; Tannenbaum, 2000

53 Terman, 1926-1959

54 Hollingworth, 1926

55 Klein, 2002

56 Marland, 1972

57 U.S. Department of Education, 2001

58 Gentry, 2007

59 New evidence suggests that even those labeled "mentally retarded" or "developmentally delayed" can learn much more than was ever thought possible. See, for example, Doidge, 2007.

60 Ontario Ministry of Education and Training, 2000, p. 33

61 New York State, 1982

62 The more that scientists learn about brain development (especially neural plasticity), the clearer it is that we have to be very careful when setting any kinds of limits on people's potential for learning. We are only starting to discover all that the brain can do and its considerable impact on learning (Kalbfleisch, 2008; Willis, 2009). However, we do know that developmental pathways are highly variable—as individual as fingerprints. Benjamin Bloom (1985), after chronicling the lives of world-class performers in such diverse fields as neurology, mathematics, tennis, art, and concert piano, concluded that "there is enormous human potential in each society [and] only a small amount of this human potential is ever fully developed. We believe that each society could vastly increase the amount and kinds of talent it develops" (p. 549). Certainly we would agree with Bloom and others who have observed that there is much more human potential than is ever developed. But educators, and parents, too, are on firmer ground when discussing gifted-level ability as a need for special education at a certain point in time.

63 Heward, 2002

64 Balchin, 2009; Gottfried et al., 2009; Hymer et al., 2009

65 Whitney & Hirsch, 2007, p. 106

66 This comment is from a teacher in the course of discussion during a learning session.

Chapter 2

1 Attributed to Kornei Chukovsky, Russian author of children's books, poet, literary critic, language theorist, and translator.

2 Feldman, 1991, p. 45.

3   Toynbee, 1967

4   Amabile, 1996; Balchin, 2009; Csikszentmihalyi, 1996; Feldhusen, 2005; Gardner, 1993, 2007; Keating, 1980; Perkins, 1981; Piirto, 2003; Simonton, 1997; Sternberg, 2009; Weisberg, 2006

5   Csikszentmihalyi, 1996; Feldman, 1991; Piirto, 2003

6   Keating, 1980

7   Csikszentmihalyi & Wolfe, 2000

8   Csikszentmihalyi, 1991

9   Piirto, 2003

10   Balchin, 2009, p. 205

11   Balchin, 2009

12   The Talent Assessment Process (Oreck, Owen, & Baum, 2003) is an observational scale that was designed to identify performing arts talent in diverse populations, including those with no prior instruction.

13   Personal communication, 2004

14   Robinson, Shore, & Enersen, 2007, p. 79

15   VanTassel-Baska, 2004

16   Bereiter & Scardamalia, 1993

17   Subotnik, 2009

18   Ericsson, 2006; Weisberg, 2006

19   Lohman, 2005a; Worrell, 2009

20   Sternberg, 2009

21   Sternberg, 2000

22   Dweck, 2006b; Piirto, 2003; Sternberg, 2009

23   Cropley & Urban, 2000, p. 496

24   Keating, 1980

Chapter 3

1   Davis, 2006, p. 70

2   Borland, 2005; Dweck, 2009a; Hymer et al., 2009; Keating, 2009

3   Claxton & Meadows, 2009; Hymer et al., 2009; Reis, 2009

4   VanTassel-Baska, 2008

5   N. Robinson, 2008; VanTassel-Baska, 2008; Webb et al., 2007

6   Webb et al., 2007

7   Webb et al., 2007

8   Robinson et al., 2007

9   Roid, 2003

10   Wechsler, 2003

11   Woodcock, McGrew, & Mather, 2001

12 The comparison population matters here. If a six-year-old scored at the 99th percentile of a test designed for four-year-olds, it would not mean the same thing as scoring at the 99th percentile for her own age group.

13 Roid, 2003

14 Wechsler, 2003

15 Reis, 2009, p. 324

16 If you are a teacher or parent who has received a psychoeducational report and one of these components is missing, it is reasonable to request that it be supplied.

17 The major relevant scores vary from one jurisdiction to another. In some circumstances, it is IQ; in others, it is a combined score comprised of several subject-specific subtest scores, such as mathematical reasoning, computation, and problem solving.

18 Ruf, 2005; Winner, 1996

19 Gottfried et al, 2009

20 It still may be possible to retest sooner using a different, equivalent test, but that depends on jurisdictional policies.

21 Dweck, 2009b

22 Dai & Renzulli, 2008

Chapter 4

1 Dai & Renzulli, 2008; VanTassel-Baska, 2008

2 Hunt & Seney, 2009

3 Johnsen, 2008

4 Riley, 2009

5 Schipper & Rossi, 1997, p. 4

6 Wright & Borland, 1993

7 Hunt & Seney, 2009; Riley, 2009

8 VanTassel-Baska, 2008, p. 285

9 Parks, 2009, p. 287

10 Feng & VanTassel-Baska, 2008, p. 130

11 McTighe & Wiggins, 2005

12 The connections between these features of performance assessment and fostering giftedness in minority populations are reviewed in VanTassel-Baska, 2008.

13 Lohman & Lakin, 2008; N. Robinson, 2008

14 Stanford Achievement Tests, 2003

15 www.eduratio.be

16 Gould, 1981

17 Ceci, 1996; Gottfried et al., 2009; Howe, 1999; Wahlsten, 1997

18 Gardner, 1998; Sternberg, 2009

19 Dweck, 2009b, p. 314

20 Claxton & Meadows, 2009; Sattler, 2001

21 Raven, Court, & Raven, 1998

22 Lohman & Hagen, 2001

23 Borland, 2003; Claxton & Meadows, 2009; Ford, 2003a; Hymer et al., 2009; Worrell, 2009

24 Wechsler, 1989

25 Wechsler, 2003

26 Wechsler, 1981

27 Roid, 2003

28 Raven et al., 1998

29 Naglieri, 1996

30 Bracken & McCallum, 1998

31 Bracken, 2008; Naglieri, 2008; Naglieri & Ford, 2003

32 Lohman, 2005b; Lohman & Lakin, 2008

33 Keating, 2009; Lohman, 2005b

34 Lohman, 2005a; Warwick & Matthews, 2009; Worrell, 2009

35 Perkins, 1981; Piirto, 2003

36 Amabile, 1996; Czikszentmihalyi, 1996; Feldman & Goldsmith, 1986; Gardner, 1993; Perkins, 1981; Piirto, 2003; Sternberg, 1998

37 Oreck et al., 2003

38 Ohio Department of Education, 2000

39 Moon & Dixon, 2006; Peterson, 2008; Robinson et al., 2007; Webb et al., 2007

40 Schipper & Rossi, 1997

41 Lohman & Lakin, 2008, p. 43

42 Motivation and drive are similar but worth distinguishing and mentioning separately. Motivation fuels drive, but without drive, motivation is not enough for high-level achievement. Drive is connected to energy and personality factors such as intensity. For more on this topic, see Winner, 1996.

43 Corno et al., 2002; Lohman & Lakin, 2008

44 Lohman, 2005a, p. 337

45 Dweck, 2006b, 2009a; Horowitz et al. 2009

46 Lohman, 2005a; Lohman & Lakin, 2008

47 Lohman, 2005a; Lohman & Lakin, 2008

48 National Association for Gifted Children, 2006; Robinson et al., 2007; VanTassel-Baska, 2008

49 For more information on interpreting test scores, including components of a typical psychoeducational assessment, translation of standard scores into percentiles, score conversion, mitigating circumstances with score interpretation, and scoring patterns among high-ability learners, refer to Appendix I.

Chapter 5

1   Dweck, 2009b, p. 314

2   Vygotsky, 1978

3   Jarvin, Newman, Randi, Sternberg, & Grigorenko, 2008; Matthews et al., 2009; VanTassel-Baska, 2008

4   VanTassel-Baska & Little, 2003; Vygotsky, 1978

5   Dweck, 2006b; Hargreaves & Earl, 1990

6   Joseph & Ford, 2006; Ortiz, 2002

7   Ontario Ministry of Education, 1984

8   Armstrong, 1991, p. 221

9   Foster, 2000; Matthews & Foster, 2008; Matthews & Kitchen, 2007

10   Dweck, 2006b, 2009a; Feldhusen & Jarwan, 2000

11   Foster, 2000

12   Matthews & Foster, 2008

13   Borland, 1989, 2003, 2005; Matthews & Foster, 2006, 2008; Reis, 2009; Renzulli & Reis, 1985

14   Matthews, Foster, Gladstone, Schieck, & Meiners, 2007

15   Hansford, Bonar, Scally, & Burge, 2001, p. 39

16   National Association for Gifted Children, 2006; Robinson et al., 2007; VanTassel-Baska, 2008

17   Lohman & Hagen, 2001

18   Lohman, 2005a

19   Matthews et al., 2009; VanTassel-Baska, 2008; Worrell, 2009

20   Dweck 2006b; Lohman & Lakin, 2008; Reis, 2009

21   Bloom, 1985; Gardner, 1991; Horowitz et al., 2009; Howe, 1999; Lieberman, 1993

22   Borland, 2005; Claxton & Meadows, 2009; Dweck, 2006b; Hymer et al., 2009; Keating, 2009; Matthews & Foster, 2009

23   Bloom, 1985; Gardner, 1991; Horowitz et al., 2009; Howe, 1999; Lieberman, 1993

24   Gottfried et al., 2009

25   Lohman & Korb, 2006

26   See *A Nation Deceived: How Schools Hold Back America's Brightest Students* (Colangelo, Assouline, & Gross, 2004; www.nationdeceived.org). Also, an instrument has been developed to identify good candidates for such an intervention, *The Iowa Acceleration Scale, 3rd Edition* (Assouline, Colangelo, Lupkowski-Shoplik, Lipscomb, & Forstadt, 2009).

27   Colombo, Shaddy, Blaga, Anderson, & Kannass, 2009; Gottfried et al., 2009

28   Courtney, 1989, p. 27

29   Armstrong, 1991, p. 206

Chapter 6

1   We are grateful to Karen Rogers for her groundbreaking work in this area. She conducted meta-analyses of academic effect size for different educational options provided for gifted students for the National Research Center on Gifted and Talented, reported on in journal articles and in her book *Re-Forming Gifted Education: How Parents and Teachers Can Match the Program to the Child* (2002). She clearly makes the case that identified-gifted learners are diverse in their needs, and different options must be used for different children. She also argues that the best approach for a child can vary from one time to another, and she illustrates the importance of ongoing assessment. In addition, she describes how to implement the options we discuss here, as well as how to evaluate their effectiveness.

2   National Association for Gifted Children, 2006

3   Tomlinson, 2003

4   Tieso, 2003

5   Roberts & Inman, 2009; VanTassel-Baska & Stambaugh, 2005

6   Dixon & Moon, 2006; Tomlinson et al., 2006; Winebrenner, 2001; Winebrenner & Brulles, 2008

7   Weinfeld, Barnes-Robinson, Jeweler, & Roffman Shevitz, 2006

8   Tomlinson et al., 2001

9   Wright & Borland, 1993, p. 591

10 At the same time, we don't want to be blindly idealistic. Differentiation requires extensive training and support, and very few teachers are given the time and tools they need to do it well. (We discuss teacher training in Chapter 12.)

11 Cox, Daniel, & Boston, 1985

12 Beales, 2008

13 Renzulli & Reis, 2008

14 Rogers, 2002

15 Blumenfeld et al., 1991

16 Bereiter & Scardamalia, 1993; Bransford, Brown, & Cocking, 2000; Keating, 2009; Reis, 2009

17 Matthews & Steinhauer, 1998

18 Lubinski & Benbow, 2006; Stanley & Benbow, 1983; Stanley et al., 1974

19 Robinson et al., 2007; VanTassel-Baska, Cross, & Olenchak, 2009

20 Fullan, 1991, p. 91

21 Salmon, 2000, p. 11

22 Besnoy, Housand, & Clarke, 2009; Renzulli & Reis, 2009

23 Palloff & Pratt, 2001, p. 25

24 Renzulli, 1976; Renzulli & Reis, 2008, 2009

25 The National Research Center on the Gifted and Talented offers many resources and publications about SEM, as well as other approaches to differentiation, through its website (www.gifted.uconn.edu).

26 Such differentiated learning experiences are key for a mastery model in gifted education, and many resources by VanTassel-Baska are available at http://cfge.wm.edu.

27 VanTassel-Baska & Brown, 2009; VanTassel-Baska & Stambaugh, 2006

28 Tomlinson et al., 2006

Chapter 7

1 Assouline et al., 2009, p. 1

2 Assouline et al, 2009. See also Feldhusen, Proctor, & Black, 2002

3 Cross & Coleman, 2005; Robinson et al., 2007; Rogers, 2002; VanTassel-Baska & Sher, 2003

4 Rogers & Kimpston, 1992

5 Colangelo et al., 2004

6 If a highly capable child experiences a sense of failure after being placed in a challenging program, it can be used as an opportunity to reinforce a growth mindset. Parents and teachers should help the child realize that all learning is incremental and that failure and challenge are the best way to learn what she needs to work on. At the same time, however, if a child has been moved into a program that is too challenging, she should be moved back into a program where there is a better fit, where perhaps her education can be supplemented with extracurricular learning. This should be interpreted within the context of meeting current learning needs rather than one of her innate ability—or lack thereof.

7 This document is available to schools, the media, and parents and has been translated into several languages (including Japanese, German, French, Spanish, Arabic, Chinese, and Russian). Research information, personal stories about acceleration, summaries of discussions, questions and answers, findings about educational practices, and a host of resources can be accessed online at www.nationdeceived.org.

8 This is also available online at www.nationdeceived.org.

9 Colangelo et al., 2004; Feldhusen, 1995; Robinson et al., 2007; Rogers, 2002; VanTassel-Baska & Sher, 2003

10 Hurwitz, 2007, p. 1

11 Robinson, 2003, p. 256

12 Quart, 2006

13 Cox et al., 1985; Robinson, 2003

14 Robinson et al., 2007, p. 201

15 Foster, Porath, & Smyth, in press

16 Hughes, 2009; Koshy, 2009; Rogers, 2002

17 Cloud & Morse, 2001, p. 45

18 Rivero, 2002

19 Kunzman, 2008

20 Rivero, 2002; Webb et al., 2007

21 Kunzman, 2008, p. 258

22 National Center for Education Statistics, 2004

23 Kunzman, 2008

24 Whitney & Hirsch, 2007, p. 20

25 Rogers, 2002, p. 318

26 Renzulli & Reis, 2009

27 Many other global options are reviewed in Gillian Eriksson's chapter on global education issues in *Diversity in Gifted Education: International Perspectives on Global Issues* (Wallace & Eriksson, 2006).

28 Foster, in press a; Kitano, 2007; VanTassel-Baska, 2007

29 More information on these and other possibilities can be found through the Internet, in local newspapers, and from active parent associations.

30 Riley & Karnes, 2007; Tallent-Runnels & Candler-Lotven, 2008

31 Olszewksi-Kubilius, 2007

32 Adams & Olszewksi-Kubilius, 2007; Renzulli & Reis, 2009

33 Siegle, McCoach, & Wilson, 2009, p. 554

34 Feng, 2007

35 Disney's *Fantasia*

36 Subotnik, 2009, p. 157

37 Reilly, 1992

38 Clasen & Clasen, 2003; Davidson Institute for Talent Development, n.d.; Reilly, 1992. Some organizations that match mentors with mentees include the National Mentoring Partnership, iMentor, the Mentoring Group, the International Telementor Program, and UConn Mentor Connection.

39 For more on designing and evaluating mentorships, including finding a good match between mentors and mentees, see Siegle et al., 2009.

40 Callahan & Dickson, 2008; Dixon & Moon, 2006; Feldhusen, 2005; Feng, 2007; Robinson et al., 2007; Siegle et al., 2009; Subotnik, 2009

41 Feng, 2007; Siegle et al., 2009

42 Callahan & Dixon, 2008; West-Burnham, 2006

43 Treffinger et al., 2009, p. 211

44 Moon & Dixon, 2006; Peterson, 2008; Robinson et al., 2007; Webb et al., 2007

45 Willis, 2009; Wolf, 2007

46 Judith Halsted has written a resource guide titled *Some of My Best Friends Are Books: Guiding Gifted Readers from Preschool to High School* (2002). In it, she offers advice and suggestions for children reading at various levels, as well as annotated bibliographies and foundational references.

47 Additional information about bibliotherapy, its origins, benefits, and processes, as well as recommended book titles for use with gifted learners, can be found in Halsted, 2002.

48 Juster, 1961, pp. 14-17

49   Westphal, 2001

50   Hymer, 2009; Sternberg, 2009

51   Silvertown, n.d.

Chapter 8

1   Neihart, 2008, p. 59, quoting William Warren, basketball coach and author

2   Graham, 2009, p. 111

3   Whitney & Hirsch, 2007, p. 25

4   Gottfried et al., 1994; Gottfried, Gottfried, Cook, & Morris, 2005; Gottfried et al., 2009

5   Graham, 2009

6   Dweck, 2006b, 2009b; Graham, 2009; Matthews et al., 2009; Whitney & Hirsch, 2007

7   Informal survey conducted by teacher candidate Martin Choi

8   Bransford et al., 1999; A. Robinson, 2008

9   Webb, Meckstroth, & Tolan, 1982, p. 35

10   Willis, 2009

11   Bowd, McDougall, & Yewchuk, 1998

12   Alexander & Schnick, 2008; Sternberg, 2009

13   Elster, 2001, p. 18

14   Renzulli & Reis, 2009

15   Scardamalia & Bereiter, 2005

16   Mitchell, 2003, p. F1

17   Alexander & Schnick, 2008; Neihart, 2008; Whitney & Hirsch, 2007

18   Folsom, 2009; Matthews & Folsom, 2009

19   Whitehead & McNiff, 2006

20   Huxtable, 2009; Hymer, 2009; Hymer et al., 2009

21   Subotnik, 2009, p. 165

22   Whitney & Hirsch, 2007, p. 31

23   The research of Sandra Graham (2009), Carol Dweck (2006b), and Rena Subotnik (2009) on motivation suggests that there is a distinction between valuing hard work on the one hand and actual competence on the other. Both are intrinsic motivators, but the combination is much more potent than just valuing hard work.

24   Dweck, 2006b; Graham, 2009; Subotnik, 2009; Willis, 2009

25   Csikszentmihalyi, 1996; Dweck, 2006b; Keating, 2009

26   R. Upitis, cited in Ferguson, 2003, p. 17

27   Alexander & Schnick, 2008, p. 423

28   Dweck, 2009a, p. xiii

29   Ford, 2003a, 2003b; Graham, 2009; Wallace & Eriksson, 2006; Worrell, 2009

30   Aronson, Fried, & Good, 2002; Dweck, 2006b, 2009b; Walton & Cohen, 2007

31   Reis, 2009, p. 321

32   McCoach & Siegle, 2008, p. 729

33   Jarvin et al., 2008

34   In Chapter 1, we discussed Carol Dweck's work on mindsets (2006b), in which she distinguishes between a fixed mindset and a growth mindset and its application to a mastery model perspective on giftedness.

35   Piper, 1930

36   Dweck, 2006b, 2009b

37   Ruf, 2005

38   Rimm, 2007; Webb et al., 2007

39   One of the best online resources for some of the skills that students may discover they need is OWL, the Online Writing Lab at Purdue University (http://owl.english.purdue.edu).

40   Whitney & Hirsch, 2007

41   Hymer et al., 2009

42   Pyryt, 2007, p. 278

43   Foster, 2007; Sapadin & Maguire, 1999; Stober & Joorman, 2001

44   Dweck, 2006b

45   Foster, 2007

46   Dweck, 2006b; Mendaglio, 2007; VanTassel-Baska & Stambaugh, 2006

47   Goleman, 1995

48   Brophy, 2004

49   John F. Kennedy, n.d.

50   Adapted from sources noted throughout this chapter, and also from Stipek, 2002

51   Luc Kumps, personal correspondence, February 26, 2009

Chapter 9

1   Dai & Renzulli, 2008, p. 119

2   Kalbfleisch, 2008, p. 162

3   Horowitz, 2009; Kalbfleisch, 2008; Willis, 2009

4   Horowitz, 2009

5   Bloom, 1985; Feldman & Goldsmith, 1986; Gottfried et al., 2009; Howe, 1990

6   Keating, 2009

7   Howe, 1990, p. 57

8   Dweck, 2009a, p. xii

9   The important roles of experience and environment in human development and intelligence are currently subjects of interest in the popular media. See, for example, Doidge, 2007; Gladwell, 2008; Nisbett, 2009.

10   Horowitz, 2009

11 Gottfried et al., 2009, p. 50

12 Colombo et al., 2009; Gottfried et al., 2009

13 Gottfried et al., 2009; Keating, 2004

14 Keating, 2004; Rutter, 2001; Willis, 2009

15 Colombo et al., 2009; Gottfried et al., 2009; Webb et al., 2007

16 Attributed to American director and playwright Nagle Jackson

17 Quart, 2006

18 Oatley & Jenkins, 1996

19 Mitchell, 2003, p. 10

20 Subotnik, 2009

21 Borowitz, 2003, p. 3

22 Dweck, 2009a, p. xiii

23 Horowitz, 2009; Keating, 2009

24 Keating, 1990

25 Moon, 2006

26 Brown, 2004

27 Steinberg, 2005

28 Keating, 2004

29 Keating, 2004; Steinberg, 2005

30 Hébert & Kelly, 2006; Moon, 2006

31 Moon, 2006

32 Baum, Rizza, & Renzulli, 2006

33 Eide & Eide, 2006, p. 447

34 Dixon & Moon, 2006

35 Kerr & Foley Nicpon, 2003, p. 502

36 Galambos, 2004, p. 255

37 Renzulli, 2003

38 Galambos, 2004; Kerr & Foley Nicpon, 2003; Kitano, 2008; Reis, 2006; Robinson et al., 2007; VanTassel-Baska & MacFarlane, 2008

39 Kitano, 2008

40 Kitano, 2008; Lubinski & Benbow, 2006

41 Kerr & Foley Nicpon, 2003

42 Ford & Moore, 2006; Freeman, 2009; Gentry, Hu, & Thomas, 2008; Graham, 2009; Kitano, 2008

43 Pipher, 1994, p. 20

44 Freeman, 2009, p. 144

45 Kitano, 2008

Being Smart about Gifted Education

46 Kerr, 2000; Reis, 2009

47 Dweck, 2006a

48 Freeman, 2004, 2009

49 Kerr & Cohn, 2001, p. 106

50 Kerr & Cohn, 2001; Kerr & Foley Nicpon, 2003

51 Ford, Harris, Tyson, & Trotman, 2000

52 Graham, 2009, p. 122

53 Reis, 2006

54 Noble, Subotnik, & Arnold (1999)

55 Steinberg (2005) and others show that the best developmental outcomes occur in families where adolescence is characterized by lots of arguments and conflict in a context of warmth, responsiveness, respect, and solid guidelines and standards. There are many reasons for this, including that "Authoritative parents encourage children's autonomy and independence appropriate for their age with the result that children develop social competence" (Meece & Daniels, 2008, p. 466).

56 Higgins-Biss, 1995, p. 58

57 Eide & Eide, 2006, p. 447

58 Attributed to early 20th century humorist W.C. Fields

59 Higgins-Biss, 1995

60 Higgins-Biss, 1995

61 Purkey, 2006

62 Attributed to Mozart

63 Butterworth, 2006, p. 564

64 Winner, 1996, 2009

65 Butterworth, 2006

66 Mendaglio, 2008

67 Sternberg, 2000; Wallace, 2009

68 Matthews, 2009, p. 93

69 Subotnik, 2009, p. 162

70 Lubinski & Benbow, 2006, p. 316

71 Ericsson, 2006; Ericsson et al., 2006

72 Dweck, 2006b

73 Margaret Mead, cited in Pipher, 1994, p. 22

74 Castellano, 2003, p. 76

75 Borland, 2003, p. 116

76 Ford & Moore, 2006; Gentry et al., 2008; Graham, 2009; Wallace & Eriksson, 2006; Warwick & Matthews, 2009

77 Ford, 2003a, p. 147

374

78 Ford, 2003b, p. 507

79 The Javits Act includes those from racial minorities, those who are economically disadvantaged, those who have limited English proficiency, and those with other learning exceptionalities.

80 Castellano, 2003; Ford, 2003b; Graham, 2009; Richert, 2003

81 Aguirre, 2003; Worrell, 2009

82 Borland & Wright, 2000; Ford, 2003a, 2003b; Matthews et al., 2009; Worrell, 2009

83 Castellano, 2003; Ford, 2003a; Richert, 2003

84 Gentry et al., 2008; Graham, 2009; Worrell, 2009

85 Dweck, 2009a, p. xii

86 Feldman, 2008, p. 528

87 Gross, 2008, p. 241

88 Feldman, 2008

89 For more detailed exploration of the concerns relating to extreme giftedness, see Ruf, 2005. The author describes developmental milestone data, as well as differences in IQ.

90 Winner, 1996

91 Webb, 2009

92 A variety of educational options are described by Karen Rogers in her book *Re-Forming Gifted Education: How Parents and Teachers Can Match the Program to the Child* (2002).

93 Baum et al., 2006, p. 138

94 Eide & Eide, 2006, p. 463

95 Ferri & Connor, 2006; Weinfeld & Davis, 2008

96 For more information on any of these exceptionalities, see Cohen, 2006; Kalbfleisch & Banasiak, 2008; Kaufmann, Kalbfleisch, & Castellanos, 2000; Silverman & Weinfeld, 2007; Weinfeld & Davis, 2008. You can also go to the websites for Children and Adults with Attention Deficit Hyperactivity Disorder (CHADD; www.chadd.org), the Council for Exceptional Children (CEC; www.cec.sped.org), or the Education Resources Information Center (ERIC; www.eric.ed.gov).

97 Baum et al., 2006; Robinson et al., 2007; Webb, Amend, Webb, Goerss, Beljan, & Olenchak, 2005

98 Kalbfleisch & Iguchi, 2008

99 Webb et al., 2005

100 When students score very high in one area and very low in another, they will appear to be "average" if those scores are combined to yield one composite score, such as IQ.

101 Brody & Mills, 1997

102 VanTassel-Baska, 2000, p. 358

103 Robinson et al., 2007, p. 208

104 Colangelo & Assouline, 2000, p. 605

105 See Hébert & Kelly (2006) for a discussion of the conflicting findings on multi-potentiality. These authors draw a conclusion that it is "not a defining characteristic of gifted students" (p. 53). Others, however, such as Robinson, Shore, & Enersen (2007), conclude that multipotentiality is a reality for many gifted learners.

106 Robinson et al., 2007

107 Kaufmann, 1981

108 Some references to consult about college planning include Berger (2006) and Wissner-Gross (2006).

Chapter 10

1 Treffinger et al., 2009, p. 210

2 Dweck, 2009a, p. xii

3 Borland, 2005; Hymer, 2009

4 Books like *Cradles of Eminence* (Goertzel, Goertzel, Goertzel, & Hansen, 2004) and *Smart Girls* (Kerr, 1997) point out that many children who later grow up to be eminent did not adapt to their school environment or even to age peers, and the authors argue that this independence of being is a necessary skill that later allowed those individuals to be eminent.

5 Peterson, 2008

6 Robinson et al., 2007, p. 19

7 Alexander & Schnick, 2008; Peterson, 2008; Webb et al., 2007

8 Some sources of information on Asperger's and Nonverbal Learning Disabilities include Cohen, 2006; Silverman & Weinfeld, 2007; Stewart, 2002.

9 Pyryt, 2008, p. 599

10 For a thoughtful discussion of the theoretical foundations of social/emotional development as it applies to giftedness and to working with high-ability learners, see Moon, 2009.

11 Dweck, 2006b

12 Harter, 1999

13 Peterson, 2008; Robinson et al., 2007

14 Alexander & Schnick, 2008; Coleman & Cross, 2005

15 Pyryt, 2008; Robinson & Clinkenbeard, 1998

16 Alexander & Schnick, 2008

17 Dweck, 2006b; Hymer et al., 2009; Webb et al., 2007; Wilson, 2009

18 Graham, 2009

19 Mendaglio, 2007, pp. 229-30

20 Mendaglio, 2007

21 Alexander & Schnick, 2008; Peterson, 2008; Pyryt, 2007

22 Goertzel et al., 2004

23 Dweck, 2006b

24 Webb et al., 2007

25 Cross, 2008, pp. 634, 637

26 Cross, 2008

27 Webb et al., 2007

28 Cross, Frazier, & McKay, 2009, p. 324

29 Fleith, 2001. For more information and resources on suicide and giftedness, visit the website for SENG (Supporting Emotional Needs of the Gifted) at www.sengifted.org.

30 Cross et al., 2009, pp. 334, 341

31 Purkey, 2006

32 Webb et al., 2005

33 Good professional practice requires that, before diagnosing ADD/ADHD or a conduct disorder, a child have a physical evaluation, including screening for allergies and other metabolic disorders, as well as a psychoeducational evaluation, including an assessment of intelligence, achievement, and social/emotional factors such as self-concept and learning styles. Any diagnoses and recommendations should take into account the child's personality, learning styles, and domain-specific abilities and interests. Consider the situations in which the problem behaviors occur, recognizing that a child's inability to stay on task (particularly in school) may be caused by a combination of high ability and personality characteristics rather than ADD/ADHD. Some apparent ADD/ADHD problems are rooted in the environment and not in the child. For more on this, see Webb, Amend, Webb, Goerss, Beljan, & Olenchak, 2005.

34 Meece & Daniels, 2008

35 Peterson, 2006

36 Coloroso, 2007

37 Li, 2007; Stover, 2006. There are also many websites containing information about cyberbullying, including www.cyberbullying.ca, www.netcrimes.net, and www.bullying.org.

38 There are many resources to help parents and educators who wish to support tolerance development in children. For example, the Southern Poverty Law Center provides free copies of the twice-yearly magazine *Teaching Tolerance* to parents (visit www.tolerance.org/teach/magazine/index.jsp). There are museums of tolerance, operated by the Friends of Simon Wiesenthal Foundation, located in several cities around the world. The New York Tolerance Center is a premiere facility for training and professional development, and also for teaching children about tolerance, social justice, and the dynamics of hatred (visit www.wiesenthal.com/newyork).

39 Those who wish to learn more about bullying, conflict resolution, and tolerance may wish to read Barbara Coloroso's books on these topics (Coloroso, 2002, 2003, 2007).

40 Goleman, 1995

41 Folsom, 2008; Matthews & Folsom, 2009; VanTassel-Baska et al., 2009

42 Peterson, Betts, & Bradley, 2009

43 VanTassel-Baska, Buckingham, & Baska, 2009

44 Hébert, 2009

45 There have been several publications in the past few years on Dabrowski's theory of positive disintegration and overexcitabilities (e.g., Mendaglio, 2008; Piechowski, 2006) and an entire issue of *Roeper Review* dedicated to it (volume 31, issue 2, June 2009). It is what Mendaglio (2008) calls a "grand theory of personality" (p. 17) and is based on an observation that personality is not a fixed attribute but rather is shaped by an individual to reflect his or her character. Personality development, according to this theory, involves a process of disintegration of the early mental organization that is aimed at gratifying biological needs and conforming to social norms, which is followed by a reintegration of the personality at a higher level of functioning, which is more autonomous. There are some aspects of this approach that are more aligned with a mystery model than a mastery model (including the focus on innate characteristics that predispose some children to giftedness and others not so much). However, there are some dimensions of this approach that align very well with the mastery model, including the emphasis on the motivation, persistence, and effort required to achieve at a gifted level.

46 Rena Subotnik and colleagues have done considerable work on talent development in different domains, illustrating the importance of psychosocial factors such as persistence and motivation (Subotnik, 2009; Subotnik et al., 2007).

47 Dweck, 2009a, 2009b

48 Anders Ericsson and colleagues have demonstrated the importance of curiosity, persistence, and motivation in the development of expertise in many different domains (Ericsson et al., 2006).

49 Wallace, 2009, p. 282

50 Chan, 2009, p. 120

51 Chan, 2009; Sternberg, 2009

52 Renzulli, 2009; Treffinger et al., 2009

53 Wallace, 2009

54 Jarvin & Subotnik, 2006; Subotnik, 2009

55 Dweck, 2009b; Folsom, 2008; Matthews & Folsom, 2009; VanTassel-Baska et al., 2009; Webb et al., 2007

Chapter 11

1 Robinson et al., 2007, p. 7

2 In Canada and the United States, an Individual Education Plan (IEP) is a written plan outlining the special education program or services that a child requires. It provides a framework for monitoring student progress and for communicating updated information and learning expectations across various subject areas. An IEP identifies learning expectations that differ from those described in policy documents for the child's normal grade expectations. It is *not* a daily lesson plan detailing every aspect of a students' education. It *does* list important information on individual accommodations and programming modifications that are needed in order to assist a student to achieve optimally.

3 Webb et al, 2007

4   Webb, Gore, Karnes, & McDaniel, 2004

5   In *Raising a Gifted Child* (2008), blog author and gifted education expert Carol Fertig provides information for parents on different publications and websites to access, as well as targeted resources and practical suggestions on a variety of topics.

6   Ferguson, 2004

7   Rogers (2002) identifies important criteria for considering various educational options, and she also profiles students of various ages and abilities, showing how certain kinds of programming might be suitable for them.

8   Rogers (2002) offers a selection of inventories pertaining to student interests, learning style preferences, and attitudes about specific subjects, as well as teacher and parent inventories designed to reveal information that can be useful during these kinds of meetings.

9   Additional components of the IEP may include transition plans, consultation specifics, timelines, and alternative informational sources. Most districts have established standards and documentation for IEPs, and schools are expected to comply with them.

10 Delcourt, 2003, p. 27

11 For detailed information, plans, and suggestions for advocating for gifted learners, see Gilman (2008) and Lewis & Karnes (2009).

12 Enersen, 2003, p. 38

13 Robinson et al., 2007, p. 11

14 Parents have the right to know how students are selected for special programming, as well as the findings of any assessments that are done. Parents need to be well informed in order to understand the implications, to explain things to their child, and to participate intelligently in decision-making and advocacy processes.

15 Inquire about core and supplementary programs being offered locally. What are the governing administrative policies, programs, and provisions for gifted learners? Is there a special education coordinator with whom you could speak, or a gifted resource specialist who can provide information about the various services available? Is there a parent advocacy group? If not, consider starting one.

16 Parents can make appointments to visit promising schools and take a tour of them. Talk to the principal. Listen. Observe. Be respectfully inquisitive. Do academic programs appear to be responsive to students' individual profiles of subject-specific abilities, learning styles, and interests? Do the children seem happily engaged and motivated? Does the learning environment seem like a positive place that supports children's emotional and social growth? Are children receiving individualized attention as needed? Do staff members look like they are enjoying their work with students?

17 Sometimes the perfect educational match for a child is in the regular program at the neighborhood public school, or there may be something else that works for the time being. Or parents may decide to become an advocate of more student learning opportunities in their child's current educational setting.

18 Lewis & Karnes, 2009, p. 697

19 Robinson et al., 2007

20 Neihart, 2008; Whitney & Hirsch, 2007

21   For example, the Association for Bright Children (ABC) in Canada, or the National Association for Gifted Children (NAGC) in the United States

22   Several such journals are listed on www.beingsmart.ca, as well as in many other sources, such as in *A Love for Learning: Motivation and the Gifted Child* (Whitney & Hirsch, 2007).

23   You can find more discussion of issues concerning siblings and giftedness in Webb, Gore, Amend, & DeVries, 2007.

24   Webb et al., 2007, p. 204

25   Steinberg, 2005

26   Lyrics from *L'Chaim, Fiddler on the Roof*

27   Serenity prayer

28   Webb, 2004. Additional tips for selecting a counselor or therapist for a gifted child are provided at www.giftedbooks.com.

29   Webb, Amend, Webb, Goerss, Beljan, & Olenchak (2005) discuss these problems at length in their book *Misdiagnosis and Dual Diagnoses of Gifted Children and Adults.*

30   VanTassel-Baska, 2000, p. 358

Chapter 12

1   Robinson et al., 2007, p. 263

2   Baldwin, Vialle, & Clarke, 2000, p. 571

3   Foster, in press b; Robinson et al., 2007; Starko, 2008

4   Ginott, 1972, p. 13

5   Dettmer, Landrum, & Miller, 2006

6   Some examples of systems for working with gifted learners include the Differentiated Model of Giftedness and Talent (Gagné, 2009), the Schoolwide Enrichment Model (Renzulli & Reis, 2008), the Parallel Curriculum Model (Tomlinson et al., 2006), the Talent Development Planning Approach (Treffinger, Young, Nassab, Selby, & Wittig, 2008), the Integrated Curriculum Model (VanTassel-Baska & Stambaugh, 2006), and the cluster grouping approach (Winebrenner & Brulles, 2008).

7   Dettmer et al., 2006; Matthews & Foster, 2005

8   Dettmer et al., 2006

9   Dettmer et al., 2006 (see pp. 626-627 for other possible themes based on needs assessment)

10   Ontario College of Teachers, 1999 (Ethical Standards)

11   National Association for Gifted Children, n.d.

12   Geake, 2009, p. 17

13   Starko, 2008

14   Adapted from Andrews & Lupart, 2000

15   Dweck, 2006b

16   National Association for Gifted Children, n.d.

17   The Ontario College of Teachers

18   Ontario College of Teachers, 1999 (Ethical Standards and Standards of Practice); Ontario College of Teachers, 2008 (Standards of Practice: Commitment to Students and Student Learning; Professional Knowledge; Teaching Practice; Leadership and Community; Ongoing Professional Learning). Members are guided by learning, which is developed through collaborative practices and professional interactions.

19   National Association for Gifted Children, n.d. NAGC's lists of guiding principles, minimal standards, and exemplary standards can be viewed online at www.nagc.org. There are recommendations for comprehensive professional development programs that address the nature and needs of gifted learners, certification processes, and support mechanisms such as time, opportunity, and funding. NAGC offers resources, conferences, programming models, and hands-on sessions for educators at all grade levels. This organization also provides resource information for parents who want to learn more about provisions for gifted education or who have gifted-related concerns. Canada has no such national organization at this time, but Canadians are welcome at NAGC conferences and can readily access their many resources.

20   Dettmer et al., 2006

21   Matthews & Foster, 2005

22   Matthews & Foster, 2005; Matthews et al., 2007

23   Bransford et al., 2000; Shonkoff & Phillips, 2000

24   Moon & Rosselli, 2000

25   Matthews & Foster, 2005; Matthews et al., 2007

26   Hogan & Pressley, 1997

27   Bernie Beales (Gifted Coordinator for the Durham District School Board in Ontario, Canada) exemplifies the kind of proactive leadership we discuss here.

28   Johnsen, Haensly, Ryser, & Ford, 2002

29   Moon & Rosselli, 2000

30   Alter & Foster, 2007

31   Thomas Carroll, cited in Schouten, 2003

32   Schouten, 2003

33   Matthews et al., 2009; National Association for Gifted Children, n.d.

Chapter 13

1   Dweck, 2009a, p. xi

2   Keating, 2009; Rutter, 2001

3   Bransford, Brown, & Cocking, 1999

4   Matthews & Foster, 2003; Robinson et al., 2007; Willis, 2009

5   Renzulli & Reis, 2009; Wallace, 2009; Worrell, 2009

6   Meier, 2002

7   Worrell, 2009

8   Robinson et al., 2007

9   Hymer, 2009; Matthews & Menna, 2003; Reis, 2009; Renzulli, 2002

10   Matthews & Foster, 2005; Matthews et al., 2007

11   There are several models that can assist educators or parents interested in implementing this kind of collaborative approach. These include Barry Hymer and colleagues' Living Theory Approach to Gift-Creation (Huxtable, 2009; Hymer, 2009; Hymer et al., 2009); Joe Renzulli and colleagues' Schoolwide Enrichment Model (Renzulli & Reis, 2008) and the Renzulli Learning System (Renzulli & Reis, 2009); Don Treffinger and colleagues' Levels of Service model (Treffinger et al., 2009; Treffinger et al., 2008); and Belle Wallace and colleagues' Thinking Actively in a Social Context model (Wallace, 2009).

12   Some of these include the Belin-Blank Center at The University of Iowa; the Center for Gifted Education at the University of Calgary; the Center for Gifted Education at the College of William and Mary; the Center for Talent Development at Northwestern University in Illinois; the Center for Talented Youth at Johns Hopkins; the Gifted Education Resource Institute at Purdue University; the Hunter College Center for Gifted Studies and Education, City University of New York; and the Neag Center for Gifted Education and Talent Development at the University of Connecticut.

13   Professors and graduate students can be wonderful mentors for advanced learners and constitute an enormous pool of usually-untapped expertise and possibility.

14   *Gifted Education International* is a journal that considers issues, policies, and practices relating to gifted education around the world. See also Balchin et al., 2009; Heller, Monks, Sternberg, & Subotnik, 2000; Kerr, in press; Wallace & Eriksson, 2006

15   Reis, 2009

16   Jarvin & Subotnik, 2006; Matthews et al., 2009; Subotnik, 2009

17   Renzulli & Reis, 2009; Witt, 2009

18   Geake, 2009; Kalbfleisch, 2008; Willis, 2009

19   Balchin, 2009; Treffinger et al., 2009; Wilson, 2009

20   Renzulli & Reis, 2008; Tomlinson et al., 2006; Treffinger et al., 2008; VanTassel-Baska & Stambaugh, 2006; Winebrenner & Brulles, 2008

21   Rizza & Gentry, 2001

22   Klapp & Porath, 2000, p. 34

23   Kalbfleisch, 2008; Willis, 2009

24   Dweck, 2009b, p. 316

Appendix I

1   Kamphaus, 2005

2   Kamphaus, 2005

3   The right to a clear interpretation is described in Standard 11.6 of the *Standards for Educational and Psychological Testing* (the standards in official use by registered psychologists in the U.S. and Canada) (American Educational Research Association, American Psychological Association, & National Council on Measurement in Education, 1999).

Appendix II

1   This concept of carefully focused, ongoing attention to special learning needs is actually written into special education practice and law in both the United States and Canada; exceptional learners' Individual Education Plans (IEPs) must be reviewed and revised at least yearly. Parents can find out more about these documents by contacting their local school or district education office or by going online to government information sites.

References

Adams, C. M., & Olszewksi-Kubilius, P. (2007). Distance learning and gifted students. In J. L. VanTassel-Baska (Ed.), *Serving gifted learners beyond the traditional classroom* (pp. 169-188). Waco, TX: Prufrock Press.

Aguirre, N. (2003). ESL students in gifted education. In J. A. Castellano (Ed.), *Special populations in gifted education: Working with diverse learners* (pp. 17-28). Boston: Allyn & Bacon.

Alexander, J. M., & Schnick, A. K. (2008). Motivation. In J. A. Plucker & C. M. Callahan (Eds.), *Critical issues and practices in gifted education: What the research says* (pp. 423-448). Waco, TX: Prufrock Press.

Alter, S., & Foster, J. F. (2007, November). *A tale of two specialists.* Paper presented at the annual meeting of the National Association for Gifted Children, Minneapolis, MN.

Amabile, T. M. (1996). *Creativity in context: Update to the social psychology of creativity.* Boulder, CO: Westview.

American Educational Research Association, American Psychological Association, & National Council on Measurement in Education. (1999). *Standards for educational and psychological testing.* Washington, DC: American Educational Research Association.

Andrews, J., & Lupart, J. (2000). *The inclusive classroom: Educating exceptional children* (2nd ed.). Toronto, ON: Nelson.

Armstrong, T. (1991). *Awakening your child's natural genius: Enhancing curiosity, creativity, and learning ability.* New York: Putnam.

Aronson, J., Fried, C., & Good, C. (2002). Reducing the effects of stereotype threat on African American college students by shaping theories of intelligence. *Journal of Experimental Social Psychology, 38,* 113-125.

Assouline, S. G., Colangelo, N., Lupkowski-Shoplik, A. E., Lipscomb, J., & Forstadt, L. (2009). *Iowa acceleration scale* (3rd ed.). Scottsdale, AZ: Great Potential Press.

Balchin, T. (2009). Recognising and fostering creative production. In T. Balchin, B. Hymer, & D. J. Matthews (Eds.), *The Routledge international companion to gifted education* (pp. 203-209). Abingdon, UK: Routledge.

Balchin, T., Hymer, B. J., & Matthews, D. J. (Eds.). (2009). *The Routledge international companion to gifted education.* Abingdon, UK: Routledge.

Baldwin, A., Vialle, W., & Clarke, C. (2000). Global professionalism and perceptions of teachers of the gifted. In K. A. Heller, F. J. Monks, R. J. Sternberg, & R. F. Subotnik (Eds.), *International handbook of giftedness and talent* (2nd ed., pp. 565-572). Oxford, UK: Elsevier Science.

Baum, S. M., Rizza, M. G., & Renzulli, S. (2006). Twice exceptional adolescents: Who are they? What do they need? In F. A. Dixon & S. M. Moon (Eds.), *The handbook of secondary gifted education* (pp. 137-164). Waco, TX: Prufrock Press.

Beales, B. (2008, November). *Five hundred parents reveal the needs of identified gifted learners.* Paper presented at the annual meeting of the National Association for Gifted Children, Tampa, FL.

Berger, S. L. (2006). *College planning for gifted students.* Waco, TX: Prufrock Press.

Bereiter, C., & Scardamalia, M. (1993). *Surpassing ourselves: An inquiry into the nature and implications of expertise.* Chicago: Open Court.

Besnoy, K. D., Housand, B. C., & Clarke, L. W. (2009). Changing nature of technology and the promise of educational technology for gifted education. In F. A. Karnes & S. M. Bean (Eds.), *Methods and materials for teaching the gifted* (3rd ed., pp. 783-802). Waco, TX: Prufrock Press.

Birren, J. E. (2009). Gifts and talents of elderly people: The persimmon's promise. In F. D. Horowitz, R. F. Subotnik, & D. J. Matthews (Eds.), *The development of giftedness and talent across the life span* (pp. 171-186). Washington, DC: American Psychological Association.

Bloom, B. S. (Ed.). (1985). *Developing talent in young people.* New York: Ballantine.

Blumenfeld, P. C., Soloway, E., Marx, R. W., Krajcik, J. S., Guzdial, M., & Palincsar, A. (1991). Motivating project-based learning: Sustaining the doing, supporting the learning. *Educational Psychologist, 26,* 369-398.

Borland, J. H. (1989). *Planning and implementing programs for the gifted.* New York: Teachers College Press.

Borland, J. H. (2003). *Rethinking gifted education.* New York: Teachers College Press.

Borland, J. H. (2005). Gifted education without gifted children: The case for no conception of giftedness. In R. J. Sternberg & J. E. Davidson (Eds.), *Conceptions of giftedness* (pp. 1-19). Cambridge, UK: Cambridge University Press.

Borland, J. H., & Wright, L. (2000). Identifying and educating poor and under-represented gifted students. In K. A. Heller, F. J. Monks, R. J. Sternberg, & R. F. Subotnik (Eds.), *International handbook of giftedness and talent* (2nd ed., pp. 587-594). Oxford, UK: Elsevier Science.

Borowitz, S. (2003). *When we're out in public pretend you don't know me: Surviving your daughter's adolescence so you don't look like an idiot and she still talks to you.* New York: Warner Books.

Bowd, A., McDougall, D., & Yewchuk, C. (1998). *Educational psychology for Canadian teachers* (2nd ed.). Toronto, ON: Harcourt Brace.

Bracken, B. A., & McCallum, R. S. (1998). *Universal Nonverbal Test of Intelligence.* Itasca, IL: Riverside.

Bracken, B. A. (2008). Nontraditional strategies for identifying nontraditional gifted and talented students. In J. L. VanTassel-Baska (Ed.), *Alternative assessments with gifted and talented students* (pp. 17-40). Waco, TX: Prufrock Press.

Bransford, J. D., Brown, A. L., & Cocking, R. R. (Eds.). (1999). *How people learn: Bridging research and practice.* Washington, DC: National Academy Press.

Bransford, J. D., Brown, A. L., & Cocking, R. R. (Eds.). (2000). *How people learn: Brain, mind, experience, and school.* Washington, DC: National Academy Press.

Brody, L. E., & Mills, C. J. (1997). Gifted children with learning disabilities: A review of the literature. *Journal of Learning Disabilities, 30*(3), 282-286.

Brophy, J. (2004). *Motivating students to learn* (2nd ed.). Mahwah, NJ: Lawrence Erlbaum Assoc.

Brown, B. B. (2004). Adolescents' relationships with peers. In R. M. Lerner & L. Steinberg (Eds.), *Handbook of adolescent psychology* (pp. 363-394). Hoboken, NJ: Wiley.

Butterworth, B. (2006). Mathematical expertise. In K. A. Ericsson, N. Charness, P. J. Feltovich, & R. R. Hoffman (Eds.), *The Cambridge handbook of expertise and expert performance* (pp. 553-568). Cambridge, UK: Cambridge University Press.

Callahan, C. M., & Dickson, R. K. (2008). Mentoring. In J. A. Plucker & C. M. Callahan (Eds.), *Critical issues and practices in gifted education: What the research says* (pp. 409-423). Waco, TX: Prufrock Press.

Callahan, C. M., & Reis, S. M. (Eds.). (2004). *Program evaluation in gifted education* (Essential Readings in Gifted Education Series). Thousand Oaks, CA: Corwin Press.

Castellano, J. A. (2003). The "browning" of American schools. In J. A. Castellano (Ed.), *Special populations in gifted education: Working with diverse learners* (pp. 29-43). Boston: Allyn & Bacon.

Ceci, S. J. (1996). *On intelligence: A bioecological treatise on intellectual development.* Boston: Harvard University Press.

Chan, D. W. (2009). Lay conceptions of giftedness among the Chinese people. In T. Balchin, B. Hymer, & D. J. Matthews (Eds.), *The Routledge international companion to gifted education* (pp. 115-124). Abingdon, UK: Routledge.

Clasen, D. R., & Clasen, R. E. (2003). Mentoring the gifted and talented. In N. Colangelo & G. A. Davis (Eds.), *Handbook of gifted education* (3rd ed., pp. 254-267). Boston: Pearson Education.

Claxton, G., & Meadows, S. (2009). Brightening up: How children learn to be gifted. In T. Balchin, B. Hymer, & D. J. Matthews (Eds.), *The Routledge international companion to gifted education* (pp. 3-9). London: Routledge.

Cloud, J., & Morse, J. (2001, August 27). Home sweet school. *Time Magazine* (Canadian edition), *158*(8), 45.

Cohen, S. (2006). *Targeting autism: What we know, don't know, and can do to help young children with autism spectrum disorders* (3rd ed.). Berkeley, CA: University of California Press.

Colangelo, N., & Assouline, S. G. (2000). Counseling gifted students. In K. A. Heller, F. J. Monks, R. J. Sternberg, & R. F. Subotnik (Eds.), *International handbook of giftedness and talent* (2nd ed., pp. 595-607). Oxford, UK: Elsevier Science.

Colangelo, N., Assouline, S. G., & Gross, M. U. M. (2004). *A nation deceived: How schools hold back America's brightest students* (Vols. I & II). Iowa City, IA: The University of Iowa.

Coleman, L. J., & Cross, T. L. (2005). *Being gifted in school: An introduction to development, guidance, and teaching* (2nd ed.). Waco, TX: Prufrock Press.

Colombo, J., Shady, D. J., Blaga, O. M., Anderson, C. J., & Kannass, K. N. (2009). High cognitive ability in infancy and early childhood. In F. D. Horowitz, R. F. Subotnik, & D. J. Matthews (Eds.), *The development of giftedness and talent across the life span* (pp. 23-42). Washington, DC: American Psychological Association.

Coloroso, B. (2002). *The bully, the bullied, and the bystander: From preschool to high school – How parents and teachers can help break the cycle of violence.* Toronto, ON: HarperCollins, Canada.

Coloroso, B. (2003). *Kids are worth it.* Toronto, ON: Penguin, Canada.

Coloroso, B. (2007). *Just because it's not wrong doesn't make it right.* Toronto, ON: Penguin, Canada.

Corno, L., Cronbach, L. J., Kupermintz, H., Lohman, D. F., Mandinach, E. B., Porteus, A. W., et al. (2002). *Remaking the concept of aptitude: Extending the legacy of Richard E. Snow.* Mahwah, NJ: Erlbaum.

Courtney, R. (1989). *Play, drama and thought: The intellectual background to drama education.* Toronto, ON: Simpon & Pierre.

Cox, J., Daniel, N., & Boston, B. (1985). *Educating able learners: Programs and promising practices.* Austin, TX: University of Texas Press.

Cropley, A. J., & Urban, K. K. (2000). Programs and strategies for nurturing creativity. In K. A. Heller, F. J. Monks, R. J. Sternberg, & R. F. Subotnik (Eds.), *International handbook of giftedness and talent* (2nd ed., pp. 485-498). Oxford, UK: Elsevier Science.

Cross, T. L. (2008). Suicide. In J. A. Plucker & C. M. Callahan (Eds.), *Critical issues and practices in gifted education: What the research says* (pp. 629-640). Waco, TX: Prufrock Press.

Cross, T. L., & Coleman, L. J. (2005). School-based conception of giftedness. In R. J. Sternberg & J. E. Davidson (Eds.), *Conceptions of giftedness* (pp. 52 63). Cambridge, UK: Cambridge University Press.

Cross, T. L., Frazier, A. D., & McKay, S. M. (2009). Preventing suicide among students with gifts and talents. In J. L. VanTassel-Baska, T. L. Cross, & F. R. Olenchak (Eds.), *Social-emotional curriculum with gifted and talented students* (pp. 321-344). Waco, TX: Prufrock Press.

Csikszentmihalyi, M. (1991). *Flow: The psychology of optimal experience.* New York: Harper Collins.

Csikszentmihalyi, M. (1996). *Creativity: Flow and the psychology of discovery and invention.* New York: Harperperennial.

Csikszentmihalyi, M., & Wolfe, R. (2000). New conceptions and research approaches to creativity. In K. A., F. J. Monks, R. J. Sternberg, & R. F. Subotnik (Eds.), *International handbook of giftedness and talent* (2nd ed., pp. 81-93). Oxford, UK: Elsevier Science.

Dai, D. Y., & Renzulli, J. S. (2008). Snowflakes, living systems, and the mystery of giftedness. *Gifted Child Quarterly, 52*, 114-130.

Davidson Institute for Talent Development. (n.d.). *Getting started for mentors.* Retrieved April, 2009, from www.davidsongifted.org

Davis, G. A. (2006). *Gifted children and gifted education.* Scottsdale, AZ: Great Potential Press.

Delcourt, M. A. B. (2003). Five ingredients for success: Two case studies of advocacy at the state level. *Gifted Child Quarterly, 47*(1), 27.

Dettmer, P. A., Landrum, M. S., & Miller, T. N. (2006). Professional development for the education of secondary gifted students. In F. A. Dixon & S. M. Moon (Eds.), *The handbook of secondary gifted education* (pp. 611-648). Waco, TX: Prufrock Press.

Dixon, F. A., & Moon, S. M. (Eds.). (2006). *The handbook of secondary gifted education.* Waco, TX: Prufrock Press.

Doidge, N. (2007). *The brain that changes itself.* New York: Penguin.

Dweck, C. S. (2006a). Is math a gift? Beliefs that put females at risk. In S. J. Ceci & W. M Williams (Eds.), *Why aren't more women in science? Top researchers debate the evidence* (pp. 47-55). Washington, DC: American Psychological Association.

Dweck, C. S. (2006b). *Mindset: The new psychology of success.* New York: Random House.

Dweck, C. S. (2009a). Foreword. In F. D. Horowitz, R. F. Subotnik, & D. J. Matthews (Eds.), *The development of giftedness and talent across the life span* (pp. xi-xiv). Washington, DC: American Psychological Association.

Dweck, C. S. (2009b). Self-theories and lessons for giftedness: A reflective conversation. In T. Balchin, B. Hymer, & D. J. Matthews (Eds.), *The Routledge international companion to gifted education* (pp. 308-316). London: Routledge.

Eide, B., & Eide, F. (2006). *The mislabeled child.* New York: Hyperion.

Elster, A. (2001). Learning through the arts: Program goals, features, and pilot results. *International Journal of Education and the Arts, 2*(7).

Enersen, D. (2003). The art of bridge building: Providing for gifted children. *Gifted Child Quarterly, 47*(1), 38-45.

Ericsson, K. A. (2006). The influence of experience and deliberate practice on the development of superior expert performance. In K. A. Ericsson, N. Charness, P. J. Feltovich, & R. R. Hoffman (Eds.), *The Cambridge handbook of expertise and expert performance* (pp. 683-703). New York: Cambridge University Press.

Ericsson, K. A., Charness, N., Feltovich, P. J., & Hoffman, R. R. (Eds.). (2006). *The Cambridge handbook of expertise and expert performance.* New York: Cambridge University Press.

Feldhusen, J. F. (1995). Talent development: The new direction in gifted education. *Roeper Review, 18,* 92.

Feldhusen, J. F. (2003). Beyond general giftedness: New ways to identify and educate gifted, talented, and precocious youth. In J. H. Borland (Ed.), *Rethinking gifted education* (pp. 34-45). New York: Teachers College Press.

Feldhusen, J. F. (2005). Giftedness, talent, expertise, and creative achievement. In R. J. Sternberg, & J. E. Davidson (Eds.), *Conceptions of giftedness* (2nd ed., pp. 64-79). New York: Cambridge University Press.

Feldhusen, J. F., & Jarwan, F. (2000). Identification of gifted and talented youth for educational programs. In K. A. Heller, F. J. Monks, R. J. Sternberg, & R. F. Subotnik (Eds.), *International handbook of giftedness and talent* (2nd ed., pp. 271-282). Oxford, UK: Elsevier Science.

Feldhusen, J. F., Proctor, T. B., & Black, K. N. (2002). Guidelines for grade advancement of precocious children. *Roeper Review, 24,* 169-171.

Feldman, D. H. (1991). Why children can't be creative. *Exceptionality Education Canada, 1*(1), 43-51.

Feldman, D. H. (2003). A developmental, evolutionary perspective on giftedness. In J. H. Borland (Ed.), *Rethinking gifted education* (pp. 9-33). New York: Teachers College Press.

Feldman, D. H. (2008). Prodigies. In J. A. Plucker & C. M. Callahan (Eds.), *Critical issues and practices in gifted education: What the research says* (pp. 523-534). Waco, TX: Prufrock Press.

Feldman, D. H., & Goldsmith, L. T. (1986). *Nature's gambit: Child prodigies and the development of human potential.* New York: Basic Books.

Feng, A. X. (2007). Developing personalized learning experiences: Mentoring for talent development. In J. L. VanTassel-Baska (Ed.), *Serving gifted learners beyond the traditional classroom* (pp. 189-212). Waco, TX: Prufrock Press.

Feng, A. X., & VanTassel-Baska, J. L. (2008). Identifying low-income and minority students for gifted programs: Academic and affective impact of performance--based assessment. In J. L. Van Taska-Baska (Ed.), *Alternative assessments with gifted and talented students* (pp. 129-146). Waco, TX: Prufrock Press.

Ferguson, S. (2003, September 22). The ABCs of classroom fun. *Maclean's Magazine, 116*(38), 17-22.

Ferguson, S. (2004, August 23). Canada's best schools. *Maclean's Magazine, 117*(34), 17-22.

Ferri, B. A., & Connor, D. J. (2006). *Reading resistance: Discourses of exclusion in desegregation and inclusion debates.* New York: Peter Lang.

Fertig, C. (2008). *Raising a gifted child: A parenting success handbook.* Waco, TX: Prufrock Press.

Fleith, D. S. (2001). *Suicide among gifted adolescents: How to prevent it.* Retrieved March 8, 2009, from www.gifted.uconn.edu/nrcgt/newsletter/spring01/sprng012.html

Folsom, C. (2008). *Teaching for intellectual and emotional learning (TIEL).* Lanham, MD: Rowman & Littlefield.

Ford, D. Y. (2003a). Desegregating gifted education: Seeking equity for culturally diverse students. In J. H. Borland (Ed.), *Rethinking gifted education* (pp. 143-158). New York: Teachers College Press.

Ford, D. Y. (2003b). Equity and excellence: Culturally diverse students in gifted education. In N. Colangelo & G. A. Davis (Eds.), *Handbook of gifted education* (pp. 506-520). Boston: Allyn & Bacon.

Ford, D. Y., Harris, J., Tyson, C., & Trotman, M. (2000). Beyond deficit thinking: Providing access for gifted African American students. *Roeper Review, 24*, 52-58.

Ford, D. Y., & Moore, J. L., III. (2006). Being gifted and adolescent: Issues and needs of students of color. In F. A. Dixon & S. M. Moon (Eds.), *The handbook of secondary gifted education* (pp. 113-132). Waco, TX: Prufrock Press.

Foster, J. (2000). *A case study approach to understanding the gifted experience: Children's and parents' perceptions of labeling and placement.* Unpublished doctoral dissertation, Ontario Institute for Studies in Education of the University of Toronto, Toronto, ON.

Foster, J. F. (2007). Procrastination and perfectionism; Connections, understandings, and control. *Gifted Education International, 23*(3), 132-140.

Foster, J. F. (in press a). Extracurricular activities. In B. A. Kerr (Ed.), *Encyclopedia of giftedness, creativity, and talent.* Thousand Oaks, CA: Sage.

Foster, J. F. (in press b). Teacher development. In B. A. Kerr (Ed.), *Encyclopedia of giftedness, creativity, and talent.* Thousand Oaks, CA: Sage.

Foster, J. F., Porath, M., & Smyth, E. M. (in press). Canada, gifted education. In B. A. Kerr (Ed.), *Encyclopedia of giftedness, creativity, and talent.* Thousand Oaks, CA: Sage.

Freeman, J. (2004). Cultural influences on gifted gender achievement. *High Ability Studies, 15*(1), 7-23.

Freeman, J. (2009). Morality and giftedness. In T. Balchin, B. Hymer, & D. J. Matthews (Eds.), *The Routledge international companion to gifted education* (pp. 141-148). Abingdon, UK: Routledge.

Fullan, M. (1991). *The new meaning of educational change* (2nd ed.). New York: Teachers College Press.

Gagné, F. (2009). Talent development as seen through the differentiated model of giftedness and talent. In T. Balchin, B. Hymer, & D. J. Matthews (Eds.), *The Routledge international companion to gifted education* (pp. 32-41). Abingdon, UK: Routledge.

Galambos, N. L. (2004). Gender and gender role development in adolescence. In R. M. Lerner & L. Steinberg (Eds.), *Handbook of adolescent psychology* (2nd ed., pp. 233-262). Hoboken, NJ: Wiley.

Gardner, H. (1983). *Frames of mind.* New York: Basic Books.

Gardner, H. (1991). *The unschooled mind: How children think and how schools should teach.* New York: Basic Books.

Gardner, H. (1998). A multiplicity of intelligences. *Scientific American, 9,* 18-23.

Gardner, H. (2007). *Five minds for the future.* Cambridge, MA: Harvard Business School Press.

Geake, J. (2009). Neural interconnectivity and intellectual creativity: Giftedness, savants, and learning styles. In T. Balchin, B. Hymer, & D. J. Matthews (Eds.), *The Routledge international companion to gifted education* (pp. 10-17). London: Routledge.

Gentry, M. (2007). No Child Left Behind: Neglecting excellence. *Roeper Review, 29,* 24-27.

Gentry, M., Hu, S., & Thomas, A. T. (2008). Ethnically diverse students. In J. A. Plucker & C. M. Callahan (Eds.), *Critical issues and practices in gifted education: What the research says* (pp. 195-212). Waco, TX: Prufrock Press.

Gilman, B. J. (2008). *Academic advocacy for gifted children: A parent's complete guide.* Scottsdale, AZ: Great Potential Press.

Ginott, J. G. (1972). *Teacher & child: A book for parents and teachers.* New York: Avon.

Gladwell, M. (2008). *Outliers: The story of success.* New York: Little, Brown.

Goertzel, V., Goertzel, M. G., Goertzel, T. G., & Hansen, A. M. W. (2004). *Cradles of eminence: Childhoods of more than 700 famous men and women* (2nd ed.). Scottsdale, AZ: Great Potential Press.

Goleman, D. (1995). *Emotional intelligence.* New York: Bantam.

Gottfried, A. W., Gottfried, A. E., Bathurst, K., & Guerin, D. W. (1994). *Gifted IQ: Early developmental aspects.* New York: Plenum Press.

Gottfried, A. W., Gottfried, A. E., Cook, C., & Morris, P. (2005). Educational characteristics of adolescents with gifted academic intrinsic motivation: A longitudinal study from school entry through early adulthood. *Gifted Child Quarterly, 49,* 172-186.

Gottfried, A. W., Gottfried, A. E., & Guerin, D. W. (2009). Issues in early prediction and identification of intellectual giftedness. In F. D. Horowitz, R. F. Subotnik, & D. J. Matthews (Eds.), *The development of giftedness and talent across the life span* (pp. 43-56). Washington, DC: American Psychological Association.

Gould, S. J. (1981). *The mismeasure of man.* New York: W.W. Norton.

Graham, S. (2009). Giftedness in adolescence: African American gifted youth and their challenges from a motivational perspective. In F. D. Horowitz, R. F. Subotnik, & D. J. Matthews (Eds.), *The development of giftedness and talent across the life span* (pp. 43-56). Washington, DC: American Psychological Association.

Gross, M. U. M. (2008). Highly gifted children and adolescents. In J. A. Plucker & C. M. Callahan (Eds.), *Critical issues and practices in gifted education: What the research says* (pp. 241-251). Waco, TX: Prufrock Press.

Guilford, J. P. (1967). *The nature of human intelligence.* New York: McGraw-Hill.

Halsted, J. W. (2002). *Some of my best friends are books: Guiding gifted readers from preschool to high school* (2nd ed.). Scottsdale, AZ: Great Potential Press.

Hansford, S. J., Bonar, A. M., Scally, J. M., & Burge, N. A. (2001). Student identification. In M. S. Landrum, C. M. Callahan, & B. D. Shaklee (Eds.), *Aiming for excellence: Gifted program standards* (pp. 39-52). Waco, TX: Prufrock Press.

Hargreaves, A., & Earl, L. (1990). *Rights of passage: A review of selected research about schooling in the transition years.* Toronto, ON: Queen's Printer for Ontario.

Harter, S. (1999). *The construction of the self: A developmental perspective.* New York: The Guilford Press.

Hébert, T. P. (2009). Guiding gifted teenagers to self-understanding through biography. In J. L. VanTassel-Baska, T. L. Cross, & F. R. Olenchak (Eds.), *Socialemotional curriculum with gifted and talented students* (pp. 259-288). Waco, TX: Prufrock Press.

Hébert, T. P., & Kelly, K. R. (2006). Identity and career development in gifted students. In F. A. Dixon & S. M. Moon (Eds.), *The handbook of secondary gifted education* (pp. 35-63). Waco, TX: Prufrock Press.

Heller, K. A., Monks, F. J., Sternberg, R. J., & Subotnik, R. F. (Eds.). (2000). *International handbook of giftedness and talent* (2nd ed.). Oxford, UK: Elsevier Science.

Heward, W. L. (2002). *Exceptional children: An introduction to special education* (7th ed.). Upper Saddle River, NJ: Prentice Hall.

Higgins-Biss, K. (1995). *The importance of being humorous: The implications for social competence and self-concept in high level cognitive development.* Unpublished master's thesis, Ontario Institute for Studies in Education of the University of Toronto, Toronto, ON.

Hogan, K., & Pressley, M. (Eds.). (1997). *Scaffolding student learning: Instructional approaches and issues.* Cambridge, MA: Brookline Books.

Hollingworth, L. (1926). *Gifted children: Their nature and nurture.* New York: Macmillan.

Horowitz, F. D. (2009). Introduction: A developmental understanding of giftedness and talent. In F. D. Horowitz, R. F. Subotnik, & D. J. Matthews (Eds.), *The development of giftedness and talent across the life span* (pp. 3-20). Washington, DC: American Psychological Association.

Horowitz, F. D., Subotnik, R. F., & Matthews, D. J. (Eds.). (2009). *The development of giftedness and talent across the life span.* Washington, DC: American Psychological Association.

Howe, M. J. A. (1990). *The origins of exceptional abilities.* Oxford, UK: Basil Blackwell.

Howe, M. J. A. (1999). *Genius explained.* Cambridge, MA: Cambridge University Press.

Hughes, J. (2009). Teaching the able child...or teaching the child to be able? In T. Balchin, B. Hymer, & D. J. Matthews (Eds.), *The Routledge international companion to gifted education* (pp. 161-168). Abingdon, UK: Routledge.

Hunt, B. G., & Seney, R. W. (2009). Planning the learning environment. In F. A. Karnes & S. M. Bean (Eds.), *Methods and materials for teaching the gifted* (3rd ed., pp. 37-74). Waco, TX: Prufrock Press.

Hurwitz, B. (2007, Spring). Just say yes to acceleration. *Association for Bright Children Newsletter*, 1-4.

Huxtable, M. (2009). Creating inclusive and inclusional understandings of gifts and talents through living educational theory research. In T. Balchin, B. Hymer, & D. J. Matthews (Eds.), *The Routledge international companion to gifted education* (pp. 292-298). Abingdon, UK: Routledge.

Hymer, B. (2009). Beyond compare? Thoughts towards an inclusional, fluid, and non-normative understanding of giftedness. In T. Balchin, B. Hymer, & D. J. Matthews (Eds.), *The Routledge international companion to gifted education* (pp. 299-307). Abingdon, UK: Routledge.

Hymer, B., Whitehead, J., & Huxtable, M. (2009). *Gifts, talents, and education: A living theory approach.* Chichester, UK: Wiley-Blackwell.

Jarvin, L., Newman, T., Randi, J., Sternberg, R. J., & Grigorenko, E. L. (2008). Matching instruction and assessment. In J. A. Plucker & C. M. Callahan (Eds.), *Critical issues and practices in gifted education: What the research says* (pp. 345-366). Waco, TX: Prufrock Press.

Jarvin, L., & Subotnik, R. F. (2006). Understanding elite talent in academic domains: A developmental trajectory from basic abilities to scholarly productivity/artistry. In F. A. Dixon & S. M. Moon (Eds.), *The handbook of secondary gifted education* (pp. 203-220). Waco, TX: Prufrock Press.

Johnsen, S. K. (2008). Portfolio assessment of gifted students. In J. L. VanTassel-Baska (Ed.), *Alternative assessments with gifted and talented students* (pp. 227-258). Waco, TX: Prufrock Press.

Johnsen, S. K., Haensly, P. A., Ryser, G. R., & Ford, R. F. (2002). Changing general education classroom practices to adapt for gifted students. *Gifted Child Quarterly, 46,* 1.

Joseph, L. M., & Ford, D. Y. (2006). Nondiscriminatory assessment: Consideration for gifted education. *Gifted Child Quarterly, 50*(1), 42-51.

Juster, N. (1961). *The phantom tollbooth.* New York: Random House.

Kalbfleisch, M. L. (2008). Getting to the heart of the brain: Using cognitive neuroscience to explore the nature of human ability and performance. *Roeper Review, 30,* 162-170.

Kalbfleisch, M. L., & Banasiak, M. (2008). ADHD. In J. A. Plucker & C. M. Callahan (Eds.), *Critical issues and practices in gifted education: What the research says* (pp. 15-30). Waco, TX: Prufrock Press.

Kalbfleisch, M. L., & Iguchi, C. M. (2008). Twice-exceptional learners. In J. A. Plucker & C. M. Callahan (Eds.), *Critical issues and practices in gifted education: What the research says* (pp. 707-719). Waco, TX: Prufrock Press.

Kamphaus, R. W. (2005). *Clinical assessment of child and adolescent intelligence* (2nd ed.). New York: Springer.

Kaufmann, F. A. (1981). The 1964-1968 Presidential Scholars: A follow-up study. *Exceptional Children, 48,* 2-10.

Kaufmann, F. A., Kalbfleisch, M. L., & Castellanos, F. X. (2000). *Attention deficit disorders and gifted students: What do we really know?* (Research Monograph No. 00146). Storrs, CT: National Research Center on the Gifted and Talented, University of Connecticut.

Keating, D. P. (1980). The four faces of creativity: The continuing plight of the underserved. *Gifted Child Quarterly, 24*(2), 56-61.

Keating, D. P. (1990). Adolescent thinking. In S. S. Feldman & G. R. Elliott (Eds.), *At the threshold: The developing adolescent* (pp. 54-89). Cambridge, MA: Harvard University Press.

Keating, D. P. (1991). Curriculum options for the developmentally advanced. *Exceptionality Education Canada, 1,* 53-83.

Keating, D. P. (2004). Cognitive and brain development. In R. M. Lerner & L. Steinberg (Eds.), *Handbook of adolescent psychology* (2nd ed., pp. 45-83). Hoboken, NJ: Wiley.

Keating, D. P. (2009). Developmental science and giftedness: An integrated life span framework. In F. D. Horowitz, R. F. Subotnik, & D. J. Matthews (Eds.), *The development of giftedness and talent across the life span* (pp. 189-208). Washington, DC: American Psychological Association.

Kerr, B. A. (1997). *Smart girls: A new psychology of girls, women, and giftedness.* Scottsdale, AZ: Great Potential Press.

Kerr, B. A. (2000). Guiding gifted girls and young women. In K. A. Heller, F. J. Monks, R. J. Sternberg, & R. F. Subotnik (Eds.), *International handbook of giftedness and talent* (2nd ed., pp. 649-657). Oxford, UK: Elsevier Science.

Kerr, B. A. (in press). *Encyclopedia of giftedness, creativity, and talent.* Thousand Oaks, CA: Sage.

Kerr, B. A., & Cohn, S. J. (2001). *Smart boys: Talent, manhood, and the search for meaning.* Scottsdale, AZ: Great Potential Press.

Kerr, B. A., & Foley Nicpon, M. (2003). Gender and giftedness. In N. Colangelo & G. A. Davis (Eds.), *Handbook of gifted education* (pp. 493-505). Boston: Allyn & Bacon.

Kitano, M. K. (2007). The value of out-of-school programs for gifted youth from diverse backgrounds. In J. L. VanTassel-Baska (Ed.), *Serving gifted learners beyond the traditional classroom* (pp. 33-54). Waco, TX: Prufrock Press.

Kitano, M. K. (2008). Gifted girls. In J. A. Plucker & C. M. Callahan (Eds.), *Critical issues and practices in gifted education: What the research says* (pp. 225-241). Waco, TX: Prufrock Press.

Klapp, J., & Porath, M. (2000). Past, present, and future of gifted education in British Columbia. *Alberta Gifted and Talented Education, 14*(2), 26-35.

Klein, A. G. (2002). *A forgotten voice: A biography of Leta Stetter Hollingworth.* Scottsdale, AZ: Great Potential Press.

Koshy, V. (2009). Too long neglected. In T. Balchin, B. Hymer, & D. J. Matthews (Eds.), *The Routledge international companion to gifted education* (pp. 155-160). Abingdon, UK: Routledge.

Kunzman, R. (2008). Homeschooling. In J. A. Plucker & C. M. Callahan (Eds.), *Critical issues and practices in gifted education: What the research says* (pp. 253-260). Waco, TX: Prufrock Press.

Lewis, J. D., & Karnes, F. A. (2009). Public relations and advocacy for the gifted. In F. A. Karnes & S. M. Bean (Eds.), *Methods and materials for teaching the gifted* (3rd ed., pp. 673-716). Waco, TX: Prufrock Press.

Li, Q. (2007). New bottle but old wine: A research of cyberbullying in schools. *Computers in Human Behavior, 23*(4), 1777-1791.

Lieberman, A. F. (1993). *The emotional life of the toddler.* New York: The Free Press.

Lohman, D. F. (2005a). An aptitude perspective on talent: Implications for identification of academically gifted minority students. *Journal for the Education of the Gifted, 28,* 333-360.

Lohman, D. F. (2005b). The role of nonverbal ability tests in the identification of academically gifted students: An aptitude perspective. *Gifted Child Quarterly, 49,* 111-138.

Lohman, D. F., & Hagen, E. P. (2001). *Cognitive Abilities Test.* Riverside.

Lohman, D. F. & Korb, K. A. (2006). Gifted today but not tomorrow? Longitudinal changes in ability and achievement during elementary school. *Journal for the Education of the Gifted, 29,* 451-484.

Lohman, D. F., & Lakin, J. (2008). Nonverbal test scores as one component of an identification system: Integrating ability, achievement, and teacher ratings. In J. L. VanTassel-Baska (Ed.), *Alternative assessments with gifted and talented students* (pp. 41-66). Waco, TX: Prufrock Press.

Lubinski, D., & Benbow, C. P. (2006). Study of mathematically precocious youth after 35 years. *Perspectives on Psychological Science, 1,* 316-345.

Marland, S. P. (1972). *Education of the gifted and talented* (Vol. 1). Report of the Congress of the United States by the U.S. Commissioner of Education. Washington, DC: Government Printing Office.

Matthews, D. J. (2009). Developmental transitions in giftedness and talent: Childhood to adolescence. In F. D. Horowitz, R. F. Subotnik, & D. J. Matthews (Eds.), *The development of giftedness and talent across the lifespan* (pp. 89-108). Washington, DC: American Psychological Association.

Matthews, D. J., & Folsom, C. (2009). Making connections: Cognition, emotion, and the shifting paradigm in gifted education. In T. Balchin, B. Hymer, & D. J. Matthews (Eds.), *The Routledge international companion to gifted education* (pp. 18-25). Abingdon, UK: Routledge.

Matthews, D. J., & Foster, J. (2003, April 10). Helping children cope with circumstances in difficult times. *Canadian Jewish News.* (Reprinted with permission at www.beingsmart.ca).

Matthews, D. J., & Foster, J. (2005). A dynamic scaffolding model of teacher development: The gifted education consultant as catalyst for change. *Gifted Child Quarterly, 49*(3), 222-230.

Matthews, D. J., & Foster, J. F. (2006). Mystery to mastery: Shifting paradigms in gifted education. *Roeper Review, 28*(2), 64-69.

Matthews, D. J., & Foster, J. F. (2008). Wrestling with misconceptions: Is the gifted label good or bad? *Understanding Our Gifted, 20*(4), 3-7.

Matthews, D. J., & Foster, J. F. (2009, Spring). The gifted label: Person or program? *Newsletter of Conceptual Foundations Strand, National Association for Gifted Children.*

Matthews, D. J., Foster, J. F., Gladstone, D., Schieck, J., & Meiners, J. (2007). Respecting professionalism, diversity, and context: A flexible collaborative approach to gifted education. *Journal of Educational and Psychological Consulting, 17,* 315-334.

Matthews, D. J., & Kitchen, J. (2007). Allowing idiosyncratic learners to thrive: Policy implications of a study of school-within-a-school gifted programs. *Journal of School Choice, 1*(4), 27-53.

Matthews, D. J., & Menna, R. (2003, Winter). Solving problems together: The importance of parent/school/community collaboration at a time of educational and social change. *Education Canada, 43*(1), 20-23.

Matthews, D. J., & Steinhauer, N. (1998). Giftedness, girls, others, and equity: Theory-based practical strategies for the regular classroom. *Exceptionality Education Canada, 8*(2), 41-56.

Matthews, D. J., Subotnik, R. F., & Horowitz, F. D. (2009). A developmental perspective on giftedness and talent: Implications for research, policy, and practice. In F. D. Horowitz, R. F. Subotnik, & D. J. Matthews (Eds.), *The development of giftedness and talent across the lifespan* (pp. 209-226). Washington, DC: American Psychological Association.

McCoach, D. B., & Siegle, D. (2008). Underachievers. In J. A. Plucker & C. M. Callahan (Eds.), *Critical issues and practices in gifted education: What the research says* (pp. 721-734). Waco, TX: Prufrock Press.

McTighe, J., & Wiggins, G. P. (2005). *Understanding by design.* Alexandria, VA: Association for Supervision and Curriculum Development.

Meece, J. L., & Daniels, D. H. (2008). *Child and adolescent development for educators* (3rd ed.). New York: McGraw-Hill.

Meier, D. (2002). *The power of their ideas: Lessons for America from a small school in Harlem.* New York: Beacon Press.

Mendaglio, S. (2007). Should perfectionism be a characteristic of giftedness? *Gifted Education International, 23*(3), 229-230.

Mendaglio, S. (Ed.). (2008). *Dabrowski's theory of positive disintegration.* Scottsdale, AZ: Great Potential Press.

Mills, J. R., & Jackson, N. E. (1990). Predictive significance of early giftedness: The case of precocious reading. *Journal of Educational Psychology, 82,* 410-419.

Mitchell, A. (2003, September 27). Slow schooling: It makes mainstream education look like fast food. *The Globe and Mail,* F1, F10.

Moon, S. M. (2006). On being gifted and adolescent: An overview. In F. A. Dixon & S. M. Moon (Eds.), *The handbook of secondary gifted education* (pp. 1-5). Waco, TX: Prufrock Press.

Moon, S. M. (2009). Theories to guide affective curriculum development. In J. L. VanTassel-Baska, T. L. Cross, & F. R. Olenchak (Eds.), *Social-emotional curriculum with gifted and talented students* (pp. 11-40). Waco, TX: Prufrock Press.

Moon, S. M., & Dixon, F. A. (2006). Conceptions of giftedness in adolescence. In F. A. Dixon & S. M. Moon (Eds.), *The handbook of secondary gifted education* (pp. 7-34). Waco, TX: Prufrock Press.

Moon, S. M., & Rosselli, H. C. (2000). Developing gifted programs. In K. A. Heller, F. J. Monks, R. J. Sternberg, & R. F. Subotnik (Eds.), *International handbook of giftedness and talent* (2nd ed., pp. 499-521). Oxford, UK: Elsevier Science.

Naglieri, J. A. (1996). *Naglieri Nonverbal Ability Test*. San Antonio, TX: The Psychological Corp.

Naglieri, J. A. (2008). Traditional IQ: 100 years of misconception and its relationship to minority representation in gifted programs. In J. L. VanTassel-Baska (Ed.), *Alternative assessments with gifted and talented students* (pp. 67-88). Waco, TX: Prufrock Press.

Naglieri, J. A., & Ford, D. Y. (2003). Addressing underrepresentation of gifted minority children using the Naglieri Nonverbal Ability Test (NNAT). *Gifted Child Quarterly, 47*, 155-160.

National Association for Gifted Children. (2006). *CEC-NAGC initial knowledge and skill standards for gifted and talented education*. Retrieved February 9, 2009, from www.pagiftededucation.info/documents/ NCATEFinalInitialStandards4-14-06.pdf

National Association for Gifted Children. (n.d.). *Gifted education programming criterion: Professional development*. Retrieved February, 2009, from www.nagc.org/table6.htm

National Center for Education Statistics. (2004). *1.1 Million homeschooled students in the United States in 2003* (NCES publication no. 2004115). Washington, DC: National Center for Education Statistics.

Neihart, M. (2008). *Peak performance for smart kids*. Waco, TX: Prufrock Press.

Nelson, C. A. (1999). Neural plasticity and human development. *Current Directions in Psychological Science, 8*, 42-45.

New York State. (1982). *Education Law, Article 90, Section 4452*. Albany, NY: Author.

Nisbett, R. E. (2009). *Intelligence and how to get it: Why schools and cultures count*. New York: Norton.

Noble, K. D., Subotnik, R. F., & Arnold, K. D. (1999). To thine own self be true: A new model of female talent development. *Gifted Child Quarterly, 43*, 140-149.

Oatley, K., & Jenkins, J. M. (1996). *Understanding emotions*. Cambridge, MA: Blackwell.

Ohio Department of Education. (2000). *Project Start ID: Statewide arts talent identification and development project.* Columbus, OH: Author.

Olszewksi-Kubilius, P. (2007). The role of summer programs in developing the talents of gifted students. In J. L. VanTassel-Baska (Ed.), *Serving gifted learners beyond the traditional classroom* (pp. 13-32). Waco, TX: Prufrock Press.

Ontario College of Teachers. (1999). *The standards of practice for the teaching profession.* Retrieved June 29, 2004, from www.oct.ca/en/CollegePublications/PDF/standards.pdf

Ontario College of Teachers. (2008). *Foundations of professional practice.* Retrieved April 22, 2009, from www.edu.gov.on.ca/publications/PDF/foundation_e.pdf

Ontario Ministry of Education. (1984). *Special education handbook.* Toronto, ON: Author.

Ontario Ministry of Education and Training. (2000). *Individual education plans: Standards for development, program planning, and implementation.* Toronto, ON: Author.

Oreck, B. A., Owen, S. V., & Baum, S. M. (2003). Validity, reliability, and equity issues in an observational talent assessment process in the performing arts. (Article includes the *Talent Assessment Process.*) *Journal for the Education of the Gifted, 27*(1), 62-94.

Ortiz, S. O. (2002). Best practices in nondiscriminatory assessment. In A. Thomas & J. Grimes (Eds.), *Best practices in school psychology* (Vol. IV, pp. 1321-1336). Bethesda, MD: National Association of School Psychologists.

Palloff, R. M., & Pratt, K. (2001). *Lessons from the cyberspace classroom: The realities of online teaching.* San Francisco: Jossey-Bass.

Parks, S. (2009). Teaching analytical and critical thinking skills in gifted education. In F. A. Karnes & S. M. Bean (Eds.), *Methods and materials for teaching the gifted* (3rd ed., pp. 261-300). Waco, TX: Prufrock Press.

Perkins, D. N. (1981). *The mind's best work.* Cambridge, MA: Harvard University Press.

Peterson, J. S. (2006). Superintendents, principals, and counselors: Facilitating secondary gifted education. In F. A. Dixon & S. M. Moon (Eds.), *The handbook of secondary gifted education* (pp. 649-672). Waco, TX: Prufrock Press.

Peterson, J. S. (2008). Counseling. In J. A. Plucker & C. M. Callahan (Eds.), *Critical issues and practices in gifted education: What the research says* (pp. 119-138). Waco, TX: Prufrock Press.

Peterson, J. S., Betts, G., & Bradley, T. (2009). Discussion groups as a component of affective curriculum for gifted students. In J. L. VanTassel-Baska, T. L. Cross, & F. R. Olenchak (Eds.), *Social-emotional curriculum with gifted and talented students* (pp. 289-320). Waco, TX: Prufrock Press.

Piechowski, M. M. (2006). *Mellow out.* Madison, WI: Yunasa Books.

Piirto, J. (2003). *Understanding creativity.* Scottsdale, AZ: Great Potential Press.

Piper, W. (1930). *The little engine that could.* New York: Platt & Munk.

Pipher, M. (1994). *Reviving Ophelia: Saving the selves of adolescent girls.* New York: Ballantine.

Purkey, W. W. (2006). *Teaching class clowns (and what they can teach us).* Thousand Oaks, CA: Corwin Press.

Pyryt, M. C. (2007). The giftedness/perfectionism connection. *Gifted Education International, 23,* 273-279.

Pyryt, M. C. (2008). Self-concept. In J. A. Plucker & C. M. Callahan (Eds.), *Critical issues and practices in gifted education: What the research says* (pp. 595-602). Waco, TX: Prufrock Press.

Quart, A. (2006). *Hothouse kids: The dilemma of the gifted child.* New York: Penguin.

Raven, J. C., Court, J. H., & Raven, J. (1998). *Standard Progressive Matrices.* London: Lewis.

Reilly, J. (1992). *Mentorship: The essential guide for schools and business.* Scottsdale, AZ: Great Potential Press (formerly Ohio Psychology Press).

Reis, S. M. (2006). Gender, adolescence, and giftedness. In F. A. Dixon & S. M. Moon (Eds.), *The handbook of secondary gifted education* (pp. 87-112). Waco, TX: Prufrock Press.

Reis, S. M. (2009). Turning points and future directions in gifted education and talent development. In T. Balchin, B. Hymer, & D. J. Matthews (Eds.), *The Routledge international companion to gifted education* (pp. 317-324). Abingdon, UK: Routledge.

Renzulli, J. S. (1976). The enrichment triad model: A guide for developing defensible programs for the gifted and talented. *Gifted Child Quarterly, 20,* 303-326.

Renzulli, J. S. (2002). Expanding the conception of giftedness to include co-cognitive traits and to promote social capital. *Phi Delta Kappan, 84*(1), 33-58.

Renzulli, J. S. (2003, November). *Senior scholars speak out.* Paper presented at annual meeting of the National Association for Gifted Children, Indianapolis, IN.

Renzulli, J. S. (2009). Operation houndstooth: A positive perspective on developing social intelligence. In J. L. VanTassel-Baska, T. L. Cross, & F. R. Olenchak (Eds.), *Social-emotional curriculum with gifted and talented students* (pp. 79-112). Waco, TX: Prufrock Press.

Renzulli, J. S., & Reis, S. M. (1985). *The schoolwide enrichment model: A comprehensive plan for educational excellence.* Mansfield Center, CT: Creative Learning Press.

Renzulli, J. S., & Reis, S. M. (2008). *Enriching curriculum for all students* (2nd ed.). Thousand Oaks, CA: Corwin Press.

Renzulli, J. S., & Reis, S. M. (2009). A computerized strength assessment and internet-based enrichment program for developing giftedness and talent. In T. Balchin, B. Hymer, & D. J. Matthews (Eds.), *The Routledge international companion to gifted education* (pp. 185-193). Abingdon, UK: Routledge.

Richert, E. S. (2003). Excellence with justice in identification and programming. In N. Colangelo & G. A. Davis (Eds.), *Handbook of gifted education* (pp. 146-158). Boston: Allyn & Bacon.

Riley, T. L. (2009). Teaching gifted and talented students in regular classrooms. In F. A. Karnes & S. M. Bean (Eds.), *Methods and materials for teaching the gifted* (3rd ed., pp. 631-676). Waco, TX: Prufrock Press.

Riley, T. L., & Karnes, F. A. (2007). Competitions for gifted and talented students: Issues of excellence and equity. In J. L. VanTassel-Baska (Ed.), *Serving gifted learners beyond the traditional classroom* (pp. 145-168). Waco, TX: Prufrock Press.

Rimm, S. (2007). *Keys to parenting the gifted child.* Scottsdale, AZ: Great Potential Press.

Rivero, L. (2002). *Creative home schooling: A resource guide for smart families.* Scottsdale, AZ: Great Potential Press.

Rizza, M. G., & Gentry, M. (2001). A legacy of promise: Reflections, suggestions and directions from contemporary leaders in the field of gifted education. *The Teacher Educator, 36,* 167-188.

Roberts, J. L., & Inman, T. F. (2009). *Strategies for differentiating instruction: Best practices for the classroom.* Waco, TX: Prufrock Press.

Robinson, A. (2008). Teacher characteristics. In J. A. Plucker & C. M. Callahan (Eds.), *Critical issues and practices in gifted education: What the research says* (pp. 669-680). Waco, TX: Prufrock Press.

Robinson, A., & Clinkenbeard, P. R. (1998). Giftedness: An exceptionality examined. *Annual Review of Psychology, 49,* 117-139.

Robinson, A., Shore, B. M., & Enersen, D. L. (2007). *Best practices in gifted education: An evidence-based guide.* Waco, TX: Prufrock Press.

Robinson, N. M. (2003). Two wrongs do not make a right: Sacrificing the needs of gifted students does not solve society's unsolved problems. *Journal for the Education of the Gifted, 26*(4), 251-273.

Robinson, N. M. (2008). The value of traditional assessments as approaches to identifying academically gifted students. In J. L. VanTassel-Baska (Ed.), *Alternative assessments with gifted and talented students* (pp. 157-174). Waco, TX: Prufrock Press.

Robinson, N. M., & Robinson, H. B. (1982). The optimal match: Devising the best compromise for the highly gifted student. In D. Feldman (Ed.), *New directions for child development: Developmental approaches to giftedness and creativity* (pp. 79-94). San Francisco: Jossey-Bass.

Rogers, K. B. (2002). *Re-forming gifted education: How parents and teachers can match the program to the child.* Scottsdale, AZ: Great Potential Press.

Rogers, K. B. (2003). A voice of reason in the wilderness. *Journal for the Education of the Gifted, 26*(4), 314-320.

Rogers, K. B., & Kimpston, R. D. (1992, Oct.). The acceleration of students: What we do vs. what we know. *Educational Leadership.*

Roid, G. H. (2003). *Stanford-Binet Intelligence Scale* (5th ed.). Itasca, IL: Riverside.

Ruf, D. L. (2005). *Losing our minds: Gifted children left behind.* Scottsdale, AZ: Great Potential Press.

Rutter, M. (2001). *Research and innovation on the road to modern child psychiatry.* London: RCPsych Publications.

Salmon, G. (2000). *E-moderating: The key to teaching and learning online.* Sterling, VA: Stylus.

Sapadin, L., & Maguire, J. (1999). *Beat procrastination and make the grade: The six styles of procrastination and how students can overcome them.* New York: Penguin.

Sattler, J. M. (2001). *Assessment of children: Cognitive applications* (4th ed.). San Diego, CA: Jerome Sattler.

Scardamalia, M., & Bereiter, C. (2005). Does education for the knowledge age need a new science? *European Journal of School Psychology, 3*(1), 263-282.

Schipper, B., & Rossi, J. (1997). *Portfolios in the classroom: Tools for learning and instruction.* York, MA: Stenhouse.

Schoon, I. (2000). A life span approach to talent development. In K. A. Heller, F. J. Monks, R. J. Sternberg, & R. F. Subotnik (Eds.), *International handbook of giftedness and talent* (2nd ed., pp. 213-225). Oxford, UK: Elsevier Science.

Schouten, F. (2003, January 30). *High turnover worsens teacher shortage.* Retrieved July 2, 2004, from www.detnews.com/2003/schools/0301/30/a01-72737.htm

Shonkoff, J. P., & Phillips, D. A. (2000). *From neurons to neighborhoods: The science of early childhood development.* Washington, DC: National Academy Press.

Siegle, D., McCoach, D. B., & Wilson, H. E. (2009). Extending learning through mentorships. In F. A. Karnes & S. M. Bean (Eds.), *Methods and materials for teaching the gifted* (3rd ed., pp. 519-564). Waco, TX: Prufrock Press.

Silverman, S. M., & Weinfeld, R. (2007). *School success for kids with Asperger's syndrome.* Waco TX: Prufrock Press.

Silvertown, R. (n.d.). *Virtuoso: The Travel Network Corp.* Retrieved June 28, 2004, from www.virtuoso.com/ge/active_0404a.html

Simonton, D. K. (1994). *Greatness: Who makes history and why.* New York: Guilford Press.

Simonton, D. K. (1997). Creative productivity: A predictive and explanatory model of career trajectories and landmarks. *Psychological Review, 104,* 66-89.

Smutny, J. F., Walker, S. Y., & Meckstroth, E. A. (2007). *Acceleration for gifted learners, K-5.* Thousand Oaks, CA: Corwin Press.

Spearman, C. (1927). *The abilities of man: Their nature and measurement.* New York: Macmillan.

Stanford Achievement Tests. (2003). *Stanford Achievement Tests* (10th ed.). San Antonio, TX: Harcourt Educational Measurement.

Stanley, J. C., & Benbow, C. P. (1983). Educating mathematically precocious youths: Twelve policy recommendations. *Educational Researcher, 11*(5), 4-9.

Stanley, J. C., Keating, D. P., & Fox, L. (1974). *Mathematical talent.* Baltimore: Johns Hopkins Press.

Starko, A. J. (2008). Teacher preparation. In J. A. Plucker & C. M. Callahan (Eds.), *Critical issues and practices in gifted education: What the research says* (pp. 681-694). Waco, TX: Prufrock Press.

Steinberg, L. (2005). *Adolescence* (7th ed.). New York: McGraw-Hill.

Sternberg, R. J. (1998). Principles of teaching for successful intelligence. *Educational Psychologist, 33*(2/3), 65-72.

Sternberg, R. J. (2000). Identifying and developing creative giftedness. *Roeper Review, 23*, 60-65.

Sternberg, R. J. (2009). Wisdom, intelligence, creativity, synthesised: A model of giftedness. In T. Balchin, B. Hymer, & D. J. Matthews (Eds.), *The Routledge international companion to gifted education* (pp. 255-264). Abingdon, UK: Routledge.

Stewart, K. (2002). *Helping a child with nonverbal learning disorder or Asperger's syndrome.* London, UK: New Harbinger Publications.

Stipek, D. (2002). *Motivation to learn: Integrating theory and practice* (3rd ed.). Boston: Allyn & Bacon.

Stober, J., & Joormann, J. (2001). Worry, procrastination, and perfectionism: Differentiating amount of worry, pathological worry, anxiety, and depression. *Cognitive Therapy and Research, 25*, 49-60.

Stover, D. (2006). Treating cyberbullying as a school violence issue. *The Education Digest, 72*(4), 40-43.

Subotnik, R. F. (2009). Developmental transitions in giftedness and talent: Adolescence into adulthood. In F. D. Horowitz, R. F. Subotnik, & D. J. Matthews (Eds.), *The development of giftedness and talent across the life span* (pp. 155-170). Washington, DC: American Psychological Association.

Subotnik, R. F., Edmiston, A., & Rayhack, K. (2007). Developing national policies in STEM talent development: Obstacles and opportunities. In P. Csermely, K. Kormevic, & K. Sulyok (Eds.), *Science education: Models and networking of student research training under 21* (pp. 28-38). Netherlands: IOS Press.

Subotnik, R. F., Olszewski-Kubilius, P., & Arnold, K. D. (2003). Beyond Bloom: Revisiting environmental factors that enhance or impede talent development. In J. H. Borland (Ed.), *Rethinking gifted education* (pp. 227-238). New York: Teachers College Press.

Tallent-Runnels, M. K., & Candler-Lotven, A. C. (2008). *Academic competitions for gifted students* (2nd ed.). Thousand Oaks, CA: Corwin Press.

Tannenbaum, A. J. (1983). *Gifted children: Psychological and educational perspectives.* New York: Macmillan.

Tannenbaum, A. J. (2000). A history of giftedness in school and society. In K. A. Heller, F. J. Monks, R. J. Sternberg, & R. F. Subotnik (Eds.), *International handbook of giftedness and talent* (2nd ed., pp. 23-53). Oxford, UK: Elsevier Science.

Terman, L. M. (Ed.). (1925-1959). *Genetic studies of genius* (Vols. 1-5). Stanford, CA: Stanford University Press.

Thurstone, L. L. (1938). *Primary mental abilities.* Chicago: University of Chicago Press.

Tieso, C. L. (2003). Ability grouping is not just tracking anymore. *Roeper Review, 6*(1), 29-36.

Tomlinson, C. A. (2003). *Differentiated instruction: The critical issue of quality.* Paper presented at the annual meeting of the National Association for Gifted Children, Indianapolis, IN.

Tomlinson, C. A. (Ed.). (2004). Differentiation for gifted and talented students. In S. M. Reis (Series Ed.), *Essential readings in gifted education.* Thousand Oaks, CA: Corwin Press.

Tomlinson, C. A., Kaplan, S. N., Purcell, J. H., Leppien, J. H., Burns, D. E., & Strickland, C. A. (2006). *The parallel curriculum in the classroom: Book 2.* Thousand Oaks, CA: Corwin Press.

Tomlinson, C. A., Kaplan, S. N., Renzulli, J., Purcell, J., Leppien, J., & Burns, D. (2001). *The parallel curriculum.* Thousand Oaks, CA: Corwin Press.

Toynbee, A. (1967). Is America neglecting her creative talents? In C. W. Taylor (Ed.), *Creativity across education* (pp. 23-29). Salt Lake City, UT: University of Utah Press.

Treffinger, D. J., & Feldhusen, J. F. (1996). Talent recognition and development: Successor to gifted education. *Journal for the Education of the Gifted, 16,* 181-193.

Treffinger, D., Nassab, C. A., & Selby, E. C. (2009). Programming for talent development: Expanding horizons for gifted education. In T. Balchin, B. Hymer, & D. J. Matthews (Eds.), *The Routledge international companion to gifted education* (pp. 210-217). Abingdon, UK: Routledge.

Treffinger, D. J., Young, G. C., Nassab, C. A., Selby, E. C., & Wittig, C. V. (2008). *The talent development planning handbook.* Thousand Oaks, CA: Corwin Press.

U.S. Department of Education. (2001). *No Child Left Behind Act of 2001*. Washington, DC: Author.

VanTassel-Baska, J. (2000). Theory and practice in curriculum development for the gifted. In K. A. Heller, F. J. Monks, R. J. Sternberg, & R. F. Subotnik (Eds.), *International handbook of giftedness and talent* (2nd ed., pp. 345-366). Oxford, UK: Elsevier Science.

VanTassel-Baska, J. L. (2004, April). Creativity as an elusive factor in giftedness. *Update*. Electronic magazine of the School of Education at the College of William and Mary (www.cfge.wm.edu).

VanTassel-Baska, J. L. (Ed.). (2007). *Serving gifted learners beyond the traditional classroom*. Waco, TX: Prufrock Press.

VanTassel-Baska, J. L. (2008). Using performance-based assessment to document authentic learning. In J. L. VanTassel-Baska (Ed.), *Alternative assessments with gifted and talented students* (pp. 285-308). Waco, TX: Prufrock Press.

VanTassel-Baska, J. L., & Brown, E. F. (2009). An analysis of gifted education curriculum models. In F. A. Karnes & S. M. Bean (Eds.), *Methods and materials for teaching the gifted* (3rd ed., pp. 75-106). Waco, TX: Prufrock Press.

VanTassel-Baska, J. L., Buckingham, B. L. E., & Baska, A. (2009). The role of the arts in the socioemotional development of the gifted. In J. L. VanTassel-Baska, T. L. Cross, & F. R. Olenchak (Eds.), *Social-emotional curriculum with gifted and talented students* (pp. 227-258). Waco, TX: Prufrock Press.

VanTassel-Baska, J. L., Cross, T. L., & Olenchak, F. R. (2009). *Social-emotional curriculum with gifted and talented students*. Waco, TX: Prufrock Press.

VanTassel-Baska, J. L., & Little, C. A. (2003). *Content-based curriculum for high-ability learners*. Waco, TX: Prufrock Press.

VanTassel-Baska, J. L., & MacFarlane, B. (2008). Writing. In J. A. Plucker & C. M. Callahan (Eds.), *Critical issues and practices in gifted education: What the research says* (pp. 749-760). Waco, TX: Prufrock Press.

VanTassel-Baska, J. L. & Sher, B. (2003). Accelerating learning experiences in core content areas. In J. L. VanTassel-Baska & C. A. Little (Eds.), *Content-based curriculum for high-ability learners* (pp. 27-46). Waco, TX: Prufrock Press.

VanTassel-Baska, J. L., & Stambaugh, T. (2005). Challenges and possibilities for serving gifted learners in the regular classroom. *Theory into Practice, 44,* 211-217.

VanTassel-Baska, J. L., & Stambaugh, T. (2006). *Comprehensive curriculum for gifted learners* (3rd ed.). Boston: Allyn & Bacon.

Vygotsky, L. S. (1978). *Mind in society*. Cambridge, MA: Harvard University Press. (Original work published 1930.)

Wahlsten, D. (1997). The malleability of intelligence is not constrained by heritability. In B. Devlin, S. E. Fienberg, & D. P Resnick (Eds.), *Intelligence, genes, and success* (pp. 71-87). New York: Springer-Verlag.

Wallace, B. (2009). Developing pupils' problem-solving and thinking skills. In T. Balchin, B. Hymer, & D. J. Matthews (Eds.), *The Routledge international companion to gifted education* (pp. 281-291). Abingdon, UK: Routledge.

Wallace, B., & Eriksson, G. (2006). *Diversity in gifted education: International perspectives on global issues.* London: Routledge.

Walton, G. M., & Cohen, G. L. (2007). A question of belonging: Race, fit, and achievement. *Journal of Personality and Social Psychology, 92,* 82-96.

Warwick, I., & Matthews, D. J. (2009). Fostering giftedness in urban and diverse communities: Context-sensitive solutions. In T. Balchin, B. Hymer, & D. J. Matthews (Eds.), *The Routledge international companion to gifted education* (pp. 265-272). Abingdon, UK: Routledge.

Webb, J. T, (2004). *Tips for selecting the right counselor or therapist for your gifted child.* Retrieved June 29, 2004, from www.giftedbooks.com/aart_webb3.html

Webb, J. T. (2009). *Dabrowski's theory and existential depression in gifted children and adults.* Retrieved April 20, 2009, from www.sengifted.org/articles_counseling/webb_dabrowski_s_theory.shtml

Webb, J. T., Amend, E. R., Webb, N. E., Goerss, J., Beljan, P., & Olenchak, F. R. (2005). *Misdiagnosis and dual diagnoses of gifted children and adults: ADHD, bipolar, OCD, Asperger's, depression, and other disorders.* Scottsdale, AZ: Great Potential Press.

Webb, J. T., Gore, J. L., Amend, E. R., & DeVries, A. R. (2007). *A parent's guide to gifted children.* Scottsdale, AZ: Great Potential Press.

Webb, J. T., Gore, J. L., Karnes, F. A., & McDaniel, A. S. (2004). *Grandparents' guide to gifted children.* Scottsdale, AZ: Great Potential Press.

Webb, J. T., Meckstroth, E. A., & Tolan, S. S. (1982). *Guiding the gifted child: A practical source for parents and teachers.* Scottsdale, AZ: Great Potential Press (formerly Gifted Psychology Press).

Wechsler, D. (1981). *Wechsler Adult Intelligence Scale – Revised.* San Antonio, TX: The Psychological Corp.

Wechsler, D. (1989). *Wechsler Preschool and Primary Scale of Intelligence – Revised.* San Antonio, TX: The Psychological Corp.

Wechsler, D. (2003). *Wechsler Intelligence Scale for Children* (4th ed.). San Antonio, TX: The Psychological Corp.

Weinfeld, R., Barnes-Robinson, L., Jeweler, S., & Roffman Shevitz, B. (2006). *Smart kids with learning difficulties: Overcoming obstacles and realizing potential.* Waco, TX: Prufrock Press.

Weinfeld, R., & Davis, M. (2008). *Special needs advocacy resource book.* Waco, TX: Prufrock Press.

Weisberg, R. W. (2006). Modes of expertise in creative thinking. In K. A. Ericsson, N. Charness, P. J. Feltovich, & R. R. Hoffman (Eds.), *The Cambridge handbook of expertise and expert performance* (pp. 761-787). New York: Cambridge University Press.

West-Burnham, J. (2006). Understanding learning: Creating a shared vocabulary. In B. Wallace & G. Eriksson (Eds.), *Diversity in gifted education: International perspectives on global issues* (pp. 45-55). Abingdon, UK: Routledge.

Westphal, C. (2001). *A family year abroad: How to live outside the borders.* Scottsdale, AZ: Great Potential Press.

Whitehead, J., & McNiff, J. (2006). *Action research living theory.* London: Sage.

Whitney, C. S. (with Hirsch, G.). (2007). *A love for learning: Motivation and the gifted child.* Scottsdale, AZ: Great Potential Press.

Willis, J. A. (2009). *Inspiring middle school minds: Gifted, creative, and challenging.* Scottsdale, AZ: Great Potential Press.

Wilson, H. (2009). Challenge and creativity: Making the links. In T. Balchin, B. Hymer, & D. J. Matthews (Eds.), *The Routledge international companion to gifted education* (pp. 235-242). Abingdon, UK: Routledge.

Winebrenner, S. (2001). *Teaching gifted kids in the regular classroom.* Minneapolis, MN: Free Spirit.

Winebrenner, S., & Brulles, D. (2008). *The cluster grouping handbook.* Minneapolis, MN: Free Spirit.

Winner, E. (1996). *Gifted children: Myths and realities.* New York: Basic Books.

Winner, E. (2009). Toward broadening our understanding of giftedness: The spatial domain. In F. D. Horowitz, R. F. Subotnik, & D. J. Matthews (Eds.), *The development of giftedness and talent across the life span* (pp. 59-74). Washington, DC: American Psychological Association.

Wissner-Gross, E. (2006). *What colleges don't tell you.* New York: Hudson Street Press.

Witt, D. (2009). *Strategies for the tech-savvy classroom.* Waco, TX: Prufrock Press.

Wolf, M. (2007). *Proust and the squid: The story and science of the reading brain.* New York: Harper.

Woodcock, R. W., McGrew, K. S., & Mather, N. (2001). *Woodcock-Johnson III.* Itasca, IL: Riverside.

Worrell, F. C. (2009). What does gifted mean? Personal and social identity perspectives on giftedness in adolescence. In F. D. Horowitz, R. F. Subotnik, & D. J. Matthews (Eds.), *The development of giftedness and talent across the life span* (pp. 131-152). Washington, DC: APA Publications.

Wright, L., & Borland, J. H. (1993). Using early childhood developmental portfolios in the identification and education of young, economically disadvantaged, potentially gifted students. *Roeper Review, 15,* 205-210.

Index

About the Authors

Dona Matthews, Ph.D., has been teaching, writing, counseling, consulting, and conducting research on giftedness-related issues since 1985. She holds an M.Ed. in Counseling Psychology and a Ph.D. in Special Education (Gifted), both from the Ontario Institute for Studies in Education of the University of Toronto. From 2003 to 2007, she was Director of the Center for Gifted Studies and Education at Hunter College, City University of New York, where she taught graduate courses to teachers and worked with the New York City Department of Education on gifted education policies and practices. She has published and presented extensively on gifted education and development, including having written dozens of journal articles and book chapters. In addition to the award-winning *Being Smart about Gifted Children*, which she co-authored with Joanne Foster, recent projects include co-editing *The Development of Giftedness and Talent across the Life Span* with Frances Degen Horowitz and Rena Subotnik (2009, American Psychological Association), and *The Routledge International Companion to Gifted Education*, (2009, Routledge) with Tom Balchin and Barry Hymer. In 2008, Dr. Matthews received the Upton Sinclair Award, given annually by *Education News* to 10 "heroes of American Education" in recognition of their outstanding contributions to the field of education.

Joanne Foster, Ed.D., began teaching at the elementary level in 1975, and shortly thereafter started working in the field of gifted education. Over the years, she has refined special education programming initiatives, developed curricular frameworks for advanced learners, consulted on education advisory committees, and led countless teacher training and development sessions. She completed a Master's degree in Special

Education and Adaptive Instruction, and a Doctoral degree in Human Development and Applied Psychology, both from the University of Toronto, where she now teaches Educational Psychology, as well as Gifted Education. The focus of her research, writing, and consulting is on understandings of giftedness and high-level development and meeting the needs of high-ability learners. She also provides professional learning programs on innovative and best practice, working alongside teams of educators within districts, boards, and individual school settings, and with teachers acquiring accreditation in Special Education. In addition to conducting presentations across North America addressing a broad range of gifted-related issues, she has written many articles, some with Dona Matthews, with whom she co-authored the award-winning *Being Smart about Gifted Children*. Together they write a regular column in the journal *Understanding Our Gifted*, and they are currently involved in several other projects.